About the editor

Shahrzad Mojab is professor in the Department of Leadership, Higher and Adult Education and is the former director of the Women and Gender Studies Institute at the University of Toronto. Her areas of research and teaching include educational policy studies; gender, state, diaspora and transnationality; women, war, militarization and violence; feminism, anti-racism, colonialism and imperialism; and Marxism, feminism and revolution.

MARXISM AND FEMINISM

edited by Shahrzad Mojab

Zed Books
LONDON

Marxism and Feminism was first published in 2015 by Zed Books Ltd,
7 Cynthia Street, London N1 9JF, UK

www.zedbooks.co.uk

Set in FFKievit and Monotype Plantin by Ewan Smith, London
Printed and bound by CPI Group (UK) Ltd, Croydon, CR0 4YY
Index: ed.emery@thefreeuniversity.net
Cover designed by Liam Chapple

A catalogue record for this book is available from the British Library

ISBN 978-1-78360-323-7 hb
ISBN 978-1-78360-322-0 pb
ISBN 978-1-78360-324-4 pdf
ISBN 978-1-78360-325-1 epub
ISBN 978-1-78360-326-8 mobi

CONTENTS

ACKNOWLEDGEMENTS

This collection is the outcome of many conversations with the contributors, sometimes one on one but most often collectively and over many months, years and decades. I am enormously grateful to them for enriching my feminist understanding of Marxism and Marxist centring of class in feminism. Thanks are also due to graduate students who prodded me to keep on organizing 'radical' or 'Marxist' reading groups where we discussed and thought through concepts/keywords covered in the book. A summer Marxist theory group, held in Europe over the last few years, has been a valuable reading and discussion space. In this group, I learned to read dialectical and historical materialism as science, philosophy, method and, most significantly, as a mode of understanding and interpreting Marx and feminism. My gratitude to all participants for sitting through hours of debate and for their palpable love for humanity and revolution.

I am grateful to Stephan Dobson for his superb editorial work, his intellectual generosity, his affection for books, and for always walking in with yet another book for me to read! Shirin Haghgou's diligent work on the preparation of the manuscript was indispensable; I owe her gracious thanks. Philip Taucher's assistance with Frigga Haug's chapters is greatly appreciated. I am also grateful for his creative contribution to the website 'Marxism and feminism: research, teaching, and praxis' (www.oise.utoronto.ca/marxfem/index.html). Special thanks are due to Karen Ruoff Kramer, who translated for this volume the poem that begins Frigga Haug's Chapter 3. Special gratitude is due to Kim Walker, the enthusiastic and supportive editor at Zed Books.

The constructive comments by anonymous reviewers on the manuscript proposal certainly improved its content, for which I am grateful. I also thank Palgrave Macmillan, publisher, for permission to reprint Himani Bannerji's chapter 'Building from Marx: reflections on "race", gender and class'. I am indebted to Teresa L. Ebert for advancing the theorization of materialist feminism and to Paradigm Publishers for permitting the reprint of her chapter 'Gender after class' as the Epilogue for this book. I am most grateful to Frigga Haug, who kindly permitted us to publish her two important chapters, 'Gender relations' and 'The Marx within feminism'. With all the support and assistance that I have received in preparing this collection, certainly any errors remaining are mine.

1 | INTRODUCTION: MARXISM AND FEMINISM

Shahrzad Mojab

Histories, theories and possibilities

This book goes to press in 2014, the centenary of the 'Great War' in which capitalist states brought immense destruction of life and property to every corner of the world. Another world war recurred on a more destructive scale within the lifespan of a generation, and it has continued to our day in an area extending from the Balkans to the Middle East to Africa, and it threatens other parts of the world. While states, media, academia and many non-state organizations have a stake in commemorating the First World War, it is unlikely that anyone will remember what Mary White Ovington (1865–1951), a socialist and feminist, said four months before the launch of the mass slaughter:

> Socialism and Feminism are the two greatest movements of to-day. The one aims to abolish poverty, the other to destroy servitude among women. Both are world movements. No matter how backward the nation may be that you visit, you will find your revolutionist there preaching that poverty is unnecessary, and that a great organization is working to destroy private capital and to build a co-operative commonwealth. And throughout western civilization, and even in the heart of the Orient, you also find the woman revolutionist telling her enslaved sisters of the effort among women to attain their freedom, to gain the right to live, not according to man's, but according to their own, conception of happiness and right. Ideas fly swiftly about the globe, and we are learning to think on the lines not of family or nation or race but of common interests and common suffering. (Ovington 1914: 143)

Ovington emphasized that 'the relation of Feminism to Socialism is a matter of profound importance to many women Socialists …' She was right. Three years earlier, socialist women had launched 8 March as International Working Women's Day (IWWD), and three years later the first socialist state was established – and women played an active role in it. On the theoretical front, twenty years before Ovington, Friedrich Engels had published *The Origin of Family, Private Property and the State* (1884), and years before this major milestone, August Bebel's *Woman and Socialism* (1879) was published. I do not intend to write the history of relations between feminism and socialism or Marxism. It is well known that this relationship has been both conflictual and constructive, and today they are evidently apart. Floyd Dell, while defending Ovington, who had been criticized by an anti-feminist, wrote: 'If there is no necessary connection between Feminism and Socialism, it may yet be advisable to invent one' (Dell 1914: 353).

Socialism and feminism have changed radically since Ovington, but her ideas, simple and significant as they are, remain on the agenda of many who yearn for an end to both 'poverty' and 'servitude'. The October 1917 revolution in Russia was for many the realization of this dream. This revolution made Marxism the dominant trend in the theory and practice of socialism, and divided the world into socialist and capitalist camps. However, in spite of great leaps towards women's emancipation, the socialist experiments of the last century came to an end when capitalism was restored first in the Soviet Union (1956) and, within two decades, in China (1976).[1] The collapse of the Soviet Union and eastern Europe in the late 1980s and early 1990s was trumpeted by the bourgeoisie as the 'end of history', one in which socialism (almost always conflated with 'communism' in the media and in popular parlance) was buried and capitalism emerged triumphant. During the past century, every success of socialism had attracted many to the cause of freedom, and each retreat has resulted in the turning away of many enthusiasts.[2] After the fall of the Soviet Union, which in its last decades was critiqued by many Marxists as a 'state capitalist' or 'social imperialist' country, the theory and practice of socialism and with it of Marxism came under a new wave of scrutiny and rejection by, among others, feminists.[3] Today, many advocates of capitalism seek to justify the way this socio-economic system produces wealth as well as poverty, hunger and destruction of the environment.

Feminism's trajectory has not been as tumultuous, but not quite dissimilar either. Unlike Marxism, which rose to state power and guided the construction of socialism for a few decades in a number of countries, feminism contributed prominently to reforming patriarchy through women's movements for equal rights within the contours of the state. While Marxism was hesitantly tolerated in the margins of capitalist academe, feminism was spreading out, by the early 1970s, from the privacy of individual theorists and the publicity of street politics to degree-granting programmes, and has grown into a credible, if still-resisted, international realm of knowledge. Feminist scholarship has seriously challenged the patriarchal nature of all previous knowledge. In stark contrast to Marxism, it comes today with hundreds of women's and gender studies programmes, hundreds of academic journals, and a powerful publishing industry, enabling it to train new generations of feminist scholars and intelligentsia. However, if Marxism was derailed by the 'socialist' state that was meant to plan its own 'withering away', feminism has been, according to some feminists, co-opted by its rise to academic status (Eisenstein 2009). Today, while gender and women's studies programmes proliferate in higher education in Western countries, anti-feminism is hegemonic in popular culture and the mass media, wherein feminism is rejected, even by some self-styled feminists, as 'extremist' and as exhibiting an 'anti-male bias' (Hammer 2002). In other contexts – for example, in Iran and Turkey – there is considerable interest in feminist theory and research as a venue of struggle against the patriarchal gender politics of the state and its anti-feminist agenda. In Iran, the Islamic theocracy makes use of the anti-feminism of American Christianity in its offensive against feminism (Mojab 2015).

The interest in merging the theoretical positions of Marxism and feminism, which has not subsided since the beginning of the last century, is fuelled by their prominence as two major emancipatory projects.[4] This political affinity is, however, constrained by divergent theoretical commitments that are themselves political and ideological. Theoretically, Marxism and feminism have never been so far apart as at present.

The idea of a society without gender oppression and class exploitation pre-dates both feminism and Marxism. Indeed, conflicts over gender and class weave together the entirety of human history. Put in the span of the long history of *Homo sapiens* (a few hundred thousand years), gender and class conflicts (as well as private property, family, trade, war, armies, states, laws, writings) are social constructions of recent origins, dating back about eight to ten millennia. This nearness in time invites a simple but crucial question: Why do class and patriarchal gender relations survive and even thrive in spite of widespread resistance and theoretical advances?

Feminism is both the product and a producer of the Enlightenment and its bourgeois democratic revolutions, whereas Marxism emerged in the context of the assumption of power by the bourgeoisie and the rise of the working class. Two *class* positions, one seeking emancipation within the legal and political frameworks of the capitalist system and the other seeking the same through the negation of bourgeois relations, separate the two. Summing up the experience of the first two years of socialist revolution, Lenin noted that 'one of the principal distinguishing features of capitalism' is that it 'combines formal equality with economic and, consequently, social inequality' (Lenin 1982: 84). Even formal equality, to the extent it has been achieved in capitalist societies, did not come without resistance. It took a century of women's organized struggle to persuade the state to grant them suffrage rights. Although socialist countries readily granted women extensive legal equality and took steps towards their economic and social equality, the transformation of gender relations was marked by compromise and retreat, and patriarchy survived through to the restoration of capitalism.

Marxist theory has provided clues for understanding the intricacies involved in the dismantling of class and patriarchy. Society is a whole, and class, gender, race, religion and other social phenomena, far from being independent, exist in relationships of determination and conflict as a system, a social formation, or a mode of production. Equally significant is the way this system and its components persist only by reproducing themselves. In his study of capitalist production, for example, Marx noted that 'When viewed … as a connected whole, and as flowing on with incessant renewal, every social process of production is, at the same time, a process of reproduction' (Marx 1983: 531). From this perspective, patriarchy may be seen as a connected whole, a social process for producing and reproducing the gender hierarchy characterized by male domination. Male power, much like class rule, is exercised through both coercion and consent; consent is created through family, religion, ideology, culture, language, literature, art, folklore, education and all other cultural institutions, while physical violence is perpetrated by males, the police, armies, the law and courts. There is no clear-cut separation between the two; the family, for instance, perpetrates violence while it generates consent. Dialectics predicts that such a system will be fraught with contradictions, with the two genders existing in relations of conflict and dependence. Class, race and religion, among other social formations, also endure only if they reproduce themselves. It happens that these dynamics of producing and reproducing, indispensable in any system, cannot be adequately accounted for by the idea that class, gender, race or sexuality 'intersect' (Aguilar 2012; Bannerji 2001).

The experience of socialism in the last century revealed the complexities of negating the capitalist system's dynamics of production and reproduction and replacing them with a communist system. Socialism was, in Marx's understanding, a long transition period between capitalism and communism, in which classes and capitalist relations would persist in conflict with communist relations, which have to be consciously created. It involves the dismantling of one social system by building its opposite. This transition for Marx was to involve nothing less than what he called the abolition of class distinctions, 'the abolition of all the relations of production on which they rest', 'the abolition of all the social relations that correspond to these relations of production' and 'the revolutionizing of all the ideas that result from these social relations' (Marx 1969). Such intervention in social reality calls for some theoretical breakthrough. Politically, such disruptions in the dynamics of production and reproduction invite hostility, both nationally and internationally, from those who have a stake in the survival of capitalism. If this conflict is visibly political, dealing with relations of power, it is no less significant in the realms of philosophy and ideology. This struggle is what Marxist textbooks call 'the fundamental question of philosophy' – that is, the dialectics of matter and consciousness, as well as other dialectical relations, such as those between necessity and freedom, essence and phenomenon, and universal and particular.[5] Ideologically, the question of alternatives to capitalism drops anchor in class positions.

Feminist theory, in all its diversity today, is not committed to the negation of capitalism, and some theorists do not see gender relations as a system (patriarchy), while others reject the idea of women's emancipation or liberation as 'grand narratives'. Even more reductionist is feminism's delinking of gender relations and capitalism and reducing gender to questions of culture. This is a feminism that finds solace in discarding the conceptual framework of twentieth-century women's movements, including the concepts of oppression, exploitation, subjugation, subordination, solidarity and internationalism at a time when religious and market fundamentalisms are engaged in a worldwide 'war on women'. These developments cannot be explained in theoretical terms only; these theoretical positions are not replacements of paradigms à la Kuhn or the falling and rising of 'waves' in feminist theory and politics. While feminism has indeed made enormous contributions to our understanding of gender relations since the theoretical twists and turns of the 1980s, its delinking of capitalism and patriarchy is a political undertaking that undermines theoretical gains in our understanding of gender relations. This politics ensures the anchoring of feminism in liberalism and – at best – democratic theory and their links to the market.

It is well known that the economic determinist trend in Marxism and, more evidently, in communist movements has reduced gender relations to class relations. This reading of Marxism, often anti-dialectical in its method, is based on conflating class with gender and reducing the political to the economic. It fails to appreciate that class is not gender and gender is not class, but that the struggle over gender relations (patriarchy) is a political struggle among and within classes. It is, thus, not difficult to find different class positions disagreeing on how and to what extent the patriarchal regime should be transformed. The class reductionist position is, however, not primarily a product of the unfamiliarity of Marxists with feminism; rather, it is related to their undialectical understanding of Marxism. Hence, while the vast knowledge produced by feminism is indispensable for the renewal of Marxism and the communist movement, a new synthesis is unlikely to happen without a dialectical approach to Marxism itself.

The political character of the struggle over two major historical divides, gender and class, is evident also in the perseverance of anti-feminism and anti-communism and their ubiquity. It is also inscribed in the endless conflicts within each theoretical perspective, Marxism and feminism, and between the two. Rather than a question of sectarianism, the politics of theorization is one of splits, ruptures, zigzags, advances and retreats and not a linear march forward. This is the case if only because, dialectically speaking, one always divides into two. I see in the diversity or richness of today's feminist knowledge seeds of conservatism. Reflecting on my lived experience of the last five decades, I have seen how, in confronting patriarchy, the major element of consciousness – that is, theory – lags behind 'material reality' or matter, and at times stays in conflict with it. For instance, I find feminism's culturalization of gender relations and its abandoning of projects of emancipation at odds with the offensive of capitalism on women throughout the world.

I have realized, following Marx, that we make our own history, but not under circumstances chosen by us; we are constrained by circumstances already existing and given and transmitted from the past (Marx 1979: 103). This dialectic reverberates in another one: 'freedom' is, according to Hegel, the recognition of 'necessity'. But necessity – that is, circumstances of the past and present – cannot be changed through recognition or interpretation only. Contemporary feminist theory engages in interpretation but, as Marx said in another context, the challenge is also to change reality. In other words, transformation occurs when matter transforms into consciousness and consciousness into matter. Feminist consciousness is the outcome of the rise of women as a new social and political force and their determination to change the material reality of oppressive and unjust gender relations. This consciousness has, through the practice of women's movements worldwide, changed gender relations through struggles for 'rights', but has failed to dismantle the hierarchy of gender relations. Let me expand on these claims by writing myself into this history.[6]

Living through imperialism and fundamentalism: the 1953 CIA coup and the 1979 'revolution'

My life is interwoven with the 1953 CIA coup and the 1979 revolution in Iran. Esmail Khoi, an Iranian poet, has beautifully, meaningfully and metaphorically captured my experience of participating in the 1979 revolution in Iran:

> The joy of a raindrop
> and the sorrow *of it* in a swamp

This reflects my experience of more than thirty years ago, 'joyously watching the life-giving raindrop [revolution], only to abruptly recognize its horrid fall into the abyss' – the coming to power of the Islamic regime in Iran.[7]

I was born in Shiraz, Iran, in 1954, a year after the CIA-led *coup d'état* which restored the failing monarchy of Mohammad Reza Shah Pahlavi and established US domination over the country. One outcome was increasing state-orchestrated modernization in the direction of the Americanization of social, political and economic life. My mother was from a middle-class background and my father came from an educated upper-middle-class family; my maternal grandfather was literate and encouraged his four granddaughters to get educated, work and have an active public life. He taught them to be independent and to immediately leave their husbands if they proved to be oppressive. My mother had the freedom to choose her future husband, my father, whom she met as her volleyball coach. She was not veiled. In fact, she is of the generation who witnessed the forced *unveiling* of her mother, under Reza Shah in 1936, and the forced *veiling* of her daughters after the establishment of the current Islamic theocracy in 1979. All my paternal and maternal aunts were among the early generation of women enjoying public education in Iran.

The thinking of my maternal grandfather was shaped by the Constitutional Revolution of Iran (1906–11), the first major democratic revolution in Asia, Africa and Latin America. During these years, women in Tehran and some major cities created educational and cultural societies, while some clerics issued religious edicts against women's presence in public life, and especially against women's education. The revolutionary press advocated women's rights, including suffrage. When my grandfather was twelve years old, a provincial delegate at the second session of Iran's new parliament submitted a petition demanding recognition of women's right to vote. By this time, only four countries had granted women suffrage rights. The London *Times* reporter in Tehran informed British readers in 1911 that 'the supporters of women's suffrage [in Britain] should be gratified to learn that even in the midst of Persia's present trials and troubles … a champion of the women's cause has been found in the Persian Mejliss [parliament]' (quoted in Afary 1996: 203).

My parents, the first beneficiaries of a fully subsidized and state-run public education system, were enchanted by the culture of modernity and envisioned an American lifestyle for their children. My siblings and I were introduced to music, art, poetry and sport with a very disciplined and organized life as had been idealized by the US 'Point Four' programme and American propaganda in the heat of Cold War in a country bordering the southern USSR. We were nurtured on American films and as of the 1960s soap operas dubbed into Persian and broadcast on national television, shows such as *Peyton Place*, *Days of Our Lives* or *Little House on the Prairie* – as well as on fashion and 'home-keeping' magazines. In this environment, I was expected to be a young 'American-like' Iranian woman. At a private and well-known girls' high school in Tehran, some of us dressed in trendy American blue jeans and tight white shirts with the American flag emblazoned on our chests. Almost fifteen years later, when I was doing research for my doctoral dissertation on the history of the Iranian student movement, I came across some archival records about a bloody suppression of one of the anti-American student riots at Tehran University. Suddenly I felt as if I had been hit by a thunderbolt. I had to sit down, squint my eyes in order to see frame-by-frame images of that day. I remembered a day when I was with my father in the vicinity of Tehran University. I had my white T-shirt with the American flag on. Suddenly I heard the voices of a group of students who were shouting anti-American slogans with reference to my T-shirt. At that moment I did not understand their reference; it was only fifteen years later at the library of the University of Illinois that a lost fragment of my life came together.

The CIA coup put an end to twelve years (between 1941 and 1953) of social movements in the country, an interlude called by some Iranians 'Incomplete Democracy' (Javid 1356 [Western calendar: 1977]), during which time women were active and had their own organizations and magazines. There was yet another unsuccessful attempt by a fraction of left parliamentarians to grant women suffrage rights. In the early 1950s, there was a popular movement, led by the popularly elected prime minister Dr Mossadeq, to nationalize the British-dominated oil industry, leading to a conflict between the United States, the United Kingdom and the Shah on one side, and Iranians on the other. The nationalization struggle encouraged similar anti-imperialist movements in the Middle East. One of my uncles was in charge of the provincial organization of the Tudeh Party (Party of the Masses of Iran), a pro-Soviet organization which advocated the rights of workers, women, peasants and minorities. Mossadeq was overthrown in a CIA-led coup in 1953, which unleashed a period of repression.

When my siblings and I were growing up, neither my uncle nor anyone else in the family talked about those years or about my uncle's prominent role in the left politics of the province. In the post-coup years, there was strict censorship of all anti-monarchical and anti-imperialist ideas. The United States had helped the Shah create a CIA-type secret police aimed at uncovering any oppositional activism.

My parents were in a position to insulate my siblings and me from the anti-monarchical and anti-imperialist dissent of the young generation. By the time I began college in the early 1970s, the political environment had changed visibly. Under the auspices of the Kennedy administration, the Shah had initiated, in 1963, a series of reforms named the 'White Revolution', aimed at consolidating his rule and preventing revolutionary struggles as they had happened in Cuba, Vietnam or Algeria. In addition to land reform, women were finally granted voting rights and were allowed into the Literacy Corps of the army and into a few higher administrative positions. The monarch, like his father, had realized that women were a new and dangerous political force that had to be tamed. Like his American allies, he was wary of women's movements as a breeding ground for communist activism.

Universities were co-educational, and the political environment was more vibrant. By the time I went to college, the student movement had moved from the reformist politics of the 'Shah should reign not rule' to a red revolutionary politics aimed at the overthrowing of the monarchy and the creation of a democratic, independent and, for some, socialist rule. In spite of unceasing suppression and the presence of the secret police on campuses, the universities could not be silenced, and they became known as *sangar-e azadi*, 'bastions of freedom'. Although both Pahlavi monarchs had suppressed independent women's organizations, the formation of a female, all-secular intelligentsia was evident by this time. Like many students, I was inspired by the poems of Forough Farokhzad (1935–67). Farokhzad was a poet and film-maker with a feminist vision not previously articulated in Persian literature and art. While the Shah recruited women into his army's Literacy Corps, a number of women, mostly students, joined the two guerrilla organizations, one Marxist and the other Islamist, which were engaged in armed struggle to overthrow the monarchy. The traditional religious opposition came under the leadership of Khomeini, who opposed both land reform and women's suffrage.

While in secondary school, we learned more about the USA and Europe than about our neighbours the USSR, Turkey, Iraq, Afghanistan, Pakistan and the Gulf states. And the presence of imperialism reached far and wide, in culture, education, arts, economy, administration, technology and science. In print culture, Marxist works were banned and their possession could lead to jail and torture. Even the names Marx, Engels, Lenin or Mao could not be mentioned in classes and were deleted when they appeared in American textbooks translated into Persian. The state-led Westernization and Americanization was, thus, carefully managed to be the introduction of bourgeois culture and social relations. This was in the 1960s when the women, youth and students of Europe and the United States were in revolt. It seemed as if the West was not the homeland of democratic revolutions, women's movements, the Paris Commune, the 1917 socialist revolution and anti-fascist resistance movements. Still, we were able to see the other side of the world we lived in, from the Cuban revolution and Che Guevara in Latin America to China and Vietnam in Asia and the national liberation movements of Africa. Although the beginnings of feminist consciousness in Iran date back to the early twentieth century (Afary 1996), the growing feminist literature of the West was not available in translation.

I received a scholarship from the Iranian government to continue my MA in the growing field of university administration. I went to the University of Illinois at Urbana-Champaign in the United States. Coming from metropolitan Tehran, a city of some five million people at the time, the small twin city of Champaign-Urbana, buried in millions of hectares of cornfield, seemed desolate and depressing. However, it did not take long for me to realize that I had entered a new world much larger than the mega-city of Tehran. The campus hosted many social movements, including one of the radical chapters of the Iranian Student Association (ISA), a member of the World Confederation of Iranian Students (WCIS). The ISA was one of the best-organized and most radical student organizations in the United States and Europe, with branches also in a number of Asian countries.

I began attending reading groups on Iranian history, national liberation movements, communist movements and Marxist philosophy. In these reading circles I learned the dialectical and historical method of analysing, synthesizing, dialogue, debating and presentation. The ISA was not preoccupied with Iran only; its members were Iranian students who were going abroad in their thousands in order to study and return to Iran as technocrats and bureaucrats in the modernization and militarization projects of the Shah and the United States. However, the ISA, budding in the revolutionary aura of the 1960s, turned from being a nationalist movement into an internationalist one, and it was an active participant in the anti-war movement, the struggles of workers, Afro-Americans, indigenous peoples and the national liberation movements, especially in Dhofar (Oman) and Palestine. The impact of ISA radicalism on the US and European student movements and the anti-war movement has been noted by many activists and scholars, including Millett (1982) and Matin-Asgari (2001). In fact, it was not in Tehran but, rather, in Champaign-Urbana that I became familiar, through the student movement, with a version of Iranian and world history that I had never been exposed to before. The dynastic history that was taught in Iranian educational institutions was nothing more than the war among the monarchs over territory and between them and the enslaved 'subjects'. The past, as narrated by the student movement, introduced the people of Iran as makers of their history. I also learned about US history from a people's perspective, something that was, due to censorship, difficult if not impossible to find out about in Iran.

The protest struggles in Iran in 1978 developed into the anti-monarchical revolt that overthrew the Shah in February 1979. The ISA was actively engaged not only in supporting these struggles, but also in being part of them through its own activism, mobilizing public opinion in the USA in favour of the overthrow of the monarchy and the independence of Iran from US imperialist domination. We would engage in diverse activities such as demonstrations, marches, sit-ins, leafleting, the organization of speaking events, and rallying support. Many students began going back to Iran in the autumn of 1978 to join the revolution. The mainstream US and European print and broadcast media covered events extensively, mostly in favour of the Shah. We, in the ISA, had a difficult time persuading the corporate media to reflect our interpretations of events. Journalists from all over the world and some intellectuals, including Michel Foucault, rushed to Iran in order to find out about what seemed to them to be a new page in history. This revolution was going to be of far more significance than the Western media or even Iranian intellectuals themselves could anticipate. It created 'Islamic feminism', and everywhere encouraged Islamic fundamentalism, one striving for theocratic power in collusion and conflict with imperialism.

I went back to Iran soon after the monarchy was replaced by theocracy on 11 February 1979. If Foucault was fascinated by discovering in political Islam an alternative to class struggle and socialist revolutions, I was appalled, as a woman, to be forcibly veiled and fully disciplined by theocrats who saw women as an effective conduit for (re-)Islamizing a society that was 'corrupted', from their perspective, by modernity.[8] The populism of the anti-monarchical revolution did not allow many observers to see that women, the campuses, the print media, nationalities (Arabs, Baluches, Kurds, Turkomans) and religious and ethnic minorities (Baha'is, Christians, Jews, Zoroastrians, and so on) were opposed to theocratic rule; some of these groups were attacked by Islamist mobs while they were participating in anti-monarchic demonstrations. Women had participated in the revolution on a mass scale, though not with the demand to advance women's rights beyond the gains made in previous decades. They were the rank and file of the male-centred and clergy-led 'revolution' (Moghissi 1994). Not surprisingly, the first assault of the new regime against the people of Iran was Khomeini's decrees on women, less than a month after assuming power, dismissing women judges (3 March 1979) and imposing hijab 'head cover' on all women, Muslim and non-Muslim (6 March 1979). The response was immediate – women judges, feeling insulted by the Islamist claim that women cannot judge, went on strike and 8 March, International Women's Day, turned into a major protest which ended after five days only when government forces attacked the rallies and marches, wounding and arresting many participants. A number of European and American feminists participated in this struggle, visited the new rulers (including Khomeini) and expressed their concerns about women's rights.[9]

Most leftist groups were, unlike Foucault, not impressed by the 'Islamic revolution', though they believed that, after the fall of the monarchy, 'American imperialism' was the major threat to the revolution. Leftists, primarily communist groups, failed to see that the coming to power of theocrats, clerical and non-clerical, amounted to the end of this revolution; they also failed to grasp how the US and European imperialist powers preferred, in the context of the fierce Cold War of the time, an Islamic regime to a nationalist or socialist one, soon after they had realized that this time the Shah could not be rescued. While leftists condemned the repression of women, they turned their back on women by inviting them to abandon their resistance and, instead, fight imperialism rather than the theocracy which it had helped come to power (Moghissi 1994; Shahidian 2002). Subsequent events, too, showed that theocrats, unlike the left, had realized the importance of women as a powerful political force and were doing everything in their power to ensure their loyalty to the

Islamic state. The left considered women's support for the cause of socialism guaranteed. Moreover, the economistic Marxist theory they advocated conflated gender with class and relegated 'the woman question' to a secondary position, one that would be resolved with the success of the revolution.

Soon after arriving in Tehran, I began teaching in a university for a semester and observed the revolutionary and predominantly secular politics of the students. After declaring war on women, the new rulers attacked the movement for Kurdish autonomy on the eve of the Iranian New Year on 20 March, and in August Khomeini ordered the army to wipe out movement members. I went to Kurdistan soon after the ceasefire in November and stayed there until the summer of the following year. In early spring of 1980, the government dispatched armed vigilante groups to subdue the universities and drive out students; this state violence, much more extensive than that of the previous regime, was named the 'Islamic Cultural Revolution'; the violence closed down the universities for two years (Mojab 1991). Meanwhile, the press, which had become independent during the revolution, was attacked and placed under government control. Kurdistan was quite different from the areas under theocratic rule. Although the Kurds are Muslims, they rejected theocracy and demanded, instead, a federal and democratic state; they boycotted the referendum that intended to legitimize the formation of the Islamic republic. Rural Kurdish women, like those in a number of rural and tribal regions in the rest of Iran, had never veiled. Communist groups were active in Kurdistan, and one of them, Komele, was the most popular political force. Young rural women were inspired by the presence of women among the armed revolutionaries who stayed in villages during the government's war against the Kurds, and many joined them. I was active together with a number of friends in establishing a revolutionary Kurdish women's organization in the spring and summer of 1980. Many women and men, young and old, were interested in continuing the failed revolution as a socialist project.

The Islamic regime was conducting a step-by-step suppression of revolutionary opposition throughout the country. Thousands of activists were rounded up and many were executed. I was forced into exile in 1983 but tried not to freeze in it; I chose not to draw my poetry from the past, but only from the future.[10] In the early post-revolution years, there was considerable consensus among Iranians of diverse political persuasions about the need to resist the Islamic state's policies and practices of misogynism and gender apartheid. In fact, the emerging generation of academic feminists indicted the gender politics of the regime (Tabari and Yeganeh 1982). While the situation was hardly improving for women, many of these feminists had gone through a theoretical and political metamorphosis by the early 1990s. Critique and political resistance were lost in a turn to ideas of 'understanding', 'tolerance', 'difference', 'particularity', 'voice', 'negotiation' and 'accommodation'. This transformation was, in part, the outcome of a major shift in social theory and in feminism, which itself was a response to a larger global disruption in the wake of the collapse of the short-lived experiments with socialism in the Soviet Union, China and eastern Europe, and the rise of neoliberalism. It was also a consequence of the suppression or waning of the social movements of the 1960s, including the women's, students', workers' and – most significantly – the radical black movements in the United States, and also the anti-colonial and national liberation movements throughout Asia, Africa and Latin America.

I returned to a chilly academic environment in January 1984 on the campus of the University of Illinois. It was a frightening and depressing return to a place I had left with much revolutionary hope. The ISA office on the second floor of the student union building was no longer there; friends were gone – some had been executed in Iran or were in prison. The sense of guilt and defeat was inescapable. I began my doctoral programme in education, but neither the programme nor any particular course was of interest to me until I took 'Women and education in the Third World'. We studied Maria Mies' *Patriarchy and Capital Accumulation on a World Scale: Women in the International Division of Labour*, a book at that time just recently published, but we studied it only as a text for understanding feminist theorizations of 'development' and South/North women's struggles and solidarity against capitalism. I soon found out about a relatively new programme, 'Women's studies'. I went to the relevant office and talked to the director of the programme, Berenice Carroll, and proposed taking a reading course with her and doing my research assistantship in that programme. She became my mentor in women's studies. It was in that programme that I got to know Ann Russo and Lordes Torres, the co-editors with Chandra Mohanty of *Third World Women and the Politics of Feminism*. Besides them, a group of radical lesbians and African-Americans became part of my social, political and intellectual circle. It was through them that I gradually grounded myself in the school work and adapted to my role as a graduate student, mother and wife. The group gave me encouragement and coached me in public speaking and conference presentations.

The academic environment in which I have lived, first as a graduate student from 1984 and then as a faculty member from 1993, is a record of far-reaching changes in the knowledge and power relations of higher education. Back in Illinois, after having experienced the defeat of an important revolution, I wanted to write and talk about women, students and nationalities under theocratic rule. The women of Iran were now a topic of interest in media and popular culture, human rights and women's rights groups, and soon in courses and the publishing industry. I wanted to talk about the relationship between state, ideology, patriarchy, religion, class, ethnicity, nationalism and feminism. But I was often encouraged to speak about my 'identity', 'body' or 'culture'. I was being constructed as a 'Muslim' woman and the region of the world that I came from as a 'Muslim society'. Before 1979, I was never considered or treated as a 'Muslim' woman. Post-1979, a host of theoretical claims, old and new, trapped me into an identity that did not belong to me, that I could not identify with. Cultural relativism, identity politics, post-structuralism, postmodernism and other turns and shifts in language and culture worked to confine my horizons to 'authenticity', 'religion', 'nativism' and 'ethnicity'. In this theoretical environment, political belonging to internationalism, feminism, socialism, communism, atheism or secularism is not welcomed, especially for those who appear to be the 'other'.

I resisted this theoretical conservatism, which was in line with the political conservatism of neoliberalism and which was spreading by the early 1990s to every corner of the world. While this perspective was, in my understanding, serving the interests of capital and religion, many individuals and oppressed groups picked up the language of belonging and identity. Theorists inspired all, from women to students to oppressed aboriginal, racial, ethnic and national groups, to avoid 'grand narratives' of freedom and class struggle. While capitalism systemically evades borders and creates new ones, and women's movements and feminist consciousness are increasingly international, theorists push for a 'micro-political' understanding in this globalizing world. Since this internationalization is, indeed, difficult to deny, it is often presented as 'transnationalism', a conceptual frame that remains within the boundaries of nationalism (Grewal and Kaplan 1994).

Moving from the conservatism of non-Marxist social theory to the conformism of the Marxist left, of which I was part, I focus now on the contradiction between their theory and practice of gender politics. Communist groups in Iran, as elsewhere, have been the most persistent advocates of women's rights. However, their theoretical approach to patriarchy reduced gender oppression to class exploitation, and found the solution to oppression in a socialist revolution which would overthrow capitalism and, with it, patriarchal oppression. They failed to appreciate that gender is not class and that exploitation is a relationship between capitalists and workers, whereas male oppression is a trans-class political relationship in which men of all classes, including workers, oppress women. Also, they failed to grasp the dialectics of this struggle: while gender cannot be reduced to class, the struggle over gender relations – that is, the dismantling of patriarchy – is inescapably political and, therefore, constitutes class struggle. Thus, the left's prioritizing of improving workers' lives and of independence from imperialist domination over women's emancipation is a political position, one that underestimates the crucial role of women in revolutionary change, and by doing so overlooks the destructive nature of the exercise of power by the male gender. Similarly, the Shah's denigration of women and Khomeini's Islamization of gender relations are as political as their suppression of workers, peasants, students, minorities, artists and journalists. The left failed to understand that women's oppression has been crucial in creating the conditions for capitalist/imperialist exploitation of all working people. This I regard as an economistic/workerist approach among most left tendencies.

Economistic theory linked with nationalistic understanding of imperialism did not allow the left to grasp the Islamization project as class struggle. In other words, they failed to interpret the attack on women as a full assault on the working class, both women and men. The left's analysis of the regime's rhetoric of anti-US imperialism also revealed their economistic/workerist approach, in which the dialectics of the inner relations of religion, patriarchy and capitalism was obscured in the simplistic binary of the internal/external enemy. Still, although 'the woman question' was given a secondary status, thousands of women persisted in their resistance and fought the theocratic regime without a clear political agenda, and thousands were imprisoned in the 1980s and thousands were forced into exile.[11]

Coming to the end of an endless story about the struggle for women's emancipation, I have arrived at the conclusion that the capitalist and patriarchal order today is an obstacle not only to women's emancipation but, together with it, to human emancipation. I see neither in today's Marxist theory nor in feminist theory much hope for making history through what Ovington called the abolition of poverty and the destruction of servitude among women. There is increasing interest in Marxism in the wake of the continuing economic crisis of capitalism; however, Marxism needs an overhaul, a serious renewal which involves, in part, a dialectical understanding of what Engels called the first great divide in history – the division of human society into two genders that form a hierarchical, patriarchal system.

Overcoming the hyphenation in Marxist-feminism

The life story briefly and partially charted above implies that a century of struggle to link the two major emancipatory projects, Marxism and feminism, involved more than a preoccupation with theoretical interests. It provides evidence about the way in which resistance against patriarchy in a country like Iran is inseparable from the rest of the world. This struggle is rooted in the material and intellectual conditions that have emerged since the nineteenth century, as well as worldwide resistance to class and gender rule. This story reveals both the universality and the particularity of oppression (gender, race, ethnicity, etc.), its political and ideological character, as well as the internationalization of feminist knowledge and women's struggle for emancipation. This account calls into question nativist, nationalist and religious reductions of social relations of gender to questions of identity. Theory and politics are products of an international division of labour in which capitalism-patriarchy-racism rules.

I have pointed so far to two conflictual trends – one that is theoretical and moves away from synthesizing feminism and Marxism, the other political – that is, the escalating gender oppression and class exploitation that call out for a blending of the two. In hyphenated relations since the 1960s, Marxism and feminism have coexisted, debated, interacted and maintained their realms. In fact, with or without hyphenation, the two world views have shaped each other since the end of the nineteenth century without creating a theoretical breakthrough. A glimpse of this history reveals flexibility for renovation and inclusion more in Marxism than in feminism. Marxism since its inception has incorporated many advances in the (social) sciences – for example, Marx and Engels' integration of Darwin's theory of evolution or Henry Lewis Morgan's anthropological work, or Lenin's embracing of John Hobson's study of imperialism, which amounted to a major shift in the Marxist theory of capitalism and the strategy for socialist revolution. In fact, this kind of liaison between Marxism and non-Marxist knowledge and art was underscored by Mao when he emphasized that Marxism 'embraces but cannot replace', for instance, realism in art or theory in physics (Mao 1971: 281).

One may argue along the same lines that Marxism should embrace feminist contributions to the understanding of patriarchy. Feminisms come with their own dynamics, social bases, theories, methodologies, ideologies, epistemologies and visions. Marxism's emphasis on oppression and exploitation appeals to some feminists, while the epistemological and methodological persuasions of many feminists are in conflict with dialectics, which distinguishes Marxism from other social theories. Feminist theories are, thus, in a difficult position for absorbing Marxism. In addition to theoretical and epistemological incongruity, the political repression of Marxism has left its mark on the theoretical front. For instance, in the wake of the restoration of capitalism in China and the fall of the Soviet Union, many socialist-feminists or feminist Marxists abandoned Marxism,[12] and those still committed to the critique of capitalism tend to identify themselves as 'materialist feminists'. Materialism, in this context, is often taken to mean 'political economy', which is placed in opposition to 'culture', 'language' or 'discourse'. However, this understanding of matter and materialism is not Marxist insofar as Marxism understands matter as 'the external reality' – that is, all that exists outside our mind, thus forming a dialectical relationship of unity and struggle with consciousness; in this philosophical understanding, all cultural, linguistic and 'spiritual' phenomena are, like economic relations, also part of matter or of material or external reality.

My inclination to remove the hyphen in Marxist-feminism should not be interpreted as a desire for parting the two. Rather, I have tried to delineate a more constructive and enduring relationship between these two major realms of knowledge, two sites of struggle, and two horizons of emancipation. Inessa Armand (1874–1920), the

Russian Marxist feminist, said what many Marxists have repeatedly said in different words and contexts: 'If the emancipation of women is unthinkable without communism, then communism is unthinkable without the full emancipation of women' (quoted in Clements 1979: 155). There was no illusion, at least in theory, about the intricate nature of emancipation.

Armand and Ovington realized, theoretically, that 'servitude' and 'poverty' would not end within the framework of the regime of bourgeois rights. Equally significant is Lenin's repeated emphasis, after the 1917 revolution, that the full legal equality of women and men immediately granted by the Soviet government could not and would not bring about extralegal (social and economic) equality overnight, a goal which could be achieved only 'in the complete triumph of communism' (Lenin 1982: 84–5). This view is rooted in a historical materialist understanding of the past and future and of the nature of socialist revolution, which treats the equality of genders, classes, races or nations not as a legal question but more profoundly as also social and economic. Building on Marx, Lenin emphasized that socialism is a long period of transition between capitalism and communism, and necessarily combines the features and properties of both systems. Socialism is, in this understanding, a class society, in which the proletariat is the ruling class holding a vision to eventually abolish itself – and all classes – through protracted class struggle (Lenin 1971: 295). The restoration of capitalism in the USSR in 1956 led Mao to theorize the dynamics of class struggle in socialism; he emphasized that the Communist Party, itself a product of class society and the site of a 'new bourgeoisie', is the main ideological and political source for the restoration of capitalism. In these theorizations, (re)production in capitalism is exceedingly complex, and this mode of production does not readily lend itself to transformation into communism. In sharp contrast to this view, we find more recent theorizations of communism as a new order that is already emerging more or less spontaneously without recourse to revolution and, commanded by the dynamics of capitalism, transformed into 'Empire', through new production and labour processes.[13] All of this points to momentous theoretical and political struggles under conditions of unceasing change in the contemporary capitalist world order. Today, interpreting the past and present and charting the future are a heavy burden on both Marxists and feminists.

I opened up this introductory essay by reminding us of the imperialist war of a century ago, when a new phase in the colonization and redivision of Africa, Asia and Latin America began. Consider the massacre of Gaza by the settler colonial and Zionist state of Israel, which came into existence only in 1948 through the forced expulsion and dispossession of the Palestinian population. The birth of the state of Israel is known to Palestinians as *Nakba Day* (the Day of the Catastrophe). Thinking through the horror of our time, a world that is messy, chaotic and riddled with injustice, violence, war and lawlessness, I observe traces of an order in this anarchy. At the core of this (dis)order is the logic of patriarchal racist capitalism/imperialism, in which women's bodies and sexuality are its battleground. In this anarchical social (dis)order, women inhabit contradictory relations of being the subject/object, possessors/dispossessors or saviour/betrayers of culture and social relations; this social disorder creates both the condition of women's liberation and of their subjugation.

Resistance to this colonial order and to the states carved up by imperialist powers out of the remnants of older empires began immediately and everywhere on the three continents – and continues in our time. Women participated, actively and on a mass scale, in the uprisings in Arab countries that began in December 2010 in Tunisia and spread throughout the Middle East and North Africa. They were organizers, leaders and cyberactivists. However, most women did not take part in these protests as members of organized women's movements demanding the dismantling of patriarchal gender relations. They, together with males and side by side with them, called for the replacement of dictators with parliamentary democracy and thus left the socio-economic system and the class structure intact. Even worse was the centre-less and leaderless politics that was proudly advocated by many, including secular youth groups. While the poverty-stricken majority did not gain any ground, women lost even more as they were subjected to male violence even in the streets and squares. Within a period of two years, the dictators were toppled in Tunisia, Egypt, Yemen and Libya and were succeeded by well-organized groups advocating another form of dictatorship in the form of theocracy. Not long after in Egypt – the main centre of political power in the Middle East and North Africa – the army ignored the popular quest for parliamentarianism and installed a military dictator at the helm of the state. In Syria, the diverse groups opposed to Assad's dictatorial regime relied on regional and imperialist powers for military and political support. Within a year, the country had turned into a battlefield between the Assad regime, Islamic fundamentalists, Western imperialism and Arab and Islamic states in the region. In the absence of revolutionary politics, the uprisings led to yet more theocratic rule in which women, the labouring masses, ethnic and religious minorities and freedom of opinion and association were seriously threatened. It seemed as if people in the Arab streets were replicating the 1979 Iranian revolution. In the case of both the Iranian revolution and the so-called 'Arab Spring', the absence of revolutionary consciousness – that is, theory, politics and organizing – made it possible for imperialism and Islamic fundamentalism to suppress any struggle for revolutionary change. At the time of writing in the summer of 2014, the conflict between and coexistence of these two obsolete forces have devastated the peoples and countries of the Middle East and North Africa. Here as elsewhere in the world, women and men are ready for a transformation of this horrible reality into a bright future for the majority of the people. However, consciousness or subjective factors lag behind objective reality, playing into the hands of a minority who have monopolized violence as well as political and economic power.

How to read this book

> The work that I want to do in my maturity, could not be done without the existence of the growing women's culture, or without the support of a women's movement … We need courage, and we draw on each other for courage, but we have to remember that there have been women who did not have the kind of networks, the kind of culture, the kind of politics surrounding them that we have. And this in itself is an immense step forward, and it's something we have to protect, we have to further, we have to defend, in order for all of us to do the kind of work we want to do, and that the world needs us to do. Adrienne Rich (quoted in Langdell 2004: 149)

This book examines, within the frameworks of feminism and Marxism, a selection of major concepts in social theory and politics. The contributors were not given a blueprint for writing their chapters, although I have been familiar with their work. Some of the authors assess the divide between Marxism and feminism, while others illustrate the usefulness of synthesis by way of examining the concept they have chosen for this book. The contributors come from diverse backgrounds, and their writing reflects the internationalization of both feminist and Marxist scholarship as well as the urge to build one upon the other. They write from different Marxist perspectives, including non-Western ones that are often excluded or derided in Eurocentric Marxist literature. The majority of the chapters were written specifically for this book, while some, such as the two chapters by Haug, 'Gender relations' and 'The Marx within feminism', Bannerji's chapter 'Building from Marx: reflections on "race", gender and class' and the Epilogue by Ebert called 'Gender after class', have been previously published.

The book is intended for scholars, students and activists who are curious about the tenuous relationship between Marxism and feminism; for those who are interested in engaging in a project of 'naming' – that is, in naming what is bourgeois and racist about feminism and what is patriarchal and racist about Marxism; for those who are curious about the hyphenation in Marxist-feminism, in the feminist analysis of class, and in the analysis of race and difference in both. It is also intended for those who strive to advance our knowledge and praxis of revolutionary feminism. The book is aimed at theoretical remembering – that is, recalling the contribution of the many feminists before us whose work was indispensable in shaping our thoughts. As Adrienne Rich puts it so eloquently, this is only possible if we have the courage to engage with each other's ideas and be ready to (re)think, revise and (re)build Marxism and feminist theory and revive their revolutionary promise.

The book is also a theoretical departure from the 'marriage' or 'divorce' metaphors which were fashioned in the 1980s following the publication of Heidi Hartmann's seminal chapter 'The unhappy marriage of Marxism and Feminism', which became the subtitle in Lydia Sargent's edited book, *Women and Revolution: The Unhappy Marriage of Marxism and Feminism*, published in 1981. Hartmann suggested that these two approaches were incompatible in explicating gender and class relations. At the core of this departure is the desire to arrive at a revolutionary feminist project which is well grounded in the knowledge and experience of feminism as an oppositional force; a feminist knowledge that understands the universality of patriarchy, racist capitalism and, in/with it, its multiple particularities – a form of feminist knowledge which is not intimidated by cultural forms and does not reduce politics to culture, nor deculturalizes politics.

As I have discussed so far, the post-1980s feminist theory developed largely in the direction of post-structuralism and postmodernism and mainstream Marxism continued to overlook both the centrality of racist patriarchy to the capitalist system, and the importance of women and their struggles in changing the racist capitalist system of power. Thus, *Marxism and Feminism* is opening up the argument that a new synthesis of Marxist and feminist thought is not only possible but also necessary in order to generate an effective challenge to all forms of oppression and exploitation. In short, the goal of the book is twofold. One aim is a careful recording of the epistemological and methodological debates on feminist ideas for revolutionary social transformation. The second aim is to present a renewed Marxist-feminist analysis of these ideas. Ultimately, the book is intended to present an analysis of feminism and Marxism that is fully coherent and integrated through dialectical and historical materialism, which can serve as a basis for both scholarship and activism.

The book is divided into two main sections. The first section, 'Class and race in Marxism and feminism', contains three chapters which I regard as foundational in understanding the renewed and historicized Marxist-feminist approaches being advanced in this book. Two chapters are by the German Marxist-feminist scholar Frigga Haug; these have not been widely available in English until the present volume. The third chapter in this section is by the anti-racist feminist and Marxist scholar Himani Bannerji. Crucially, her chapter argues for an integrative understanding of gender, class and race, and it represents a dialectical materialist account of Marxist-feminist ontology and epistemology.

The second main section of the book, 'Marxist-feminist keywords', includes the contribution of twelve scholars and is organized in alphabetical order of the keywords. Each author has written a concise piece on their chosen concept. These chapters have been generated through a number of collaborative workshop sessions and conference symposia, with the goal of theorizing issues that are essential to the work of revolutionary social transformation. In selecting 'keywords', our goal has not been to cover a comprehensive list of concepts; rather, they represent a small sample of the core conceptual – and unresolved – debates within Marxism and feminism. We also recognize that the concepts selected are not *discrete*, but are related to one another and are best understood in clusters and in conversation with each other. In short, the book presents a clear and rigorous case for the synergy of Marxist and feminist thought by building on, yet nonetheless going beyond, previous theoretical debates. As stated above, it intends to open up discussion instead of concluding or enfolding them. It applies a renewed Marxist-feminist framework to a series of key concepts essential to the work of revolutionary feminism and appealing to a broad and growing global audience of scholars and activists currently engaging with such ideas. The epilogue, 'Gender after class', written by Teresa L. Ebert, applies dialectical materialism to the theorization of women's oppression and exploitation, and critiques current trends in feminism.

In reading this book, keep in mind that the goal of each chapter is not necessarily to present a broad literature review on each topic, nor is it meant to cover the entire corpus of Marxist and feminist literature. Each chapter creates a concise point of entry into the most important issues that have been debated in and between Marxism and feminism around a given keyword. Authors have explained *why* certain issues have become so prominent in Marxism and feminism. They have explained *how* Marxist theory has addressed the keyword and the problems/lacunae raised around the relationships of capitalism with gender, class, race and sexuality. It is important to note that the theoretical nuances in each chapter may be treated as continuing dialogues within Marxism and feminism.

I encourage the reader to actively engage with the book by using the following questions as a reading guide: How can we retheorize capitalist patriarchy through a full analysis of racism, colonialism and imperialism? How would a Marxist-feminist conceptualization enable us to develop a revolutionary feminist understanding of the anarchy of capitalism and the forces of change? What is it that a Marxist-feminist project makes visible that would not otherwise be seen? To put it differently, what invisible relations will be fully, rather than partially, unearthed by our collective effort at retheorizing Marxism and feminism? I encourage you to look into the dialectical and historical materialist method of analysis and argumentation employed in the book. This method is key in the learning suggested by the essays. One last word: in keeping with the philosophical and methodological orientation of this work, it would be useful to debate the issues, push the theoretical boundaries framed here, try them out in practice, and, most importantly, see whether it offers learning for the purpose of building the better world that we all deserve.

Notes

1 The building of socialism and the restoration of capitalism constitute processes of struggle on many fronts, and cannot be traced to an exact date. However, in the case of the USSR, the Twentieth Congress of the Communist Party in 1956 became a watershed after Nikita Khrushchev launched, in a 'secret report', a major theoretical and ideological shift, which the Communist Party of China assessed as a project of restoration of capitalism. The conflict over this shift led, by 1963/64, to the first major split in the post-1917 international communist movement. The party in China initiated the Great Proletarian Cultural Revolution (1966–68, and continuing unofficially until 1976) as a means to prevent the restoration of capitalism in the way it had happened in the USSR. In both 1956 and 1976, the architects of restoration resorted to violence against the advocates of socialism. Before 1956, critics had explained the limitations of Soviet socialism as a product of bureaucratization (state capitalism), the personality or psychology of Stalin (dictatorship), or the retarded development of productive forces (economism). Mao provided a different explanation by emphasizing the nature of socialism as a class society, its transitional position between capitalism and communism, the prominence of class struggle especially in the party, the role of a political and ideological line, and the determining nature of the superstructure in the course of transition from capitalism to socialism. In China much more than in the USSR, restoration happened in the wake of intensive political and ideological struggles between 'socialist roaders' and 'capitalist roaders'. See, for instance, Foreign Languages Press (1973), Gao (2008) and Hinton (1990).

2 For instance, six years after the formation of the People's Republic of China (in October 1949), Simone de Beauvoir visited the country and wrote in detail about the progress made in the life of the Chinese people, especially women (De Beauvoir 2001). To give another example, Julia Kristeva visited China in the wake of the Cultural Revolution and depicted the Chinese Revolution as a 'women's revolution' (Kristeva 1991). See also Note 12, below.

3 For a critique of this theoretical shift, see Ebert (1996).

4 Marxism's preoccupation with women's emancipation is widely acknowledged. Michèle Barrett, for instance, has noted that 'Outside feminist thought itself there is no tradition of critical analysis of women's oppression that could match the incisive attention given to this question by one Marxist thinker after another' (1983: 164).

5 For more on this, see Carpenter and Mojab (2011).

6 See also Mojab (2000, 2006).

7 I have borrowed this metaphor from Hammed Shahidian (2002: 1).

8 For a study and documentation of Foucault's reports and other writings on Iran, see Afary and Anderson (2005), who argue that his enthusiasm for the 'Islamic revolution' was rooted in his understanding of modernity and secularism. In his review of this book, Toscano disconnects Foucault's understanding of the revolution from his theoretical position and reduces his relatively detailed writing on Iran to a 'brief, if fraught,

intellectual episode' (2006: 57), as if Foucault had abandoned his theoretical and political commitments during the year he was preoccupied with Iran even while he was being challenged by and responding to the criticism he received from, among others, an Iranian feminist, Atoussa H., and Marxist scholar of Islam Maxime Rodinson. Toscano believes that Foucault's position on Iran's political Islam was shaped by his 'anti-Marxism of the late 1970s' (ibid.: 57).

9 For a detailed record of this round of resistance and international solidarity, see Matin and Mohajer (2013).

10 I am quoting Marx's remarks about the 1848 revolutions in Europe: 'The social revolution of the nineteenth century cannot take its poetry from the past but only from the future' (1979: 106).

11 The extensive archive of the literature and reports on political prisoners can be accessed through my website, 'Political prisoners: the art of resistance in the Middle East' (womenpoliticalprisoners.com/).

12 For instance, Claudie Broyelle (1977), who wrote enthusiastically about progress in dismantling patriarchal gender relations in the wake of the Cultural Revolution in China, failed to make sense out of the restoration of capitalism and retracted her writing (see Broyelle et al. 1980).

13 These are ideas of Hardt and Negri (2000, 2004); for a critique, see K.J.A. (2006). For recent thought, of a philosophical nature, on communism, see Douzinas and Žižek (2010).

References

Afary, J. (1996) *The Iranian Constitutional Revolution, 1906–1911: Grassroots Democracy, Social Democracy, and the Origins of Feminism*, New York: Colombia University Press.

Afary, J. and K. Anderson (2005) *Foucault and the Iranian Revolution: Gender and the Seductions of Islamism*, Chicago, IL: University of Chicago Press.

Aguilar, D. (2012) 'From triple jeopardy to intersectionality: the feminist perplex', *Comparative Studies of South Asia, Africa and the Middle East*, 32(2): 415–28.

Bannerji, H. (2001) *Inventing Subjects: Studies in Hegemony, Patriarchy and Colonialism*, London: Anthem.

Barrett, M. (1983) 'Feminism', in T. Bottomore, L. Harris, V. G. Kiernan and R. Miliband (eds), *A Dictionary of Marxist Thought*, Cambridge, MA: Harvard University Press, pp. 163–5.

Broyelle, C. (1977) *Women's Liberation in China*, trans. M. Cohen and G. Herman, Atlantic Highlands, NJ: Humanities Press.

Broyelle, C., J. Broyelle and E. Tschirhart (1980) *China: A Second Look*, trans. S. Matthews, Atlantic Highlands, NJ: Humanities Press.

Carpenter, S. and S. Mojab (eds) (2011) *Educating from Marx: Race, Gender and Learning*, New York: Palgrave Macmillan.

Clements, B. (1979) *Bolshevik Feminist: The Life of Alexandra Kollontai*, Bloomington: University of Indiana Press.

De Beauvoir, S. (2001) *The Long March: An Account of Modern China*, trans. A. Wainhouse, London: Phoenix.

Dell, F. (1914) 'Socialism and feminism', *New Review: A Weekly Review of International Socialism*, 2(6): 349–53.

Douzinas, C. and S. Žižek (2010) *The Idea of Communism*, London: Verso.

Ebert, T. L. (1996) *Ludic Feminism and After: Postmodernism, Desire, and Labor in Late Capitalism*, Ann Arbor: University of Michigan Press.

Eisenstein, H. (2009) *Feminism Seduced: How Global Elites Use Women's Labor and Ideas to Exploit the World*, London: Paradigm Publishers.

Foreign Languages Press (1973) *Three Major Struggles on China's Philosophical Front (1949–64)*, Peking: Foreign Languages Press.

Gao, M. (2008) *The Battle for China's Past: Mao and the Cultural Revolution*, London: Pluto.

Grewal, I. and C. Kaplan (eds) (1994) *Scattered Hegemonies: Postmodernity and Transnational Feminist Practices*, Minneapolis: University of Minnesota Press.

Hammer, R. (2002) *Anti-feminism and Family Terrorism: A Critical Perspective*, Lanham, MD: Rowman and Littlefield.

Hardt, M. and A. Negri (2000) *Empire*, Cambridge, MA: Harvard University Press.

— (2004) *Multitude*, New York: Penguin.

Hinton, W. (1990) *The Great Reversal: The Privatization of China, 1978–1989*, New York: Monthly Review Press.

Javid, M. A. (1356 [1977]) *'Demokrasi-ye Naqes': Barresi-ye Sal-ha-ye 1320–32* ['Incomplete democracy': survey of the years 1941–53], Daftar-e 1. N.p.: Etehad-iye-ye Komonist-ha-ye Iran.

K.J.A. (2006) 'On empire: revolutionary communism or "communism" without revolution?', *A World to Win*, 32: 66–88.

Kristeva, J. (1991) *About Chinese Women*, New York: Marion Boyars.

Langdell, C. C. (2004) *Adrianne Rich: The Moment of Change*, Westport, CT: Praeger.

Lenin, V. I. (1971) 'Economics and politics in the era of the dictatorship of the proletariat', in V. I. Lenin, *Selected Works in Three Volumes*, vol. III, Moscow: Progress Publishers, pp. 289–97.

— (1982) *On the Emancipation of Women*, Moscow: Progress.

Mao Tsetung (1971) 'Talks at the Yenan Forum on Literature and Art', in *Selected Readings from the Works of Mao Tsetung*, Peking: Foreign Languages Press, pp. 250–86.

Marx, K. (1969) 'The class struggles in France, 1848 to 1850', in K. Marx and F. Engels, *Selected Works*, vol. 1, Moscow: Progress, pp. 186–299.

— (1979) 'The Eighteenth Brumaire of Napoleon Bonaparte', in K. Marx and F. Engels, *Collected Works*, vol. 11, Moscow: Progress, pp. 99–197.

— (1983) *Capital: A Critique of Political Economy*, vol. 1, Moscow: Progress.

Matin, M. and N. Mojaher (2013) *Iranian Women's Uprising: March 8th 1979*, vol. 1: *Renaissance*, vol. II: *International Solidarity*, Berkeley, CA: Noghteh.

Matin-Asgari, A. (2001) *Iranian Student Opposition to the Shah*, Costa Messa, CA: Mazda.

Mies, M. (1986) *Patriarchy and Capital Accumulation on a World Scale: Women in the International Division of Labour*, New York: Zed Books.

Millett, K. (1982) *Going to Iran*, New York: Coward, McCann & Geoghegan.

Moghissi, H. (1994) *Populism and Feminism in Iran: Women's Struggle in a Male-defined Revolutionary Movement*, New York: St Martin's Press.

Mohanty, C. T., A. Russo and L. Torres (eds) (1991) *Third World Women and the Politics of Feminism*, Bloomington: Indiana University Press.

Mojab, S. (1991) 'The state and university: the "Islamic Cultural Revolution" in the institutions of higher education of Iran, 1980–87', Doctoral thesis, Urbana: University of Illinois at Urbana-Champaign.

— (2000) 'Civilizing the state: the university in the Middle East', in S. Inayatullah and J. Gidley (eds), *The University in Transformation: Global Perspectives on the Futures of the University*, Westport, CT: Greenwood, pp. 137–48.

— (2006) 'Feminist studies in focus', *Atlantis: A Women's Studies Journal*, 31(1): 85–7.

— (2015) 'The state and women's studies: the Islamization-indigenization of anti-feminism', *Iran Nameh*, 29(4) (in Persian).

Ovington, M. W. (1914) 'Socialism and the feminist movement', *New Review: A Weekly Review of International Socialism*, 2(3): 143–7, www.marxists.org/history/usa/pubs/newreview/1914/v2n03-mar-1914.pdf.

Shahidian, H. (2002) *Women in Iran: Gender Politics in the Islamic Republic*, Westport, CT: Greenwood.

Tabari, A. and N. Yeganeh (eds) (1982) *In the Shadow of Islam: The Women's Movement in Iran*, London: Zed Books.

Toscano, A. (2006) 'Dossier for the prosecution', *Radical Philosophy*, 136: 54–7.

PART ONE

CLASS AND RACE IN MARXISM AND FEMINISM

2 | GENDER RELATIONS

Frigga Haug

'Gender relations' is a common expression in many fields of research, yet it is hardly ever clearly defined in conceptual terms. At the same time as there is a discussion of different versions of and approaches to gender relations, therefore, the clarification of the concept of 'gender relations' itself also needs to be advanced. The concept should be suitable to investigate critically the structural role which genders play in social relations in their totality. It presupposes that which is a result of the relations which are to be investigated: the existence of 'genders' in the sense of historically recognizable men and women. Complementarity in procreation is the natural basis upon which what has come to be regarded as 'natural' has been socially formed in the historical process. In this way genders emerge from the social process as unequal. Their inequality then becomes the foundation for further transformations, and gender relations become fundamental regulating relations in all social formations. No field can be investigated meaningfully without complementary research into the ways in which gender relations shape and are shaped. When these are ignored (as is traditionally the case), an image of all relations as implicitly male gains general acceptance. Opposing this tendency and forcing the sciences to research the 'forgotten women' was the great contribution of the feminist movement of the last third of the twentieth century. Often, though, this perspective is obscured to some extent by the phenomenology of men and women as they relate to each other as effects of gender relations, which thus focuses analysis on relations between particular individuals, as if these were able to be founded upon themselves. In German this is particularly noticeable when the concept of gender relations is expressed in the singular as 'the gender relation', which appears in almost all scientific studies (of the 145 relevant titles which, according to an internet search, appeared in German in the period 1994–2000, only four use the concept in the plural); in English, the plural is used exclusively, while 'gender' appears only in the singular. The singular may be appropriate, if it is a matter of the proportional representation of men and women in selected areas. Whoever uses it in a broader sense consequently has difficulties avoiding an assumed certainty regarding what genders are. In order to define the concept in such a way that it is able to comprehend the moving and transformative aspects of its object, the plural is appropriate. In the widest sense, gender relations are, like relations of production, complex praxis relations. The analysis of such relations must consider both the process of formation of actors and the reproduction of the social whole.

French Revolution: Olympe de Gouges

During the French Revolution, Olympe de Gouges wrote a manifesto entitled 'Declaration of the rights of woman and the female citizen' (1979); she was born in 1748 and executed in 1793 on account of her protests and her organization of women's clubs. Without having an expression such as 'gender relations' at her disposal, she effectively thought total social reproduction as being determined by such relations. Public misery and corruption of governments, she declared, were a product of 'the lack of rights of women' (ibid.: 36). 'A revolution is being prepared which will raise up the spirit and the soul of the one and the other sex, and both will work together in the future for the common good' (ibid.: 35). Without social and political equality of the sexes the revolution would become a farce. Gender relations appropriate to forms of domination were enforced by the law; thus the law would also be a means for the enforcement of emancipatory gender relations. The 'unnatural' domination of men over women was derived by de Gouges psychologically: the male, 'extravagant, blind ... bloated and degenerated, wants to command despotically a sex which possesses all intellectual capacities' (ibid.: 35). Women, kept like slaves in the contemporary society, would consequently, however, begin to rule as slaves over men (Friedrich Nietzsche later took up this point from an opposed standpoint, when he depicted the slave rebellion of women). De Gouges characterized that doubled reversal as the very quintessence of general ruination. The female sex, whose formation had been neglected, developed treacherous forms of domination in such a position without rights. Women thus became more harmful than good; as a 'political' means they dedicated their charm to the cultivation of corrupt power over men; their weapon was poison. In all previous politics there had been a de facto domination of women in cabinet, in the embassy, in the command of the armed forces, in the ministries, in the presidency, in the bishoprics and in the sacred college of cardinals, and 'everything which constitutes the stupidity of men … was subject to the greed and ambition of the female sex' (ibid.: 41). De Gouges did not pursue, therefore, a discourse of the victim; she thought at an early stage of the interpenetration of domination and oppression in the assumption of a fundamental equality of capacity of the sexes. More far-sightedly than later feminisms, she diagnosed the necessity of the inclusion of the concrete social situation in the idea of the social construction of gender. The form of gender relations decided on morality (*Sittlichkeit*), justice and freedom. Brutes developed in deformed relations. The fact that women used their beauty as a lever for the acquisition of power and money was a consequence of their exclusion from regular participation in these goods: 'Yet mustn't we admit that in a society where a man buys a woman like a slave from the African coast, any other way to gain prosperity is closed to her?' (ibid.: 42). Brecht later judged in a similar way (Brecht 1967: 474).

De Gouges linked the oppression of women with their function in the reproduction of the species and further articulated both of these with the law of inheritance and women's lack of rights regarding the free expression of opinion. On the basis of their bondage (they were not allowed to name the father of their child), many women and, with them, their children were thrown into poverty, ideologically supported by sanctimonious prejudices against the open confession of fatherhood. 'The rich, childless Epicurean has no problem with going to his poor neighbour and augmenting his family' (de Gouges 1979: 44). The mingling which was actually occurring was hushed up in order to maintain the class barriers. However, de Gouges also declared marriage to be 'the grave of trust and love' (ibid.: 43). She demanded the entry of women into the national assembly (ibid.: 36), access to all public offices for all according to their capabilities, as well as equal rights in paid occupations. The state's expenditure was to be publicly accounted for, the use of budgetary funds by women according to their needs to be sued for. A 'social contract' between the sexes was supposed to protect the free decision of individuals on the basis of affections, protect their rights regarding joint assets, and also give recognition to children born outside of wedlock. The opponents of these politics were 'the hypocrites, the prudes, the clergy and their entire infernal following' (ibid.: 44).

The following elements can be gained from de Gouges which strengthen a concept of gender relations: egalitarianism in relation to the sexes is heuristically fruitful; relations of subordination of one sex lead to brutality and the ruination of society; it is important to think of actors in gender relations in their particular structures of power and subjugation (slave morality) and their consequences; law as a form in which the dominant relations are reproduced is to be noted in the *dispositif* of gender relations. The assignment of the reproduction of the species to women as a private affair instead of a social solution is accorded a fundamental status.

Bourgeois ethnological studies

Ethnological studies on gender relations in the development of humanity emerged with the evolutionism of the nineteenth century. They referred in the first instance to matriarchy and patriarchy. The most well-known representatives are Johann Jakob Bachofen and Lewis Henry Morgan. The Jesuit Joseph-François Lafitau (1983), who associated the image of feminine domination in antiquity and in Native American groups with specific forms of social regulation such as autonomous self-governance of villages and a type of council system, is regarded as a precursor. He showed the connections between systems of inheritance and descent founded upon the mother's side, political rights of women, and a differentiated spectrum of activities which undermined the focus upon the mother.

While preparing for his work *The Origin of the Family, Private Property and the State*, Engels read Bachofen, alongside Marx's excerpts from Morgan and others. It was Bachofen who became the most influential for the reception of this field of research in Marxism. Among others, Paul Lafargue, August Bebel, Franz Mehring, Max Horkheimer, Walter Benjamin and Ernst Bloch referred to him, and he also played a decisive role in later feminist discussions.

Bachofen (1975) presented (from 1861) material studies on the basis of a rereading primarily of classical mythology. Central was the idea that the maternal principle was expressed in love, peace, freedom, equality, humanity and commonality, and therefore that the dominance of women which was based upon matriarchy represented the 'civilized' part of humanity's history. He portrayed development as a violent-subversive dialectical process. Monogamous marriage was represented as a women's victory after a long drawn-out struggle against the humiliating institution of hetaerism. It was a victory which was difficult to win, because marriage as an exclusive association seemed to injure the divine decree. Hetaerism thus also appeared as accompanying atonement. Accordingly, he read Greek mythology as a history of the struggle between powers which affirmed the legality of marriage (Demeter) and those which sought to undermine it (those related to the hetaerism). The hard road from mothers to the domination of women conflicted, according to Bachofen, with the sensual and erotic dimensions of the 'life of women'; the latter undermined 'necessarily more and more the Demetrian morality and ultimately reduced matriarchal existence back to an Aphroditean hetaerism patterned after the full spontaneity of natural life' (ibid.: 102, trans. modified). 'The progress from the maternal to the paternal conception of man forms the most important turning point in the history of the relations between the sexes' (ibid.: 109); 'the triumph of paternity brings with it the liberation of the spirit from the manifestations of nature, a sublimation of human existence over the laws of material life' (ibid.: 109). Bachofen's criteria became decisive for the further debates concerning matriarchy: female lines of descent, group sexuality with the impossibility of determining the father; and social and political communal participation, complemented by communal property, and including the contradictory gender stereotype of the woman-mother, morally superior, on the one hand, natural on the other. This final element served further to transfigure the matriarchy into the originary form of social organization.

Bachofen used the concept of 'gender relations' alternately in the singular or in the plural. He thought the sexes as fixed in their determinate qualities and limited his interpretations primarily to legal and religious forms. Departing from a strict attribution of that which is naturally female and male, he 'found' in classical mythology precisely those commonly accepted thought-forms: the opposition of reason and emotion, nature and sensuality, spirit (*Geist*) and culture. Here it can be observed how veneration of women and enthusiastic attribution of a feminine nature can function as the reverse side of the oppression of women, by transfiguring them in compensation. Ernst Bloch diagnosed that Bachofen's heart was for the matriarchy, his head for the patriarchy (Bloch 1968: 119), so that at the end he finally foresaw the detested communism as a return to the figures of the mother. Because Bachofen derived the real relations of life out of their celestial forms (myths, religion) instead of vice versa, the real work – that is, of deciphering domination and oppression in gender relations and the utopian forms in which they were figured – remained still to be done.

Morgan (1987) combined a rereading of ancient and particularly Greek and Roman sources as well as those of the Old Testament with ethnological reports about tribes in Asia, Africa and North and South America (his fundamental reference was the Iroquois). He depicted two lines of history: technical-civilizing progress (invention and discovery) and the development of institutions from group marriage to the monogamous family and the state. The description of invention included livestock breeding, agriculture, pottery – in short, the whole of human life, since the question of the spread of humans over the whole of the earth depended on progresses in the forms of sustenance of life. Morgan did not speak of matriarchy, but of descent in the female line; his chief criteria were economic: occupation of land in common, work in common, a budget of a communist type. According to his view, there had been an originary community which consisted of equals. The development of private property led to the undermining of collective structures. A chief focus of his researches was the process of separation of family forms and lines of kinship; he comprehended the latter as passive, the family as active, and kinship structures as fossils of earlier forms of organization. Forms founded upon descent in the female line interested Morgan because they preceded the emergence of property and its accumulation. A theory of gender relations can gain from Morgan the ideas of the development of the forces of production, of the obtaining of the means of sustenance of life and of the forms in which procreation and rearing are organized, all of which are to be thought in their mutual interpenetrations.

Karl Marx and Friedrich Engels

In his first sketch of a critique of political economy, the 'Economic and philosophic manuscripts of 1844', Marx spoke of 'both sexes in their social relations' (Marx 1975: 243), a formulation which can be used for a theory of gender relations. The early Engels spoke of the relation of the sexes, but he meant essentially the relationship between men and women. From their early writings, both Marx and Engels were concerned with man–woman relations free of domination which they anchored integrally in their project of social emancipation. The famous sentence, taken up from Fourier, in which they argue that the 'degree of female emancipation' is 'the natural measure of general emancipation' (Marx and Engels 1975a: 195), established the principle that the development of humanity can be read off from the development of the relationship of the sexes, 'because here, in the relation of woman to man, of the weak to the strong, the victory of human nature over brutality is most evident' (ibid.: 195). According to the 'Economic and philosophic manuscripts of 1844', 'the relation of the man to the woman' determines 'to what extent man's need has become a human need, to what extent man has become, in his most individual being, at the same time a social being' (Marx 1975: 294).

The scenario of 'The German ideology' moves the problematic of the sexes on to centre stage. Among the 'moments' 'which have simultaneously existed from the beginning of history' is the one in which 'humans, who daily reproduce their material life, start to produce other humans, to procreate … This family, which in the beginning is the only social relation, later becomes subordinated when the increased needs create new social relations and the increased number of individuals creates new needs' (Marx and Engels 1975b: 35). And from the beginning they state:

> The production of life, both of one's own in work and of others in procreation, already appears immediately as a double relationship – on the one hand a natural one, on the other hand a social one – social, in the sense that we can understand it as a cooperation of several individuals. From this we conclude that a certain mode of production or industrial stage is always connected with a certain mode of cooperation or social stage … [T]herefore 'the history of humanity' always has to be written and elaborated in interrelation with the history of industry and exchange. (Ibid.: 35)

Not noted here is only that the complementary rule must also be regarded as valid – namely, that political-economic history is never to be studied in abstraction from the history of those natural-social relations. The remark that 'the family' becomes a 'subordinated relation' demands that the process of this subordination is specially to be investigated. 'The German ideology' contains a series of remarks regarding how development in this area proceeds. The 'unequal, quantitative just as much as qualitative, distribution of labour and of its products … [namely] property, which has its seed, its first form, in the family where women and children are the slaves of men' (ibid.: 35), is regarded as fundamental. The 'latent slavery in the family' was comprehended as 'the first property', which, the authors emphasized, 'here already corresponds perfectly to the definition of modern economists, according to which it is the power of disposing of the labour-power of others' (ibid.: 35). The division of labour developed further together with needs on the basis of surpluses which generated, in their turn, further surpluses, just as independent production of the means of life was both a result of an 'increase in population' and in its turn promoted this (ibid.: 30). The division of labour further contained the possibility of the possession by different individuals of 'pleasure and labour, production and consumption' (ibid.: 33); it was therefore at the same time a precondition of domination and of development. Two forms of domination which overlap each other had determined the progress of history: the power of some to dispose of the labour-power of many in the production of the means of life and the power of (the majority of) men of disposing of women's labour-power, reproductive capabilities and the sexual body of women in the 'family'. The contradictory interpenetration caused the development of community to advance at the same time as the destruction of its foundations, supported and borne by gender relations, in which, for reasons bound up with domination, the socially transformed was claimed to be natural and the sensuous-bodily substance was subordinated with nature.

In their works on the critique of political economy Marx and Engels time and again ran into blockages which were forms in which gender relations were played out. Both noted carefully the composition of the new factory personnel according to sex. Marx made the following excerpt: 'The English spinning mills employ 196,818 women and only 158,818 men … In the English flax mills of Leeds, for every 100 male workers there were found to be 147 female workers. In Dundee and on the east coast of Scotland as many as 280 … In 1833, no fewer than 38,927 women were employed alongside 18,593 men in the North American cotton mills' (Marx 1975: 244). After the analysis of a multitude of statistics, Engels came to the conclusion that in the English factory system in 1839 at least two-thirds of the workers were women. He called this a 'displacement of male workers', 'an over-turning of the social order', which would lead to the dissolution of the family and neglect of children. At this stage he did not further consider the gendered division of labour which led him to view the labour force as essentially male (Engels 1975: 434). A little later he discovered that in the social division of domestic and non-domestic labour the agent of the first, independently of the respective genders, was dominated by the agent of the second. Such a discovery grasped a fundamental element of gender relations of domination. Nevertheless, Engels gave an account of the outrage over the situation of the factory workers essentially with categories of morality (deterioration of morals). This made it difficult to see the interrelation as an effect of gender relations specific to conditions of capitalist exploitation. He recognized 'that the sexes have been falsely placed against one another from the beginning. If the reign of the wife over the husband, as inevitably brought about by the factory system, is inhuman, the original rule of the husband over the wife must have also been inhuman' (ibid.: 438). He located the problem in the community of goods with unequal contributions. He concluded that private property undermined the relationships of the sexes. Conversely, he thought that the proletarian family, because it was without property, was free of domination. 'Sex-love in the relationship with a woman becomes, and can only become, the real rule among the oppressed classes, which means today among the proletariat ... Here there is no property, for the preservation and inheritance of which monogamy and male domination were established' (Engels 1990: 180). The idea functioned as an ethical ideal in the workers' movement. As a pronouncement on an actual here and now it was always contradicted by the facts. It missed theoretically the function of the division of labour between house and factory and therefore the role of gender relations in the reproduction of capitalist society. Engels' further interest was directed in particular to the man–woman relation, not the investigation of how gender relations traverse all human practices. He expected from communist society that it would 'transform the relations between the sexes into a purely private matter ... into which society has no occasion to intervene. It can do this since it does away with private property and educates children on a communal basis, and in this way removes the two bases of traditional marriage, the dependence rooted in private property, of the women on the man, and of the children on the parents' (Engels 1976: 332, trans. modified).

In the first volume of *Capital* Marx noted that the maintenance and reproduction of the working class as a condition for the reproduction of capital remained left 'to the labourer's instincts of self-preservation and of propagation' (Marx 1996: 572). This is the case, except for forms of 'care for the poor' and 'social welfare', but can nevertheless mislead theory into moving the process as a private matter out of the focal point of interest and possibly to treat it as a mere gift of nature. An effect of the control of men over women in the family consists in the lesser value of the labour of women compared to that of men. This situation makes women's work particularly suitable for capitalist exploitation as cheap labour.

Marx evaluated official reports in which the workers appeared grammatically, in the first instance, as gender neutral; as soon as there were women and children, they were named as extras and as a peculiarity. Thus an implicit maleness appeared in the diction; at the same time, Marx registered that male workers were being replaced by women and children. The consequence of this practice, in gender relations which remained the same, was the destruction of the natural foundations of the working class.

Because the maleness of the proletariat was implicitly assumed in the texts, it was not really made explicit that the form of wage labour actually presupposed the male wage-labourer, precisely because gender relations in which the labour of the production of the means of life (insofar as this occurred in commodity forms) is a social affair which occurs under private forms of domination. The reproduction of the workers (ibid.: 182), on the other hand, entrusted privately to individual families, did not appear to be a social affair. The interpenetration of capitalist exploitation and the division of labour in traditional gender relations demonstrated that capitalist production is based, among other elements, upon the oppression and exploitation of women. In the midst of concentrating on capitalism, Marx had a flash of inspiration: 'However it still remains true that to replace them they must be reproduced, and to this extent the capitalist mode of production is conditional on modes of production lying outside of its own stage of development' (Marx 1997: 108). (The idea was taken up by Rosa Luxemburg in *The Accumulation of Capital*).

Already in the 'Economic and philosophic manuscripts of 1844'

Marx had noted 'a greater economic independence' of women, because 'a wider area of employment opportunities has been opened up' to them by 'changes in the organization of labour', as a result of which 'both sexes [had been] brought closer together in their social relations' (Marx 1975: 243). In the first volume of *Capital* he then directed his attention to the 'peculiar composition of the body of workers, composed of individuals of both sexes' (Marx 1996: 424), and finally the placement of women 'in socially organized processes of production outside the domestic sphere' as a 'new economic foundation for a higher form of the family and of the relation between the sexes' (ibid.: 489). Here the relation (in the singular) is actually meant as an attitude or disposition to one another, emanating out from relations in work into all fields. The cooperative labour of the sexes in close quarters and at night was regarded by Marx, under the given relations of production, as a 'pestiferous source of corruption and slavery' (ibid.: 489; cf. Engels 1975: 438); the hope remained, however, that it would become a 'source of humane development' as soon as 'the process of production is for the worker' (Marx 1996: 489). This perspective was restricted in the lands of state socialism to the professional occupation of women. Since the totality of labour necessary for reproduction and its reinforcement in morality, law, politics (in shorthand: ideology), sexuality and so on did not enter into the analysis, this solution misunderstood the persistence and complexity of gender relations. In the workers' movement, that foreshortening led to the adoption of a theory of the succession of the struggles for liberation, in which it was overlooked that gender relations are always also relations of production, and thus how strong the relations of reinforcement and support for the reproduction of the current form of relations in their totality are. The relations of production cannot, therefore, be revolutionized first and the gender relations only after.

In the last three years of his life (1880–82) Marx made copious ethnological excerpts from Morgan, John Budd Phear, Henry Sumner Maine and John Lubbock. Lawrence Krader designated them as 'empirical ethnology which is simultaneously revolutionary and evolutionary' (Marx 1972: 12). He understood their perspective in the following way: 'the originary community, consisting of equals, is the revolutionary *form* of society which will have a new content after the historical transformation which humanity has experienced and after exploitation in the form of slavery, serfdom and capitalism has been overcome' (ibid.: 14–15). He thought to have found in ethnology proofs for the possibility of cooperative institutions and communal, community-oriented labour relations.

The excerpts from Morgan constituted the major share of this work. The focal points of the 'family' and kinship make them fruitful for the question of gender relations. Marx mostly followed Morgan's views, so that astonishment when gender relations are not mentioned and when they are treated applies to both authors. The material suggests the view that human development proceeded from an original communist equality to domination and oppression through the emergence of private property, that this process was accompanied by progress and, crossing stages of barbarism, led to civil society. Inventions and discoveries assured not only survival, but also the possibility of surplus and thus the foundations for the emergence of wealth, which became a historical reality to be privately appropriated.

Marx excerpted exactly the kinship lines demonstrated by Morgan – from the family related by blood to the *punaluan* and the *syndyasmian* or pairing family, to the patriarchal family (which he held, with Morgan, to be an exception) and to monogamy. That which interested him in Morgan was the idea, later to be more fully developed by Bloch, of a non-contemporaneity. 'The system has out-lived the uses from which it emerged, and survives as if those uses were still valid, even though such a system is in the main unsuited for present conditions' (ibid.: 135). Which women and which men were allowed to marry each other in group marriage thus became relevant, because the tribal lines of the gentes were determined in this way. Everywhere there were female lines of descent, and the children remained with the mother or with the gens of the mother. The father belonged to another gens. At the beginning of humanity's development inventions aimed to achieve the acquisition of the means of subsistence and were in this way easily conceivable for both sexes. 'Common estates and agriculture in common must have led to communal housing and a communistic household … Women received much, with common supplies and households, in which their own gens had a numerical predominance, provid[ing] for a great security' (ibid.: 344). The situation of women deteriorated 'with the rise of the monogamous family, which abolished the communal dwelling, placed the woman and mother in a single family dwelling in the midst of a purely gentile society and separated her from her gentile kin' (ibid.: 344). One gains the impression that regular military campaigns led to the invention of better weapons and to the formation of military leaders; the bow and arrow, the iron sword (barbarism) and firearms (civilization) were regarded as important inventions.

Inasmuch as chieftains, councils and political assemblies are considered – the selection criteria are noted as personal competence, wisdom and eloquence (ibid.: 199) – women are represented only enigmatically: the Iroquois 'women were allowed to express their wishes and opinions through a speaker which they had selected themselves. The council made the decision' (ibid.: 227). After the forms of marriage, the excerpts are concentrated on the development of the cultivation of grain, domestication of animals, military campaigns and the development of property, and later the development of political society. The activity of women, however, is conspicuous in its absence. For example, the following isolated note from Morgan's presentation of the Moqui Pueblo Native Americans appears (without commentary): 'Their women, generally, have control of the granary, and they are more provident than their Spanish neighbours about the future. Ordinarily they try to have a year's provisions on hand' (Morgan, cited in ibid.: 179). One can implicitly gather that responsibility for children – as presumably also for births; at any rate humans multiplied themselves rapidly, but even this notice only obtains a reference to increased means of consumption (ibid.: 172) – held women back from the warpaths. Such wars, however, when successfully issuing in conquests, led to an accumulation of wealth. 'Following upon this, in course of time, was the systematic cultivation of the earth, which tended to identify the family with the soil, and render it a property-making organization' (ibid.: 184). This sheds light on the seeming 'naturalness' of male property, succession according to the father's line of descent and corresponding monogamy. Finally, the head of the family (male) became 'the natural centre of accumulation' (ibid.: 184).

Concentration on the history of men occurred rather implicitly, and was often revealed in the spontaneous choice of words. Marx noted: 'The higher qualities of humanity begin to develop on the basis of the lower stages: personal honour, religious feeling, openness, masculinity and courage now become common character traits, but also cruelty, treachery and fanaticism' (ibid.: 176). He did not appear to note the androcentrism. As long as there was no private property, the line of descent according to the mother was clearly just as little problematic as was her authority. Marx wrote again without further explanation: 'as soon as more property had been accumulated … and an ever greater part was in private possession, the female line of descent (due to inheritance) was ripe for abolition' (ibid.: 342). Origin was now defined according to the father (patrilineal). This was possible due to the fact, among other reasons, that the gradually forming 'political' positions of power (chieftains, councillor, judge) were occupied by men as well.

In Morgan's reading of Fourier, Marx noted an extension of earlier definitions of the family and of its relations to the broader society:

> Fourier characterized the epoch of civilization according to the presence of monogamy and private ownership of land. The modern family contains in essence not only servitus (slavery), but also serfdom, since from the beginning it had a relation to service for agriculture. It contains in itself in miniature all of the antagonisms which later were widely developed in society and the state. (Ibid.: 53)

It can be inferred from the study of Morgan and Marx that war and private property determined gender relations which undermined the originary community and thus promoted development on the basis of inequality. Unfortunately, Marx was largely silent about a form of ethnological research which considered the activity and lives of women beyond the realities of who was allowed to marry whom and how descent in the female line and ur-communism were connected. The rereading of ethnological studies which broke this silence was the late work of Marxist and feminist ethnology. Claude Meillassoux criticized Marx's reading (and its continuation by Engels) with having stumbled 'into the ideological trap of blood kinship' and claimed that they had failed to apply their own method – namely, that of analysing the 'reproduction of life' and the relations of production as 'social relations of reproduction' (Meillassoux 1994: 318). This critique can be extended to the treatment of gender relations in all of the classics. A more sophisticated version of gender relations in the development of humanity remains almost invisible in historiography if female labour in the context of total social labour and the participation of women in politics and administration are not searched for with the attentive eye of a detective.

The Ethnological Notebooks of Karl Marx were first published in 1972 by Lawrence Krader. Engels, however, had already in 1884 gathered together Marx's excerpts from Morgan and the notes from his own reading of Bachofen in 'Origins of the family, private property, and the state', thus providing the material and the style in which the oppression of women was thought. Simultaneously, he had thus strengthened a mode of reading which, to a certain extent, comprehended gender relations as an addition to, and outside of, the relations of production. In his famous passage on monogamy (taking up an insight from 'The German ideology'), he opened up a personal relation into a social one by means of the application of the concept of class to the man–woman relationship: 'The first class conflict … coincided with the development of the antagonism between husband and wife in monogamous marriage, and the first instance of class oppression with the oppression of the female sex by the male' (Engels 1990: 175). Furthermore, with monogamous marriage began an

> epoch in which every step forward was simultaneously a relative backward step, in which the well-being and the development of the one group prevail through the misery and repression of the other. It is the cell form of civilised society in which we can already study the nature of the oppositions and contradictions which fully develop therein. (Ibid.: 175)

Marx had noted to the contrary, incidentally, that 'the family – even the monogamous family – could not form the natural basis of gentile society, just as little as today in bourgeois society the family is the unity of the political system' (Marx 1972: 285). Engels' stirring rhetoric conceals the fact that the form of monogamous marriage does not imply any specific labour relations. Concepts such as antagonism, classes, well-being and misery allowed gender relations to be regarded as mere relations of subjugation – as after a war – and not as practices of both sexes. Thus studies on gender relations did not lead to a comprehension of the connection of relations of production, but rather, on the contrary, to a separation of the terrains of the production of *life* and the production of the *means* of life. That admittedly corresponds to the development of capitalism, but nevertheless prevents seeing precisely the generalizing structures of the established state as an effect of the relations of production. In the Preface to 'Origins', Engels sketched out what was supposed to be understood by 'production and reproduction of immediate life': 'On the one hand, the production of the means of life, of the objects of food, clothing and shelter and the tools necessary for that production; on the other hand the production of human beings themselves, the propagation of the species' (Engels 1990: 135). He named both 'productions' and thereby established the starting point for a theory of gender relations. However, he impeded its further elaboration by definitions which appeared to establish all labour (nutrition, clothing and housing) on the one side, and, on the other, the family; the latter was distinguished not by specific labour connections, but rather through relations of kinship. Consistently, following Marx's notebooks of excerpts, he noted in detail in 'Origins' the variants of organization of sexual relations and reproduction, but did not note in what relation the labours carried out in the family stood to total social labour and to the reproduction of society. To this extent his work can be read as an omission for writing the history of gender relations as a dimension of the relations of production. Instead, he treated the levels of sexuality and morality – in which Engels, though, as Bloch noted, obeyed 'puritanical motives' when he proclaimed monogamy to be a female victory against 'disorderly sexual dealings' and claimed a 'mysterious seizure of power' of men on the basis of taking up, all too unconsidered, ideas from Bachofen (Bloch 1961: 118). Engels gathered much material in order to prove the humiliation of women. However, it also escaped him in this instance that gender relations determine the *whole* society and are not restricted to the domestic sphere. His most famous sentence in this connection presented women as mere victims: 'the overthrow of matriarchy was the *world-historic defeat of the female sex*' (Engels 1990: 168).

Engels' perspective for liberated gender relations was the inclusion of women in industry, a movement which he saw already becoming a reality in capitalistically organized production, because modern industry 'not only allows female labour on a large scale, but in fact formally demands it, and … strives more and more to dissolve private domestic labour into a public industry' (ibid.: 261). Since this perspective defined the state-socialist project, the problems can be studied in concrete and historical terms.

Critical conceptual summary The critical survey of Marx and Engels demonstrates the approach to comprehend gender relations as relations of production just as much as its abandonment. The greatest barrier proves to be the tendency to think of gender relations as relationships between men and women. It must obviously become a rule to investigate the different modes of production in history as always also gender relations. Neither can be comprehended without the answer to the question of how the production of life in the totality of the relations of production is regulated and in which relation they stand to the production of the means of life – in short, how they determine the reproduction of the whole society. That includes the differential shaping of genders themselves, the particular constructions of femininity and masculinity, just as much as the development of the productive forces, the division of labour, domination and forms of ideological legitimation.

Gender relations in intenational Marxism after Marx

Politics concerning gender relations emerge in the history of Marxism as a struggle against the ban on abortion and as a demand for gainful employment for women and equal wages for the same work, but also as demands for a better family life (among others, by Clara Zetkin), as a promise to raise women up out of the restrictive confinements of the domestic sphere (Lenin, alongside many others), and as an attempt to liberate also the feminine psyche from its love-prison (Alexandra Kollontai). Finally, in the late twentieth century, there was the demand to create the preconditions which would allow the combination of family work and paid employment. In short, the question of gender relations always emerged as the 'women's question', which took no account of its connection to the relations of production.

An exemplary exception stands out in Antonio Gramsci's notes on Fordism. His point of departure was the rationalization of labour on the assembly line (Taylorism), the related creation of 'a new type of man' among workers, and the political regulation of structural conditions. Gramsci introduced the concept of *historical bloc* for this process. He understood by this the combination of groups in the dominant power relation – in this context, the combination of the mode of mass production, private lifestyles and state-sponsored campaigns concerning morality (Puritanism/Prohibition). In this context gender relations emerged, in the first instance, as a particular subjugation of men under exhausting and intensified 'mechanical' work conditions for a higher pay which allowed the support of a family and recreation, and which in turn was necessary for the maintenance of precisely this Fordist labour subject. His exhausting work conditions required specific morals and ways of living, monogamy as a form of sex which did not waste time or indulge in excess, little consumption of alcohol, and the formation of housewives who watched over (and were accordingly actively engaged in promoting) the discipline, lifestyle and health and nutrition of the family – in short, the mode of consumption. One sees the disposition of the sexes and thus essential aspects of their construction, along with political regulations. Among other aspects, it can be seen how this whole structure was transformed with the change of the mode of production, and the essential points of articulation which flexibly hold capitalist society together can be recognized in this process. Related to the transition to the high-technological mode of production, Gramsci's insights teach how to investigate the transformation by the new mode of production of the relations of manual to mental labour through an examination of gender relations: the new mode of production requires less labour-force of other types and its hegemony is correspondingly differently enforced; it needs another type of intervention by the state; it produces another effect on the terrain of civil society, and so on. The question of the new labour subject must include the new determination of gender relations, precisely because it concerns lifestyle, maintenance and development, which to a certain extent represent a 'marginalized centre' of social relations (cf. Haug 1998).

Liberal bourgeoisie

The book on the subjugation of women published by John Stuart Mill together with his wife, Harriet Taylor, and their daughter Helen in 1869 caused a great sensation and was translated into German in the same year. The goal was a kind of social psychology of gender relations as a foundation for the political and legal equality of women in order to support the struggles for the right to vote, the right to work, and the education of women. Mill and Taylor used the concept of gender relations, even though it became unrecognizable in the German translation ('*Beziehungen zwischen den Geschlechtern*', 'relations between the sexes' – Mill et al. 1997: 5). The primary terrains upon which existing gender relations were thought were habits and feelings, opinions on the nature of men and women and their current positions in society which were derived from such opinions, above all in terms of their legal status. Since 'the subjugation of women by men' was 'a universal habit', every deviation from this appeared as 'unnatural' (ibid.: 24). Their research was consequently directed towards the terrains of everyday experience, towards the morality which regulated it and the law. The assumption of naturalness of the 'feminine' was criticized, and instead comprehended as a product of an education in dependency, a 'result of imposed oppression according to the one tendency, of unnatural stimulation according to the other' (ibid.: 38). The main focus of their work was the legal treatment of women: for example, the contract of marriage (ibid.: 51–2), which they portrayed historically from stages of violence to the modern form of 'slavery' in which women, to a large extent without legal status and without property, owed obedience to their husbands, 'in a chronic situation of simultaneous bribery and intimidation' (ibid.: 22), until, finally, a gradual correction in the direction of the right of divorce. Olympe de Gouges remained unnamed, but her ideas are certainly present. 'Marriage', declare Mill and Taylor, 'is the only form of serfdom still recognized by our legal system. There are no longer any slaves except for the ladies of the house' (ibid.: 131). Humanity would gain infinitely if women were allowed to develop their capabilities and to apply them (ibid.: 136–7). According to the assumption of an arbitrary masculine violence, no attempt was undertaken to establish a connection to the relations of production. Their own field of experience, the fate of women of the bourgeoisie, allowed them also to overlook the formation and education of the female proletariat. It remains to be recorded that since the end of the eighteenth century insight into the constructed nature of gender, in particular the gender of women – first in de Gouges, now in Mill/Taylor – belonged to the standard stock of knowledge. Two centuries later this insight emerged again with no sense of its own history, as if it were the most novel of all ideas.

Just seventy years after Mill/Taylor, Virginia Woolf, in bourgeois gender relations which had remained relatively the same, bid adieu to the hope that society would gain when women were placed on an equal footing with men and could take up the careers reserved for and practised by men. In this case, she argued, women would become just as 'possessive, suspicious, and quarrelsome' as men (Woolf 1938: 87). She detected in the gender relations in which the bourgeoisie reproduced itself the possibility of the capitalist mode of production, of war and of its ideological anchoring. These gender relations produced on the side of the subject 'senselessness, pettiness, malice, tyranny, hypocrisy, immorality in excess' (ibid.: 108). On the basis of the difference between the practices of the genders she came to the conclusion that the emancipation of women required another society in which, among other things, formation and development would not be 'for capitalism, market, war, but for the perfecting of spirit and body, life and society' (ibid.: 108). Although, again, limited to the bourgeois class, knowledge was here developed concerning the structural role of the sexes in the reproduction of the relations of production.

Ten years later, Simone de Beauvoir explained that the oppression of women was due to the 'capacity for reproduction' of woman; she saw feminine subalternity maintained by the socially specific construction of social gender of the time. 'The balance of the productive and reproductive powers is realised in different ways in different economic epochs of humanity's history. These, however, create the pre-conditions for the relationship of the male and female parts to their descendants and thus also to each other' (De Beauvoir 1952: 46). Her conclusion, which was influential for the later women's movement, was aimed at the employment of women in order to make them economically independent from men, the structural integration of technical progress in human reproduction, and the transformation of the ideological-psychological construction of the feminine.

Marxist anthropology

Important elements for a theory of gender relations were developed in the discussions concerning a Marxist anthropology in France in the 1960s. Insights into the connection of political and cultural dimensions in the development of modes of production were supposed to be gained from the analysis of pre-capitalist societies. A point of contention, among others, was what 'the economic in the last instance' meant. Maurice Godelier grasped the role of relationships of kinship for the regulation of the relations of production as a question of a dominance which then '"integrates" all other social relations', which in turn not only defines relations of descent and marriage, 'but also regulates the particular laws regarding the disposal of the means of production and products of labour ... and when it possibly serves as a code, as a symbolic language, which expresses the relations of humans among one another just as much as their relations to nature' (Godelier 1973: 49). Claude Meillassoux responded critically that kinship was for Godelier the 'Alpha and Omega of any explanation of primitive society, since kinship generates, as it were, its own determination. It follows from this that the economic is determined by social development … and historical materialism no longer possesses any scientific basis at all' (Meillassoux 1983: 63). The critique is unjust, since Godelier's formulation of the research question posed to the social sciences was: 'Under what conditions and according to what reasons does any particular instance assume the functions of the relations of production and control the reproduction of these relations and thus the reproduction of the social relations in their totality?' (Godelier 1973: 50). He understood this as a specification of Marx's formulation of the ultimate determination of the social and intellectual life process by the mode of production.

Meillassoux's suspicion that in this articulation kinship was given 'a doubled status of a base and a superstructure' (Meillassoux 1983: 63) and was even regarded as a key for anthropology is, however, not to be rejected out of hand. Of course, the seesaw of instances and dominances vanishes as soon as kinship relations are grasped as relations of production. Meillassoux opened the way for this by defining as the central point of departure the concept of *relations of reproduction*. With this he analysed that a society for its continuance must establish a 'satisfactory balance between the number of productive and unproductive individuals and among these … a sufficient number of members of both sexes of the right age' (ibid.: 56). Since this is not given in itself in small cells of production, the oldest, who enjoy a higher standing owing to work done in the past, develop a system of exchange of women (ibid.: 57–8); their power shifts 'from the control of the means of life to the control of women and from the management of food stuffs to political authority over individuals' (ibid.: 59). In the proto-agrarian mode of production (which was based in addition upon hunting), these instances of the eldest did not exist; there was kidnapping of women and thus the necessity to protect women, which excluded them from hunting and war. At the same time war gained the meaning of founding the domination of men.

Meillassoux agreed with the view of Marx and Engels that 'women were undoubtedly the first exploited class' (ibid.: 95), but adds that they were subjected to different relations of exploitation and subjugation according to sexual maturity. He agreed with Engels that one could speak of a 'historical defeat of the female sex', but objected that this is not to be linked to the emergence of private property. Rather, it was founded in the relations of reproduction, in which on closer inspection a multiplicity of relationships of dependence are also to be detected among men, differing according to the mode of production. He connected the necessity of marriage with farming, in which the wife became an instrument of reproduction.

Meillassoux showed as an example of the agricultural household how the 'relations of reproduction' became 'relations of production', since 'the relationships of filiation [have to] correspond to the relationships of dependence and authority which exist in production' (ibid.: 62). In this case, the relations in reproduction are politically formed, subjugated, however, to the determining constraints of production. In the central themes of the studies on primitive societies – forms of the family, female lines of descent, their dissolution by patriarchal lines of descent, authority of elders, fertility cults, compulsion to endogamy, incest taboo – he highlighted the achievement of relative independence of the organization of reproduction. 'The social reproduction of the household is no natural process, nor is it ... a consequence of war, robbery and abductions. It is a political undertaking' (ibid.: 61). Meillassoux held, with Marx, to the primacy of the relations of production and explained that 'the place which the relations of reproduction in the organization and management of the society take' establishes the meaning 'which the juridical-ideological idea, i.e., kinship has', so that relations of reproduction 'have the tendency to become accepted in a non-egalitarian class society as fundamental "values"' (ibid.: 62).

The domestic mode of production, the economic centre of primitive societies, continued, according to Meillassoux, until the late phases of imperial capitalism and was assimilated to the laws of capitalist class society as a meagre basis of production of life and labour-power, preserved there and at the same time destroyed. Accordingly, Meillassoux opposed Marx's view (Marx 1996: 565) that there was no longer any inflow without costs into developed capitalism at all after the phase of primitive accumulation, overlooking of course Marx's comment to the contrary (Marx 1997: 105–6).

Following Meillassoux, studies became possible which allowed the structural role of the sexes in the regulation of total reproduction (determined by the state of material production) and, in this, the role of politics, ideology, morality and their relative independence to be analysed. Nevertheless he did not keep completely to his approach to think of the relations of production on the basis of the relations of reproduction, so that, for example, the power of the oldest appeared to him as masculine, conditioned by production. Here the inclusion of gender relations is to be added.

Feminist ethnology

Feminist ethnology concentrated on the treatment of gender relations. Thus Olivia Harris and Kate Young gave as a reason for their turn from women's studies to research on gender relations the fact that the relationships between different actors only become understandable in connection to the relations of production (Harris and Young 1981: 111). As a terrain of analysis they suggested changing from the general terrain of the mode of production to the more concrete one of the 'conditions of reproduction of historically-located productive systems' (ibid.: 117).

Engels' 'Origins' has regularly been a starting-point or critical point of departure for feminist ethnologists. One of the first, Eleanor Leacock, following Engels' proposal to connect the oppression of women to the emergence of private property, began in the 1950s to research into non-class societies in order to grasp in a new way the position of women in relations of production, distribution and consumption. Her fields of research are, among others, organized hunter-gatherer societies before the emergence of the state. In her rereading of the studies of Morgan, Wright and Lafiteau, but also later authors like Landes (1938), Leacock criticized both their inadequate research of the self-transformative socio-economic conditions and their ethnocentric points of view (Leacock 1989: 47). Instead of equality, she spoke of an autonomy of the sexes (ibid.: 134). She criticized the generalization of the division, common in class societies, of the public and private, doubted the universal representation of the family and noted the absence of leaders, markets and private landownership as essential dimensions of hunter-gatherer societies (ibid.: 140). The division of labour between the sexes was accompanied by a high reputation for women because of their ability to give birth to children. To be noted, according to Leacock, is the fact that women in every society make an important economic contribution, but their status is dependent upon 'whether or not they can control the conditions under which they work and the distribution of the goods which they have produced' (ibid.: 152). Her conclusion is that in societies in which the domestic economy makes up the whole economy, gender relations were not determined by relations of domination (ibid.: 144) and that 'household management' was decisive in council assemblies which decided on war and peace.

Inside feminist ethnology there consequently developed three tendencies in opposition to the thesis of the binary division of the history of humanity into a matriarchy and – after a break – a patriarchy as precondition of progress. The idea of women as victims was positively taken up, or rather updated in a slightly modified form, by a first tendency. Thus the view of Claude Lévi-Strauss (e.g. 1971, 1980), among others, that men everywhere behaved towards women just as culture to nature and that women represented the non-cultural wild element also enjoyed feminist recognition (cf., e.g., Ortner 1974; Rosaldo 1974; Benard and Schlaffer 1984). Sherry B. Ortner, for example, inspired in equal measure by both Simone de Beauvoir and Lévi-Strauss, claimed that universal oppression of women stems from the fact that 'woman's body seems to doom her to mere reproduction of life; the male, in contrast, lacking natural creative functions, must … assert his creativity externally, "artificially," through the medium of technology and symbols'; the male creates in this way 'relatively lasting, eternal, transcendent objects, while the woman creates only perishables – human beings' (Ortner 1974: 75).

A second group regarded the victim discourse as a result of a masculine mode of research which did not notice (or, owing to the separateness of women's culture, could not even perceive) the activities of women. Carol P. MacCormack criticized the constructed nature of such a model as a product of the late eighteenth century and demonstrated at the same time the dominatory uses of this mode of thought: 'If women are defined as ""belonging to nature," the domination of men over women begins to be regarded in high esteem or even have ascribed to it moral virtue, analogous to the virtue of human domination over natural sources of energy or the libidinal energies of individuals' (MacCormack 1989: 75). The perception of non-European women and their symbolical appropriation by means of Western ethnology was treated in a similar way. 'The conscious and unconscious symbolic reification of the "primitive" woman in the everyday life, art and science of the metropoles has legitimated her actual subordination and encouraged an activity which continues it' (Arbeitsgruppe Ethnologie Wien 1989: 9).

A third tendency of critical-feminist research was directed towards the search for gender-egalitarian societies. Equality was here understood as equal value, because the division of functions is not necessarily accompanied by hierarchy. Ilse Lenz (1995), who spoke of 'gender-symmetrical societies', criticized the conclusion which was suggested by Engels' binary division of history into a matriarchal phase of reproduction and a patriarchal epoch determined by production – namely, that women could only liberate themselves through participation in the latter (ibid.: 38–9): 'Gender and domination are simply seen in relation to each other in this binary division of epochs, and the necessary steps of mediation of the economy, society and thought are lacking' (ibid.: 44). The question for ethnological research, on the other hand, had to be 'in which form women and men are active in these socio-political processes and which power they derive from them' (ibid.: 45). Research questions were directed towards production, reproduction and sexuality, knowledge of the body, political authority, and symbolic order. Lenz rejected the usual concept of power (for example, that of Max Weber) as masculine, since it one-sidedly referred to the opportunity to enforce one's will over and against others and was thus limited from the outset to the victor. She comprehended power as determination over processes and resources. Only this allowed the multiplicity of gender relations to be comprehended, to discover, for example, women's power also in patriarchal societies on the 'underside' of official power (ibid.: 55), and thus to think in terms of a 'power balance' rather than having to envisage a complete subjugation of one gender by the other (ibid.: 64).

The thesis 'that forms of marriage give an excellent insight into the organization of relations of production specifically relevant to gender in all classless societies' (Collier and Rosaldo 1981: 278) was contested by Ute Luig (1995), who pushed rites of sexual maturity and of access to economic, political and religious resources back on to centre stage. Her main conclusion: a gender-specific division of labour does not have to be accompanied by hierarchy, dependence and exploitation. 'Egalitarian relationships do not correspond to any natural, originary situation, but are perpetuated by conscious, social strategies and control mechanisms and are continually formed anew' (ibid.: 95). As preconditions of equality she named the absence of accumulation – that is, the immediate consumption of foodstuffs – and, accompanying this, autonomy as a capacity to provide for oneself. For the most part, Luig used the concept of gender relations in the singular. This mode of formulating the question produced the effect that the different practices into which the sexes enter were not seen in connection to the reproduction of society, but rather, on the contrary, social production, hunting and gathering were comprehended as moments of determination of the interaction of the sexes – as if the genders as such were antecedent and as if society were additionally produced as a particular (e.g. egalitarian) relation of both to each other.

The study of distant cultures and their gender relations led at times to a kind of sophisticated tolerance for which all material evidence appeared to be unimportant. Thus Ina Rösing (1999) reported from an investigation of an Andean village in which she claimed to have discovered ten instead of the normal two genders. She demonstrated this in the multiple and changing 'gender' allocations of space, time, field and public offices, and so on – thus, for example, the sun is masculine in the morning, but feminine in the evening. Research into gender relations was here dissolved into a multiplicity of discourses. Nonetheless, even in this many-stranded fabric there is a central thread to be discovered: 'The fundamental, everyday division of labour, family life and sexuality are not affected by symbolic genderness' (ibid.: 56). The conspicuous gender symbolism was explained by her materialistically as a recharging of the sexual, in the sense of entreaties for fertility made necessary by the hard conditions of survival in the Andes.

Maxine Molyneux, in her rereading of studies on Gouro-formation – which had been studied by Emmanuel Terray (1974) and Georges Dupré and Pierre Philippe Rey (1978) – demonstrated that leaving the status of women out of an account led to more general conceptual and epistemological problems. The point of contention was the question of whether or not this was already class society. The focus of the analysis was the relation of elders to the younger men who found themselves in an ambivalent exploitative relation. Molyneux showed that opponents and supporters of the thesis of class society departed from a vision of a purely male society (Molyneux 1989: 107). Central for the analysis of any mode of production, however, according to Molyneux, was the comprehension of the gender-specific division of labour (ibid.: 112). Among the Gouros, the women's surplus production was appropriated by the eldest, so that they would have represented a class for Terray, whose point of departure was observed exploitation rather than property. Attention to women, however, could also have corrected Terray's concept of class: in the separation of women from the land and from the product of their work one could have seen 'the dissolution of collective property in land and the emergence of relations of private property' (ibid.: 121–2) and consequently the transition from ur-communism to a class society (ibid.: 120). In opposition to Engels, Molyneux did not see the subordination of women founded in their marginalization by the development of social production. Rather, she argued that it consisted precisely in the fact that they were supposed 'to remain a central factor for production' (ibid.: 128), because they brought prosperity. Women and their labour were thus essential for the dissolution of community. Molyneux used the concept of gender relations, but this was made unrecognizable by the translator as 'relations between the sexes' (*Beziehungen zwischen den Geschlechtern*) (ibid.: 132).

The study of feminist ethnology demonstrates, among other elements, that a historical materialism of the thing itself demands that gender relations are comprehended as relations of production – that is, demands research into the participation of the genders in different modes of production and thus the investigation of the many and diverse practices and their symbolic expression, and their reinforcement in determinant customs, traditions and value systems. If the standpoint of the reproduction of society is abandoned, the phenomena appear as arbitrary. In the rereading of existing research it becomes apparent that doubts are appropriate, owing to the ethnocentrism and/or androcentrism in language and concepts; this is also the case for feminist research.

Capitalism and patriarchy

The discovery that there was a further system of domination beyond that of capitalism – namely, the patriarchy – raised the question for the feminism of the second wave of the women's movement of how the interaction of the two types of domination was to be thought. The discussions about principal and secondary contradictions, influenced by Maoism, sought to claim a totality. Its analysis, however, was simultaneously blocked by this same conceptual paradigm. The discussion was conducted within Marxism, by which Marx was understood as standing for the centrality of class relations. After the struggles beginning in the 1970s concerning the recognition of housework, the question was further developed into a problematic of the total social economy. The debate was conducted under the name of 'dual economy'.

Linda Phelps was one of the first who sought to comprehend capitalism and patriarchy as different relations of production:

> If sexism is a social relationship in which males have authority over females, *patriarchy* is a term which describes the whole system of interaction arising from that basic relationship, just as capitalism is a system built on the relationship between capitalist and worker. Patriarchal and capitalist social relationships are two markedly different ways human beings have interacted with each other and have built social, political and economic institutions. (Phelps 1975: 39)

Zillah Eisenstein proposed to speak of two different modes of production which mutually supported one another (1979: 27); Sheila Rowbotham (1973) regarded such a coexistence as merely specific to capitalism; Ann Ferguson (1979) coined the term 'sex/affective production' in relations of reproduction as a term for the mode of production occupied dominantly by women. The most well known was Heidi Hartmann's attempt of 1981 – in connection to the theses of Marx and Engels that the seed of patriarchy is the power to dispose of female labour power (Marx and Engels 1975b: 37) – to establish a materialist theory of gender relations. This was aimed against the view proposed by, for example, Juliet Mitchell, that there were 'two autonomous areas, the economic mode of capitalism and the ideological of patriarchy' (Mitchell 1974: 409). Roisin McDonough and Rachel Harrison insisted that patriarchy could only be comprehended if it was defined historically and concretely in the interaction of 'relations of human reproduction' and the relations of production (McDonough and Harrison 1978: 26). This meant for capitalism the introduction of class relations into the analysis of gender relations. Gabriele Dietrich questioned the priority of commodity production, since 'the production of life is a indispensable condition for every further production process'; in a socialist perspective, this involved 'not only the problem of how we want to get to the association of free producers, but also of how we want to shape that which was called "reproduction" for the society of free humans' (Dietrich 1984: 38).

Iris Maria Young proposed to overcome the 'dual system' approaches in the direction of a single theory 'that can articulate and appreciate the vast differences in the situation, structure, and experience of gender relations in different times and places' (Young 1997: 105). Michèle Barrett (1983) summarized the debate for her foundation of a Marxist-feminism.

The concept of gender relations

The analysis of gender relations presupposes the category of gender. The possibility available in English of distinguishing between biological *sex* and social *gender* was the basis for a conjuncture which lasted more than twenty years in which gender was comprehended as socially constructed, to the extent that the concept of 'gender' was also adopted in other languages. However, the analysis of gender which – not least of all due to the decline of the women's movement – had dissolved the apparent naturalness of previous thematics of questions concerning women had also dispensed with the connection to relations of production which had still been dominant in the debate concerning housework; thus the discussion centred upon the concept of gender, but not gender relations.

The fall of state socialism made it absolutely necessary for Marxist feminists to think of the relation of gender relations and modes of production in a new way, not least of all because the now obvious demolition of women's rights in the former state socialist lands caused by bringing them into line with those offered by capitalism was accompanied by the claim that state socialism had oppressed women just as much as capitalism, and, at the same time, the claim that fallen state socialism's mode of production was entirely different from capitalism's mode of production, with which it had not been able to compete. The mode of posing the problem assumed that gender relations and a mode of production do not have any internal connection. It was not the time for social theory, and thus thinking of gender relations as relations of production could be made out to be a relic of thought from days gone by.

The following thesis led to intense controversy:

> The dominant economy of exchange, the market, profit and growth is setting out upon an extensive exploitation, not only of employed labour power, but just as much other (third) worlds which do not

> produce according to the same principles. It is neglecting care for life and its commitment to the people who do these things out of love, out of a feeling of 'humanity' and who therefore cannot be treated as the same. The symbolic order, the fields of art and science and the entire model of civilisation are all equally imbued and legitimated by such gender relations as relations of production. That is also the case for subjects themselves as personalities. (Haug 1996: 151)

Hildegard Heise saw in this a maceration of the concept of relations of production suited to such unhappy times (Heise 1993: 235), while Ursula Beer detected the reduction of 'Marxist conceptual paradigms' to 'a purely illustrative character' (Beer 1993: 231). Such conceptions of gender relations as relations of production would result in 'one of the most essential concepts of Marxism being comprehended in an *anti-* or *un-*Marxist way' and 'the necessary, in Marxist terms, transformation of capitalist relations of production' would be seen as 'a contradiction between male production and female appropriation' (Rech 1993: 258–9). Beer regarded it as arbitrary whether the concept of gender relations was used in the singular or the plural; in order to avoid an 'unnecessary addition ... of gender relations ... to the capital relation' (Beer 1993: 230), she spoke of 'moments of sexual inequality which are spread across the whole system ... e.g. the exclusion of women from positions of influence and power, the gender-specific division of labour in the family and at work, cultural production as, to a large extent, men's business' (ibid.: 231). Such definitions overlook both that in the lands of state socialism women were almost fully integrated into working life, and that the multitude of female writers can be taken as an indicator that cultural production was also women's business.

The following concepts were suggested in the place of gender relations: 'gender inequality to the disadvantage of women' and 'gender domination', analogous to class domination (ibid.: 231). Classes, however, can be abolished, they are not a 'natural' phenomenon; genders, on the other hand, are (although socially formed) also a 'natural' phenomenon; the existence of genders is thus not simply an element of 'gender domination' as the existence of classes is an element of class domination. The concept of 'gender inequality' is dubious, because 'gender equality' would be understandable at the best as an expression of political slang. To speak of genders is to speak of the differences between genders. Or even further: difference is too weak a term for thinking of the complementarity which is conditioned by the naturally unequal contribution of the two genders to procreation. Equal rights before the law for women and men places them on the same level as legal subjects, abstracted, that is, from gender. Where equal rights are not really realized and compensatory measures such as quota regulations are resorted to, the members of the individual genders are in fact treated in individual cases, departing from inequality, as 'unequal', in order to arrive at an average equal treatment in a determinate respect. To speak of 'asymmetrical power relations' (Bader 1993: 228) or 'masculine supremacy' (Becker-Schmidt, cited in Beer 1993: 230) is too weak, because power relationships could only have any effect at all as asymmetrical, and supremacy is a shifting phenomenon, while domination is something structural. 'Gender opposition' (Heise 1993: 235), formulated following the opposition between classes, is similarly not fully conceptualized. Sexual complementarity is the natural form of mammals, but the dominative development of relations between complementary genders is a historically variable form of human society. Heise feared that thinking of gender relations as relations of production instigated 'the substitution of genders for classes' (ibid.: 235). Her general concept was the concept of a 'combinatory of genders', which, however, would only have sense if one sought to model the reality and the mode in which gender relations find their field-specific forms in all social fields. To think all of these forms as a 'combinatory' (to be comprehended as a strategic encoding), however, assumes the concept of gender relations.

Gender relations and the category of gender Already in 1987, Donna Haraway was registering a fundamental critique of the explanation of women's oppression by the 'sex-gender-system'. Her critique of the biological essentialism of this distinction prepared the way also for the surrender of thinking in terms of gender. This terrain was further explored primarily by Judith Butler, who rejected 'gender' as an 'identificatory site of political mobilization at the expense of race or sexuality or class or geopolitical positioning/displacement' (Butler 1993: 116). She radicalized the representation of the socially constructed nature of gender, also regarding the part which was taken for granted as biologically given, and in this way transposed the battleground to the process of the formation of identity. 'There is no "I" before the assumption of a gender ... to identify one's self with a gender means to be in a relation to an imaginary and persuasive ... threat' (ibid.: 99–100). In the symbolic the 'sexualized' subject is formed normatively by language (ibid.: 107). The displacement of power struggles in the assignment of gender allows exclusions, bans and stabilizations to be deciphered as elements of gender relations. The dispute about the respective priority of race, class and gender, which resulted in the corresponding movements falling out with each other in a depoliticizing way, can also be productively turned around by the question of the articulation of the one in – and at the cost or rather to the benefit of – the other (ibid.: 116). Butler extended this approach to a fundamental position for productive conflicts for a left which is 'universal', not in the sense of uniformity but rather in that of a perspective (Butler 1998: 36–7). This is the liberating side of Butler's intervention. She pleaded for a type of democratic coherence (following Gramsci) which individuals worked on for themselves and their identities, without always repeating exclusions through unreflected unification. Against the 'plundering of the third world' by feminists searching for examples of the 'universal patriarchal subordination of woman' (Butler 1993: 117), Butler proposed 'to find the forms in which identification is involved in that which it excludes, and ... to follow the lines of this involvement for the sake of the map of a future community' (ibid.: 119). The liquefaction of categories is easily comprehended; though the avoidance of any functionalism for the question of gender relations has the disadvantage of losing sight of how it really also concerns the reproduction of humanity. It is from the support, enabling and a contemporaneous marginalization of the necessity of the reproduction of the species that the actions decoded by Butler gain their virulence in the symbolic sphere, in language and in the imaginary.

Nancy Fraser attacked Jürgen Habermas' analysis of modern society as a paradigm of androcentric social theory. Here the capitalist economic system was comprehended as 'systematically integrated' while the small family, on the other hand, was understood as 'socially integrated' (Habermas 1981a: 457, 477–8; 1981b: 256, 266). She demonstrated the wasted opportunity in Habermas' model of different fields of material and symbolic reproduction for understanding in a genuinely new way the public and the private realms in their interpenetrating relation. Habermas' model made it difficult to analyse families as 'sites of work, exchange, calculation, distribution and exploitation' – in short, as economic systems (Fraser 1994: 183). That Habermas comprehended the raising of children as symbolic, but wage labour, on the other hand, as material, while each of these is both, made the fact that he took up the former at all in his model at once problematic and a supporting argument for the private raising of children as a form of female subordination. Fraser understood the weakness of this concept as its inability to thematize the 'gender subtext' (Smith 1984) of the described relationships and arrangements. All mediating personifications are, however, determined by gender: 'Wages were contested … as payment to a man for the maintenance of his economically dependent wife and children' (Fraser 1994: 190). With Carol Pateman (1985), Fraser demonstrated that women are not absent in paid occupation, but rather are present in a different way: for example, reduced to femininity, often to sexualized servants (secretaries, domestic servants, saleswomen, prostitutes, stewardesses); as members of the caring professions with maternal capacities (such as nursing sisters, social workers, primary school teachers); as lowly qualified workers in segregated workplaces; as part-time workers under the double burden of unpaid housework and paid employment; as additional-wage earners. Thus the official economy is not merely bound to the family by means of money for commodities, but also by the masculinity of 'normal' wage labour. Conversely, the consumer 'in classical capitalism is the companion and the helper of the worker' and 'advertising has developed an entire illusory world of greed built upon the femininity of the consumer-subject' (Fraser 1994: 191). This is of course dependent upon the product, and changes in this branch of industry which also affect men struggle not only with the attributes of the feminine, as Barbara Ehrenreich (1984) demonstrated in an analysis of *Playboy*. Habermas' dramatis personae lacked the childminder, Fraser's critique continued, which he nevertheless needed to cast in a central role in his definition of functions of the family. A consideration of them could have shown the central meaning of gender relations for the 'institutional structure of capitalism' (Fraser 1994: 192). The 'citizen's role', this connecting-position between the private and the public, is self-evidently masculine – it relates to the participant in political discourse and naturally to the soldier as defender of the community and protector of women, children and the old. It escaped Habermas how the protection/reliance structure runs through all institutions and how, finally, 'the construction of masculine and feminine gendered subjects is necessary in order to fill every role in classical capitalism' (ibid.: 195).

Fraser used the concept of gender relations only marginally, though in the German translation it becomes completely casually 'the gender relation' (*das Geschlechterverhältnis*) (ibid.: 211). Her central concepts were gender identity and gender; she thus falls behind her own analysis with her demand for 'gender sensitive categories' (ibid.: 196). Finally, she highlights practices into which humans enter for the reproduction of their life. She proposes to understand 'worker', 'consumer' and 'wages' as gender-*economic* concepts, and 'citizen' as a gender-*political* concept. But in this way only the gender-typical effects of the social relations of production are noticed. Thus the open questions which Fraser wins out of this extensive engagement appear to be comparatively harmless: should a future society which is not founded upon the subjugation of women (and which therefore needs no firm attribution in the construction of masculinity and femininity) conceive all labour under the form of wage labour, or should the political part of society (Habermas' citizen's role) be expanded through making the raising of children obligatory for all? Fraser's critique was at the same time her answer to the 'dual economy debate', whose supposition of a 'fundamental distinctness of capitalism and patriarchy, class and gender' had left unclear 'how to put them back together again' (ibid.: 8).

Feminist sociology Attempts to undertake feminist research in the terms of social theory operate with the concept of gender relations. For Ursula Beer (1990), 'the gender relation' was limited without exception to 'generative maintenance of survival' or 'generative reproduction'. As such a 'structural element' (ibid.: 77), she claimed to inscribe it in Marxist social theory which she accordingly renovated when necessary. She understood Marx's work as fundamentally a theory of structure, whose central concept was 'totality' (ibid.: 70–1). She screened off 'the production of life' conceptually against empirical practices. Nor was she concerned with praxis-relations, but rather with the status that, for example, women's ability to give birth has in a structural theory of society. The view comes from above on a theoretical order in which individuals are allocated a 'categorical' place. That individuals in reality shape their lives either in forms of resistance or those of obedience is not taken into account. The *concepts* which were suggested for 'empirical' purposes allow a sociological investigation only at the cost of marginalizing the contradictions in which actual human beings realize themselves: 'differentiation of fields of labour' (ibid.: 52) remains vague; 'forms of labour/production not mediated by the market' (ibid.: 73, 76–7) resolves only seemingly the problem of the domestic labour debate, as this sum includes not mere activities of the reproduction of life, but also, for example, left-wing theory, gardening, bowling and voluntary work of all types.

Regina Becker-Schmidt and Gudrun-Axeli Knapp (1995) wanted critically to overcome the limitedness of feminist research, which they thought had been bogged down in the analysis of the construction of gender. Moving 'the gender relation' into the centre of feminist sociology was supposed to do this. The research question was how man–woman relationships 'are organized in particular historical conjunctures' (ibid.: 7), 'to what extent predominant connections and conditions influence the relation of the genders' (ibid.: 8), and conversely, how 'gender relationships' react upon society. The way of formulating the question remained structural-theoretical, organized according to the logic of cause and effect. In this way genders themselves appeared to be fixed and society was grasped as a type of space in which human relationships merely occur. They talked of 'arrangement of the genders' (following Goffman 1994), of 'composition of gender relations' or, five years later, evading the difficulty by changing terminology, 'gender-relations' (*Gender-Relationen*) (Becker-Schmidt 2000: 45) in order to overcome the merely psychologizing research of 'gender relationships'. Becker-Schmidt and Knapp comprehend these as 'cultural, political and economic' (Becker-Schmidt and Knapp 1995: 18) and related them to 'exchange' in 'labour, performances, and satisfaction of needs' (ibid.: 17–18) or to 'exclusion' from 'spaces, terrains of praxis, resources and rituals'. In distinction, they here regarded gender relations as 'contexts of domination and power in which the social position of gender-groups is institutionally anchored and prolonged' (ibid.: 18). In this way gender relations were articulated to social reproduction like a type of administrative machine; they are to be studied additionally and appear to function according to their own rules which can simply be modified by the total social reproduction.

In the foreword to Becker-Schmidt and Knapp (2000) the use of the singular and the plural of gender relations is described in this way:

> If we want to express the mutual social relatedness of gender-groups ... epistemologically only the concept of 'gender relation' makes sense. If we come across empirically on all social levels of a society situations of disparity, if all social orders turn out to be based upon similar determinations of relation, the singular is advisable ... The plural is called for when we ... consider international variability. (Ibid.: 154, n38)

The linking of the concept of gender relations to international usage was justified by 'ethnographical diversity'; by 'the gender relation', a cultural order as an expression of structure (social fabric, symbols) was meant. In this way society can hardly be thought of practically, even though it strives to somehow bring together structure and activity by means of the concept of 'connections' (ibid.: 40). Following Beer (1990), there was an attempt to comprehend the equality of determinant mechanisms in different fields (here, families and servant and service rights) 'as an expression of the structure of the relations of production' (ibid.: 165). Alternatively a patriarchal population politics, a gendered division of labour and a masculine politics were supposed to sustain the complementary thought of envisaging gender as a structural category. The investigation of diversity, discrepancy and even the contrariness of human practices, however, is blocked by such an expressivist theory. In the end, Becker-Schmidt and Knapp summarized their argument as follows: 'Feminist research has not yet succeeded in sketching out a theory of gender relations which would be capable of itemising all of the complexes of causation and motivation-contexts which traverse the relations between gender-groups' (Becker-Schmidt and Knapp 2000: 61). But there remained the approach of 'itemising all of the motivations and causes', itself trapped in the irredeemable idea that it is possible to sketch such a model theoretically, instead of researching the practices of humans in the organization of their life and their reproduction in their interconnections.

Masculinity research Robert Connell gave the concept of gender relations a fundamental status in the field of masculinity studies: 'Knowledge of masculinity arises within the project of knowing gender relations' (Connell 1995: 44). He recognized that it is not meaningful to speak of genders without relating their foundation historically to the question of the reproduction of the species, upon which 'one of the major structures of all documented societies' (ibid.: 72) was formed. Connell argued that 'definitions of masculinity are profoundly interwoven with economic structures and the history of institutions' (ibid.: 48), and assumed that in capitalist relations of production the field of human reproduction is subordinated to that of the production of the means of life (understood in the broadest sense).

Conclusion: gender relations are relations of production

Gender relations, as 'relations into which men enter in the production of their lives', are always relations of production, just as, vice versa, relations of production are always also gender relations. The duplication of 'production' in the production of life (in the broadest sense, including rearing and care) and the production of the means of life (again, in the broadest sense, including the means of production) was the point of departure for the historical naturalization of the latter into the system of the economy and – in capitalism – its dominance over the production of life. The state stabilized this dominance inasmuch as it ensured that the economy did not destroy its own foundations. For the analysis of relations of production, the codification of the whole with overdeterminations, relations of articulation and dependencies must be treated. To research into gender relations as relations of production requires a differential combination of historically comparative studies, attentive to moments of transition, with social theoretical and subject-scientific analysis.[1] All of these aspects require clarification.

The development and capitalist utilization of gene technology, intervening in human reproduction, has now moved so decisively the boundaries between the production of life and goods, however, that the connection of gender relations as relations of production must be thought of in a new way. If it could previously be assumed that capitalism allowed, for the purposes of its diffusion, the continuance of the 'domestic mode of production' of the family or, rather, thrived from it, capitalist industry is now pushing its borders farther, into the terrain of the sexual body and its propagation. An antecedent was medical transplants, which turned the body into a usable resource of organs and opened up a new field of activity for business just as for crime. Reproductive medicine has moved the borders farther.

Sperm, eggs and embryos have become commodities; fertilization, training and implantation have become services for sale. The ability to give birth can be bought like labour power or like the right to use a body for sexual gratification. So long as the creation of children was not organized in a capitalist form, the protection of women and control of the woman's body appeared as a dimension of the second order of the relations of production. Now, however, her organs themselves – just as previously male sperm – are becoming raw material or means of production of a mode of production which has added a further form, that of the 'surrogate mother', to the former forms of individuality – such as housewife, businesswoman, wage worker and prostitute – according to which sexual bodies were active and positioned in relation to each other. This is the beginning of a development whose effect upon gender relations constitutes the task of future analysis and a politics of emancipation. In gender relations in which social interference in the lives of women with the ability to be mothers and the corresponding protective and blocking strategies were mostly negotiated and diminished, the penetration of the forms of capital into the sphere of procreation can bring all borders into flux.

At the beginning of the second wave of the women's movement great hopes of liberation were placed in reproductive technology. Shulamith Firestone (1975) regarded test-tube babies to be an indispensable revolution, because she thought the oppression of women to be biologically determined. Donna Haraway proposed in a fiercely contested manifesto 'to infiltrate gene technology with socialist-feminist principles', 'to enjoy the blurring of all boundaries (such as those between the human and the machine) and to mark them out responsibly' (Haraway 1995: 165). Haraway comprehended the 'translation of the world into an encoding-problem, into a pursuit of … a universal key which subjugates everything to an instrumental control' as an approaching 'info-tech of domination' (ibid.: 167). Since women have lost more than they have won from previous boundary consolidations, they should not withdraw to motherhood, human dignity and similar 'innocent' positions, but instead answer offensively the dimensions produced by the capitalist commissioning of this 'info-tech of domination' and the violence against women within it with their 'own biotechnological politics' (ibid.: 169). Further, they should negotiate openly the problems of gene technology, taking into account gender, race and class as well as labour, poverty, health and economic power. Feminist science fiction novels were an important medium for such negotiation (Joanna Russ, Ursula K. LeGuin, Marge Piercy). A sociological fantasy was developed regarding what a transformation of gender relations by technological and economic development would look like, in the best as well as the worst of cases, if motherhood's attachment to the female body was dissolved, if dreams of an end to all natural lack were satisfied by capitalism in the form of 'flawless' children like commodities for exchange, or the human–machine boundary became permeable. Here the threatening destruction of the earth through the unleashing of a savage capitalism by neoliberalism was anticipatorily explored. A world in which everything is subjugated to the profit principle cannot maintain itself without increasing self-destruction.

Note

1 Editorial note: 'Subject-scientific analysis' (in German, *Subjektwissenschaftliche Analyse*) refers to the work of Klaus Holzkamp, founder of German Critical Psychology. His goal was to create a critical psychology from the standpoint of the subject; see, e.g., Schraube and Osterkamp (2013).

References

Arbeitsgruppe Ethnologie Wien (1989) *Von fremden Frauen: Frausein und Geschlechterbeziehungen in nichtindustriellen Gesellschaften* [Of strange women: being woman and gender relations in non-industrial societies], Frankfurt: Suhrkamp.

Bachofen, J. J. (1975) 'Das Mutterrecht: eine Untersuchung über die Gynaikokratie der alten Welt nach ihrer religiösen und rechtlichen Natur' [Myth, religion and mother right], in K. Meuli (ed.), *Gesammelte Werke*, vol. 2(3), Frankfurt: n.p., pp. 109–13.

Bader, V. M. (1993) 'Benötigt der Kapitalismus das Patriarchat?' [Does capitalism need patriarchy?], *Ethik und Sozialwissenschaften*, 4(3): 227–9.

Barrett, M. (1983) *Das unterstellte Geschlecht: Umrisse eines materialistischen Feminismus* [Women's oppression today], Berlin: Argument.

Becker-Schmidt, R. (2000) 'Frauenforschung, Geschlechterforschung, Geschlechterverhältnisforschung' [Women research, gender research, gender relation research], in R. Becker-Schmidt and G.-A. Knapp (eds), *Feministische Theorien zur Einführung*, Hamburg: Junius, pp. 14–62.

Becker-Schmidt, R. and G.-A. Knapp (eds) (1995) *Das Geschlechterverhältnis als Gegenstand der Sozialwissenschaften* [Gender relation as object of social sciences], Frankfurt: Campus.

— (eds) (2000) *Feministische Theorien zur Einführung* [Introduction to feminist theories], Hamburg: Junius.

Beer, U. (1990) *Geschlecht, Struktur, Geschichte: Soziale Konstituierung des Geschlechterverhältnisses* [Gender, structure, history: social constitution of the gender relation], Frankfurt: Campus.

— (1993) 'Die kleinen Fallstricke von großen Entwürfen' [The small pitfalls of big designs], *Ethik und Sozialwissenschaften*, 4(3): 230–2.

Benard, C. and E. Schlaffer (1984) *Die Grenzen des Geschlechts: Anleitungen zum Sturz des Internationalen Patriarchats* [Limits of gender: instructions for the overthrow of international patriarchy], Reinbek: Rohwolt.

Bloch, E. (1961) 'Bachofen, Gaia-Themis und Naturrecht' [Bachofen, Gaia-Themis and natural law], in E. Bloch, *Naturrecht und menschliche Würde*, vol. 6, Frankfurt: Suhrkamp, pp. 115–29.

— (1968) 'Astralmythos und babylonisch-ägyptischer Einschlag' [Astral myth and the Babylonian-Egyptian impact], in E. Bloch, *Atheismus im Christentum*, Frankfurt: Suhrkamp, pp. 254–8.

Brecht, B. (1967). *Gesammelte Werke* [Collected works], vol. 12, Frankfurt: Suhrkamp.

Butler, J. (1993) *Bodies that Matter: On the Discursive Limits of Sex*, New York: Routledge.

— (1998) 'Merely cultural', *New Left Review*, 227(39): 33–44.

Collier, J. and M. Rosaldo (1981) 'Politics and gender in simple societies', in S. H. Ortner and H. Whitehead (eds), *Sexual Meanings. The Cultural Construction of Gender and Sexuality*, Cambridge: Cambridge University Press, pp. 275–329.

Connell, R. (1995) *Masculinities*, Cambridge: Polity.

De Beauvoir, S. (1952) *The Second Sex*, New York: Vintage.

de Gouges, O. (1979) 'Deklaration der Rechte der Frau und Bürgerin' [Declaration of the rights of woman and the female citizen], in H. Schröder (ed.), *Die Frau ist frei geboren: Texte zur Frauenemanzipation*, vol. 1: *1789–1870*, Munich: Beck, pp. 32–49.

Dietrich, G. (1984) 'Die unvollendete Aufgabe einer marxistischen Fassung der Frauenfrage' [The unfinished task of a Marxist framing of the women's question], in Projekt Sozialistischer Feminismus (ed.), *Geschlechterverhältnisse und Frauenpolitik*, West Berlin: Argument, pp. 24–41.

Dupré, G. and P. P. Rey (1978) 'Reflections on the relevance of a theory of the history of exchange', in D. Seddon (ed.), *Relations of Production: Marxist Approaches to Economic Anthropology*, London: Frank Cass, pp. 171–208.

Ehrenreich, B. (1984) *The Hearts of Men: American Dreams and the Flight from Commitment*, New York: Anchor.

Eisenstein, Z. (ed.) (1979) *Capitalist Patriarchy and the Case for Socialist Feminism*, New York: Monthly Review Press.

Engels, F. (1975) 'The condition of the working-class in England', in *Marx–Engels Collected Works*, vol. 4, trans. R. Dixon et al., Moscow: Progress, pp. 295–597.

— (1976) 'The principles of communism', in *Marx–Engels Collected Works*, vol. 6, trans. R. Dixon et al., Moscow: Progress, pp. 341–57.

— (1990) 'Origins of the family, private property, and the state', in *Marx–Engels Collected Works*, vol. 26, trans. R. Dixon et al., Moscow: Progress, pp. 129–276.

Ferguson, A. (1979) 'Women as a new revolutionary class', in P. Walker (ed.), *Between Labor and Capital*, Boston, MA: South End, pp. 279–309.

Firestone, S. (1975) *Frauenbefreiung und sexuelle Revolution* [The dialectic of sex: the case for the feminist revolution], Frankfurt: Fischer.

Fraser, N. (1994) *Widerspenstige Praktiken. Macht, Diskurs, Geschlecht* [Unruly practices: power, discourse and gender in contemporary social theory], Frankfurt: Suhrkamp.

Godelier, M. (1973) Ökonomische Anthropologie: Untersuchungen zum Begriff der sozialen Struktur primitiver Gesellschaften [Perspectives in Marxist anthropology], Reinbek: Rohwolt.

Goffman, E. (1994) *Interaktion und Geschlecht* [Interaction and gender], Frankfurt: Campus.

Habermas, J. (1981a) *Theorie des kommunikativen Handelns* [Theory of communicative action], vol. 1, Frankfurt: Suhrkamp.

— (1981b) *Theorie des kommunikativen Handelns* [Theory of communicative action], vol. 2, Frankfurt: Suhrkamp.

Haraway, D. (1987) 'Geschlecht, Gender, Genre. Sexualpolitik eines Wortes' [Sex, gender, genre: sexual politics of a word], in K. Hauser (ed.), *Viele Orte überall?*, Berlin: Argument, pp. 22–41.

— (1995) 'Lieber Kyborg als Göttin!: Für eine sozialistisch-feministische Unterwanderung der Gentechnologie' [A manifesto for cyborgs: science, technology and socialist feminism in the 1980s], in *Monströse Versprechen*, Hamburg: Argument, pp. 165–84.

Harris, O. and K. Young (1981) 'Engendered structures: some problems in the analysis of reproduction', in J. S. Kahn and J. R. Llobera (eds), *The Anthropology of Pre-capitalist Societies*, London: Macmillan, pp. 109–47.

Hartmann, H. (1981) 'The unhappy marriage of Marxism and feminism: towards a more progressive union', in L. Sargent (ed.), *Women and Revolution: A Discussion of the Unhappy Marriage of Marxism and Feminism*, Boston, MA: South End, pp. 1–41.

Haug, F. (1996) 'Knabenspiele und Menschheitsarbeit' [Boys' games and human labour], in F. Haug (ed.), *Frauen-Politiken*, Hamburg: Argument, pp. 125–45.

— (1998) 'Gramsci und die Produktion des Begehrens' [Gramsci and the production of desire], *Psychologie und Gesellschaftskritik*, 22(2/3): 75–92.

Heise, H. (1993) 'Am Anfang steht die Unterwerfung (der Frauen)?' [At the beginning is the subjection (of women)?], *Ethik und Sozialwissenschaften*, 4(3): 235–8.

Lafitau, J.-F. (1983) *Moeurs des sauvages américains: Comparées aux moeurs des premiers temps* [Customs of the American Indians compared with the customs of primitive times], Paris: Maspero.

Landes, R. (1938) *The Ojibwa Woman*, New York: Columbia University Press.

Leacock, E. (1981) *Myths of Male Dominance*, New York: Monthly Review Press.

— (1989) 'Der Status der Frauen in egalitären Gesellschaften: Implikationen für die soziale Evolution' [Myths of male dominance], in Arbeitsgruppe Ethnologie Wien (ed.), *Von fremden Frauen: Frausein und Geschlechterbeziehungen in nichtindustriellen Gesellschaften*, Frankfurt: Suhrkamp, pp. 29–67.

Lenz, I. (1995) 'Geschlechtssymmetrische Gesellschaften. Neue Ansätze nach der Matriarchatsdebatte' [Gendersymmetric societies: new approaches after the matriarchy debate], in I. Lenz and U. Luig (eds), *Frauenmacht ohne Herrschaft: Geschlechterverhältnisse in nichtpatriarchalen Gesellschaften*, Frankfurt: Fischer, pp. 26–87.

Lévi-Strauss, C. (1971) *Strukturale Anthropologie* [Structural anthropology], 2 vols, Frankfurt: Suhrkamp.

— (1980) *Mythos und Bedeutung* [Myth and meaning], Frankfurt: Suhrkamp.

Luig, U. (1995) 'Sind egalitäre Gesellschaften auch geschlechtsegalitär?' [Are egalitarian societies also gender-egalitarian?], in I. Lenz and

U. Luig (eds), *Frauenmacht ohne Herrschaft*, Frankfurt: Fischer, pp. 88–169.

MacCormack, C. P. (1989) 'Natur, Kultur und Geschlecht: Eine Kritik' [Nature, culture and gender], in Arbeitsgruppe Ethnologie Wien (ed.), *Von fremden Frauen: Frausein und Geschlechterbeziehungen in nichtindustriellen Gesellschaften*, Frankfurt: Suhrkamp, pp. 68–99.

Marx, K. (1972) *The Ethnological Notebooks of Karl Marx*, ed. L. Krader, Assen: Van Gorcum.

— (1975) 'Economic and philosophic manuscripts of 1844', in *Marx–Engels Collected Works*, vol. 3, trans. R. Dixon et al., Moscow: Progress, pp. 229–348.

— (1996) *Capital: Volume 1*, in *Marx–Engels Collected Works*, vol. 35, trans. R. Dixon et al., Moscow: Progress.

— (1997) *Capital: Volume 2*, in *Marx–Engels Collected Works*, vol. 36, trans. R. Dixon et al., Moscow: Progress.

Marx, K. and F. Engels (1975a) 'The holy family or critique of critical criticism', in *Marx–Engels Collected Works*, vol. 4, trans. R. Dixon et al., Moscow: Progress, pp. 5–244.

— (1975b) 'The German ideology', in *Marx–Engels Collected Works*, vol. 5, trans. R. Dixon et al., Moscow: Progress, pp. 19–584.

McDonough, R. and R. Harrison (1978) 'Patriarchy and relations of production', in A. Kuhn and A. Wolpe (eds), *Feminism and Materialism: Women and Modes of Production*, London: Routledge, pp. 11–48.

Meillassoux, C. (1983) *Die wilden Früchte der Frau. Über häusliche Produktion und kapitalistische Wirtschaft* [Maidens, meals and money: capitalism and the domestic community], Frankfurt: Suhrkamp.

— (1994) 'Anthropologie' [Anthropology], in W. F. Haug, F. Haug, P. Jehle and W. Kuettler (eds), *Historisch-kritisches Wörterbuch des Marxismus*, vol. 1, pp. 309–20.

Mill, J. S., H. Taylor Mill and H. Taylor (1997) *Die Hörigkeit der Frau* [The subjection of women], Frankfurt: Suhrkamp.

Mitchell, J. (1974) *Psychoanalysis and Feminism*, New York: Pelican.

Molyneux, M. (1989) 'Androzentrismus in der marxistischen Anthropologie' [Androcentrism in Marxist anthropology], in Arbeitsgruppe Ethnologie Wien (ed.), *Von fremden Frauen: Frausein und Geschlechterbeziehungen in nichtindustriellen Gesellschaften*, Frankfurt: Suhrkamp, pp. 100–36.

Morgan, L. H. (1987) *Die Urgesellschaft: Untersuchungen über den Fortschritt der Menschheit aus der Wildnis durch die Barbarei zur Zivilisation* [Ancient society], Fulda: n.p.

Ortner, S. H. (1974) 'Is female to male as nature is to culture?', in M. Z. Rosaldo and L. Lamphère (eds), *Woman, Culture, and Society*, Stanford, CA: Stanford University Press, pp. 67–88.

Pateman, C. (1985) 'Women and democratic citizenship: the personal and the political: can citizenship be democratic?', Jefferson Memorial Lectures, University of California, Berkeley, February.

Phelps, L. (1975) 'Patriarchy and capitalism', *Quest* 2(2): 35–48.

Rech, P. W. (1993) 'Eine/Meine Paraphrase als "das Ende vom Lied"' [A/my paraphrase as 'the end of it'], *Ethik und Sozialwissenschaften*, 4(3): 258–60.

Rosaldo, M. Z. (1974) 'Woman, culture, and society', in M. Z. Rosaldo and L. Lamphère (eds), *Woman, Culture, and Society*, Stanford, CA: Stanford University Press, pp. 17–42.

Rösing, I. (1999) *Geschlechtliche Zeit – Geschlechtlicher Raum* [Gendered time – gendered space], Heidelberg: Winter.

Rowbotham, S. (1973) *Women's Consciousness, Men's World*, Harmondsworth: Penguin.

Schraube, E. and U. Osterkamp (2015) *Psychology from the Standpoint of the Subject: Selected Writings of Klaus Holzkamp*, Critical Theory and Practice in Psychology and the Human Sciences, New York: Palgrave Macmillan.

Smith, D. (1984) *The Conceptual Practices of Power*, Toronto: University of Toronto Press.

Terray, E. (1974) *Zur politischen Ökonomie der 'primitive' Gesellschaften* [Marxism and 'primitive societies': two studies], Frankfurt: Suhrkamp.

Woolf, V. (1938) *Die drei Guineen* [Three guineas], Munich: Frauenoffensive.

Young, I. M. (1997) 'Socialist feminism and the limits of dual systems theory', in R. Hennessy and C. Ingraham (eds), *Materialist Feminism*, London: Routledge, pp. 95–106.

3 | THE MARX WITHIN FEMINISM

Frigga Haug

What toils he spared us,
this desk-chair Hercules …
Yet what he bequeathed us.
What dearth of illusions.
What worldwide loss
of dependable values. What widespread
refusal to subjugate ourselves!
And how impossible, between you and me,
not to question it all. Since then,
all our successes were mere down payments
of history. The time to hold back
has passed,
how impossible, not to fight to the end:
and not to see it as the beginning.

Volker Braun, 'Karl Marx'[1]

I want to show what we can inherit from Marx and where we have critically to go beyond him: in short, how to make him useful for a feminist project. To that end, and rather than repeating the old argument between Marxism and feminism, I want to draw three lessons from Marx that are fruitful, even indispensable, for contemporary, practical feminism: (1) the role of 'real life', where Marx's theses on Feuerbach are significant for feminist criticism of mainstream science; (2) how Marx's concept of work has shaped feminist debates and resonates with the current 'crisis of working society',[2] and thus deserves more attention; and (3) the elaboration of a Marxian theory of family and housework to overcome a widespread blindness to their importance, a blindness that weakens the critique of modern capitalism. Since I already considered myself a Marxist at the beginning of the women's movement, there is an autobiographical aspect to this essay, which I indicate below.

Marx's critique of Feuerbach

In his shortest important work, *Concerning Feuerbach*, Marx wrote:

> The chief defect of all hitherto existing materialism – that of Feuerbach included – is that the thing, reality, sensuousness, is conceived only in the form of the *object or of contemplation*, but not as *sensuous human activity*, *practice*, not subjectively. Hence, in contradistinction to materialism, the *active* side was developed abstractly by idealism – which, of course, does not know real, sensuous activity as such.
>
> Feuerbach wants sensuous objects, really distinct from the thought objects, but he does not conceive human activity itself as *objective* activity. Hence, in *The Essence of Christianity*, he regards the theoretical attitude as the only genuinely human attitude, while practice is conceived and fixed only in its dirty-judaical manifestation. Hence he does not grasp the significance of 'revolutionary,' of 'practical-critical', activity. (Marx 1969: 13, emphasis in original)

This critique of existing materialism had little significance for the reception of Marxian thought in the labour movement, but it now reads like direct instruction for the feminist theory and practice of today. The disconnection of science from the real practices of people, the deducing of all human activity from the most abstract categories, and the neglect of sensuous human activity are major critical points that feminist-informed science asserts against the scientific canon. That the dominant social sciences were conceptualized without regard for the experiences and practices of women was one of the first critiques made by the women's movement. It thus intervened in existing traditions of thought in revolutionary ways, even though the women did not connect their criticisms to Marx's critique of Feuerbach.

The remaining paragraphs in this section are based on my personal experience in the women's movement. I had earlier studied Marx's theses on Feuerbach and found them useful for the slowly strengthening women's movement. During the late 1960s and early 1970s, mass rallies of women occurred regularly in large cities across Western capitalist countries. They articulated their protests, tribunal-style, denouncing degrading treatment by men. Violence against women was one theme that moved these burgeoning throngs of women to rage and indignation. Since I then considered that such gatherings contributed mainly to despair, not to the actions that were needed,

I wrote 'Women: victims or actors?'[3] In applying what I had learned from Marx, I drew certain conclusions from his 'Theses on Feuerbach' (numbers three and six) that I still find fundamental today. From thesis three:

> The materialist doctrine concerning the changing of circumstances and upbringing forgets that circumstances are changed by men and that it is essential to educate the educator himself. This doctrine must, therefore, divide society into two parts, one of which is superior to society.
>
> The coincidence of the changing of circumstances and of human activity or self-changing can be conceived and rationally understood only as *revolutionary practice*. (Marx 1969: 13)

I concluded, first, that personal transformation was a necessary moment and an essential component of altering oppressive conditions, and secondly, that every intervention in society (i.e. each political act) had to be carried out by individuals whose own liberation was at stake. In the words of Peter Weiss: 'Liberation cannot be handed to us, we have to conquer it ourselves. If we fail to conquer it ourselves, then it will have no consequences for us' (2005: 199). This simple idea indicated how crucial it was for women to take their history into their own hands and not wait for liberation through others, such as workers. Moreover, this idea connected personal, subjective issues to societal interventions for political change. Thus, neither our own personal struggles nor our efforts to transform society would get lost or separated for us.

To my surprise, this double movement of women taking self-change as a dimension of their revolutionary practice aroused an unexpectedly violent reaction in many labour movement organizations. Their opposition was furiously voiced over the next ten years in various journals and newspapers. I was accused of 'bourgeois deviance', among other things, by those less concerned about the women's movement than about their own interests and privileges. They included male leaders of the labour movement who sometimes even occupied chairs of women's committees. Proclaiming women as particular political subjects was a heresy against the male labour organizations' claims to be the only legitimate representatives of the political struggle for everyone's liberation. 'Capital as the principal enemy', as it was then termed, must first be fought jointly. The woman question, 'a subordinate contradiction', was to take its place later on the agenda of the new society. Thus the labour movement ultimately directed its criticism at the very existence of the women's movement, which was treated as an aloof, bourgeois troublemaker. This meant that its real revolutionary dimensions went unrecognized, while the connection between capitalism and women's oppression was never grasped at all.

The self-righteous tone and hostile intensity in the attacks by labour movement intellectuals against the women's movement very quickly pushed the latter into an oppositional stance towards the socialist movement out of which it had sprung. The crisis soon became so acute that many women's groups in England, Italy, France and Germany withdrew from labour organizations, some even reorganizing as parallel groups in what Italian feminists called 'double militancy'. These groups identified and exposed men's dominance over women as historically and politically powerful alongside and interwoven with capitalist exploitation; they also often articulated notions of women's essentially higher nature and victim status in modern society. However, with few exceptions, the women's critiques of the labour movement neither drew even a little from Marx nor appealed to his authority. For the few women's groups who did remain connected to Marxism, their work was ineffectively 'derivative' and abstract without much apparent contact with women's lived realities and thus without much influence.[4]

In response to the conflicts separating feminism and Marxism, I found a basis for a useful dialogue between them in Marx's sixth thesis on Feuerbach:

> Feuerbach resolves the religious essence into the human essence. But the human essence is no abstraction inherent in each single individual. In its reality it is the ensemble of the social relations. Feuerbach, who does not enter upon a criticism of this real essence, is consequently compelled: To abstract from the historical process and to fix the religious sentiment as something by itself and to presuppose an abstract – isolated – human individual. Essence, therefore, can be comprehended only as 'genus,' as an internal, dumb generality which naturally unites the many individuals. (Marx 1969: 14)

This turn from speaking of humanity in the singular, behind which gender relations inevitably disappear, seems to me to remain fundamental for every attempt to formulate the problematic of women in our societies. I read it as a research mandate to study the participation of women in their own oppression, their engagement in social relations, and their need for self-change. In short, the problematic of women is a historical production in which women themselves have been and are actors. Their position in society could not, therefore, be understood without taking their own involvement into account. Understanding the connection between different societal practices and the culturally supported formation of gender seemed like a research task that could show, more pointedly than ever before, the gaps left by the absence of the female from the production of knowledge. At the same time, this approach would link knowledge about women's socialization to their liberation, thereby breaking from the abstract objectivism so deeply ingrained in the prevailing traditions in social scientific research. Feminist research could and should become the process of turning the objects of research into its subjects, as experts of their own socialization, utilizing women's remembered history as a basic research tool and raw material.

I thus endeavoured to develop an empirical methodology that would advance research in which women, as subjects, could collectively figure out the problematic of their position in society, their participation in the reproduction of their own oppression, so that they themselves could determine where change was necessary and possible. With this methodology, which I called 'memory work', I developed a praxis from Marx's 'Theses on Feuerbach' which aimed to overcome the problem of robbing women of their practical-subjective inclusion – that is, of making them research objects on the order of insects. It was important to bring women's implicit knowledge to the fore and make it public. This methodology also worked against the essentialism then emerging in feminism (i.e. the 'higher nature of women' thematic) by attempting instead to track a connection between self-change and societal change. The Feuerbach theses provided a space in which the vexed questions of a developing feminism could be posed, questions that are no less valid today and that continue to be urgent for feminist research. Since concrete research on them has only just begun, in fact, they are by no means fully answered yet. With respect to Marx, however, it is always better to study him not as a theorist who has already done our thinking for us, but rather as one whose ways of intervening in conventional thought can teach us the art of shifting the subject of knowledge for the sake of a greater knowledge.

Marx and work

The initial feminist wrath against Marx, which finally resulted in a renunciation of Marxist thought, was not directed, however, at his 'Theses on Feuerbach' (the importance of which for a scientific feminism has never been elaborated anywhere, so far as I know), but rather at Marx's concept of work and his theories of the production of surplus-value.[5] What are we to make of feminist concerns that Marx's concept of work excludes women and prevents them from perceiving the reality of their oppression? Feminist criticism has focused primarily on Marx's arguments about the 'dual character of work'. The idea of work as a force which can create both use-value and exchange-value is fundamental to his analysis of capitalism and its dynamic as well as to his theory of revolution. A society driven by the desire to turn living labour into dead labour (to use Marx's own imagery) and then to endow that dead labour with power over the living in the form of capital, machines and factories would manoeuvre itself into catastrophe unless radical measures were taken. Such measures would have to destroy the basic structures of social regulation – that is, profit as the driving force and the corresponding domination of incremental value over living labour on the basis of the division of labour and the rule of property. In his analysis of the dual character of work, Marx focuses on wage labour as the dominant mode of life-deforming activity, with the first step towards change being the abolition of private ownership of the means of production. His analysis had the effect of focusing too narrowly on the male worker's historical role as family breadwinner and on the working class as the political subject. Women's protests against this theoretical configuration seem justified, for even if we agree that such a situation is the product of capitalist society rather than the creation of Marx's analysis of it, his terms are remarkable for a certain vacuity and silence on the subject of women.

The domestic-labour debate of the late 1960s – and still percolating with Lise Vogel's 'Domestic labour revisited' (2014) – broadened the scope of a complaint about the centrality of the male worker into an evaluation of the validity of Marx's theory of value as a whole.[6] Beginning in 1973 with an article by Mariarosa Dalla Costa (1973), Marx's theory was extended to include domestic labour as 'productive' because, by reproducing male labour-power as a commodity, it thereby enables the surplus value appropriated from the male labourer. While 'invisible' as work inside the family, women's work produces more than necessary for her own reproduction, an excess that eventually accrues to the capitalist as profits. Marx had not analysed this process (domestic labour was called the 'blind spot' in the critique of political economy). Yet the analysis showed that the family was central to social production.

However, wage discrimination against women was supposedly justified by their producing less value than men, for although women reproduced men, this entailed a withdrawal of their own reproduction from their labour-power. In this respect, men literally had more value for their employers, since in purchasing the commodity male labour-power they also got a bonus ration of women's work. This overlooking of the work performed by women in the home was based on disregarding an essential component of the surplus value appropriated by the capitalist. If the secret of the commodity labour-power was its ability to produce more than it needed for its own reproduction, then this must also be true of women's labour-power; what remained to be discovered was how it contributed to the capitalist-manufactured commodity (Pohl 1984).

One practical consequence of this analysis was the demand for domestic labour's compensation as wage labour, on the one hand, and for simply doing away with this sphere of unpaid female labour altogether, on the other. In 1985, Christel Neusüß (1985: 25) added a further twist to the argument when she calculated that the commodity labour-power, as something belonging to the worker, could not figure in any account of commodity production and value because it rendered the work of mothers (i.e. giving birth to children) invisible together with domestic labour (her book includes a survey of ideas from the history of the labour movement, all of which show an absolute ignorance of the production of life, as well as domestic labour). While the plausibility of such arguments cannot be denied, it seems problematic to me that they should have been put forward in a purely academic way, as bereft of consequences as the passion that went into the struggle over the value of domestic labour but led to no corresponding political strategy. The other line of argument pursued in the domestic-labour debate – namely, that housework was productive and should be socially acknowledged as such by being compensated like any other form of wage labour – proved to have political potential: the demand that wages be paid for domestic labour was embraced by the more conservative parties in West Germany because it enabled them both to promote 'family values' and, in the face of rising unemployment, to uphold their seemingly ever more justified opposition to women's professional activity. But with this support for compensating domestic labour that took shape as a straightforward idea of the equivalence of housework to waged labour, almost everything else with which the women's movement had begun its struggle was given up: the critiques of family form, of the gendered division of labour, of the alienated form of wage labour, and of capitalism itself. Claiming that domestic labour was productive could presumably – if only by the magic force of conceptualization – remove the stain from a division of labour that denied women the possibility of existing without a male breadwinner as long as they remained housewives.

The debate continued for the most part in the United States. In 1994, Fraad, Resnick and Wolff published *Bringing It All Back Home: Class, Gender and Power in the Modern Household*, in which they tried to apply the concept of class to household practices and concluded that such an approach was a fertile one. As these authors saw it, two different modes of class production from two different eras were operating together in the present: a feudal mode alongside a capitalist one. This point of entry allowed them to depict separate practices as possibly self-contradictory and the structure of demands by those who inhabit both the domestic and the public sphere as non-homologous. Their hope is that there could develop a potential of protest (Fraad et al. 1994). While not incompatible with Marx, this representation shifts the analytic weight from the critique of the ruling mode of domination and economy to the problematic of the coexistence of differently organized power relations. But Marx had also spoken of the fact that being a productive worker would be bad luck and no luck. Before I suggest another approach to the question of the function of unpaid housework for the reproduction of capitalist society as a critique of Marx, however, let me return to the original series of arguments that arose from the domestic-labour debate in relation to his concept of work. In my opinion, they relate less to Marx than to the Marxism of the labour movement. That would in itself pose no problem had not Marx made some important points for feminists to take into account precisely on the question of work – which therefore brings me to a rereading of Marx.

From the philosophical tradition and the latter-day developments in political economy (e.g. Smith, Ricardo) Marx drew a concept of work in relation to a significantly controversial sphere. Work was the activity of the poor: it was laborious toil that exhausted people's lives; indeed, for many it had replaced life. But work was also the source of wealth and of all value:

> but it is the interest of all rich nations, that the greatest part of the poor should never be idle, and yet continually spend what they get. Those that get their living by their daily labour have nothing to stir them up to be serviceable but their wants which it is prudence to relieve, but folly to cure. From what has been said, it is manifest, that, in a free nation, where slaves are not allowed of, the surest wealth consists in a multitude of the laborious poor. (Mandeville, cited in Marx 1977: 765)

Work as the connecting link between poverty and wealth, as the contradictory foundation of both – Marx begins by elaborating on the position of work in this provocative contradiction. He sees it as a dimension of domination: 'the emancipation of society … is expressed in the political form of the emancipation of the workers' because 'the whole of human servitude is involved in the relation of the worker to production, and all relations of servitude are nothing but modifications and consequences of this relation' (Marx 1992: 333).

In Marx's early writings, we find a number of statements that, in the language of the day, define work as alienation: 'For in the first place labour, life activity, productive life itself appears to man only as a means for the satisfaction of a need, the need to preserve physical existence. But productive life is species-life' (ibid.: 328); and 'all human activity up to now has been labour, i.e. industry, self-estranged activity' (ibid.: 354).

This idea that labour is domination does not yet make a difference between the material side and the economic forms and thus comes to the logical conclusion that work itself should be abolished:

> One of the greatest misunderstandings is to speak of free, social, human work, of work without private property. 'Work' is by nature un-free, inhuman, unsocial, activity which is both controlled by

> private property and which creates it. The abolition of private property, therefore, only becomes reality when it is seen as the abolition of work. (Marx 1972: 25)

Finally, from the conception of history we have sketched, we obtain these further conclusions: 'In all revolutions up till now the mode of activity always remained unscathed and it was only a question of the distribution of this activity, a new distribution of labour to other persons, whilst the communist is directed against the preceding mode of activity, does away with labour' (Marx and Engels 1965: 87). A counter-concept to alienated labour is in this context 'universal producing', shaping or forming 'along the laws of beauty'. If labour is capital's power over humans, capital 'is man completely lost to himself' (Marx 1992: 334–5).

I do not think that Marx actually contemplated the abolition of work as man's metabolic interchange with nature, promising eternal idleness, or that he imagined the abolition of industry to be compatible with the survival of the race. But thinking of work in formal conceptual terms compels us to reconstruct what has become deformed in his concept of work, and hence what 'substance' remains to be liberated. In work's alienated form Marx found the free expression and enjoyment of life, the free, spontaneous activity of the human community, the opportunity to know oneself affirmed in the thought and love of another; the development of each individual into a whole person, the intercourse of individuals as such (Marx and Engels 1965: 86–7), and free, conscious life activity as species-life (Marx 1992: 329). The emphasis is on 'free activity', or 'self-activity', and this is always connected to the life of the species as a species-specific characteristic. As species-beings, people are active on each other's behalf, which determines their intercourse with one another and with the community, as well as their development as individuals. This free activity is a pleasure; life itself is a pleasurable, productive activity.

Taking such statements as our starting point, we could posit self-activity as 'the primary need of life', conceive of the community as a productive framework, and speak of the development of individuals through their own free activity; but we would never thereby arrive at the modern, defensive sociological reaction to work as what should no longer stand at the centre of social theory (as it allegedly did for Marx), but rather as what is to be replaced by 'communication' or 'way of life' (life-world). It is crystal clear that Marx never distinguished between life-world and 'work-world', having been more concerned with revolutionizing what is nowadays called our 'way of life', which he understood as the collectively active, enjoyable union of the individuals in a community (including the form of their intercourse, love and life itself, although by 'life' he always meant active life).

> Our way of life is distorted by the relations of production, the means by which people produce their material lives as they have done throughout the course of history, initially so that some could indulge in free activity whilst their material existence was produced by others. (Marx and Engels 1965: 84–5)

> While in the earlier periods self-activity and the production of material life were separated, in that they devolved on different persons, and while, on account of the narrowness of the individuals themselves, the production of material life was considered as a subordinate mode of self-activity, they now diverge to such an extent that finally material life appears as the end, and what produces this material life, labour (which is now the only possible but, as we see, negative form of self-activity), as the means. (Ibid.: 67)

Self-activity, as a perspective on liberation, is related to the production of material life, and this relationship is essential to conceiving the possibility of life without domination. The production of material life passes through a number of stages and forms, one of which is work: the most direct form of perversion, the 'negative form of self-activity' (ibid.: 67). Thus does life become divided against itself. Enfolded in this negative form are the analytical categories that Marx would later deploy in *Capital* (the passage that follows is from the 'Economic and philosophical manuscripts'):

> Thus through *estranged, alienated labour* the worker creates the relationship of another man, who is alien to labour and stands outside it, to that labour. The relation of the worker to labour creates the relation of the capitalist or whatever other word one chooses for the master of labour to that labour. *Private property* is therefore the product, result and necessary consequence of *alienated labour*, of the external relation of the worker to nature and to himself. (Marx 1992: 331–2)

We can already see here his later linguistic usage, in subsequent writings, where Marx will substitute the global condemnation of work by a differentiation in which the being of work is determined by forms on the one side, their necessity on the other. About work, Marx would go on to say in *Capital*: 'Labour, then, as the creator of use-values, as useful labour, is a condition of human existence which is independent of all forms of society; it is an eternal necessity which mediates the metabolism between man and nature, and therefore human life itself' (Marx 1977: 133).[7] Work always has an anthropological dimension: while the working individual changes nature outside himself, he changes at the same time his own nature (see ibid.: 283). In its alienated form work has a dual nature. On the one hand, it is a producer of use-values, purposive and, in that sense, independent of social formations. On the other, it produces exchange-values and creates wealth, but only under certain social conditions. The distortions or alienations that arise as a consequence are thoroughly analysed in *Capital*. The dual nature of work is fundamental to capitalism as a system that produces commodities, but what remains decisive in Marx is the production of material existence as a form of free activity. It includes the idea of production without domination and hence the elimination of private property (the accumulation of exchange-values) as a regulative principle, as well as the reconciliation with nature which comes from understanding its laws. People's emancipation lies within the developing production of material existence – its developing forces of production – leading towards a communal, self-determined goal. This connects the early writings with the later ones.

At stake in the idea of free activity, conceived as a process, is the relationship between freedom and necessity. As an aspect of material production, the bounds of necessity should be pushed back as far as possible for the sake of free activity. Work, in the realm of necessity, is a problem of distribution – everyone should perform an equal share of necessary labour. In the realm of freedom, however, the activity is of a different kind, one to which the traditional divisions of labour – above all, its division into mental and manual labour – no longer apply. The route from one realm to the other proceeds via the development of the productive forces that will moderate the aspect of necessity in the production of material existence. And it proceeds likewise through the division of human labour, its alienation, for alienated labour has to be overcome in a process whereby human beings take comprehensive possession of the productive forces that they themselves have created. All the relations of production have to be overturned, since these have distorted the human species to the point where all development, all wealth and culture, and the actual conditions of work have become objective realities that oppose the workers and gain power over them. This contradiction can be resolved only by rupture.

In the 'Critique of the Gotha programme', Marx sketches the cooperative phase of society (social ownership of the means of production), which – precisely because it has emerged from capitalist society – bears the birthmarks of that society 'in every respect, economically, morally, intellectually'. He goes on to describe a more advanced 'communist society', a community in which the distortions of labour have been overcome, and it is in this context that we encounter the reference to work as 'the primary need of life':

> when the enslaving subjugation of individuals to the division of labour, and thereby the antithesis between intellectual and physical labour, have disappeared; when labour is no longer just a means of keeping alive, but has itself become the primary need of life; when the all-round development of individuals has also increased their productive powers and all the springs of cooperative wealth flow more abundantly only then can society wholly cross the narrow horizon of bourgeois right and inscribe on its banner: From each according to his abilities, to each according to his needs! (Marx 1974: 347)

These remarks have led to widespread misunderstandings. On Marx's authority individuals could be accused of a 'work-shy' mentality and then 're-educated' as people for whom work was 'the primary need of life'. Worse yet, the final proclamation, 'to each according to his needs', triggered both hopes and fears. Had Marx been expressing a yearning for a society in which needs which had been moulded by capitalism and superfluous production, on the one hand, and by poverty, on the other, should be satisfied? The context, however, makes his meaning unambiguously clear. If human beings succeeded in liberating themselves from material want and domination, the production of material life would become a source of productive pleasure and an opportunity for people to experience this 'primary need' and, to that extent, realize their humanity. This would include the abolition of those divisions of labour which had served to institute our social formations: manual versus mental labour, men's versus women's labour, urban versus rural labour, and finally the dominating pseudo-division of labour, the class division of society between those who work and those who do not. With these considerations in mind, let's turn to our previous questions.

It is self-evident that when we speak of work we should take its (frequently overlooked) formal character into account. The failure to make distinctions when we think and talk about work is the source of most misunderstandings. We speak of 'wage labour', imagining it as the be-all and end-all of the matter, and – with this understanding in mind – are critical of any talk about work as 'the primary need of life'. But conversely, educating people to view work as this primary need is not only senseless; for the most part it is no more than educating them to accept wage labour in its various guises, which is to say, teaching them to submit to the discipline of industry. When we speak of work's 'substance', which in our societies has been submitted to paid work in a division-of-labour system, we really ought to use the cumbersome phrase 'self-activation in the production of material existence'.

Feminist issues My own studying and rethinking of the arguments in the domestic-labour debate since the 1960s has led me to develop Marx's arguments about work more consistently and to look at them from a feminist perspective. Consequently, I have underlined and stressed here some of his ideas that have been forgotten in the heat of debate and to which we should give more weight. Instead of hastily consigning Marx to the rubbish bin of history, we should step back and see whether the women's movement could not make good use of his formulation of enjoyable free activity in the production of material existence, for Marx in fact placed the question of women's oppression squarely in the context of alienated labour: 'This latent slavery in the family, though still very crude, is the first property, but even at this early stage it corresponds perfectly to the definition of modern economists who call it the power of disposing of the labour-power of others' (Marx and Engels 1965: 44).

I have great difficulties in finding a foundation for the accusations of the women's movement against Marx in the writings of Marx. It is correct that he rather wants to get rid of all work (in his early writings) instead of including women's non-paid domestic work in it, but it is out of the question that he thinks the reification and alienation of parts of human work activities by subjecting them to the wage form is fundamental for his analysis of capitalist societies and not applicable to all social work. Is not the framework Marx proposed for human society and the individuals who live in it so constructed as to enable the oppression of women, with its mixture of 'natural' and social origins, to acquire a tremendous dynamism? The sexual division of labour is inscribed in an altogether diabolical fashion as the division between the production of life and the production of the means of life, as well as in the major division between work and free activity. The sphere of actual life is marginalized from the vantage point of the social production of the means of life, and with it those people – women – who largely inhabit it. Meanwhile, at the centre of society, activity is alienated such that all hope of liberation is displaced on to the living activity at the margins of society. Women, who are still being oppressed, are irrationally expected to bear the weight of society's hopes for a better life, for enjoyment and sensuous pleasure.

In Marx we find the worker described as 'at home when he is not working, and not at home when he is working' (Marx 1992: 326). Not without some justification, feminists have made this remark a target of criticism. Does Marx not speak here from the standpoint of the male worker while overlooking the situation of the other half of humankind, who do indeed work at home and therefore are at home when they are working?[8] However, this criticism overlooks the problems hinted at by Marx, particularly the double cleavage of sensuous pleasure and the meaning of life from work, along with paid work, from work that (apparently) counts for naught. This is implicit in the metaphor of the worker who 'is not at home when he is working'. In this deformation women occupy the home, the marginal realm which is also a refuge, a deformed place of hope. The oppressive idealization of women becomes essential to the survival of the male wage-labourer – an idealization that is then reinforced by the cooperation of the two sexes within the family. Would it not be a revolutionary act to introduce some disorder into this system so as to establish the basis for a new order? If we are to salvage the marginalized realms of life, they must be universalized and hence revalorized. At the same time, the privileged realm of social labour must now be occupied by women and its authority weakened. The very sharing of the different spheres of activity by both sexes would deal a blow to one element of domination that has up to now affirmed the old destructive order. In my view, this is a precondition for bringing love back into the realm of work, a rehumanization of society for which the women's movement is crucial.

Although the domestic-labour debate has introduced a considerable number of necessary and healthy rebellious notions into established Marxism, this very rebellion should be used to rethink the role and function of women's oppression in the reproduction of capitalist society. Both Marx's early hopes concerning labour and his sharp analysis of its fate as wage labour (i.e. the main source of profit and hence of capitalist progress) are of real value now in this time of modern capitalism. I do not think that the situation of women would be improved by smuggling domestic labour in under the laws of wage labour and thereby attributing to Marx's analysis the problematic of unpaid female labour in the home. Rather, our critique should proceed the other way around, beginning with an understanding of housework and its role in the different stages of capitalism, which will uncover another problematic in Marx.

Family work/housework and domestic labour While the feminist argument with Marx, initiated by Dalla Costa's 1973 intervention on the meaning of the separation of the spheres of household labour and factory work for women's oppression, subsequently took issue with his analysis of wage labour, no connection was made to Marx's or Engels' position on housework (a critical deficit that I hope to remedy here). Marx and Engels conceptualized housework primarily as wage labour performed in the home, treating as 'family work' what in the twentieth century has generally been understood as housework. (In order to account for this difference, we need to formulate it as a 'double concept': family work/housework.) It is nonsensical in the context of such work to limit the discussion – and the critique – to Marx when the ongoing reception of Engels' ideas within feminism makes it obvious that the latter should be addressed as well.

In his preface to the first edition of *The Origin of the Family, Private Property and the State*, Engels sketches what he considers the 'production and reproduction of immediate life' (1986: 35): 'On the one side, the production of the means of existence, of food, clothing and shelter and the tools necessary for that production; on the other side, the production of human beings themselves, the propagation of the species' (ibid.: 36). In using 'production' in both cases, Engels provided a starting point for a theory of women's oppression, the elaboration of which he blocked, however, by formulating the two forms of production as 'labour on the one hand and of the family on the other' (ibid.: 36). Dividing the labour of producing food, clothing, shelter, and so on, from the family rendered the latter, for Engels and thus for any theory of women's oppression he might have developed, exclusively a matter of biological processes and their incorporation into the law and the state; family labour was not a consideration. Consequently, he examines the organization of procreation, but not how the work performed within the family relates to the totality of labour and to the reproduction of society.

Elsewhere, Engels makes his awareness that labour is also performed within the family perfectly clear. In *Anti-Dühring*, he takes a historical perspective:

> The entire development of human society beyond the stage of animal savagery dates from the day when the labour of the family creates more products than were necessary for its maintenance, from the day where a part of the labour, no longer used in the production of bare means of subsistence could be diverted to production of means of production. (Engels 1935: 198)

Engels was not interested in the consequences of this diversion for the remaining part, which he calls 'production of bare means of subsistence', but only in whatever social effects might come out of the surplus produced by labour over the cost of labour's maintenance, which he considered the basis of all 'continued social, political and intellectual progress' (ibid.: 198).

Marx is a different story. In the first volume of *Capital* he recognizes family work, if only in passing, and describes the organization of work typical of a manufactory; performed in small, family-operated workshops, this 'family work' is still distinguished from agriculture today. It involves the transformation of the 'life time' of all family members, even children, into 'work time'. In connection with the achievement of factory legislation, Marx wrote about the 'regulating [of] so-called "domestic labour" as a direct attack on the *patria potestas*, or, in modern terms, parental authority', a step which the 'tender-hearted English parliament long affected to shrink from taking': 'The power of facts, however, at last compelled it to acknowledge that large-scale industry, in overturning the economic foundation of the old family system, and the family labour corresponding to it, had also dissolved the old family relationships' (Marx 1977: 620). Marx also speaks here of the 'rights of the children' (ibid.: 620), his target being the decomposition of the family through commodity production and, with it, the collision of two different modes of production and ways of life – the logic of the market, which presupposes the free commodity owner, and family work, with the relative disenfranchisement of women and children: 'Previously the worker sold his own labour-power, which he disposed of as a free agent, formally speaking. Now he sells wife and child. He has become a slave-dealer' (ibid.: 519); and, in a footnote to the same page, he observes that 'in relation to this traffic in children, working-class parents have assumed characteristics that are truly revolting and thoroughly like slave-dealing' (ibid.: 519, n40). Marx quotes a number of factory reports specifically on children, all of which show how 'the spheres of handicrafts and domestic industry become, in what is relatively an amazingly short time, dens of misery' (ibid.: 621). Then we come to his well-known perspective sentence:

> However terrible and disgusting the dissolution of the old family ties within the capitalist system may appear, large-scale industry, by assigning an important part in socially organized processes of production, outside the sphere of the domestic economy, to women, young persons and children of both sexes, does nevertheless create a new economic foundation for a higher form of the family and of relations between the sexes. (Ibid.: 620–1)

Marx's gaze here is focused ahead to the societal organization of production and the necessary elimination of old, interfering forms. He takes absolutely no account of labour performed within the family, aside from the production of commodities, nor of how such labour of caring for humankind and nature contributes to the societalization process. He conceptualizes wage labour within the household as 'household trade', and in this context he also speaks of 'domestic industry', meaning an 'external department of the factory, the manufacturing workshop, or the warehouse' (ibid.: 591; see also p. 645, where he shows some interest in housework as a 'hybrid form' that is not directly subordinated to capital, but is susceptible to pressure from 'usurers' or 'merchants'). Finally, references to family work as separate from and in conflict with wage labour outside the home can be found in two footnotes. Writing of a report on the cotton crisis during the American Civil War, Marx says:

> He [Dr Edward Smith] reported that from a hygienic point of view, and apart from the banishment of the operatives from the factory atmosphere, the crisis had several advantages. The women now had sufficient leisure to give their infants the breast, instead of poisoning them with 'Godfrey's Cordial' (an opiate). They also had the time to learn to cook. Unfortunately, the acquisition of this art occurred at a time when they had nothing to cook. But from this we see how capital, for the purposes of its self-valorization, has usurped the family labour necessary for consumption. (Ibid.: 518, n38)

The conceptual proposition 'family labour necessary for consumption' makes it possible to understand family labour as distinct from wage labour, yet Marx does not elaborate on this or on the 'leisure' necessary for breastfeeding babies who would otherwise be 'poisoned' instead of nourished. In other words, the question of what qualities of life are destroyed through the time-saving measures that rule in a capitalist economy is not pursued. Marx treats the issue of breastfeeding only in terms of wages or profitability:

> Since certain family functions, such as nursing and suckling children, cannot be entirely suppressed, the mothers who have been confiscated by capital must try substitutes of some sort. Domestic work, such as sewing and mending, must be replaced by the purchase of ready-made articles. Hence the diminished expenditure of labour in the house is accompanied by an increased expenditure of money outside. (Ibid.: 518, n39)

What interests Marx here is that since women's inclusion in the capitalist production process brings no additional revenue into the family, it is not really worth the cost. Nevertheless, the repeated mention of 'substitutes' opens up a space for further analysis.

In Marx's analysis of the division of labour, we can discern the beginnings of a theory of family work:

> For an example of labour in common, i.e. directly associated labour, we do not need to go back to the spontaneously developed

> form, which we find at the threshold of the history of all civilized peoples. We have one nearer to hand in the patriarchal rural industry of a peasant family which produces corn, cattle, yarn, linen and clothing for its own use. These things confront the family as so many products of its collective labour, but they do not confront each other as commodities. The different kinds of labour which create these products such as tilling the fields, tending the cattle, spinning, weaving and making clothes are already in their natural form social functions; for they are functions of the family which, just as much as a society based on commodity production, possesses its own spontaneously developed division of labour. The distribution of labour within the family and the labour-time expended by the individual members of the family are regulated by differences of sex and age as well as by seasonal variations in the natural conditions of labour. The fact that the expenditure of the individual labour-powers is measured by duration appears here, by its very nature, as a social characteristic of labour itself, because the individual labour-powers, by their very nature, act only as instruments of the joint labour-power of the family. (Ibid.: 171)

It is astonishing that Marx made no further examination of this finding that the various products were not measured and estimated as more or less valuable according to the time spent on them, even though it certainly had consequences not only for the sexual division of labour, but also for the capitalist model of civilization. After all, the calculation of time spent also makes value a curse for some products, which then have to be protected. In the end, the only things that can withstand the social test of capitalism are those that eat up as little time as possible, making this a model of both progress and pauperization. At the same time, we get a hint of the still-existent yearning to validate the family and to guarantee its continued existence, for it is the one place where production is not calculated solely in terms of labour costs.

Nowhere in Marx is there any analysis of the problem arising from the subordination of all those activities not subject to the wage structure under the logic of cost/benefit calculations as a problem in terms of both human needs and the development of humankind itself (i.e. of that which is regarded and acknowledged as socially meaningful). In his enthusiasm for comprehensive economizing, Marx basically subordinates all work and its valuation to the rationalization that he considers necessary for the further satisfaction of 'life claims':

> The more the productivity of labour increases, the more the working day can be shortened, the more the intensity of labour can increase. From the point of view of society the productivity of labour also grows when economies are made in its use. This implies not only economizing on the means of production, but also avoiding all useless labour. (Ibid.: 667)

This statement conflicts with the belief (expressed in his 'Critique of the Gotha programme') that in some future society time will no longer be geared to wealth.

The gender-specificity of the division of labour emerges only at the margins of Marx's analysis of work under capitalism. He describes it as 'naturally' springing up and, 'based on a purely physiological foundation' (ibid.: 471), as developing through exchange into two, mutually dependent branches, but he does not pursue the configuration of these separate spheres that proved so crucial to the capitalist model of civilization. It seems equally odd that Marx and Engels failed to work out their dominative notion of the gender-specific division of labour articulated in *The German Ideology*: 'This latent slavery in the family, though still very crude, is the first form of property, but even at this stage it corresponds perfectly to the definition of modern economists, who call it the power of disposing of the labour-power of others' (Marx and Engels 1965: 46). For it was on this basis that a social formation developed in which only those things that proved more or less profitable were produced and that any work which could not be accommodated to this logic of time – and thus could not be rationalized, automated or accelerated, such as cherishing and nurturing nature or humankind – came to be neglected or left to women's (unpaid) provision. Today, we can proceed on the assumption that the crisis associated with both the unrestrained (and now uncontrollable) development of the forces of production and the ruinous exhaustion of nature is due to the logic of profit, which rests on women's oppression. We can put to the record the critique of Marx to the effect that the one-sided analysis of wage labour – instead of analysing the interrelation of socially necessary labour and its superordination and subordination – leads to an insufficient analysis of the reproduction of capitalist societies (and consequently of their duration and of the forces which support them). Here some reworking and changes have to be undertaken from a feminist standpoint.

There was no further analysis of the relationship between family labour and wage labour by Marxists. The study of 'women's work' within the family was taken up instead by ethnologists such as Claude Meillassoux (1983). Rosa Luxemburg pretty much followed Marx's lead on this issue, seeing the family as something out of which proletarian women are 'seized': 'It was Capitalism, which has torn her out of the family and subjugated her under social production drove her on foreign land, into workshops, on construction sites, into offices, industries, and warehouses' (Luxemburg 1973: 410).[9] And Lenin was interested in the family only as a site of stupidity from which women had to be removed. He thinks it the main task for the proletarian women's movement to 'include the woman into the socially productive work, to tear her from the "slavery at home"' (Lenin 1961: 401). It was not until the late 1970s that women's studies emerged and began to take up the analysis of family work in the general context of social relations. This was the period during which Maria Mies, Veronica Bennholdt-Thomsen and Claudia von Werlhof (Werlholf et al. 1983), among others, suggested that a practical generalization of subsistence work could provide a solution to the global problem arising from the production of commodities and extending to the exploitation of the Third World.

From today's standpoint, the development of humankind in relation to those products and activities that could pass the market test – and on which it therefore seemed worthwhile to spend time – led to the corresponding situation whereby those products and activities requiring extensive amounts of time without yielding anything sufficiently grand fell by the wayside. Most agricultural and nature-conservational activities, not to mention the rearing of children, were deemed incompatible with the logic of continually reduced expenditures of time. (Efforts to industrialize agricultural production have yielded those horrible products that Brecht predicted in warning: 'You will no longer recognize the fruits by their taste' – Brecht 1967: 162). Although many such products may be indispensable for even the short-term survival of humankind, their development has also widened the gap between those members of the species who can pass the market test and those 'partial people' who live at a level considerably lower than is now typical of the industrialized world. Here we find the Third

World countries, with their continued immiseration becoming even worse in the wake of neoliberal globalization. The First World, on the other hand, is experiencing different and apparently more complex developments, while the women in these countries are still being kept economically dependent on the same breadwinner discussed by Marx and Engels more than a century ago, though he himself ceases to exist. Most women, if employed, fill low-paying 'female' jobs and perform time-consuming tasks that would otherwise simply remain undone.

In this respect, humankind has not progressed; on the contrary, as the forces of production have developed with industrialization, creating ever new human needs in the capitalist West, a monstrous brutalization of humankind has occurred. Crime, drug addiction and alcoholism, and child abuse (including the prostitution of children) are just the visible signs of a model of civilization in which human development has been utterly subordinated to rationalization and market forces, to the needs devised and the products generated to satisfy them under the rule of profit. The material progress realized by enhanced forces of production, far from freeing people to take up their development as human beings, has rather made such human development a mere by-product of industrial development and of the work done by women. In this context it was not unreasonable for Gorbachev to have hoped that the trend towards an increasingly demoralized youth could be countered by sending women back into the family. To this extent, the claim that human liberation can be measured by the degree of liberation women achieve is completely realistic today. For women's liberation affects human interaction at every level, as well as human needs related to sensuality, to nature, to the work of hands and heads, and to women themselves as human beings.

Conclusion

Marx within feminism – the title wanted two things: to show where Marxian ideas were already part of feminism or had been criticized from a feminist point of view, and where we could inherit from him, where to repudiate his ideas or to improve them. His methodological and theoretical break with metaphysics is above all a fundament without which feminist research is hardly to be conceived. We speak of it as an approach which starts with the experiences of women – in Marxian terms this is 'the language of real life', which he brought into research. Therefore, the theses against Feuerbach are fundamental for a productive feminism; at the same time it is obvious why they had so little been taken up into the politics of state-socialist countries and the workers' movement; women's politics was meaningless for them.

Nobody interested in the relationship between Marxism and feminism can avoid the discussion on the Marxian concept of labour and the theory of surplus value. Ironically this critique has led to an uncoupling of feminist criticism from a comprehensive critique of capitalism. A new reading of Marxian thoughts on labour shows that it is useful for feminist thinking in all dimensions, goes beyond most of the complaints, and never falls into the trap of welcoming a subjection of all work under the form of wage labour (as is the case in the feminist demand for 'wages for housework'). Here we can still win a lot for current feminism.

This is different with the passages on family work/domestic work, which have not been taken into account by feminism at all. Here we can observe Marx, patriarch from top to toe, forget the qualitative side of domestic labour, the real actions, the language of real life, to hasten to the fate of such labour, which has been subjected to wage labour. This has consequences for the critics of political economy – that is, for the analysis of capitalism. Because here Marx does not understand that it belongs to the essential moments of capitalism to subject the production of life and does not understand the work on the living as a disruptive element for the production of profit, to marginalize it, to destroy it. It is the analysis of the relationship of both productions, the one of the means of life and the one of life itself, which gives us a sound critique of the capitalist mode of production in which the feminist questions are self-understood and fundamental.

Notes

1 Translated for this volume by Karen Ruoff Kramer.

2 By 'crisis of working society', I refer to the enormous development of the productive forces through microelectronics and the resulting growth of structural unemployment as described mainly in contemporary sociology and political science.

3 This essay, originally published in *Das Argument* (Haug 1980), was based on a talk I gave at the first people's university in Berlin. It has since been translated into eleven languages and has appeared in approximately twenty publications, including, most recently, as 'Women, actors or culprits?' (Haug 1992).

4 Other relatively early exceptions to the prevailing tendency to overlook Marx were the feminist efforts to inscribe the woman's question into Marxism and the studies on ideology by the 'Project Ideology-Theory', published as *Theorien über Ideologie* (Projekt

Ideologie-Theorie 1979), and the studies on work and automation by the 'Project Automation and Qualification' (1974–87, 7 vols).

5 In summarizing the discussion I do not include all literature, which has been published, especially in the United States and in England, in abundance – it can easily be found in the main publications and would here unnecessarily make the list of literature far too long.

6 Lise Vogel (2014) argues that the domestic labour debate had already started in the United States in 1940, with Mary Inman's analysis of women's oppression.

7 For another, almost identical expression of this view, see Marx (1971: 36).

8 See Ivekovic (1984: 103–12).

9 The entirety of Luxemburg's *Die Proletarierin* (1973) is relevant here.

References

Albers, D., E. Altvater, and V. Braun (1983) *Aktualisierung Marx* [The actualization of Marx], Hamburg: Argument.

Brecht, B. (1967) 'Der Dreigroschenprozess' [The threepenny trial], in E. Hauptmann and W. Hecht (eds), *Schriften zur Literatur und Kunst, Gesammelte Werke*, vol. 18, Frankfurt: Suhrkamp, pp. 139–209.

Dalla Costa, M. R. (1973) 'Die Frauen und der Umsturz der Gesellschaft' [Women and the revolution of society], in S. James (ed.), *Die Macht der Frauen und der Umsturz der Gesellschaft*, Berlin: Merve, pp. 22–66.

Engels, F. (1935) *Herrn Eugen Dührings Umwälzung der Wissenschaft (Anti-Dühring)*, Chicago, IL: Charles H. Kerr.

— (1986) *The Origin of the Family, Private Property and the State*, Harmondsworth: Penguin.

Fraad, H., S. Resnick and R. Wolff (1994) *Bringing it All Back Home: Class, Gender and Power in the Modern Household*, London: Pluto.

Haug, F. (1992) *Beyond Female Masochism*, London: Verso.

Haug, W. F. (ed.) (1980) *Das Argument*, 22(123) http://www.amazon.de/Argument-Emanzipation-Problematik-Sexualit%C3%A4t-Herrschaft/dp/B00I60C1J4.

Inman, I. M. (1940) 'In woman's defense', Los Angeles, CA: Committee to Organize the Advancement of Women.

Ivekovic, R. (1984) 'Noch einmal zum Marxismus und Feminismus' [Once again about Marxism and feminism], in Projekt Sozialistischer Feminismus (ed.), *Geschlechterverhältnisse und Frauenpolitik*, Argumentsonderband 110, Berlin: Argument.

Lenin, V. I. (1961) *Gesammelte Werke* [Collected writings], vol. 30, Berlin: Dietz.

Luxemburg, R. (1973) 'Die Proletarierin' [The proletarian], in *Gesammelte Werke* [Collected writings], vol. 3, Berlin: Dietz.

Marx, K. (1969) 'Theses on Feuerbach', trans. W. Lough, in K. Marx and F. Engels, *Selected Works*, Vol. 1, Moscow: Progress, pp. 13–15.

— (1971) *A Contribution to the Critique of Political Economy*, London: Lawrence and Wishart.

— (1972) 'Über F. List's Buch *Das nationale System der Politischen Ökonomie*' [About List's book *The National System of Political Economy*], in K. Marx and F. Engels, *Kritik der bürgerlichen Ökonomie:* Neues Manuskript von Marx und Rede von Engels über F. List, Berlin: VSA, pp. 7–43.

— (1974) 'Critique of the Gotha programme', trans. J. de Bres, in D. Fernbach (ed.), *The First International and After, Political Writings*, vol. 3, Harmondsworth: Penguin.

— (1977) *Capital: A Critique of Political Economy*, vol. 1, New York: Vintage.

— (1992) 'Economic and philosophical manuscripts (1844)', in K. Marx, *Early Writings*, trans. R. Livingstone and G. Benton, Harmondsworth: Penguin, pp. 279–400.

Marx, K. and F. Engels (1965) *The German Ideology*, New York: Lawrence and Wishart.

Meillassoux, C. (1983) *Die wilden Früchte der Frau: Über häusliche Produktion und kapitalistische Wirtschaft* [Women's wild fruits: about domestic production and capitalist economy], Frankfurt: Suhrkamp.

Neusüß, C. (1985) *Die Kopfgeburten der Arbeiterbewegung: oder die Genossin Luxemburg bringt alles durcheinander* [Figments of the labour movement: or Comrade Luxemburg confounds everything], Hamburg: Rasch und Röhring.

Pohl, S. (1984) *Entwicklung und Ursachen der Frauenlohndiskriminierung: Ein feministisch-marxistischer Erklärungsansatz* [Development and origin of women's wage discrimination: a feminist-Marxist approach], Frankfurt: M. P. Lang.

Projekt Ideologie-Theorie (1979) *Theorien über Ideologie* [Theories about ideology], Berlin: Argument.

Vogel, L. (2014) 'Domestic labour revisited', in D. McNally and S. Ferguson (eds), *Marxism and the Oppression of Women: Toward a Unitary Theory*, Chicago, IL: Haymarket, pp. 183–98.

Weiss, P. (2005) *The Aesthetics of Resistance*, trans. J. Neugroschel, Durham, NC: Duke University Press.

Werlhof, C., M. Mies and V. Bennholdt-Thomsen (eds) (1983) *Frauen, die letzte Kolonie* [Women, the last colony], Reinbek: Rohwolt.

Young, I., C. Wolkowitz and R. McCullagh (eds) (1981) *Of Marriage and the Market: Women's Subordination in International Perspective*, London: CSE.

4 | BUILDING FROM MARX: REFLECTIONS ON 'RACE', GENDER AND CLASS

Himani Bannerji

> I know I am not alone. There must be hundreds of other women, maybe thousands, who feel as I do. There may be hundreds of men who want the same drastic things to happen. But how do you hook up with them? How can you interlink your own struggle and goals with these myriad, hypothetical people who are hidden entirely or else concealed by stereotypes and/or generalities of 'platform' such as any movement seems to spawn? I don't know. I don't like it, this being alone when it is clear that there will have to be multitudes working together, around the world, if radical and positive change can be forced upon the heinous status quo I despise in all its overwhelming power. (June Jordan, 'Declaration of an independence I would just as soon not have', in Jordan 1989)

It is conventional in academic and political circles now to speak of 'race' in the same breath as gender and class. It is more or less recognized that 'race' can be combined with other social relations of power and that they can mediate and intensify each other.[1] This combination of 'race', gender and class is often expressed through the concept of 'intersectionality', in which three particular strands of social relations and ideological practices of difference and power are seen as arising in their own specific social terrain, and then criss-crossing each other 'intersectionally' or aggregatively.[2] It is a coming together of social issues to create a moment of social experience.

Yet, speaking of experience, both non-white and white people living in Canada/the West know that this social experience is not, as lived, a matter of intersectionality. Their sense of being in the world, textured through myriad social relations and cultural forms, is lived or felt or perceived as being all together and all at once. A working-class non-white woman's (Black, South Asian, Chinese, etc.) presence in the usual racialized environment is not divisible separately and serially. The fact of her blackness, her sex and her gender-neutral personhood of being working class blend into something of an identity simultaneously and instantaneously (see Terkel 1992; see also Bannerji 1995: 121–58). This identification is both in the eye of the beholder and in her own sense of social presence captured by this gaze. The same goes for a white woman, yet when confronted with this question of 'being' and experience we are hard put to theorize them in terms of a social ontology. What could be the reason for this inadequacy of conceptualization that fails to capture such formative experientiality? If it is lived, then how can it be thought, and how can we overcome our conceptual shortcomings? It is my intent here to suggest a possible theorization that can address these questions, or at least to grasp the reasons for why we need to ask them in the first place. This is not a matter of responding simply to a theoretical challenge, but to a political one as well. This is a basic piece of the puzzle for the making of social democracy.

If democracy is to be more than a mere form consisting of political rituals that only serve to entrench the rule of capital and sprinkle holy water on existing social inequalities, it must have a popular and actually participatory content. This content should be of social and cultural demands concentrating in social movements and organizations working through political processes that aim at popular entitlement at all levels. Such politics needs a social understanding which conceives social formations as complex, contradictory and inclusive phenomena of social interactions. It cannot be a simple arithmetical exercise of adding or intersecting 'race', gender and class in a stratificatory mode. It cannot posit 'race' as a cultural phenomenon and gender and class as social and economic. It needs to overcome the overall segmentation of the social into such elementary aspects of its composition. For example, a trade union cannot properly be said to be an organization for class struggle if it thinks of class only in economic terms without broadening the concept of class to include 'race' and gender in its intrinsic formative definition. Furthermore, it has to make its understanding actionable on this socially composite ground of class.[3]

Outside of the trade unions, which are explicitly 'class' organizations, the usual practice in current social-justice movements is to adopt what is called 'coalition' politics without discriminating among the platforms on which these organizations have been put together.[4] This coalitionist activism is not only a tactical matter, but also reflects the pluralist aggregative logic of social understanding. Organizations that are class based and those that are not come together because of their shared interest in certain issues. But in what would be called 'new social movements', the very issues of class and capital are considered unnecessary, if considered at all.[5] As such, popular demands on grounds of gender, 'race', sexuality, identity and so on have to be primarily formulated outside of class and capital and in cultural terms. In this political framework, 'anti-racism' becomes more a question of multiculturalism and ethnicity, as the socially relational aspects of racialization embedded in the former are converted into a cultural demand. It is not surprising that, of late, there has been a sharp decline in work on 'race' that combines hegemonic/cultural common sense with the workings of class and state.[6] The turn to postmodernism and the turn away from Marxism and class analysis have resulted in increasing valorization of cultural norms and forms and have made theories of discourse into vehicles for 'radical' politics. If, in the past, we had to deal with the economism and class reductionism of positivist Marxists, now our battle is with 'cultural reductionism'. Neither of these readings of social ontology allows us to do justice to politics for social justice. Our theoretical journey must begin somewhere else to reach another destination.

Theorizing the social

The theorization and politics I suggest are not exercises in abstraction. They do not eschew thinking or organizing on specific issues relating to economy, culture or politics. They can be highly specific or local in their scope – about neighbourhoods or homelessness in Toronto, for example – or can speak to cultural problems. But, using these different entry points into the social, they have to analyse and formulate their problems in terms of political problematics which show how these particular or local issues arise only in a wider or extra-local context of socio-economic and cultural relations. If they are 'specific' issues, we have to realize that it is because they are 'specific' to a general, larger set of social, structural and institutional relations.[7] Can, for example, the type of homelessness experienced in Toronto be possible outside of the way capitalist economic and social development have proceeded in Canada as a whole? In redressing the wrongs in this case, one has to think and ask questions on grounds that go beyond the immediate situation; one has to go above and behind it. It would not do, either, to think of 'poverty' as an issue or problem by itself (only to be added to 'race', class or gender) or to conceive of these outside of capital.

In spite of frequent lip-service paid to reflexive social theorization, and even some excellent works on class, slavery, colonialism and imperialism, especially by historians, we need to venture, therefore, into a more complex reading of the social, where every aspect or moment of it can be shown as reflecting others; where each little piece of it contains the macrocosm in its microcosm – what Blake called 'the world in a grain of sand'. What we have instead is a thriving theory industry which ruptures the integrity of the social and joyously valorizes 'fragments', preferring to posit a non-relational inchoateness or to add them whenever necessary. By such accounts, as I said before, the social amounts to an ordering of regulatory parts – the old utilitarian arithmetic – and, properly speaking, is inconceivable. Marxists and neo-Marxists have also succumbed to a ceaseless debate on modernism and postmodernism, allowing the aesthetic, moral category of the 'modern' to distract them. Seeking to bypass the terms of this debate, I would like to come back to Marx's own formulation of 'the social', the ontological or the existential, in different terms or concepts. Here, I assume 'the social' to mean a complex socio-economic and cultural formation, brought to life through myriad finite and specific social and historical relations, organizations and institutions. It involves living and conscious human agents and what Marx called their 'sensuous human activity, practice' (Marx 1976: 615).[8] Here, culture and society are not in a mechanical relation of an economic base and a cultural superstructure. All activities of and in the social are relational and are mediated and articulated with their expressive as well as embedded forms of consciousness. Here, signifying and communicative practices are intrinsic moments of social being. Using such a formulation of the social here, it is my primary concern to perform a Marxist critique of what 'race' in particular means to 'class' and gender. In other words, I am trying to socialize the notion of 'race'.

Before articulating my theory of the social, I would like to pause over the habit of fragmentive or stratified thinking so prevalent among us, which ends up by erasing *the social* from the conception of ontology. This same habit can also produce an evaluative gesture whereby 'the cultural', for example, becomes secondary, apparent or illusory, and 'class', understood as a function of 'economy', becomes the 'real' or the fundamental creative force of society. Culture as superstructure 'reflects' or 'corresponds to' the economic base. Alternatively, we have the reverse conceptual habit, whereby the formative power of discourse determines the social. By becoming primarily discursive, the social becomes a thought object. Epistemologies reach a proportion of exclusivity, which is of course not new and about which Marx speaks in his first thesis on Feuerbach (1976).[9] Through both of these reductive modes, class politics can ignore 'race' or gender, or politics based on any of these others can ignore class. Positivist Marxism can also rank the importance of social issues of struggle by relegating gender relations to the status of 'secondary contradictions', while 'race' or caste are seen as mere 'cultural' forms of inequality. Currently, the mainstream Western labour movements often dismiss issues of 'race' as politics of discourse or ethnic/cultural identity. Conversely, 'race' activists may dismiss class or anti-imperialist politics as 'white' politics. Gender or patriarchy may be considered as entirely redundant by both groups, while feminists who can theorize community on grounds of being women may find 'race' and class both redundant or of no intrinsic significance.[10] Furthermore, all groups might find what they do not consider important to be also divisive and detrimental for the advancement of their movements. My primary concern, on the other hand, is to bypass these conceptual positions and to offer an inclusive Marxist critique with a social interpretation of difference, especially in regard to what 'race' means to class and gender – in other words, how class can be transformed from an economic to a social concept which constitutively implicates both social relations and forms of consciousness. What I intend is best presaged by Edward P. Thompson in *The Making of the English Working Class* (1974), when he discusses class and class consciousness as active creations of social individuals.[11]

It is not news to hear that the culture of positivist thinking that pervaded the nineteenth-century European (especially English) intellectual world and the prestige accorded to a measuring scientifism changed the tenor of social thought from the earlier philosophical tone. Notions such as 'knowledge' and 'science' took on a definitely technological and quantitative aspect, and to this were added strict notions of causality as well as the idea of social 'laws' parallel to 'natural laws' – an offshoot of the study of human evolution. If we look at the later work of Engels, for example, we can see how later Marxism absorbed this culture of utilitarian positivism and scientifism

(Engels 1969). As economics emerged as a science, since it could lend itself most fully to quantification, Marxism changed from being a 'critique' of political economy as attempted by Marx to *becoming* political economy. The notion of economy came to substitute for notions of the social. As such, social organization and society became enunciations or functions of the economy. Lived social relations and experiencing subjects became subjected to one-dimensional views of the social; that is, of economic relations or structures. This habit of scientifism has endured, erupting in Louis Althusser's claim, for example, regarding an 'epistemological break' in Marx's opus – periodizing it into philosophical and scientific. The concept and practice of 'scientific' Marxism or socialism became a credo of communist parties throughout the world.[12]

This scientific or positivist Marxism, with its truncated and reified understanding of the social, interestingly relied much more on some characteristics of eighteenth-century liberal thought rather than Marx's own writings. Not the least of these is a compartmentalizing way of thinking which ruptures the formative, complex integrity of the social whole and creates segments or spheres of 'the economic', 'the political' and 'the cultural', which are in reality ontologically inseparable. This separation of social spheres was essential for the rising bourgeois state and society. In bourgeois or liberal democracy, in spite of its universalist claims, equality could only be *formal*, and thus the notions of 'liberality' and 'democracy' could not be actually realized. But this way of thinking in self-contained spheres has become hegemonic or naturalized enough that programmatic, political Marxism can, unconsciously perhaps, fall back upon the same separation of spheres. Broadly speaking, 'class' thus becomes an overarching economic category, gender/patriarchy a social one, and 'race', 'caste' and 'ethnicity' categories of the cultural. It is not hard to see then how class struggle or class consciousness can be theorized and acted on minus 'race' and gender, or vice versa.

But not all Marxists submitted to this liberal/bourgeois fragmentary and economistic reading of the social. So called for their difference from others, 'cultural Marxists' such as, for example, Georg Lukács, Walter Benjamin and Raymond Williams actively explored the formative relations between culture and society in their broadest sense, while Antonio Gramsci theorized relations between these and the institutions of the state and civil society (Gramsci 1971).

Socializing 'race'

At the outset, I need to state that the social phenomenon that I refer to as 'race' is not a biological distinction actually inhering in people themselves. It is a way, and a power-inscribed way, of reading or establishing difference and for finding long-lasting ways to reproduce such readings, organization and practice. Roughly, this is what people signal to when they say that 'race' is a construct. The non-existence of 'race' as a physical entity has been remarked on by critical Darwinians such as Stephen J. Gould, for example (Gould 1981). This accounts for my use of quotation marks, hedging the term from the danger of becoming considered as an actual fact of nature. 'Race', therefore, is neither more nor less than an active social organization, a constellation of practices motivated, consciously and unconsciously, by political or power imperatives with implied cultural forms – images, symbols, metaphors and norms which range from the quotidian to the institutional. This is the view that I wish to sustain through my theorization here.

If we consider 'race' as a connotative, expressionist cluster of social relations in the terrain of certain historical and economic relations, and class as an ensemble of property-oriented social relations with signifying practices, it is easy to see how they are formatively implicated. From this standpoint, one could say that modern 'race' is a social culture of colonialist and imperialist capitalism. 'Race', therefore, is a collection of discourses of colonialism and slavery, but firmly rooted in capitalism in its different aspects through time. As it stands, 'race' cannot be disarticulated from 'class' any more than milk can be separated from coffee once they are mixed, or the body divorced from consciousness in a living person. This inseparability, this formative or figurative relation, is as true for the process of extraction of surplus value in capitalism as it is a commonsense practice at the level of social life. Economic participation, the value of labour, social and political participation and entitlement, and cultural marginalization or inclusion, are all part of this overall social formation.

This integrity of 'race' and class cannot be independent of the fundamental social organization of gender – that is, the sex-specific social division of labour, with mediating norms and cultural forms. Various proprietorial relations, including of bodies, productive and reproductive labour, and normative institutional and commonsensical cultural relations, are thus in a reflexive and constitutional relation.[13] It is this that multinational corporations fall back on in the Third World when they hire an overwhelmingly female labour force to raise their profit margin. In every social space, there is a normalized and experiential as well as ideological knowledge about whose labour counts the least. The actual realization process of capital cannot be outside a given social and cultural form or mode. There is no capital that is a universal abstraction. Capital is always a practice, a determinate set of social relations – and a cultural one at that. Thus, 'race', gender and patriarchy are inseparable from class, as any social organization rests on intersubjective relations of bodies and minds marked with socially constructed difference on the terrain of private property and capital.

Going back to Marx

> In all modes of society there is one specific kind of production which predominates over the rest, whose relations thus assign rank and influence to others. It is a general illumination which bathes all the other colours and modifies their particularity. It is a particular ether which determines the specific gravity of every being which has materialized within it. (Marx 1973: 106)

To perform a reflexive theorization of the social, it helps to go back to some key concepts used by Marx himself. Of the many he used, at times with Engels, I will primarily concentrate on three: the 'concrete' (in *Grundrisse*), 'civil society' (in *The German Ideology*, *The Communist Manifesto*) and 'ideology' (in *The German Ideology*, *The Holy Family* and *On the Jewish Question*). On a related note, we could use notions such as 'mediation', 'reification' and 'fetishism', which, though only partially articulated by Marx himself, were developed by Marxists. It is interesting that, of these Marxists, such as Lukács, Benjamin, Althusser, Dorothy E. Smith and Fredric Jameson, to name a few, none was a political economist. As critical social and cultural theorists, they sought to break free from an economistic or class-reductionist as well as cultural-reductionist understanding of the social as elaborated in particular by capital.

Marx adapted the Hegelian concept of 'the concrete' in his notes on *Capital* compiled as *Grundrisse*. It seems to me that his treatment of this concept holds the correlates of reflexive epistemology earlier outlined as historical materialism in *The German Ideology*. About this notion, he makes the following remarks:

> The concrete is concrete because it is the concentration of many determinations, hence the unity of the diverse. It *appears* in the process of thinking, therefore, *as a process of concentration, as a result, not as a point of departure, even though it is the point of departure in reality*, and hence also the point of departure for observation … and conception. (Ibid.: 101, emphasis added)

The 'concrete' as the social, we can see, has a dual character for Marx. It is, on the one hand, a mental or conceptual category and, on the other, an existing specific social formation. Thus, it is both 'a point of departure' (as the social) and 'a point of arrival' (as theory). Something that is 'concrete' is not like an 'object' that is visible, such as a table or a chair, but nonetheless its 'concreteness' is a determinate form of social existence. It is concretized by specific social relations with mediating and expressive as well as reproductive forms of consciousness and practices. In fact, this 'concrete' social form is to be seen in contrast to a fact or an 'object', because it is not reified/fixed, hypostatized. It is a fluid, dynamic, meaningful formation created by living subjects in actual lived time and space, yet with particular discernible features that both implicate it in other social formations and render it specific. From this perspective, then, 'race', as I said before, is a connotative cluster of social relations, implicated in others coded as 'economic' and 'social' – that is, class and gender. If one were to broaden 'class' into a sociological category, thus making it stand for an entire ensemble of social relations, signifying practices and organizations, it could not be articulated within specific socio-historic formations such as ours without 'race'. For this reason, one could say that 'race' is the ideological discourse as well as cultural common sense of a patriarchal, colonial and imperialist capitalism. In such an existential historical terrain, disarticulating 'race' from 'class' is impossible. Denuded of its metaphysical trapping, the notion of the 'concrete', then, in Marx's usage, becomes one of social formation signalling a constitutive complexity. Social relations and organization, both complementary and contradictory, with historical accretion and inflection, go into the making of the social ontology of the subject-agent. But it also has a capacity for conceptualizing these in a non-mechanical, non-serialized way.

It is sensible to move from the concepts 'concrete' and 'the social' to the notion of 'civil society', which is crucial to Marx's critical epistemology,[14] and to note its intimate connection with the notion of 'mode of production'. Marx's (and at times Engels') emphasis here is on the *mode*, the organizational and social ground for production as well as reproduction and their entailed politics, administration and cultures. *The German Ideology*, where he presents his ideas on the making of the social and social change, is a rich source for understanding the complexity of modes of production as articulated by Marx. Breaking free of the qualitative and ontological separation between civil society and the state, economy and culture, and between the political and public sphere and the private and familial, he presents in this text an integrated, constantly elaborating historical/social space. It is the theatre of class struggle and revolution. This historical and social movement is not presented as evolutionist and teleological, and it is shot through with both resisting and dominating forms of consciousness. Here are some examples of what he has to say about the civil society, the ground for 'the mode' or the style and the fashion for organizing an everyday life for the production of private property and related moral and cultural propriety. For Marx, 'civil society is the true source and theatre of all history, and how absurd is the conception of history held hitherto, which neglects the real relationship and confines itself to high-sounding dramas of princes and states' (Marx and Engels 1976: 57–8). He also treats civil society as 'social organisation evolving directly out of production and intercourse, which in all ages forms the basis of the state and of the rest of the idealistic superstructure …' (ibid.: 98).

If we scrutinize Marx's statements, two issues primarily grab our attention. First, that the 'mode' of the social is a dynamic and integral one. In its character as a formative process, it cannot be an aggregative one. This processual nature requires both temporal and spatial aspects, where it is here and now a specific form, which, however, will move on to something else in the future. But some aspects of this formation which lie in the now will, therefore, be in the past as well. You cannot tear this live social way of being and its formational journey into component parts and yet expect it to live and move. Just as a dismembered and dissected human body does not yield up the secret of a conscious evolving life, neither does a 'mode' of production reveal its live social being when considered as segregated, though 'intersecting', social relations and forms of consciousness. It is this that is precisely wrong with what is called 'the intersectional method'. In this, one has to agree with those romantics of the nineteenth century with whom Marx shared much of his *weltanschauung* (world view) – that the whole is more than the sum of its parts.

The second issue of note is that of culture and consciousness. It is clear from explicit statements that consciousness is not an afterthought of existence. All activities are 'sensuous practical human' ones and, as such, of conscious agents and subjects. Hence Marx's need to put forward the notion of 'practical consciousness'[15] as a fundamental moment of all aspects of 'concrete' form of existence. In this learning, changing and transmitting process, life goes on, history moves on and is made – both consciously and subconsciously. The gesture of forging a primitive tool, rubbing two sticks together, judging the seasons by the stars, becomes the science and technology of our present times. In this schema, no apple falls out of sight of a conscious eye. It is not surprising, then, that private-property-based ways of establishing propriety and reproducing difference would be a basic part of social existence involving consciousness and institutionalization. Viewed thus, 'race' is no more or less than a form of difference, creating *a mode* of production through practical and cultural acts of *racialization*. 'Race' *is* such a difference and it cannot stand alone.[16]

If this formative integrity or 'unity' of the social is 'ruptured' (to use another of Marx's phrases in *Grundrisse*), then we have phenomenal object forms or thought objects which are fetishized. The work of Marxist theorists is to deconstruct this object form and return it to its concrete diverse social determinations. As Lukács puts it, an ontology of social being can only be appropriately understood with an epistemology that connects thought to its material socio-historical ground (Lukács 1980). As such, empiricist or positivist versions of Marxism will not do because they tend to depict the concrete as no more than a 'thing' or an 'object' – as a dead 'fact'.

Attempts to rupture mutually constitutive and diverse determinations and to present this as reality lead to the kind of problem that bedevils social movements which, for all their effectiveness, ought to integrate 'race', gender and class. Unintentionally, we produce reified thought objects which defy social understanding and are occlusive or truncated. We confuse the specificity of social forms or figurations with disconnected particularities. Thus, culture becomes non-material, asocial, solely discursive, while economy or polity lack mediatory forms of consciousness. As pointed out earlier, this fractured reading results in ideology, in bourgeois democracy's claim to offer equality of citizenship or rights while legally preserving and enhancing actual social relations of inequality and ruling. It is in the criticism of this bourgeois political economy that Marx repeatedly elaborates his theory of a mode (as style, fashion, ensemble) of production. In opposition to liberal/bourgeois thought, he shows how each specific social form serves as the microcosm of the social macrocosm, just as each physical cell of the body holds the entire genetic code. Such a mode of understanding is anti-dualist and anti-positivist. The mode of production, as he puts it in *Grundrisse*, is not 'linearly, causally organized' (Marx 1973: 97). By employing the notion of mediation, between social relations and forms of consciousness, both practical and ideological, he shows how an entire significatory/communicative and expressive social ensemble must obtain for any specific economy and polity to operate and be effective. Seen thus 'socially', class cannot be genderless or cultureless, nor can culture be genderless and classless.

It is obvious that capital is a social practice, not just a theoretical abstraction. As such, its reproductive and realization processes are rooted in civil society, in its cultural/social ground. Class in this sense, for Marx and others, is a category of civil society.[17] The exploitation of labour is not simply an arithmetical ratio of labour to technology in the terrain of means of production. Social and cultural factors, for example of gender and 'race', enter into it, and with their implied norms and forms organize the social space which comprehends capitalism as a *mode* of production, an organization of civil society (see, e.g., Marx and Engels 1976: 61). We enter a realm of extensive and subtle mediations which determine forms, values, processes and objects of production.[18] Therefore, 'class', when seen concretely, both relies upon and exceeds what we call economy. The once vocal debates on the household labour of women, on wages for housework, and about the relationship of slavery to capitalism revealed the far-flung sociocultural roots of economy. Thus, we might identify 'race' and patriarchy/gender with the so-called extra-economic or cultural/discursive but nonetheless social moments of the overall mode of capitalist production, which has its own social ontology. It is to this formative relation between production and reproduction that Marx signals when he speaks of mediation as 'the act through which the whole process again runs its course' (Marx 1973: 94). As modes of mediation, gender or 'race' therefore not only help to produce the constant devaluation of certain social groups' embodiment and labour power, but also create a 'colour coded' cultural common sense for the state and the society as a whole (see Backhouse 1999; Razack 2002).

The epistemology that ruptures the integrity of the socially concrete at a conceptual level and posits this as a property of the social is identified by Marx in *The German Ideology* as 'ideology'. In contrast to much Marxism familiar to us, he does not consider ideology only in terms of its thought content, but rather considers the very form of knowledge production that generates such content, a content that desocializes, depoliticizes and dehistoricizes our social understanding. Though Marx's primary concern is with the precise method that produces ideology, he is also deeply concerned with the thought content or ideas that are generated. As they are ideas of ruling, they need to be specifically addressed by our political organizations. As such, racializing discourses need to be considered in these terms. In a section entitled 'Ruling class and ruling ideas', Marx states:

> The ideas of the ruling class are in every epoch the ruling ideas, i.e., the class which is the ruling *material* force of society, is at the same time its ruling *intellectual* force. The class which has the means of material production at its disposal, consequently also controls the means of mental production, so that the ideas of those who lack the means of mental production are subject to it. (Marx and Engels 1976: 67, emphasis in original)

After offering this cryptic, though highly suggestive, view of the creation of a 'cultural common sense' that legitimizes and reproduces the overall relations and institutions of ruling, Marx states categorically that 'ruling ideas', or what we call generally prevalent ideas, 'are nothing more than the ideal [i.e. cultural/formal] expression of the dominant material relations, the dominant material relations grasped as ideas; hence of the relations which make the one class the ruling one, therefore, the ideas of its dominance' (Marx 1976: 67). It is not surprising that the dominant relations of patriarchal colonial capitalism would produce racist patriarchal discourses of physical, social and cultural differences. This is exactly what happens when the discourses or ideological categories of 'race' or 'human nature' are employed to 'explain' social behaviour or cultural characteristics, while in actuality no more than interpreting them.

But, most importantly, the question is how such occlusive, substitutive or displacing discourses of ideological categories are generated. In *The German Ideology*, Marx outlines this epistemological practice, connecting it with the social division of manual and mental labour. He exposes the disciplinary practices of metaphysicians whereby everyday ideas, events and experiences are decontextualized, overgeneralized or over-particularized from their originating social relations and interests. Then, these empirical bits of degrounded ideas are reconfigured into discursive systems or interpretive devices, which take on a semblance of independence and substantiveness. It is helpful to actually both paraphrase and quote Marx here. Considering ideology to be an epistemological device employed in decontextualization and extrapolation, Marx offers us a disclosure of the method. His disclosure reveals what he calls 'tricks', and there are three of them. We can begin by 'considering the course of history' by detaching 'the ideas of the ruling class from the ruling class itself and attribut[ing] to them an independent existence' (Marx and Engels 1976: 68). Having detached them from their specific social and historical locations, we now 'confine ourselves to saying that these or those ideas were dominant at a given time, without bothering ourselves about the conditions of production and the producers of these ideas' (ibid.: 68). Now we have a set of ideas or discourses independent of their social ontology. They appear to generate each other, appear even *sui generis*, but are claimed to be shaping, even creating, the very social realities that gave rise to them in the first place. Thus, consciousness gives rise to existence, rather than existence to consciousness, understood as conscious existence. Life imitates or illustrates theory. Only 'if we thus ignore the individuals and world conditions which are the source of these ideas', says Marx, can we truly produce ideology (ibid.: 68). We can blithely forget that notions such as honour and loyalty came into being in the time of aristocracy and that the dominance of the bourgeoisie produced concepts of freedom or equality (ibid.: 68). So 'ever more abstract ideas hold sway, i.e., ideas which increasingly take on the form of universality' (ibid.: 68). Hiding behind abstract universality and time-honoured metaphysicality, ideas of ruling, for example those of 'race' or gender, represent their interests 'as the common interest of all members of society' (ibid.: 68).

Intellectuals or ideologues organic to a system of ruling, guardians of property relations, then take upon themselves the task of development and systemization of these decontextualizing concepts. We know well the amount of philosophical, 'scientific' and cultural labour that has gone into the production of 'race' and of the practices that have gone into racialization of whole legal systems and polities.[19] Needless to say, diverting attention from power-organized differences in everyday life, history and social relations can only be useful for the purpose of ruling, of hegemony, not of resistance.

Ideological forms masquerade as knowledge. They simply produce discursivities incorporating bits of decontextualized ideas, events or experiences with material consciousness of a practical kind. The modus operandi of these 'ruling knowledges' relies on epistemologies creating essentialization, homogenization (i.e. despecification) and an aspatial and atemporal universalization. Given that ideology's most powerful trick is to cut off a concept from its originating and mediating social relations, even critical and resisting concepts, such as 'class' or the feminist category of 'woman', when used in such a way, can become occlusive and serve the interests of ruling relations through exclusion and the invisibility of power in relations of difference. The world of feminist theory has been riven by struggles in which it became evident that the category of 'woman' in its desocialized (class/'race') and dehistoricized (colonialism and imperialism) deployment has helped to smuggle in middle-class white women's political agenda and has hidden the relationship of dominance which some social groups of women hold with regard to other social groups.[20]

Conclusion

> Men [sic] make their own history, but they do not make it just as they please; they do not make it under circumstances chosen by themselves, but under circumstances directly found, given and transmitted from the past. (Marx 1963: 15)

What, we might ask, are the consequences of the ideological practice of the dissociation of 'race', class and gender, which both Marxists and non-Marxists have engaged in? As far as social movements are concerned, this has made them largely ignore the task of fashioning a fully socially informed politics. For Marxists, their ideological/economistic reading of class, the habit of separating class from culture and social relations of gender/patriarchy, has succeeded in creating at best compromised petty bourgeois politics. By dubbing the issue of 'race' as a non- or anti-class one, they have marginalized those sections of the people who are the most dispossessed and who provide the fodder for capital both in the West and elsewhere. Thus, issues of 'race' and gender have become mainly identified with liberal politics, with those of rights and citizenship, not of socialist struggles. Labour movements and whatever is left of the women's movement are thus unrepresentative and incomplete social or anti-capitalist movements and as such participate in replicating the organization of capital and bourgeois rule.

Another consequence has been a promiscuous mixture or coalition of class-, gender- and 'race'-based politics in which a lack of common understanding and of internal constructive grounds have created only tenuous possibilities of association and acrimonious relations. Furthermore, an inability to create socialized class or anti-capitalist movements has given room for the development of culturalist 'race' groups which, with the help of *official* multiculturalism, have held social movements hostage to 'identity' and fundamentalist politics. The oppressions created by unequal, dominating social relations do not disappear through being rendered invisible as such. They do not disappear in actuality. Denuded of their full socio-historical concreteness or reality at both the civil society and state levels, they surface in ideological forms of reified 'race' and ethnic nationalist identities or in acts of basic despair and desperation.

The best way to understand this destructive politics of ideology is to remember Marx in *The Eighteenth Brumaire of Louis Bonaparte*, where he speaks of displaced, substituted cultural identities that accomplish the work of class rule on the stage of hegemony (ibid.: 15–16, 47). The masks of god that are worn by current fundamentalist political agencies can only serve to remind us of the Roman masks worn by successive protagonists of the French revolution – until the excluded, unintegrated, class-based sociocultural forms/identities terminated in a fascism instead of social emancipation. Present-day nationalism, imperialism and official multiculturalism have all resorted to 'identity' politics and unleashed wars, genocides and general social oppression and surveillance. Bush and Blair's civilizational or Christian utterances, their capitalist and militaristic ambitions masquerading in the masks of democracy and freedom, and their co-opting feminist discourses of rescuing Muslim women, are devastating ideological identity projects.

It is only by practising a 'concrete' social analysis that these legitimizing, unificatory sleights-of-hand, which have drawn a large section of North Americans (mostly white) to identify with various myths of domination, can be challenged.

The Marxists in the West, in particular because they call for a *social* politics, need to take heed of their own implication in undercutting class struggle by furthering 'identity' politics through their defensiveness or 'tolerant' liberalism with regard to 'race'. Being quick to dismiss much popular anger at social injustice as peripheral to anti-capitalist or class struggle, they have adopted a path which cannot bring any 'real' social transformation. An inability to regard colonial capitalist and imperialist politics as racist, combined with the colonialist 'identity' politics of the last five hundred years, have rendered Western Marxists politically ineffectual. If anti-racist feminist movements challenging hegemony have in them an element of recuperation of erased cultural identity, this is not necessarily disastrous in and of itself. The major point is to assess from what standpoint this so-called 'identity' is elaborated, and what cultures, histories and social relations it evokes. Whose identity are we talking about – that of the oppressors or of the oppressed? Theorists of the left or Marxists have no reason to fear 'identity', because there is enough ground in the works of Marx himself to create social movements which do not have to choose between culture, economy and society or 'race', class and gender in order to organize politics of social revolution. Going beyond gestures of intersectionality, coalition and social cohesion, Marxists have recourse to a non-fragmentary understanding of the social which could change the world as we know it.

Notes

1 For the beginning of theorization on the relationship between 'race', gender and class, which forms the departure point for this chapter, see Davis (1983); Bannerji (1993, 1995); Smith et al. (1982); and Silvera (1983).

2 The notion of 'intersectionality' is the most common one used in critical race theories as well as in legal theories. See, for example, Crenshaw (1989), Collins (1998) and D. Aguilar's chapter in this volume.

3 There needs to be an examination of Canadian labour history or texts of labour studies to see how 'race' in its various forms has been incorporated in theorizing class, labour or class politics. It would be interesting to see whether, in that domain, there are texts comparable to Roediger's *Wages of Whiteness* (1992) or Li and Singh Bolaria's *Racial Oppression in Canada* (1988). This is an invitation to further research. Black feminist historians have started the project, but it needs to go deeper.

4 Consider, for example, the Metro

Network for Social Justice (MNSJ) in Toronto.

5 For a classic example of this formulation, see Laclau and Mouffe (2001).

6 By this I mean anthologies such as the Centre for Contemporary Cultural Studies' *The Empire Strikes Back* (CCCS 1982).

7 For an understanding of my use of the term 'specific', see the introduction to Bannerji (1995: 41–54).

8 Additionally, my use of the notion of 'the social' needs a note, an acknowledgement of the debt I owe not only to Marx's work but also to that of Dorothy E. Smith, who in all her works, but primarily in *Writing the Social* (1999), has offered a relational and constitutive view of it. In essays such as 'Ideological practices of sociology', in *Conceptual Practices of Power* (1990), Smith has also elaborated on Marx's and her own 'reflexive' method. See also Bannerji, 'But who speaks for us?' (1995: 55–98).

9 Marx says, 'The chief defect of all previous materialism ... is that things, reality, sensuousness are conceived only in the form of *the object or of contemplation*, but not as *sensuous human activity*, *practice*, not subjectively. Hence in contradistinction to materialism, the *active* side was set forth abstractly by idealism – which, of course, does not know real, sensuous activity as such' (Marx 1976: 616, emphasis in original).

10 Two interesting formulations of this exclusionary method are to be found in now classic texts: Spelman's *Inessential Woman* (1988) and Smith et al.'s *All the Women Are White* (1982).

11 In this book, Thompson *socializes* the concept of class, thus retrieving it from economism. He introduces into the social-relational aspect the element of conscious subjectivity. 'Class' for him is an 'active process which owes as much to agency as to conditioning. The working class did not rise like the sun at an appointed time. It was present in its own making' (Thompson 1974: 9). Also, I concur with his statement that class is 'a historical phenomenon, unifying a number of disparate and seemingly unconnected events, both in the raw material of experience and in consciousness' (ibid.: 9).

12 See Althusser and Balibar (1973), especially Althusser's considerations on science and theory in Part 1, 'From capital to Marx's philosophy' (ibid.: 48–70).

13 For the implication of 'proprietorial' or moral notions, as well as familial relations, and for a reflexive/constitutional view of the social, see classic statements by Marx and Engels (1976: 38–9, 48, 52, 194–5). There, discussing the family as a moment of property, they say, for example, that it is 'the first form ... where wife and children are the slaves of the husband' (ibid.: 52). See also Marx and Engel's *Communist Manifesto* (1985) and Engel's *Origin of the Family, Private Property and the State* (1984). Later theorizations retain the core of their insight; in the North American context, Davis (1983) is a good example.

14 For an expanded discussion of 'civil society', see Marx and Engels (1976: 57–8, 61–2), as well as a section on history in the same volume (ibid.: 47–51). Both sections involve discussions of the construction of the social, where the organization of social relations involves all basic aspects of life, including that of consciousness. Here, production and consumption are unthinkable in separation and without an intrinsic, active and material form of consciousness.

15 Along with discussing 'primary historical relationships', Marx speaks of 'consciousness ... which here makes its appearance in the form of agitated layers of air, sounds, in short, of language. Language is as old as consciousness, language *is* practical, real consciousness that exists also for other men as well,

and only therefore does it also exist for me; language, like consciousness, only arises from the need, the necessity, of intercourse with other men' (Marx and Engels 1976: 49).

16 For a clear understanding of the concept of difference, Gates' edited volume *'Race,' Writing, and Difference* (1985) is particularly useful. Though the authors of the essays are not Marxist, they provide examples of cultural materialism with a strong basis in cultural history.

17 See, for example, Hegel's view of 'civil society' summarized by C. J. Arthur in his introduction to Marx and Engels (Arthur 1970: 5).

18 On the importance of the concept of mediation, see Marx (1973: 331–3).

19 This ideological process that Marx talks about is addressed in different ways in the chapters in Harding (1993) and Dua and Robertson (1999).

20 This issue has been also addressed in post-colonial feminist writings; see Midgley (1998); Ware (1993); McClintock (1995).

References

Althusser, L. and É. Balibar (1973) *Reading Capital*, trans. B. Brewster, London: Verso.

Arthur, C. J. (1970) 'Editor's introduction', in K. Marx and F. Engels, *The German Ideology*, ed. C. J. Arthur, New York: International, pp. 4–34.

Backhouse, C. (1999) *Colour-Coded: A Legal History of Racism in Canada, 1900–1950*, Toronto: University of Toronto Press.

Bannerji, H. (ed.) (1993) *Returning the Gaze: Essays on Racism, Feminism and Politics*, Toronto: Sister Vision.

— (1995) *Thinking Through: Essays on Feminism, Marxism, and Anti-racism*, Toronto: Women's Press.

CCCS (Centre for Contemporary Cultural Studies) (1982) *The Empire Strikes Back: Race and Racism in 70s Britain*, Birmingham: Hutchinson.

Collins, P. H. (1998) *Fighting Words: Black Women and the Search for Justice*, Minneapolis: University of Minnesota Press.

Crenshaw, K. (1989) 'Demarginalizing the intersection of race and sex: a black feminist critique of antidiscrimination doctrine, feminist theory and antiracist politics', *University of Chicago Legal Forum*, 139: 139–67.

Davis, A. Y. (1983) *Women, Race and Class*, New York: Vintage.

Dua, E. and A. Robertson (eds) (1999) *Scratching the Surface: Canadian Anti-racist Feminist Thought*, Toronto: Women's Press.

Engels, F. (1969) *Socialism: Utopian and Scientific*, trans. E. Aveling, New York: International.

— (1984) *The Origin of the Family, Private Property and the State*, Harmondsworth: Penguin.

Gates, H. L. (ed.) (1985) *'Race,' Writing, and Difference*, Chicago, IL: Chicago University Press.

Gould, S. J. (1981) *The Mismeasure of Man*, New York: Norton.

Gramsci, A. (1971) *Selections from the Prison Notebooks*, trans. Q. Hoare, London: Lawrence & Wishart.

Harding, S. (ed.) (1993) *The 'Racial' Economy of Science: Toward a Democratic Future*, Bloomington: Indiana University Press.

Jordan, J. (1989) *Moving Towards Home: Political Essays*, London: Virago.

Laclau, E. and C. Mouffe (2001) *Hegemony and Socialist Strategy: Towards a Radical Democratic Politics*, London: Verso.

Li, P. S. and B. Singh Bolaria (1988) *Racial Oppression in Canada*, Toronto: Garamond.

Lukács, G. (1980) *The Ontology of Social Being*, trans. D. Fernbach, London: Merlin.

Marx, K. (1963) *The Eighteenth Brumaire of Louis Bonaparte*, New York: International.

— (1972) *On the Jewish Question* (excerpts), in R. C. Tucker (ed.), *The Marx–Engels Reader*, New York: Norton, pp. 24–51.

— (1973) *Grundrisse: Foundations of the Critique of Political Economy (Rough Draft)*, trans. M. Nicolaus, London: Penguin.

— (1976) 'Theses on Feuerbach', in K. Marx and F. Engels, *The German Ideology*, 3rd edn, Moscow: Progress, pp. 615–17.

Marx, K. and F. Engels (1972) *The Holy Family* (excerpts), in R. C. Tucker (ed.), *The Marx–Engels Reader*, New York: Norton, pp. 104–6.

— (1976) *The German Ideology*, 3rd edn, Moscow: Progress.

— (1985) *The Communist Manifesto*, trans. S. Moore, Harmondsworth: Penguin.

McClintock, A. (1995) *Imperial Leather: Race, Gender, and Sexuality in the Colonial Contest*, London: Routledge.

Midgley, C. (ed.) (1998) *Gender and Imperialism*, Manchester: Manchester University Press.

Razack, S. (2002) *Race, Space, and the Law: Unmapping a White Settler Society*, Toronto: Between the Lines.

Roediger, D. R. (1992) *The Wages of Whiteness: Race and the Making of the American Working Class*, London: Verso.

Silvera, M. (1983) *Silenced: Caribbean Domestic Workers Talk with Makeda Silvera*, Toronto: Williams-Wallace.

Smith, B., G. T. Hull and P. Bell-Scott (1982) *All the Women Are White, All the Blacks Are Men, but Some of Us Are Brave*, New York: Feminist Press.

Smith, D. E. (1990) *Conceptual Practices of Power: A Feminist Sociology of Knowledge*, Toronto: University of Toronto Press.

— (1999) *Writing the Social: Critique, Theory, and Investigations*, Toronto: University of Toronto Press.

Spelman, E. V. (1988) *Inessential Woman: Problems of Exclusion in Feminist Thought*, Boston, MA: Beacon.

Terkel, S. (1992) *Race: How Blacks and Whites Think and Feel about the American Obsession*, New York: New Press.

Thompson, E. P. (1974) *The Making of the English Working Class*, Harmondsworth: Penguin.

Ware, V. (1993) *Beyond the Pale: White Women, Racism and History*, London: Verso.

PART TWO

MARXIST-FEMINIST KEYWORDS

5 | DEMOCRACY

Sara Carpenter

The concept of democracy is subject to many of what Marx referred to as 'errors of bourgeois thought' that result in the 'violent abstraction' of our social world (Sayer 1987). It is often treated transhistorically, as if there is a clear line between the direct democracy of ancient Greece and the caucuses of Iowa. It is often fetishized in the most acute sense of the term; democracy as a concept is given the agency and power of people, to move and act in the world as if it were a living, breathing human being. Given this generalized mode of political consciousness, it is no wonder that according to various anxious sources, democracy has been 'in crisis' for more or less the last half-century. This notion of 'crisis' has often been used to encapsulate all material, political, social and cultural domains characterized by a persistent sense of instability. Following the Vietnam War and the global social movements of the 1960s, the Trilateral Commission declared democracy to be 'in crisis' because there was too much of it (Crozier et al. 1975). There were too many demands from below, too many mobilizations in the streets, and too much instability in governance. Following the suppression of social reforms in the 1960s, through the brute force of neoliberalism during the Reagan and Thatcher governments, democracy was again 'in crisis' because neoliberalism accomplished its aims: poor people were starving and living on the streets while the privileged avoided any and all bonds of communal life (Bellah et al. 1985; Putnam 1995). The democracies of advanced capitalism were competitive, individualistic and fragmented. Further, they were increasingly inactive in the public sphere, demonstrating that the legitimacy of the electoral system was threatened by low voter participation and corruption through ties to corporate dollars (Nace 2005). Again, democracy was in a different kind of 'crisis', one that remains intricately related to the crises of democracy identified abroad (Mojab and Carpenter 2011).

The events of September 11th provided another interpretation of the crisis of democracy. According to the Bush administration and its allies, the lack of democracy in the Middle East had allowed a fundamentalist ideology to proliferate unchecked, one which now sought to squash the 'freedoms' so hard won by capitalist democracy. This pitted a fundamentally undemocratic regime against free and democratic states (Huntington 1996). This became the most recent in a string of wars and occupations launched with the intention of 'installing democracy' outside the central capitalist powers of Europe and North America, and through this imperialist democratic project, the attenuating gain of capital, markets and labour was accomplished through war (Bricmont 2007; Wood 2006). As has been widely noted, it is revealing and ironic that the rights and freedoms of women, in particular, came to be emblematic of the need for this imperialism (Mohanty 2006; Mojab 2009; Riley et al. 2008; Stabile and Kumar 2005; Zangana 2007). This imperialist-driven 'crisis of democracy' turns away from the reality of capitalist patriarchy and crisis, namely that

> crisis has never been the exception to the rule for the subalternatized subjects and collectives. Rather, it has been the rule for the majority of humankind around the globe for at least 500 years, even as various elites have successfully obfuscated oppression and dominance by making use of changing concepts of 'emancipation.' (Brunner et al. 2013: 268)

Once again it is on the backs of women that the ideology of capitalist imperialist democracy begins to crack open. The most radical engagement by feminists with the problems of bourgeois democracy emerges in the feminist response to imperialism. For example, the ongoing debate over NGOs is emblematic of the emergence of this critique (Funk 2006; Jad 2004; Mojab 2007). The feminist critique of imperialism and colonization intersects with, but is distinct from, the critique of feminism *as* imperialism (Amos and Parmar 1984; Mohanty 1988). Rather, in the last decade and a half, feminist scholars have reinvigorated their engagement with the relations between occupation, dispossession, violence, imperialism and the ideology of democracy (Butler 2006; Cockburn 2007; Smith 2005, 2006).

The imperialist mandate of permanent war brings into sharp relief the crises of democracy that are of deepest concern to feminists: bottomless poverty, fundamentalist patriarchies, obscene acts of degradation against women and children, destruction of the planet, insensate eroticization of violence, occupation and dispossession – the list can continue on. The true nature of crisis, as experienced by billions on the planet, is often disguised in the debate around democracy, which is never held responsible for the emergence of these forms of violence. Democracy, as a political ideal, is meant to deliver something more humane than the barbarism of monarchy or despotic rule. And yet, democracy is an undisturbed constant, always carrying with it, despite difficulties, the best of intentions. Our imagination about democracy seems to always be truncated by this reality, which Žižek has referred to as a 'prohibition on thinking' (2002: 167). Imagine that you continue to prick your finger upon a thorn and explain this reality by arguing that while it is in the thorn's nature to be sharp, it doesn't really want to be.

In what follows, I hope to contribute to the dismantling of this 'prohibition', particularly within feminist theory, by putting forth Marx's classic, and crucial, critique of bourgeois democracy. Elaborated through his engagement with notions such as freedom, equality and rights, bourgeois democracy, otherwise known as capitalist democracy, is shown to have a complex inner relation with capitalism. This is due to the historical specificity of the mode of democracy that arose, coincidentally, with capitalism from the seventeenth century onwards. While some argue that democracy is an ancient concept (*dēmokratía* in Ancient Greece, *dēmocratia* in Latin, *démocratie* in Middle French), these modes of thinking are specific to their historical moments and forms of empire (Wood 2003). What we are most concerned with here is what has come to be known as *liberal democracy*, the democracy that emerged following the collapse of feudalism in Europe and the establishment, through centuries of revolution, of the bourgeois state. After outlining Marx's critique, I will review some of the primary struggles within and against the bourgeois state that have been taken up by feminists in order to understand better the limits of this democratic form for a revolutionary feminist project. I end with some considerations for feminist praxis.

Marx's critique of bourgeois democracy

In order to elaborate Marx's critique of bourgeois democracy, we must focus our attention on its foundational concepts: freedom, equality and rights, which are intertwined with one other in their elaboration. It is important, however, to remember that Marx's critique of bourgeois democracy is not an isolated endeavour. The work emerged through his larger aim to realize the totality of social relations under capitalism. The political domain, that which we label 'democracy' and the 'state', are as important to this totality as understanding any other relation, such as the functioning of value and labour or the relation between production and reproduction. Thus, Marx's critique of democracy cannot be understood apart from his critique of capitalism and the wholeness of bourgeois social relations. The discussion that follows here begins by elaborating a bit more on Marx's method of engagement with the categories of democratic thought before continuing with his method of examination of these modes of consciousness in relation to actual existing material social relations and his emphasis on elaborating irresolvable contradictions between democracy and capitalism.

Marx's engagement with the problem of democracy is taken up through a larger exploration of the nature, assumptions and uses of what he referred to as 'bourgeois categories of thought'. Many of these categories were those he saw emerging in the context of the transition from feudalism to capitalism and were associated with the new forms of democracy and secular state formation; these include notions of freedom, equality and liberty, foundational categories for the theorization of democracy and citizenship which are also the foundational categories of feminist political theory (Barrett 1987). Marx saw these notions as dialectically related to one another, and he sought to understand them through a process of critique; often his analysis comes in the form of a critique of policy proposals or historical interpretation and in his engagement with ongoing debates in European socialism. Two of his most important works on democracy, 'On the Jewish question' (1978) in 1843 and 'Critique of the Gotha programme' (1970) in 1875, are emblematic of this approach. Significantly, Marx's attention to the problem of democracy emerged through his active engagement with the struggle to realize a revolutionary democracy. His method involved holding the commonly understood conception of these categories, such as the notion that all are equal before the law, in tension with the material relations he saw functioning in civil society. Marx and Engels elaborated this historical materialist method in *The German Ideology* in this way:

> We do not set out from what men [sic] say, imagine, conceive, nor from men as narrated, thought of, imagined, conceived, in order to

> arrive at men in the flesh. We set out from the real, active men, and on the basis of their real life-process we demonstrate the development of the ideological reflexes and echoes of this life-process. (1968: 37–8)

In this way he was able to explore how these categories did not explain what was happening in everyday life, but rather how they actually obscured our understanding of the realities of social conditions and relations. Thus, in his work, a category such as 'inequality' emerges through its relation to its opposite, 'equality', and through its relation to other categories such as 'freedom' and 'necessity'. This web of contradictions between the political and the material is the conceptual framework of Marx's critique.

We must begin with life as it is *actually lived* by people under capitalism. Marx uses the concept of 'civil society' to refer to this reality (ibid.).[1] In civil society, people face one another as producers, consumers and owners of commodities organized for production through a social division of labour and the exploitation of surplus value. They engage in coordinated relations of production and reproduction, which do not hold equal social, political or material value. These coordinated relations are organized through social forms such as gender, race, ability, religion, and so on. The resulting social formation is deeply divided, profoundly violent, and intricately tied to each person's individual ability to thrive and survive. They become 'free' to live through the guarantees of the bourgeois democratic state.

This notion of civil society is not just a political entity, as it is in today's discourse, but is a material entity based in relations of production and reproduction. What is important about Marx's conception of civil society is that it reminds us, before we even begin to unpack categories of democracy, that a set of human relations exists that are not only unequal, but are *premised* on inequality. Within capitalism, the way we go about meeting our material needs and subsisting cannot be an equal process because it is *organized* to create inequality and to *privatize* that inequality. In fact, capitalism emerged through inequality, in the form of private property, in the first place, and we have much historical evidence to suggest that capitalism as a historical formation was able to emerge only through making use of existing and new forms of patriarchy, racism and violent subjugation (Federici 2004; Mies 1986; Linebaugh and Rediker 2000). It persists in these ways, growing more concentrated in its inequity. We do not begin, historically and in our objective reality, from a position of equality. Thus, any discussion of democracy, a theory of *political* or *extra-economic* equality, must be held in contradiction with the civil society of capitalism, a mode of life stinking with inequality in every possible facet of human diversity.

The bourgeois concept of equality is premised on the notions of 'freedom', 'individuality' and 'rights'; under the classical tenets of democratic thought, our 'freedoms' make us equal as these freedoms are natural rights of those we designate as 'human'. Freedom here has multiple definitions. On the one hand, it refers to the kind of freedoms we often associate with bourgeois democracy and which can be described as the 'regime of rights'. These are formal freedoms, given and ensured by the state, and made real through juridical apparatuses. The first amendment of the US constitution, a revolutionary document at the time of its writing, enshrined the foremost of these freedoms: speech, thought, association, religion, communication (press) and petition. The principle of habeas corpus, or the right to your person, makes you free from arbitrary and tyrannical incursion by a state. The individual is both the subject and object of these rights, and 'the social', when conceived, is thought of as an aggregate of individuals, such as in the right to associate. A great deal of the struggle of the oppressed within and against bourgeois democracy has been for inclusion in and expansion of these rights from those that enshrine only individual autonomy to those that guarantee some form of social welfare (Marshall 1950). A considerable number of these so-called social rights did not emerge historically until the twentieth century and have played a crucial role in the ability of capitalism to disguise its own internal mechanisms of exploitation and oppression.

Marx (1967) argued that other forms of freedom exist in civil society. One is the freedom to labour; to work free from ties and commitments to land or person. In this kind of freedom, labour is a commodity and it may move, theoretically, through the market as it sees fit. This kind of freedom is a precondition for labour within capitalism and emerges out of the historical collapse of feudalism through processes of primitive accumulation. Under the conditions of a feudal regime, the peasantry lacks freedom of person, they are not free to pursue their own interests, and do not have freedom of mobility – they may not leave the lands of their lord (Wood 2012).

They are obligated, through systems of fealty and decree, to work the lands of their lord, to produce food and some goods for exchange, and, in return, they may expect measly provision of their needs for food, shelter and well-being. The process of labour moving from this type of 'unfreedom' to a position of freedom – that is, freedom to move and work as they see fit – was the violent dispossession of the means of subsistence that Marx referred to as 'primitive accumulation' (Marx 1967). Rather than marking this process as the birth of a freedom of unfetteredness, primitive accumulation, which is an ongoing historical process, is a severing of people from land, community and the ability to reproduce one's life outside of wage relations (Harvey 2010). It is the violent establishment of another form of freedom: the right to private property. In other words, for labour to be 'free' it must also be dispossessed of the means of production and the ability to subsist; this second kind of freedom, which is intimately tied to the 'free man', is also a form of unfreedom. You may be free to work, but not to live. This condition of unfreedom is what Marx referred to as 'necessity'.

An important contradiction emerges: through the kind of freedom necessary for capitalist production, we are made 'unequal' in everyday life and yet democracy guarantees us that we are all made equal through our political status vis-à-vis the state, as 'citizens'. But what does this contradiction mean? Does it mean that we are two persons in one? That we are unfree in the world of wage labour, free only to move between varying forms of violence and exploitation? That this domain of the 'private', of property and commodities and money, is a terrain of unfreedom while in the 'public' sphere of democracy we are all formally equal to one another? It simply does not make sense that we should be two persons in one, especially when we take into consideration that what is 'unfree' in capitalism is characterized as 'free': the freedom to choose, the freedom to move, the freedom to act as one sees fit through the medium of money.

This kind of fragmentation of a human being and the social world can only be accomplished through ideology (Bannerji 1995, and see her Chapter 7 in the present volume). Marx argued time and again that the 'equality' of political freedom cannot negate the inequality of material life, meaning that no amount of liberty can address the central opposition between political freedom and material unfreedom. This 'freedom' is the freedom to aspire to be a capitalist. Marx's radical reformation of this contradiction is to argue that the equality of political freedom is *presupposed* by material inequality and *ensures* its continuity. Marx argued in 'On the Jewish question' that:

> The state abolishes, after its fashion, the distinctions established by *birth, social rank, education, occupation*, when it decrees that birth, social rank, education, occupation are *non-political* distinctions; when it proclaims, without regard, to these distinctions, that every member of society is an *equal* partner in popular sovereignty, and treats all elements which compose the real life of the nation from the standpoint of the state. But the state, none the less, allows private property, education, occupation to *act* after *their* own fashion, namely as private property, education, occupation; and to manifest their *particular* nature. Far from abolishing these *effective* differences, it only exists so far as they are presupposed. (1978: 33, emphasis in original)

His argument is twofold: the bourgeois democracy does not create equality *and* it cannot create such conditions. In the processes of creating the formal equality known as 'equal before the law', the relations of inequality in civil society are reinscribed and cemented as 'natural' components of social life and invisible components of the so-called coercive laws of competition. This extends not only to material relations of production, but *social* relations as well, including processes of race and gender (Lowe 1996). It is for this reason that many demands by feminists for equality remain unanswered; bourgeois democracy cannot regulate the most crucial and basic functioning of capital, which is its ability to privatize, accumulate, and to assign value to labour through the mediating social relations of race and gender. Said differently, the only kind of equality that bourgeois democracy can create, within capitalist social relations, is in the sphere of formal abstract relations.

The principal instrument for the imposition of this formal abstract equality is the concepts of 'rights'. The regime of rights associated with bourgeois democracy, both those we understand as positive (freedom to …) and negative (freedom from …), was classically characterized by Marx in 'Critique of the Gotha programme' (1970) as 'rights to inequality'. In 'On the Jewish question' (1978), Marx takes the time to ask what exactly these 'rights' are which define bourgeois citizenship. His answer is that the so-called immutable and natural 'rights of man' are in actuality the right to exist as an egoist individual in civil society.

These rights, which we classically associate with liberalism as 'negative' rights, are the 'freedom from' rights: the rights of equality, liberty, security and property. They protect the citizen from incursions by his fellow citizen and the state. For Marx, these are legal expressions of the social relations of the capitalist mode of production, such as the right to be separated from others in your community (the division of labour), the right to acquire and appropriate (private property), and the right to be self-interested. As Žižek provocatively argues on the subject of the international expression of legal political relations, i.e. human rights:

> As the experience of our post-political liberal-permissive society amply demonstrates, human rights are ultimately, at their core, simply rights to violate the Ten Commandments. 'The right to privacy' – the right to adultery, in secret, where no one sees me or has the right to probe my life. 'The right to pursue happiness and to possess private property' – the right to steal (to exploit others). 'Freedom of the press and the expression of opinion' – the right to lie. 'The right of free citizens to possess weapons' – the right to kill. And, ultimately, 'freedom of religious belief' – the right to worship false gods. (2001: 110)

At the same time that these rights appear to ameliorate the inequality of civil society, it is Marx's argument that they actually affirm the inequality and class antagonisms of civil society. Further, they are in a completely paradoxical relation to their expression as *common* rights of political community; they are completely predicated on the separation of individuals within community. Marx argued that in the frame of bourgeois rights, 'Man is far from being considered as a species-being; on the contrary, species-life – society – appears as a system which is external to the individual as a limitation of his original independence. The only bond between men is natural necessity, need, and private interest' (1978: 43). In this way, the bourgeois notions of citizenship and rights reduce human community to a notion of political community whose purpose is solely to protect the individual right to accumulate and to reproduce the social relations of capitalism. But again, these notions of citizenship and rights are predicated on the actual existing relations of civil society. These 'natural rights' of the citizen are actually 'the recognition of the frenzied movement of the cultural and material elements of which form the content of life' (ibid.: 45).

Marx referred to this form of equality as *political emancipation*, and while this freedom is an important reality of people's lives, it should not be confused with *human emancipation* or the freedom from necessity. This differentiation is extremely important; when combined with Marx's analysis of the capitalist mode of production we can see further how political emancipation is the limit of freedom under capitalism. In civil society, individuals co-produce under relations of inequality created through private property, the divisions of labour and the accumulation of capital. The state is unable to abolish these inequalities through the mechanism of citizenship precisely because the state exists in the first place to secure these relations; the state arises out of the contradictions of civil society, not, as Hegel argued, the other way around (Callinicos 1999). How can bourgeois democracy guarantee the right to private property, and the right to accumulate, at the same time that it guarantees the rights to life, liberty and the pursuit of happiness? It cannot, because the right to life in this context becomes itself privatized; only some may own the material conditions of labour while others own only their labour. Thus, democracy can only abolish inequality theoretically or abstractly, formally. It cannot undo how inequality is built into the ways in which we have organized our productive and social lives without a revolutionary democracy that aims to accomplish human emancipation or a kind of freedom that negates necessity. For this reason, out of contradictions of bourgeois democracy we see that political emancipation develops as the limit of freedom within capitalist society. It is further for this reason that generations of Marxists have referred to bourgeois democracy as a 'dictatorship of the bourgeoisie'.

Feminist struggles for freedom within and against bourgeois democracy

Without this critique of bourgeois democracy, feminists have worked tirelessly to carve out a space within bourgeois democratic relations for the political emancipation of women. These struggles within and against the bourgeois democratic state have been diverse, complex, violent and long. Despite gains made in many locations, but not universally, around suffrage, women continue to battle within democracy over several seemingly 'unwinnable' struggles: wages, reproduction, against violence. When legislation is passed, it is constantly under threat – such as the Violence Against Women Act (VAWA) in the United States – and access to abortion and reproductive rights remains a staggering barrier for women around the world. Women's bodies remain a location of deep ideological debate in the halls of democracy and a space of violence in civil society. Despite this reality, mainstream feminist theorization of democracy has largely left this terrain undisturbed, choosing to invest in bourgeois democracy as the process through which such violence can be brought to an end. A brief review of some of these primary areas of engagement between feminism and democratic theory reveals the reality of these limits.

The foundational political struggle of modern feminism has been to obtain recognition by the bourgeois democratic state of women as equal before the law with the same rights and entitlements as men. However, feminist historical research indicates that women violently struggled to resist the consolidation of bourgeois social relations and their expression in exclusionary democratic forms (Federici 2004). The status of 'citizen' has been doled out on a selective and incomplete basis over time, serving to reinforce the racialized and classed relations among and between women. This basic struggle emerged in Europe and the Commonwealth colonies in the eighteenth and nineteenth centuries through the context of Enlightenment-era thinking on women, which ranged from the truly radical to the reformist to the repressive. While the historical period of the Enlightenment did extend the thinking of some into the question of women's status and possible equality, notable in debates on such topics as the education of women, suffrage and their inclusion in public debate (Israel 2001), this necessarily classed and raced discussion of women's possible emancipation must be understood in relation to coincident social processes of accumulation and dispossession in the rural areas of Europe as well as chattel slavery and genocides of indigenous people in the Americas, Africa and Asia and the mass extermination of women in Europe known as the 'witch hunts' (Federici 2004). At the same time that polite society debated the 'empowerment' of elite women, it terrorized, robbed, raped, exterminated and enslaved women around the world (Linebaugh and Rediker 2000).

This political struggle, which can be understood as the struggle to gain access to this 'regime of rights' secured by the state, characterizes a major component of feminist struggle within democracy. While suffrage comprises large parts of this struggle, it is not reducible to the right to vote. Property rights have been, and remain, a similarly significant terrain of lobbying, in some cases pre-dating the enfranchisement of women (Lebsock 1977). Women have also fought to gain access to equal protection under the law – for example, with regard to discrimination and harassment in the workplace, privacy, wages, violence and equal treatment as consumers (for instance by healthcare providers). Within the logic of rights, this struggle for freedom takes on an entirely political character. It seeks to establish the material and cultural aspects of the feminine as non-political distinctions, meaning it constructs sexism as some kind of error in consciousness that need only be dispelled. This is the classical project of liberal feminism (MacKinnon 1983).

Coincident with these struggles for political recognition, women have also fought to gain access to the spheres of bourgeois political and economic power. While these efforts are intertwined, as women have had to win protections from the state in order to secure their ability to participate in the accumulation of capital, much feminist attention to the theorization of democracy has focused on the problem of access to spheres of influence. Feminist theory has contributed a great deal to the dissection of the processes and procedures through which democracy is organized and administered and has meticulously revealed the insidious workings of patriarchy in everything from women's access to political office and their popular representation as leaders to the minutiae of discursive interactions in deliberation and debate that serve to marginalize the experiences, perspective and words of women (Phillips 1998). The debate over the private versus the public sphere (Landes 1998), the elaboration of counter-publics (Fraser 1990), the development of frameworks for inclusion and participation (Young 1989, 2000), the proposal of a feminist welfare state (Sarvasy 1992), expanding of boundaries of notions of 'participation' (Sparks 1997) – all of these feminist lines of thought have sought out ways for women to gain power and access within existing democratic structures of the state while at the same time attempting to theorize a negation of the patriarchal state, but not the state as such. Here women have laboured for a vision of freedom that is fully inclusive, participatory, just and shared, that realizes the ideals of democratic society and in effect either dismantles sexism as a political and cultural force or affirms difference and builds strategies for transformation. This is a vision of freedom premised on the possibility of full equality and on the faith in democratic institutions regarding their ability to bring forth such a social state of being. The danger of this engagement with bourgeois democracy is the reduction of women to the status of 'interest group' (MacKinnon 1983: 642).

Women have also struggled extensively over the relationship between the state and reproduction, and these struggles have constituted the most radical domains of feminist engagement with bourgeois democracy. These struggles, while far reaching and interrelated, coalesce around major points of engagement. First, the ongoing struggle for control over sexuality, which includes the struggles around rape, violence, privacy, sex work and queerness (Cooper 1995; MacKinnon 1982). Secondly, there are the extensive 'cultural' wars over the reproduction of labour power, which have been raised by feminists as debates around contraception, abortion, healthcare, sterilization, and so forth (Martin 2001; O'Brien 1981). Thirdly, the very complex notion of the value of reproductive labour, notably access through debates over paid and unpaid labour, wages for housework, sex work, social entitlements for reproductive work, and redistribution and economic justice (Dalla Costa and James 1975; Fortunati 1995; Mies et al. 1988). Despite the utility of identifying these themes, these struggles have an inner relation to one another such that the sexuality of women, their role in the reproduction of labour power, and the contribution of reproductive labour to the accumulation of capital are indivisible social relations and thus points for the violent subversion and state control of women's bodies and consciousness. It is in the debate over control of reproduction that we most clearly see the limits of freedom for women with bourgeois democracy, and it is here that the 'unwinnable' struggles of feminism emerge most strongly.

Implications for revolutionary feminist democratic praxis

> A new way of life has to be created. The so-called 'racial problem' is not a problem amenable to a solution: it is not a problem at all. It is a cruel way of life for which, if we wish to survive as a free nation, a new way of life must be substituted. And such a life requires a new vision, a new grasp of the meaning of human experience. (Lillian Smith, 1949 [1994: 173])

Lillian Smith was not a revolutionary feminist. She was the queer daughter of middle-class white people from Georgia. She tried to make a space on top of a mountain where young women could try to imagine a different world, one different from the patriarchal, racist and militarist regime of capitalism in which they lived. She understood better than most in her time the ways in which the bodies and minds of women, both white and black, became part of the inner relations of the violent system known as Jim Crow. She recognized that democracy, or so it was called, could not coexist with the racist, patriarchal violence she struggled against – and that therefore she did not live in a democracy. For those interested in imagining revolutionary feminist democracy, the task is not simply a matter of carrying forward Marx's critique. It requires, as Smith implies, a new grasp on the meaning of human experience.

I want to close by suggesting that there are several key theoretical problems within feminist theory that must be addressed in order for us to move forward and not simply rehash 'unwinnable' struggles for unfreedom. The first of these is an ontological shift towards a feminist historical materialism. The primary reason for the dearth of feminist political theory aimed at dismantling bourgeois democracy is the naturalization of existing democracy through continued engagement with its concepts and categories. This problem is not exclusive to feminists; it troubles the political left more broadly. Despite their actual existing expression, we remain deeply wedded to the ideological power of notions such as freedom and equality and the claims to legitimacy made by representative government. It is for this reason that Žižek referred to this problem as 'fidelity to the democratic consensus' (2002: 167). The second is a need to theorize 'necessity' from a feminist standpoint and to articulate what the negation of necessity (i.e. freedom) will be under patriarchal capitalism. This is a robust theoretical problem, but with a now decades-long history of engagement from Marxist and socialist feminists. Feminist theory has moved far away from this debate, and its more recent attempts to 'rematerialize' feminism are only a new beginning. Thirdly, and finally, feminists interested in the problem of democracy must closely examine the relationship between reform and revolution. Feminist engagement with bourgeois democracy has largely been focused on the reform of policy and processes. While this has indeed moved many women, but not all, towards a realized vision of political emancipation, the project is incomplete without an accompanying vision of human emancipation. This requires the commitment to work through and beyond the limits of democracy.

Note

1 Marx's conception of civil society is further elaborated in 'On the Jewish question' (1978).

References

Amos, V. and P. Parmar (1984) 'Challenging imperial feminism', *Feminist Review*, (17): 3–19.

Bannerji, H. (1995) *Thinking Through: Essays on Feminism, Marxism and Anti-racism*, Toronto: Women's Press.

Barrett, M. (1987) 'Marxist-feminism and the work of Karl Marx', in A. Phillips (ed.), *Feminism and Equality*, New York: New York University Press, pp. 44–61.

Bellah, R. N., R. Madsen, W. M. Sullivan, A. Swidler and S. M. Tipton (1985) *Habits of the Heart: Individualism and Commitment in American Life*, Berkeley and Los Angeles: University of California Press.

Bricmont, J. (2007) *Humanitarian Imperialism: Using Human Rights to Sell War*, New York: Monthly Review Press.

Brunner, C., L. Burcar and M. Freudenschub (2013) 'Critical reflections on "democracy in crisis": between activism and academia', *International Feminist Journal of Politics*, 15(2): 267–76.

Butler, J. (2006) *Precarious Life: The Powers of Mourning and Violence*, London: Verso.

Callinicos, A. (1999) *Social Theory: A Historical Introduction*, New York: New York University Press.

Cockburn, C. (2007) *From Where We Stand: War, Women's Activism and Feminist Analysis*, London: Zed Books.

Cooper, D. (1995) *Power in Struggle: Feminism, Sexuality and the State*, Cambridge: Cambridge University Press.

Crozier, M., S. P. Huntington and J. Watanuki (1975) *The Crisis of Democracy*, New York: Trilateral Commission.

Dalla Costa, M. and S. James (1975) *The Power of Women and the Subversion of the Community*, Bristol: Falling Wall.

Federici, S. (2004) *Caliban and the Witch*, New York: Autonomedia.

Fortunati, L. (1995) *The Arcane of Reproduction: Housework, Prostitution, Labor and Capital*, New York: Autonomedia.

Fraser, N. (1990) 'Rethinking the public sphere: a contribution to the critique of actually existing democracy', *Social Text*, 25/26: 56–80.

Funk, N. (2006) 'Women's NGOs in central and eastern Europe and the former Soviet Union: the imperialist criticism', in J. Lukic, J. Regulska and D. Zarvisek (eds), *Women and Citizenship in Central and Eastern Europe*, Hampshire: Ashgate, pp. 265–86.

Harvey, D. (2010) *A Companion to Marx's Capital*, 2 vols, London: Verso.

Huntington, S. P. (1996) *The Clash of Civilizations and the Remaking of World Order*, New York: Penguin.

Israel, J. I. (2001) *Radical Enlightenment: Philosophy and the Making of Modernity 1650–1750*, Oxford: Oxford University Press.

Jad, I. (2004) 'The NGOisation of Arab women's movements', *IDS Bulletin*, 35(4): 34–42.

Landes, J. B. (ed.) (1998) *Feminism, the Public and the Private*, Oxford Readings in Feminism, Oxford: Oxford University Press.

Lebsock, S. D. (1977) 'Radical reconstruction and the property rights of Southern women', *Journal of Southern History*, 43(2): 195–216.

Linebaugh, P. and M. Rediker (2000) *The Many-headed Hydra: Sailors, Slaves, Commoners, and the Hidden History of the Revolutionary Atlantic*, Boston, MA: Beacon Press.

Lowe, L. (1996) *Immigrant Acts: On Asian*

American Cultural Politics, Durham, NC: Duke University Press.

MacKinnon, C. A. (1982) 'Feminism, Marxism, method, and the state: an agenda for theory', *Signs*, 7(3): 515–44.

— (1983) 'Feminism, Marxism, method, and the state: toward feminist jurisprudence', *Signs*, 8(4): 635–58.

Marshall, T. H. (1950) *Citizenship and Social Class*, Cambridge: Cambridge University Press.

Martin, E. (2001) *The Woman in the Body: A Cultural Analysis of Reproduction*, Boston, MA: Beacon Press.

Marx, K. (1967) *Capital: A Critique of Political Economy*, vol. 1, New York: International.

— (1970) 'Critique of the Gotha programme', in *Marx–Engels Selected Works*, vol. 3, Moscow: Progress, pp. 13–30.

— (1978) 'On the Jewish question', in R. C. Tucker (ed.), *The Marx–Engels Reader*, New York: W. W. Norton, pp. 26–52.

Marx, K. and F. Engels (1968) *The German Ideology*, Moscow: Progress.

Mies, M. (1986) *Patriarchy and Accumulation on a World Scale: Women in the International Division of Labour*, New York: Palgrave Macmillan.

Mies, M., V. Bennholdt-Thomsen and C. von Werlhof (1988) *Women: The Last Colony*, London: Zed Books.

Mohanty, C. T. (1988) 'Under Western eyes: feminist scholarship and colonial discourses', *Feminist Review*, 30: 61–88.

— (2006) 'US empire and the project of women's studies: stories of citizenship, complicity and dissent', *Gender, Place and Culture*, 13(1): 7–20.

Mojab, S. (2007) 'Women NGOs under conditions of occupation and war', Solidarity, www.solidarity-us.org/node/576.

— (2009) 'Post-war reconstruction, imperialism and Kurdish women's NGOs', in N. S. Ali-Ali and N. Pratt (eds), *Women and War in the Middle East: Transnational Perspectives*, London: Zed Books, pp. 99–128.

Mojab, S. and C. Carpenter (2011) 'Learning by dispossession: democracy promotion and civic engagement in Iraq and the United States', *International Journal of Lifelong Education*, 30(4): 549–63.

Nace, T. (2005) *Gangs of America: The Rise of Corporate Power and the Disabling of Democracy*, San Francisco, CA: Berrett-Koehler.

O'Brien, M. (1981) *The Politics of Reproduction*, New York: Routledge.

Phillips, A. (ed.) (1998) *Feminism and Politics*, Oxford: Oxford University Press.

Putnam, R. D. (1995) 'Bowling alone: America's declining social capital', *Journal of Democracy*, 6(1): 65–78.

Riley, R. L., C. T. Mohanty and M. B. Pratt (2008) *Feminism and War: Confronting US Imperialism*, London: Zed Books.

Sarvasy, W. (1992) 'Beyond the difference versus equality policy debate: postsuffrage feminism, citizenship, and the quest for a feminist welfare state', *Signs*, 17(2): 329–62.

Sayer, D. (1987) *The Violence of Abstraction: The Analytic Foundations of Historical Materialism*, London: Blackwell.

Smith, A. (2005) *Conquest: Sexual Violence and American Indian Genocide*, Cambridge, MA: South End.

— (2006) 'Heteropatriarchy and the three pillars of white supremacy', in A. Smith, B. E. Richie and J. Sudbury (eds), *The Color of Violence: INCITE! Anthology*, Cambridge, MA: South End.

Smith, L. E. (1994) *Killers of the Dream*, New York: W. W. Norton.

Sparks, H. (1997) 'Dissident citizenship: democratic theory, political courage, and activist women', *Hypatia*, 12(4): 74–110.

Stabile, C. A. and D. Kumar (2005) 'Unveiling imperialism: media, gender and the war on Afghanistan', *Media, Culture and Society*, 27(5): 765–82.

Wood, E. M. (2003) *Empire of Capital*, London: Verso.

— (2006) 'Democracy as ideology of empire', in C. Mooers (ed.), *The New Imperialists: Ideologies of Empire*, Oxford: OneWorld, pp. 9–23.

— (2012) *Liberty and Property: A Social History of Western Political Thought from the Renaissance to Enlightenment*, London: Verso.

Young, I. M. (1989) 'Polity and group difference: a critique of the ideal of universal citizenship', *Ethics*, 99(2): 250–74.

— (2000) *Inclusion and Democracy*, Oxford: Oxford University Press.

Zangana, H. (2007) *City of Widows: An Iraqi Woman's Account of War and Resistance*, New York: Seven Stories.

Žižek, S. (2001) *The Fragile Absolute: Or, Why is the Christian Legacy Worth Fighting For?*, London: Verso.

— (2002) 'Afterword: Lenin's choice', in S. Žižek (ed.), *Revolution at the Gates: A Selection of Writings from February to October 1917*, London: Verso, pp. 165–334.

6 | FINANCIALIZATION[1]

Jamie Magnusson

Feminist literature on the question of financialization is only now beginning to emerge, and is characterized more often than not by empirical stratification studies on the gendered and racialized impact of the global financial crisis of 2007/08.[2] One reason for this lacuna is that, although an old topic within Marxism, financialization has only recently come to occupy a much more significant role in the global accumulation process such that we can now mark our current historical formation as 'monopoly finance capitalism' – the latest phase of capitalism. In Marxist literature, imperialism is understood as a key historical manifestation of monopolized finance and is critical for understanding globalization and uneven 'development' on one hand, and the constitutive necessity of militarized territorial struggle on the other. More recent analyses have been particularly important in showing how financialization, imperialism and primitive accumulation are interconnected within the internal logic of financialized accumulation (e.g. Moyo et al. 2012).

This chapter revisits the financialization question from a contemporary perspective that brings into sharper focus both imperialism and primitive accumulation as critical to a Marxist-feminist analysis. To accomplish this aim, I have contextualized the discussion in terms of sex trafficking. Sex trafficking was chosen as a site of analysis in part because it flows from my work with women and youth who have been trafficked, but more importantly because it reveals several aspects of contemporary financialization and gender relations that are not often covered in the literature on this topic. As Bhattacharyya (2005) points out, financialization, which has produced a burgeoning unregulated shadow sector of financial services intermingled with a regulated sector of financial services, has greatly facilitated the money laundering process by which illicit capital enters into the licit economy. Flowing from this point, as the distinction between illicit and licit money diminishes in the financialized form of capital, proceeds of illegal economies, characterized by brutal forms of primitive accumulation, can become a significant source of licit accumulation through financial trading. Sex trafficking, the target of which is almost exclusively young women and girls, then, is becoming more prevalent as a form of illicit primitive accumulation that is used to produce licit wealth and to secure political power.

In the jurisdiction where I live, for example, the potential profit made by *one* trafficker who forces *one* victim into daily service can be between $168,000 and $336,000 Canadian dollars per year (HTNCC 2013). When we consider that traffickers may have more than one victim, we can see that sex trafficking is a lucrative business. Moreover, if trafficking is set up as an organized (illegal) business, the estimated revenues can be millions. A conservative estimate of the global profits from commercial sex exploitation is close to US$34 billion, and a conservative estimate of the global profits from sex trafficking is close to US$28 billion (Belser 2005). Other data sources show this figure to be much higher. For example, in one study, prostitution, the largest of the underground businesses in Thailand, was estimated to generate between US$22 billion and US$27 billion, comprising approximately 10 to 14 per cent of the country's GDP (Lim 1998). There is no empirical data available to estimate profits that can be subsequently generated from wealth initially acquired from sex trafficking and then reinvested in the financialized sector (or other sectors). When these fortunes are considered alongside accumulation through drugs, weapons trafficking and other organized crime enterprises, we can see that the amounts of wealth are extremely large. We also get a sense as to how illicit and licit accumulation work together, the one depending on the other.

Bhattacharyya (2005) explains this process by pointing out that market (neo)liberalism, globalization and the financialization of capitalism set up the conditions by which the illegal economy offered unprecedented opportunities to make a great deal of money fast, and it also set up the conditions for organized crime to expand and develop transnational networks. Tracing trends across drugs, arms trafficking, organized crime and people trafficking, she illustrates how the legal and illegal economy are not merely interpenetrated but co-constitutive. Using the example of the former Eastern Bloc, she argues that in the early stages of economic transition and neoliberal restructuring, 'few other than the corrupt, the criminal and foreigners were able to take part in the rush to buy up former state assets' (ibid.: 89). Those who made vast fortunes during what may be described as a sweep of primitive accumulation are now holders of political power.

With regard to power interests, Kempadoo (2002/03) explains that Thailand's sex industry boom emerged from the complex networks that connect the shared interests of the elite within military, business and organized crime. She further points out that the World Bank's support for an 'open economy and export oriented development strategy results in financial support of tourism' (ibid.: 144). As the scholars cited here note, the multibillion-dollar tourism industry, referred to as the 'Thai Economic Miracle', is organized around sex tourism. In reference to Cuba and the Dominican Republic, Kempadoo writes:

> In Cuba and the Dominican Republic, the specter of sex tourism has become embedded in the economy. The sexual labour of young brown women has become increasingly important to national economies, while prostitution remains condemned as degrading and destructive. In Cuba's case it is viewed as a counter-revolutionary engagement. Nevertheless, State support or tolerance of this form of tourism is evident. Sex work fills the coffers of countries whose economic survival is increasingly dependent on global corporate capitalist interests. (Ibid.: 144)

Although profits from sex trafficking and commercial sexual exploitation can wield a powerful influence within certain contexts, such as developing or transitioning economies, as described above, the industrialized economies of the global North actually have the highest profits globally, followed by the Asia and Pacific region (Belser 2005). Moreover, the United Nations Office on Drugs and Crime (UNODC) reports that sexual exploitation is the most common form of human trafficking, making up 79 per cent of all cases, predominantly women and children. Globally, children make up 20 per cent of trafficked persons, but in certain regions, such as parts of West Africa, this percentage could be as high as 100 per cent. According to the report, data shows that domestic or inter-regional movement comprises the major form of trafficking, in comparison to intercontinental movement (UNODC 2009). In other words, although international sex trafficking attracts a great deal of interest, most trafficking takes place close to home.

Given these statistics, the lopsided focus on intercontinental trafficking seems strange, particularly in light of the lack of police and government attention to pandemics of missing and/or murdered young women as a result of domestic sex trafficking that has become a disturbing reality in many international locations. In the tri-border region of Argentina, Brazil and Paraguay, 'sex with children' is included in certain travel packages, the victims of which are usually indigenous teens who have gone missing. Similarly, in Canada the lack of government and police attention to missing/murdered Aboriginal women has brought the public to the street in protest. In certain areas of Canada, Aboriginal women and youth can represent as much as 50 per cent of street-based sex workers (Shannon et al. 2009).

At the same time that so much money is being made through sex trafficking and organized crime, we are seeing an immense global expansion of the carceral state, as well as militarized infrastructure. This can take the form of regulating movement across national borders, managing militarized 'humanitarian' aid, and intervening in 'new wars' (e.g. Bhattacharyya 2005; Meiners and Quinn 2011; Sudbury 2005; Wood 2003). The United States most exemplifies this picture of both an 'outward' militarism focused on territorial control and an 'inward' militarized police state characterized by the rapid expansion of private for-profit prisons focused on providing a source of cheap labour for enterprise, including weapons parts for the military. These dually focused expansions are justified by a 'war on terrorism' ideology in the case of the outward-focused imperialist arrangement, and a 'war on crime' ideology in the case of the inward-focused imperialist arrangement. Together, these outward and inward imperialist arrangements comprise a full-spectrum dominance strategy oriented to constructing and maintaining value regimes for monopolized finance capital (e.g. Wood 2003).

One would think that with this unprecedented intensification of imperialist arrangements, if we flow with the ideological justification, we would be seeing fewer 'new wars' and less organized crime. More women and children ought to be enjoying safety, security and protection. That the opposite is true represents a fundamental contradiction through which militarized finance capital is organized. We are, rather, witnessing the successive enclosure of 'safe communities' for privatization, commodification and speculative investment. These enclosures are creating a 'planet of slums' (e.g. Davis 2006) wherein women and children are dislocated and comprise the increasing pauperized masses vulnerable to labour exploitation, including indentureship and slavery, as evidenced in the instance of sex trafficking as a lucrative source of primitive accumulation. Rather than this protecting us from 'criminals', we are witnessing a sharp increase in women – particularly indigenous and racialized women – being criminalized to fill private for-profit prisons (Sudbury 2005); rather than preventing sex trafficking, the border police are regulating gendered migrations due to dislocation of women from their communities; rather than the containment of 'terrorism', we are seeing the militarized containment of international social crises enter into the speculative orbits of stock markets and financialized trading.

From this very brief snapshot of sex trafficking, we can see the urgent need for more research, writing and struggle from a Marxist-feminist perspective on the financialization question, particularly in relation to imperialism and primitive accumulation. To summarize the main points in this section, the dominance of monopolized financial accumulation in late capitalism has exacerbated economic stagnation at the same time that it produces new investment markets (Magdoff and Bellamy-Foster 2014) that render primitive accumulation via sex trafficking (and other forms of organized crime) a very lucrative source of capital for investment in the burgeoning shadow markets (Bhattacharyya 2005). Young women and girls are the almost exclusive targets of this egregious form of primitive accumulation. These developments have to be read against the expansion of the for-profit carceral state taking place at the same time that neoliberal and austerity policies gut social infrastructure that offered spaces for community-building and social and cultural security. In the case of the United States, for-profit carceral state expansion is connected to the same weapons-dollar accumulation logic driving heightened militarization more generally. National and homeland security in the post-terror era, as well as militarized containment of international crises and new wars, offer opportunities for speculative investment (e.g. Enron) and territorial control of resource extraction (e.g. Nigeria). Women's and girls' bodies are central to these imperialist accumulation projects, as evidenced by the increasingly gendered migration to cities/slums, by primitive accumulation as an accumulation strategy within the illegal sector of sex trafficking, and by the global spike in women's carceration (e.g. Sudbury 2005).

The next section provides a historical understanding of financialization from a traditional Marxist perspective, followed by a Marxist-feminist intervention that traces the money form of capital (i.e. financialized capital) through women's bodies within the sex trafficking context. Finally, I conclude with some considerations about what can be done.

More or less traditional Marxist explanation of contemporary financialization

This section will provide a brief sketch of dynamics associated with what has come to be termed 'the financialization of late capitalism' from a Marxist perspective. 'Finance capital' existed in a pre-capitalist form as interest-bearing capital. 'Commercial capital' also existed in a pre-capitalist form as a 'buy low and sell high' exchange. Both finance and commercial capital continue to exist in capitalism, but as capitalism emerged as the dominant and ever-expanding mode of production, finance and commercial capital became subsumed to the distinctive role that market dependence plays in capitalism. For example, the industrial capitalist needs to borrow money to build factories and purchase labour power. The products, or commodities, need to enter into exchange with purchasers. Market dependence, which distinguishes capitalist from pre-capitalist modes of production, pulls this entire productive process, including social relations of finance and commercial capital, into 'laws of motion' that may best be described as a compulsion towards profit maximization, expansion and accumulation (Wood 1998). As Marx and Engels state: 'The need for a constantly expanding market for its products chases the bourgeoisie over the whole surface of the global. It must nestle everywhere, settle everywhere, establish connexions everywhere' (Marx and Engels 1945: 12). Marx explained that capital underwent metamorphoses as it cycled through the production process:

> The two forms that the capital value assumes within its circulation stages are those of money capital and commodity capital; the form pertaining to the production stage is that of productive capital. The capital that assumes these forms in the course of its total circuit, discards them again and fulfils in each of them its appropriate function, is industrial capital – industrial in the sense that it encompasses every branch of production that is pursued on a capitalist basis. (Marx 1992: 133)

He continues:

> Money capital, commodity capital and productive capital thus do not denote independent varieties of capital whose functions constitute the content of branches of business that are independent and separate from one another. They are simply particular functional forms of industrial capital, which takes on all three forms in turn. (Ibid.: 133)

Finance capital, then, is money capital, which is simply a functional form of industrial capital. Financialization can be understood as the historical process by which capital in its money form emerged dominant in the world economic and even political system. That is, in the current era of financialization, capital accumulation is dominated by what Marx referred to as 'the money circuit' rather than 'the productive circuit'. Pragmatically what this means is that it can be more lucrative to borrow money at 1 per cent interest and reinvest it in the credit market at 20 per cent interest than to take that same money and build factories. The difficulty is that if everyone were to invest in this way, the entire system would collapse as, at the end of the day, the system *is* organized around extracting surplus value from workers selling their labour power to the capitalist (Patnaik 2010).

The production cycle is characterized by three circuits, as follows:

- money circuit: borrowing money from money capital (note: the activities that comprise this circuit are what is referred to as the 'finance sector', and money capitalists have come to be referred to as the 'financial class');
- productive circuit: using the money capital to build factories and purchase labour power, transforming money capital into productive capital (note: the activities that comprise this circuit are what is referred to as the 'productive sector');
- commodity circuit: selling the commodity at a higher price than productive capital invested into production, transforming productive capital into commodity capital (noting that the activities that comprise this circuit are what is referred to as the 'commercial sector').

As we can see, and as Marx points out, the cycle is better described as 'metamorphoses' of capital, rather than separate and independent spheres.

The production cycle is constructed through some contradictions that are internal to the logic of industrial capitalism. These are too many to elaborate in this brief chapter, but they primarily originate in the 'laws of motion' set up through the complete market dependence of the entire system, and they render the entire system unstable and given to crises. For example, what happens when one capitalist has figured out a way to complete the production cycle faster and more cheaply than other capitalists? Or what happens when everyone who wants the product now has one? When the rate of profit falls, which is bound to happen, the financial class loses anticipated profit, as well as a part or all of the original capital, and cannot lend more money; the productive class is unable to borrow more money and as a result factories close and workers are laid off and cannot buy things; and because workers cannot buy things when they are laid off, the commercial class cannot offload their commodities for a profit (over-accumulation), and must sell at a loss. In short the contradictions of capitalism originating in market dependence render the entire system unstable and given to crises.

For much of industrial capitalism's brief history, capital accumulation centred the role of productive capital as evidenced in Fordism as an iconic example of a nationally organized economy characterized by assembly line factories, scientific management, vertical lines of hierarchical control, fixed production, and an extensive domestic market. Flesh out the Fordism picture with suburban houses sporting two-car garages and complete it with the assemblage of war jeeps and a massive non-profit sector, namely the Ford Foundation with its publicly known connections to the World Bank and US security, and we begin to get a picture of industrial capitalism during the post-war years after Bretton Woods: a Fordist–Keynesian militarist-accumulation regime primed for global expansion. The 'militarism' through which the industrial complex was interwoven facilitated both accumulation via the productive cycle as well as accumulation through the exercise of violence or threat of violence. To explain, I introduce the distinction used by Marx between economic coercion and non-economic coercion, concepts that are given innovative interpretation by Wood (2003).

Extra-economic coercion was used in pre-capitalist formations in the process of 'primitive accumulation' to extract labour surplus from farming families by landlords or the state by leveraging 'privileged access to military, judicial, and political power' (Wood 1998). In capitalist formations, people do not have access to the means of producing, say, food and materials for clothes, and so on, and therefore must sell their labour power to the capitalist in order to buy what they need for subsistence/reproduction. An interesting question, then, is why is privileged access to military, judicial and political power necessary in capitalism? The answer is that capitalist systems, using the example of industrial capitalism, are not quite self-contained such that economic coercion is sufficient. Owing to its own internal contradictions, as explained above, capitalism must always have an outside or periphery, and exploiting the periphery is a form of primitive accumulation that requires extra-economic coercion (e.g. Luxemburg 2003). Imperialism and colonialism go hand in hand, as do imperialism and neocolonialism. Capturing territory for access to natural resources is one important example. Also, if one thinks of the competition between two imperialist nations such as the United States and the former Soviet Union, imperialism is inherent in the violent struggle for territory connected to natural resources, trading routes, and so on. That is, capitalism is always organized through relations of imperialism and historically capitalism has always had peripheries. In the next section of the chapter, I take up this question of imperialism in connection with financialization in terms of ways to understand emergent peripheries and gender/race relations organizing primitive accumulation as an ongoing process of capitalism.

As described above, the relative stability of this instantiation of Keynesian military industrial capitalism could not last for ever, and when it began to bump up against the wall of falling profits, over-accumulation/underconsumption, and so on, the system had to morph. By the 1970s, the profit crunch was being felt across most jurisdictions in the global North characterized by military Keynesianism, as described above, but particularly in the United States, which had become an epicentre of the international economy and which found itself in a deficit for various reasons, such as the costs associated with the war in Vietnam. What unfolded in response to this crisis is the historical process by which the global economy became 'financialized'. There are entire books written on this topic and so the discussion here is extremely abbreviated and selective.

First, through neoliberal policies international finance institutions enforced structural adjustment programmes (SAPs) that violently impacted the global South by exponentially increasing indebtedness and manipulating and destroying local economies, opening them up for exploitation by the global North. Many of these 'peripheral' economies had been working towards economic independence in an era of post-colonialism, and the structural adjustment programmes orchestrated via international finance institutions severed this process. Secondly, neoliberal policies orchestrated at local and international levels made possible reorganization of production, moving parts of production to areas where labour was cheaper. The first and second points are critical events in terms of accelerating the globalization of capital accumulation through neoliberal policies. Extra-economic coercion has been most violently exerted in the case of enforcing structural adjustment programmes and subsequent neoliberal economic policies enforced by the International Monetary Fund (IMF). Militarism has also been used to contain the eruption of class struggle that we are currently seeing owing to the relatively wealthier proletariat of the rich world becoming pauperized as production moves to the global South. As I discuss in the next section, relations of imperialism have intensified through this process, as has how imperialism is organized in terms of racialized gender relations.

Thirdly, the Bretton Woods system, by which the US dollar was established as the de facto gold standard, was dismantled by Nixon – a move that McNally describes as 'the day world finance changed forever' (McNally 2011: 88). That is, since 1971 global finance has had no standard against which to value currencies, creating volatility in currency value and initiating a frenzy of currency trading as investors tried to keep up with continuous changes in value. Floating value is associated with risk, inspiring the term 'casino economy', in that investment becomes a bet. Financial products offering 'risk management', therefore, became an area of intensive innovation and investment. New forms of financial derivatives, credit debt swaps (CDSs) and hedge funds – all financial products that manage risk for a price – attracted intensive speculative interest. Recall that the money circuit is characterized by interest-bearing loans, or credit and debt. With the speculative frenzy initiated by dissolving the US dollar as the de facto gold standard, incentive increased to create new financial products focusing on the role of credit/debt, such as collateralized debt obligations (CDOs). CDOs are portfolios of various debt obligations – for example, mortgages – of varying risks. The availability of CDOs as an investment opportunity created a speculative bubble in US real estate because of the connection of CDOs to mortgages, particularly sub-prime variable mortgages (that is, mortgages with interest rates that fluctuate according to 'the market', much like 'currency value' as described above). Housing buyers and real estate developers are both caught in a speculative bubble organized through ever-expanding and sophisticated credit services, as are banks and nation-states (for example, Iceland). However, the massive expansion of a shadow sector of financial services – that is, finance services outside of the regulatory constraints of investment banking institutions or other regulated financial services – is an important aspect of the narrative that explains how illicit capital can enter into the licit economy. Suffice to say that all of the financial innovations listed above appeared in the shadow investment sector. The investment banking and shadow investment sectors are not parallel to one another, but came to be intermingled, a process in which investment banking in the City of London played a lead role.

A question one might ask is, 'Why invest in the financial sector rather than the productive sector?' Recall that by the 1970s, the 'Fordist era' (or what Patnaik refers to as 'demand management') had hit a wall. For capitalists who had accumulated great wealth from production, reinvesting by expanding production could only yield diminishing returns. On the other hand, reorganizing production by moving parts of the production process to countries where labourers would receive lower wages, work longer hours and receive fewer, if any, benefits allowed them to keep ahead of falling rates of profit. Restructuring production in this way created employment and housing precarity for those in the former Fordist jurisdictions, creating incentives for them to accept lower wages, work several part-time jobs, relinquish benefits, and work increasingly in the informal economy – sometimes referred to as the shadow economy. The credit industry expanded exponentially to keep consumption lively: everyone soon had more than one major credit card as well as a credit card from every major retail outlet. In addition, the state began to disinvest from public and civic infrastructures, offering speculative investment opportunities for investors through privatization. As the costs of, say, higher education were downloaded on to consumers, degrees were paid for via for-profit publicly traded credit that lacked many of the regulatory constraints of banking institutions. All of this is to say that lucrative investment opportunities eventually and overwhelmingly were located in the finance sector, which was quickly growing a tumour of unregulated, unconstrained credit-related financial products and investment services. The unregulated financial services and the regulated investment sector then became interpenetrated.

The final part to this abbreviated summary regards the historical tendency for financialized accumulation to become concentrated in fewer and fewer hands. Lenin was famous for mapping (empirically and conceptually) this tendency in terms of the first phase of capitalism, claiming that monopoly finance is the material basis of imperialism (e.g. militarism) as a structural feature of internationalized capital accumulation. This tendency towards monopolization in the current phase of capitalism has come to form an international financial oligarchy that originated in the nationally organized demand management policies (for which one instantiation is the Keynesian military Fordism as described above). Patnaik (e.g. 2010) argues that the concept of imperialism is more relevant than ever in the current era of neoliberalism and financialization. His thoughts on imperialism are inspired by Lenin's thesis on monopoly finance and imperialism, but he offers a critical reinterpretation that enriches our understanding of how imperialism works in connection with current financialization and peripheries. As he explains, not only does capital-as-finance act as finance, but capital-as-production also acts as finance; however, capital-as-finance is oblivious to production. After offering these characteristics of financialization, he outlines key characteristics differentiating the imperial financialized capitalism of today from Lenin's time based on the role of the state. I quote at length because I go on to use Patnaik's conceptualization of territory and peripheralized populations in my discussions on sex trafficking:

> finance capital in Lenin's time had its base within a particular nation, and its international operations were linked to the expansion of national 'economic territory.' But the finance capital of today, though of course it has its origins in particular nations, is not necessarily tied to national interests. It moves around globally and its objectives are no different from the finance capital that has its origins in some other nation. It is in this sense that distinctions between national finance capitals become misleading, and we can talk of an international finance capital, which, no matter where

> it originates from, has this character of being detached from any particular national interests, having the world as its theatre of operations, and not being tied to any particular sphere of activity, such as industry. (Ibid. 2010)

He continues later:

> In the current phase of imperialism, finance capital has become international, while the State remains a nation-State. The nation-State therefore willy-nilly must bow before the wishes of finance, for otherwise finance (both originating in that country and brought in from the outside) will leave that particular country and move elsewhere, reducing it to illiquidity and disrupting its economy. The process of globalization of finance therefore has the effect of undermining the autonomy of the nation-State. The State cannot do what it wishes to do, or what its elected government has been elected to do, since it must do what finance wants. (Ibid.)

We can see from this explanation that both imperialism and primitive accumulation are inherent to the internal logic of monopoly finance capital. What we cannot see using a traditional Marxist understanding of financialization is how women are structurally implicated in the accumulation logic. The next section addresses this question.

Marxist-feminist interventions

Marxist feminists offer a powerful analytical entry point for understanding contemporary financialization as organized through gendered and racialized transnational relations characterized by primitive accumulation and imperialism. In Marx's analysis, primitive accumulation by violent means produced the original pre-capitalist class distinction between possessors and non-possessors, which was reproduced through capitalist relations of production. However, Marxist feminists such as Maria Mies (1998), Sylvia Federici (2004), Nancy Harstock (2008) and Mariarosa Dalla Costa (e.g. 1995) have argued that gendered violence and imperialism as a means of primitive accumulation and accumulation through dispossession continue to be an ongoing and gendered structural feature of capitalism. This is evidenced in a myriad of ways, including through contemporary gendered forms of slavery, indentured labour, organ trafficking and global organization of sex trafficking.

Mies is clear that both imperialism and primitive accumulation are important analytical tools in understanding prostitution and sex trafficking within the context of capitalism. She argues that 'imperialist industrial capital follows the imperialist military, both, however, strengthen the sex industry' (Mies 1998: 139). With regard to primitive accumulation, she called for more focused analyses of 'the use of structural or direct violence and coercion by which women are exploited and superexploited' (ibid.: 145). Federici further argues that primitive accumulation was not merely productive of a concentration of workers, but was also an accumulation of 'differences and divisions within the working class, whereby hierarchies built on gender as well as "race" and age, become constitutive of class rule and the formation of the modern proletariat' (Federici 2004: 63). In this way, Federici suggests, degradation of women through primitive accumulation was the historical context for contemporary gendered and racialized forms of primitive accumulation such as sex trafficking, as well as the devaluation of women's work as unproductive and therefore unwaged. Reading across these two authors, stripping women of power with regard to waged employment combined with degradation of women generally lead to the massification of prostitution as a means of subsistence.

Selma James has pointed out that women who prostitute through economic coercion came to be criminalized because money made from sex work could be seen as an autonomous source of income threatening the social organization of labour power and super-exploitation. She argues that the motivation to legalize sex work is animated by the desire to regulate women's 'autonomy' by transferring 'pimping' to the (police) state, thereby creating a whole new set of problems for women involved in prostitution. Her political work around women and sex work involved advocating for decriminalization rather than legalization and concomitantly advocating to criminalize pimping. As she states, 'Once women are not divided by the laws, prostitutes will be in a much more protected position to take the offensive against all kinds of pimping – by landlords, taxi drivers, etc., as well as by individual men' (James 2012: 114).

That financialization has been productive of contemporary forms of slavery has been pointed out by Dalla Costa (1995), who argued that the poverty imposed on most of the globe's population via financial agencies has 'chained entire families' to debt bondage. As she suggests, women's position within capitalism was spawned by violence and, in its contemporary financialized formation, is more than ever maintained through violence. One could argue that the global connectivity of violence against women was made possible through the circulation of money and money as a commodified form.[3] Federici describes these violences under financialization as follows:

> Where 'austerity' programs and land grabbing could not reach, war has completed the task, opening new grounds for oil drilling and the harvesting of diamonds or coltan [an ore]. As for the targets of these clearances, they have become the subjects of the new diaspora, siphoning millions of people from the land to the towns, which more and more resemble encampments. Mike Davis has used the phrase 'Planet of Slums' in referring to this situation, but a more correct and vivid description would speak of a planet of ghettos and a regime of global apartheid. (Federici 2012: 103)

This passage is critical in tracing how the money form of capital circulates through women's bodies via sex trafficking in an era of monopoly finance capital. What are required are new analyses of the gendered relations organizing apartheid imperialism and primitive accumulation through the power nexus connecting organized crime, the militarized state and monopoly finance capital.

Ghetto imperialism and sex trafficking: primitive accumulation and shadow economics

The transformation of cities in the contemporary era of financialization is proceeding rapidly and marked by expansion of slum conditions wherein housing and employment precarity are only deepening. The feminization of migration is now generally acknowledged, and irrespective of whether movement is rural-to-urban, inter-regional or intercontinental (predominantly South to North), cities and, importantly, mega-cities are the primary destinations. Poor people live within, or on the periphery of, large urban centres that are undergoing unprecedented expansion, such that by the year 2000 more than half of humanity lived in cities (Lotta 2013), and the slum growth throughout the South is currently superseding urbanization (Davis 2006). In rural jurisdictions the pressures compelling movement to the cities are felt more keenly by women. However, once in the cities, women continue to fare relatively poorly as they negotiate precarious employment (wage labour) and childcare (unwaged labour). Productive stagnation has become a stable characteristic of financialization, and employment precarity has become normalized, lowering wages globally (Magdoff and Bellamy-Foster 2014). The most accessible employment opportunities, particularly for women, are increasingly in the ever-expanding informal and/or illegal sectors. The intensification of pauperization and apartheid ghetto expansion is felt more keenly in the global South regardless of the romanticized production of millionaires; however, pauperization and the apartheid expansion of ghettos are global (Khosla 2005).

Within this environment, states, led by the United States, are expanding for-profit prison systems to extract surplus from incarcerated populations. Flounders reports that, in the United States, Unicor, a quasi-public for-profit corporation run by the Bureau of Prisons, manufactures electronic equipment for land, sea and air communications (2013). Unicor is a major contractor for the US government, with 110 factories at 79 federal penitentiaries:

> The majority of Unicor's products and services are on contract to orders from the Department of Defense. Giant multinational corporations purchase parts assembled at some of the lowest labour rates in the world, then resell the finished weapons components at the highest rates of profits. For example, Lockheed Martin and Raytheon Corporation subcontract components, then assemble and sell advanced weapons to the Pentagon. (Ibid.)

In addition to working for the financialized weapons-dollar regime, Flounders goes on to report that racialized enslaved prisoners also work for Motorola, Compaq, Honeywell, Microsoft, Boeing Revlon, Chevron, TWA, Victoria's Secret and Eddie Bauer. Moreover, IBM, Texas Instruments and Dell acquire circuit boards made by Texas prisoners. Private for-profit prisons have undergone massive expansion, and inmate populations in these institutions tripled between 1987 and 2007.

We can see that the industrial-military complex and the prison-military complex work together in an arrangement by which the imperialist power of the military is primarily focused on accumulation via securing territorial power through 'new wars' and the prisons are primarily focused on containing populations for both enterprise and supporting the market-centred compulsion for territorial power via the military. Clearly the two flow together and comprise a financialized imperial arrangement by which licit power syndicalism and enterprise syndicalism have developed partnerships that enable ongoing processes of primitive accumulation. Capital investors such as Merrill Lynch, Shearson Lehman, American Express and Allstate are all beneficiaries of lucrative returns on prison bonds (ibid.).

Sudbury (2005) has discussed the gendered organization of this inhumane exploitation in pointing out that, while racialized men continue to represent the majority of the prison population, racialized and indigenous women's incarceration rates are currently far outstripping those of men. Globally, incarcerating the very poor in the ghettos represents a 'new war' that is launched against the poor world, as evidenced recently in Laventille in Trinidad when martial law and curfews were instituted to conduct a 'sweep' through the ghetto, purportedly to contain violence by incarcerating those connected to organized crime. We could also read 'sweeps' of this sort as an example of 'expulsion' of the poor from prime real estate, as discussed by Sassen (2014).

The dynamics of drug trafficking can materially shape the ways in which sex trafficking and criminalization of racialized women play out. For example, drug cartels have become increasingly organized and globally inter-territorial, with informal partnerships with illicit/licit power syndicates, including state-level power in certain jurisdictions. The more sophisticated and monopolized the drug trade, the less lucrative street-based drug selling becomes as primitive surplus extraction evolves and becomes brutally efficient. That is, if most of the street-based sales in monopolized drug transactions flow upward, there is little if any room to start up one's own enterprise or to make much money at the level of street-based sales if one is working for a cartel. Moreover, the rapid expansion of the financialized carceral state provides an incentive to launch a war on drugs, the focus of which is young racialized men. The gang culture continues to sell drugs to maintain a certain investment in the trade and develop partnerships that leverage territorial control, but for street-based traders there is very little money to be made from drugs, and the cost of incarceration is too high a price to pay. The mostly undocumented increase in sex trafficking, which affects primarily young, racialized, pauperized women who have been dislocated through migration and severe fractionalization of the sprawling city, is produced through these relations of illicit *as well as* licit imperialism. Gangs and individuals turn to sex trafficking, thereby 'downloading' the risk of incarceration to women within a primitive accumulation enterprise controlled primarily by men and a gang culture that is profoundly misogynist. The sex trade has also become extremely organized and generates billions of dollars. However, there is still space for individuals to enter into this lucrative business.

In spite of the fact that most sex trafficking is inter-regional (moving women from city to city across provinces or states) or domestic, as mentioned previously, much effort to contain or stop trafficking has focused on intercontinental trafficking. Regulating intercontinental flow is ideal in terms of maintaining territorial containment and control of women whose paid and unpaid labour increasingly support a globally organized financial oligarchy. Moreover, the ever-expanding border control that has the appearance of protecting women results in few arrests, and virtually no women are 'saved'. On the other hand, the criminalization of women contained within territories is escalating. When this scenario of enterprise syndicalism is integrated with power syndicalism associated with the political economy of new wars on the poor world, there can be no question that imperialism as well as primitive accumulation is as important in the era of financialization as it ever was.

Mobilizing for change

This chapter has tried to illustrate that violence against women as an accumulation strategy achieves international integration through the globalized circulation of capital in its money form. The rapid expansion of the shadow finance sector and its global integration into regulated finance sectors significantly enables processes by which illicit capital associated with brutal misogynist primitive accumulation becomes licit capital. These processes reveal the need for more in-depth analyses of how imperialist finance capital and illegal strategies of primitive accumulation come together as part of the organizational logic of 'a planet of ghettos and a regime of global apartheid'. Particularly in the era of financialized capitalism, much more attention must be given to illegal economies and their dialectical/constitutive relation to the formal economies that more typically form the basis of historical materialist analyses. The strength of Marxist-feminist interventions is that they extend beyond analytics restricted to formal economies in order to incorporate the significant revolutionary potential of most of the women of the world who inhabit spaces of unwaged work and whose lives are ordered through the material relations organizing legal and illegal shadow economies.

The feminist revolutionary project flowing from this analysis is therefore international in scope and centres on anti-patriarchal struggles in dismantling militarized capitalism through feminist anti-racist praxis. Coming to an understanding of financialization through the sex trafficking context reveals how globally integrated violence against women is integral to the accumulation process. A viable revolutionary project must therefore deploy internationally coordinated strategies that build solidarity across spaces of gendered violence, including brothels, prisons, encampments and ghettos.

Notes

1 The inspiration for this chapter flows from my involvement in a research project on youth and domestic sex trafficking coordinated by Jolene Heida at the All Saints Community Centre in Toronto. Many thanks to all the women and youth involved in the project and to the women who make the Friday Drop-In for Sex Workers the best part of my work week. This chapter could not have been written without the readings and discussion available to me through the Marxist Feminist Reading Group organized and guided by Shahrzad Mojab. Her editorial feedback was an important part of my writing process. Many thanks also to Amir Hassanpour, whose contributions to the reading group have been critical to my development. Beverly Bain and Punam Kholsa are my constant conversation companions who generously offer their wisdom acquired through years of feminist anti-racist activism and scholarship on colonial and state violence.

2 See, for example, the special issue of *Feminist Economics* on 'Financial and economic crises' (volume 19, issue 3). The studies in this issue provide important empirical data revealing the uneven impact of the 2008 crisis on women, with further stratification according to race, ethnicity, marital status, and so on.

3 I thank Shahrzad Mojab, who, in her editorial feedback, provided this precise summary of the connection between globally organized violence against women and the money form of capital.

References

Belser, P. (2005) 'Forced labour and human trafficking: estimating the profits', Working paper, Geneva: International Labour Office, digitalcommons.ilr.cornell.edu/cgi/viewcontent.cgi?article=1016&context=forcedlabor.

Bhattacharyya, G. (2005) *Traffick: The Illicit Movement of People and Things*, London: Pluto.

Davis, M. (2006) *Planet of Slums*, London: Verso.

Dalla Costa, M. (1995) 'Capitalism and reproduction', in W. Bonefeld, R. Gunn, J. Holloway and K. Psychopedis (eds), *Open Marxism*, vol. 3: *Emancipating Marx*, London: Pluto.

Federici, S. (2004) *Caliban and the Witch: Women, the Body and Primitive Accumulation*, New York: Autonomedia.

— (2012) *Revolution at Point Zero: Housework, Reproduction and Feminist Struggle*, Oakland, CA: PM.

Flounders, S. (2013) 'The Pentagon and slave labour in U.S. prisons', Montreal: Global Research, www.globalresearch.ca/the-pentagon-and-slave-labor-in-u-s-prisons/25376.

Harstock, N. (2008) 'Globalization and primitive accumulation: the contributions of David Harvey's dialectical marxism', in M. Castree and D. Gregory (eds), *David Harvey: A Critical Reader*, New York: Blackwell, pp. 167–90.

HTNCC (Human Trafficking National Coordination Centre) (2013) 'Project Safekeeping – domestic human trafficking for sexual exploitation in Canada', Ottawa: Royal Canadian Mounted Police, October, publications.gc.ca/collections/collection_2014/grc-rcmp/PS64-114-2014-eng.pdf.

James, S. (2012) *Sex, Race, and Class: The Perspective of Winning, a Selection of Writings from 1952–2011*, Oakland, CA: PM.

Kempadoo, K. (2002/03) 'Globalizing sex workers' rights', *Canadian Women's Studies*, 22(3/4): 143–50.

Khosla, P. (2005) 'Privatization, segregation and dispassion in Western urban space: an anti-racist, Marxist feminist reading of David Harvey', Unpublished manuscript.

Lim, L. L. (1998) *The Sex Sector: The Economic and Social Basis of Prostitution in Southeast Asia*, Geneva: International Labour Office.

Lotta, R. (2013) 'On the driving force of anarchy and the dynamics of change, a sharp debate and an urgent polemic: the struggle for a radically different world and the struggle for a scientific approach to reality', *Revolution Newspaper*, 4 November.

Luxemburg, R. (2003) *The Accumulation of Capital*, trans. A. Schwarzschild, London: Routledge.

Magdoff, F. and J. Bellamy-Foster (2014) 'Stagnation and financialization: the nature of the contradiction', *Monthly Review*, 66(1): 1–24.

Marx, K. (1992) *Capital: A Critique of Political Economy*, vol. 2, trans. D. Fernbach, London: Penguin.

Marx, K. and F. Engels (1945) *The Communist Manifesto*, New York: International.

McNally, D. (2011) *Global Slump: The Economics and Politics of Crisis and Resistance*, Oakland, CA: PM.

Meiners, E. R. and T. Quinn (2011) 'Militarism and education normal', *Monthly Review*, 63(3), monthlyreview.org/2011/07/01/militarism-and-education-normal.

Mies, M. (1998) *Patriarchy and Accumulation on a World Scale: Women in the International Division of Labour*, London: Zed Books.

Moyo, S., P. Yeros and P. Jha (2012) 'Imperialism and primitive accumulation: notes on the new scramble for Africa', *Agrarian South: Journal of Political Economy*, 1: 181–203.

Patnaik, P. (2010) 'Notes on contemporary imperialism', *Monthly Review*, 66(2), mrzine.monthlyreview.org/2010/patnaik201210.html.

Sassen, S. (2014) *Expulsions: Brutality and Complexity in the Global Economy*, Cambridge: Belknap Press.

Shannon, K., T. Kerr, S. K. Strathdee, J. Shoveller, J. S. Montaner and M. W. Tyndall (2009) 'Prevalence and structural correlates of gender based violence among prospective cohort of female sex workers', *BMJ*, 339(b2939), www.bmj.com/content/339/bmj.b2939.

Sudbury, J. (2005) *Global Lockdown: Race, Gender, and the Prison-industrial Complex*, New York: Routledge.

UNODC (United Nation Office on Drugs and Crime) (2009) *A Global Report on Trafficking in Persons*, www.unodc.org/documents/Global_Report_on_TIP.pdf.

Wood, E. (1998) 'The agrarian origins of capitalism', *Monthly Review*, 50(3), monthlyreview.org/1998/07/01/the-agrarian-origins-of-capitalism.

— (2003) *Empire of Capital*, London and New York: Verso.

7 | IDEOLOGY

Himani Bannerji

The notion of ideology is frequently found in many academic disciplines, as well as in the media and speeches of politicians, and indeed in common parlance. Though its pervasive presence indicates its importance, the meaning of the term is often vague. This diverse and indeterminate use requires a close scrutiny.

Ideology is most often associated with ideas and beliefs related to power and politics, and the use of ideology assigns culture or forms of consciousness a central role in the creation or assertion of power relations. Ideology also refers diffusely to interpretive frameworks, conscious or commonsensical, which John Berger (1972) called 'ways of seeing'. These usages show a creation and internalization of world views by social subjects and the nature of their agency. They are reminiscent of Antonio Gramsci's ideas of 'common sense' and 'hegemony'.[1] The present chapter focuses on Marxist-feminist uses of the notion of ideology, particularly with regard to social transformation and socialist politics and revolution. At the outset, we need a general introduction to ideology as a concept and must bring to the fore its epistemological dimensions. We will examine the method of its production and the content or the type of thought objects this process produces, as well as their socio-political effects.

The concept of ideology has a history prior to the advent of Marx and Marxism. Its different uses, however, consistently connected it from its inception to forms of consciousness pertaining to power and politics, combining in its conceptual import its social context and the development of its content. Any study of ideology explores the nature of certain ideas and beliefs and their organization into systems of meaning, thus creating a 'science' of ideas. The term 'ideology' was first used by Destutt de Tracey in eighteenth-century France (Williams 1977: 56) and implied a secular origin of ideas (a shift noted in the writings of Hegel and the Young Hegelians).[2] Ideology could be seen as a branch of philosophy, with a secular understanding born of the

'Enlightenment'. The notion of ideology achieved an important role during and after the French Revolution, serving as social enquiry, which enables consciously transformative politics. The view that ideas had social origins, could be studied, systematized and manipulated for social and political purposes, was indeed novel. This 'science of ideas' was developed at a time when monarchic and feudal forces and the absolutist role of the Church were being eroded. It was claimed that a system of socio-political ideas was itself a social force. It is in this context that Marx and Engels saw the importance of ideology and launched their critique.

Marx and ideology

Marx's critique of ideology, especially in *The German Ideology*, is one of the key components of historical materialism, his method of social inquiry and historiography. His understanding of the past as 'history', and not just as memorial narratives or a miscellany of events or facts, showing the connection between the writing and the making of history, relied on the critique of ideology. Marx's interest in this indicates that he placed the greatest importance on consciousness and its socio-historical and political role. This cardinal role he attributed to consciousness and epistemology, however, did not make him an idealist/cultural determinist, just as his emphasis on the economy did not render him an economic determinist. His understanding of different forms of consciousness is to be considered in relation to a material grounding of ideas in socio-historical processes. For Marx the production of ideas is as much 'real sensuous activity' (Marx and Engels 1970: 121) as any other form of labour.

Raymond Williams provides a summary of conventional views of Marx's understanding of ideology. In this context ideology is seen as: '1) a system of beliefs characteristic of a particular class or group; 2) a system of illusory beliefs – false ideas or false consciousness – which can be contrasted with true and scientific consciousness; 3) the general process of the production of meanings and ideas' (Williams 1977: 55; see also pp. 75–82). But as Williams points out, one needs to go beyond these simplifications to an in-depth account of Marx's critique of ideology. The point of departure for such an account lies in Marx's eleventh thesis on Feuerbach, which states that 'The philosophers have only *interpreted* the world in various ways; the point is to *change* it' (Marx and Engels 1976: 617, emphasis in original). Notably, Marx does not set up an antithesis between 'interpreting' and 'changing' the world; rather, we note the word 'only'. For him, interpretation must provide a knowledge which is capable of directing a social change that heralds socialist/communist revolution, thus enabling a conscious making of history. This requires a critical method for producing knowledge capable of accessing the real bases of history. Marx not only criticizes the 'ruling' ideas which oppress people, but discloses through his critique their very process or grammar of generation.

The pathway to a 'true' form of knowledge or an inquiry or a 'science' of society starts from the life activities of embodied, conscious socio-historical subjects as they produce and reproduce themselves. Any other starting point of social inquiry is ideological. Theory must therefore be rooted in the concrete reality of lives of people and their society, which they create through material forms of labour. As Marx puts it, consciousness or ideas cannot make history, but living, active people do – it is *their* history, their society and ideas, their life lived in determined time and space/place, which are the objects of social transformation. Even the stance of ideology which proclaims the 'independence' of ideas can only exist because the social and intellectual conditions implying a separation of mental and manual labour are present. In *The German Ideology*, Marx and Engels point out that production of ideology does not exhaust all the activities of consciousness. We must keep in mind *that while all ideology is a form of thought, not all forms of thought are ideological.* The production of ideology is thus a very specific form of mental activity towards a particular result.

Consciousness, according to Marx, has two main forms: practical and ideological, both subject to refinement and high specialization of labour. It is this highly specialized ramification which creates the appearance of disconnection and qualitative difference between mental and manual labour and the impression of autonomy and predominance of concepts/ideas over reality. Marx's critique of ideology is built on the axiom that human existence has never been un-conscious. From its inception, humanity is conscious. It is a 'practical consciousness' (Marx and Engels 1970: 51) which we continue to generate. Beginning with evolution of language through to the creation of concepts and categories, in creating relations to others for communication and skill transmission as well as in transforming nature, consciousness is involved as shaping and being shaped by people. It is only through this involvement that ontology becomes *social*. Human consciousness is thus both a physical and a mental capacity in an indivisible way. Marx debunks the attribution of an exalted *sui generis* nature to ideas and situates them in cumulative social-historical formations and products of consciousness.

The production of ideology requires experts in the technology of generation of ideas. These professionals are called 'philosophers' or 'metaphysicians' by Marx. They form an important part of the social organization and the legitimation of capitalist relations of accumulation and ruling. Intellectual specialization or 'disciplines' are the domains of these experts. A pervasive market begins to appear for ideas as commodities, and ideology is diffused in the upper and lower strata of society. Only then does it become possible to say that ideology or the ruling ideas of any age are those of its ruling class.[3] Belief in the autonomy of knowledge, in its transcendent or objective status, is itself an ideology which conceals the actuality of social organization and relations and the situated nature of knowledge. Marx offers a *social* ontology of epistemology. For him, 'consciousness is, therefore, from the very beginning a social product, and remains so as long as men exist at all' (Marx and Engels 1970: 51). Using the example of language, he categorizes most forms of consciousness as *practical consciousness*. Language, he says, is as old as human consciousness, and it 'exists also for other men, and for that reason alone, it really exists for me personally as well'. It is intrinsically social: 'as well language, like consciousness, only arises from the need, the necessity, of intercourse with other men' (ibid.: 51).

But the historical context of the creation of ideology and the social nature of its content notwithstanding, the question that confronts us is: how is ideology produced? What, according to Marx, is its epistemological grammar? In *The German Ideology* he presents us with the 'secret' of its production process, its syllogism. He speaks of 'three tricks' for producing ideology (ibid.: 65). It begins with an idea, a theory, or 'discourse', with the belief in the precedence and primacy of an idea over material/social conditions, in its transcendence from history. Marx shows that the first task for producing ideology is to separate ideas from their producers – that is, separate ideas from their social and individual origin. Thus 'ruling ideas' (ideas that are dominant in society) are separated from 'ruling individuals' (intellectuals who are bourgeois or at their service) who help to produce justifications for the 'ruling relations'. An epistemological act of decontextualization leading to extrapolation of ideas from their original situation evacuates their socio-historical content or concrete materiality. 'If now in considering the course of history we detach the ideas of the ruling class from the ruling class itself and attribute them an independent existence' (ibid.: 65), they become general propositions. Marx also says, 'if we confine ourselves to saying that these or those ideas were dominant at a given time, without bothering ourselves about the conditions of their production and the producers of these ideas, if we thus ignore the individuals and world conditions which are the source of the ideas' (ibid.: 65), we can do little except to produce ideology in the guise of knowledge. This process can be exemplified in notions such as 'honour' and 'loyalty' in feudal times and those such as 'freedom', 'equality' and 'individual' in capitalist times. In its fully separated state the process of production of ideas increasingly depends on dislocation, displacement and abstract formulation.

Once the evacuation of reality takes place, a substitute or 'mythical' connection has to be provided between these extrapolated bits of empirical reality. This second 'trick' of the production of ideology can be done by using metaphysical empty universalism or rational abstractions such as the ideas of 'essence', 'nature', 'human nature', 'homogeneity' and so on. The fabricated autonomy and human-like agency of ideas asserts that an 'age' or an 'epoch' is moulded by certain ideals rather than by people. This homogenizes diverse and contradictory ideas and activities into stereotypes and predictabilities. The paradigmatic uses of 'modernity' and 'tradition' are good examples, as are racist and sexist stereotypes. A homogeneity indicating ahistoricity erases the contradictory relations of an actual social formation and cultural complexities. Certain constellations of ideas are then posited as dominant ideas (for example, 'race') and offer pseudo-explanatory and descriptive services. Marx disarticulates this constellation of ideas or code into its components through historicization and socialization. In doing this, he refuses the ideological concepts their status as forms of determination *in* and *as* history.

The third 'trick' in Marx's formulation of the production of ideology occurs as the appearance of reality that ideological notions or usages convey occludes their origin in 'metaphysics', erasing an *overtly* idealistic appearance to make it seem *secular* – for example, the movement from God to 'Man' is more suited to 'modern' times (Feuerbach). There are other ideological sleights of hand, such as that of making a person out of a concept – for example, by personalizing many ideas into the *Idea* and making it the prime mover of history.[4] Common nouns or adjectives can be similarly treated, such as the ideas of 'whiteness' or 'blackness' as used in a racialized discourse. Thus concepts are treated as people with agencies, while actual people are seen as their mere bearers.

Feminism and ideology

Marx's critique of ideology should be an indispensable part of feminist analyses and political projects. Patriarchy and gender could then be treated as ideological categories in certain usages and as social categories which name particular types of social formations. The time-honoured equation of women with nature, the naturalization of gender and the sexual division of labour or the institution of the family provide examples of ideology. For that matter, the construction of a singular and fixed category called 'woman', which is extrapolated from actual women's historical and social relations, can itself be seen as an ideological practice. Marx's critique also helps to explode conventional binary paradigms encoded in notions such as masculine and feminine, which in this usage become reified and reifying conceptual devices only tenuously or contingently connected with biological differences. Likewise binary categories such as nature and culture or civilization, emotion or imagination and reason or rationality, the home and the private sphere and the world or the public sphere, should be treated as ideological formulations when they go beyond a descriptive function. These concepts and the spatializations they elaborate match a private property-based, patriarchal, ideological social organization scored with numerous ruling relations. When scrutinized through the historical materialist method, antithetical masculine–feminine categories reveal their imbrication in sexual and social division of labour as developed in history. The moral construction and regulation and economic and legal aspects of the state and society are frozen in these static categories. Marx's anti-ideological method challenges the conventional practice of attributing to men and women exclusive social ontologies and their 'natural' habitats.

We can see, therefore, that an effective and socially actionable understanding of patriarchy as a historically concrete social formation can be uncovered by anti-ideological historical materialism. This realization is essential if feminism is going to be a force for social change. The question why this insight is so frequently lacking calls for a scrutiny of the epistemological positions which underlie different types of feminist theorizations, the most dominant stream of which arises from liberal perspectives. Liberalism is not a reflexive and historically grounded epistemological position and can offer no account of social relations and ideas that inspire its own and other social thought. Liberal thought is empiricist and thus has no concept of an overall constitutive social whole. The integrity of the social is perceived by liberal thinkers as discrete issues or spheres which are to be aggregated for different purposes. Liberal approaches to social formation and transformation tie feminists who rely on them to conceptualizing social problems in terms of relational and intellectual dysfunctions, and thus to seeking only social reform. This treatment of gender or patriarchy creates a one-dimensional view of its hegemony and leaves the overall social organization and relations that form it invisible and unaddressed. It makes no distinction between the reality and the ideology of patriarchy and gender. 'Race' and 'class' are similarly understood, forcing us to rely on manipulation of concepts such as 'difference', 'intersectionality' or 'co-constitution' without accounting for their historical and social formation.[5]

The discomfort of trying to bring class, 'race' and gender together into a meaningful and formative relation with each other can be attributed to an ideological way of thinking which prevents us from seeing the social as a concrete formation.[6] This concreteness extends even to the most minuscule aspect of society. The different aspects of society are not static. They are simultaneously conscious, practical and evolving. They are what Marx calls sensuous practical human activity. The necessity of capturing formational moments involved in the production and reproduction of the social as a concrete consequence of different determinations forces us to name them and specify their categorical function. As I have written elsewhere in this context:

> The 'concrete' as the social, we can see has a dual character for Marx. It is, on the one hand, a mental or conceptual category and, on the other, an existing specific social formation. Thus, it is both 'a point of departure' (as the social) and 'a point of arrival' (as theory). Something that is 'concrete' is not like an 'object' that is

> visible, such as a table or a chair, but nonetheless its 'concreteness' is a determinate form of social existence. It is concretized by specific social relations with mediating and expressive as well as reproductive forms of consciousness and practices. In fact, this 'concrete' social form is to be seen in contrast to a fact or an 'object,' because it is not reified/fixed, hypostatized. It is fluid, dynamic, meaningful formation created by living subjects in actual lived time and space, yet with particular discernible features that both implicate it in other social formations and render it specific. (Bannerji 2011: 48–9)

These names for our present times and the global Northern context are 'class', 'gender' and 'race' – but these categorical names are not 'things' in themselves. They are congelations of historical social relations with conscious social subjects and agents securely in their formational centre. The ideological gesture has been to consider these names or categories as substantive 'things', as separate realities which then come into 'co-constitutive' or 'intersectional' relations. In this ideological practice, which asserts appearances or phenomenal forms as stable social ontologies, they substitute for the ever-forming concrete social realities. Reality then takes on a secondary life, as illustrative of this category 'things'. This is the inversion that Marx critiques throughout his opus, in one form or another. Anti-ideological critique reverses this ideological practice where ideas/categories are ideas or categories of a socio-historical, practical and intellectual formation. If we did not consider class, gender and 'race', for example, as determining realities, but as determined social formations, we could use them as names for certain formative relations.

Marxist-feminism generally uses his critique of ideology, especially the process of its production, rather cursorily, conventionally downgrading his interest in consciousness. This underuse of Marx's interest in consciousness results in ideology being treated as a neutral organization of ideas. Thus in common with non-Marxists, Marxist feminists also employ ideology as a synonym or a vehicle for political ideas.[7] The primary use of Marx's critical social analyses has been made by feminist political economy. There his analysis of the capitalist mode of production in its intricate complexity has provided a fertile ground for understanding the formation of capital, forms of social production, and the labour theory of value, among other things.

The feminist political economists have contributed to an expansion of Marx's method of analysis and pointed out his own ideological blinders through their critique of his gender unconsciousness and under-theorization of social reproduction. But feminist historical sociologists, while using the category of class for a nuanced understanding of gender and patriarchy, moral regulation and sexist stereotypes as patriarchal 'ruling ideas', have not paid much attention to how ideology is created, more how it is deployed. The most notable exception is in the sociological writings of feminist Marxist sociologist Dorothy E. Smith, for whom Marx's anti-ideological epistemology has played a crucial role. In her sociological methods of inquiry, consisting of 'social organization of knowledge' and 'institutional ethnography', Marx's critique of ideology has been pivotal.

Feminist critiques of mainstream epistemology have been generally produced by non-Marxist theorists, such as Catherine MacKinnon (1982), Sandra Harding, Lorrain Code and Nancy Fraser, among others. They have addressed women's lives, experiences and the marginalization of their knowledges, as well as their invisibility created through patriarchal omissions and commissions. But not even the anti-capitalist materialist Marxists, including Maria Mies or Sylvia Federici, have paid the notion of ideology any sustained attention as being important for theorizing. Of the two, Mies, who is more explicitly a Marxist thinker and engaged with patriarchal capitalist accumulation on a global scale, has productively drawn upon Marx's concept of social division of labour and the devaluation of women's labour. She emphasized the importance of ideological forms of consciousness in producing and reproducing women's subordination. Her critique of the conventional women–nature equation is a version of an anti-ideological critique from a materialist viewpoint, as she offers an in-depth disclosure of patriarchy's relationship to property relations, extending to women being social property. Mies' feminist critique of 'development' operates at the levels of both political economy and critical epistemology.

Smith considers prevailing patriarchal ideas as 'ruling ideas' which mediate and textualize the ruling relations of capitalism. Her specific use of Marx's epistemological critique of ideology is pioneering not only for women's studies but for sociology as a field of social inquiry. Through the application of Marx's method, Smith discovers the 'social organization' of knowledge and the constitutive role of ideological knowledge in developing bourgeois institutions or ruling apparatuses. Her critical sociology, including her innovation of 'institutional ethnography', allows for an anti-racist feminist extension for both Marxist and feminist thinking. The wide scope of Smith's contribution in critical sociology extends from her initial stage of writing a 'sociology for women' (1987) to one for 'people' (2005).

Confining the challenge of patriarchal ideology to the realm of consciousness alone, the linguistic or discursive approach to social relations endangers the very project of feminism. It itself becomes an ideological venture and attributes to consciousness the power of self- and social reproduction. Concrete realities of daily lives, experiences, activities and social interrelations are thus linguistically/discursively overdetermined. Articulated discursively, the project of feminism mainly becomes a pedagogic one of trying to change consciousness without changing the world. Feminist politics framed within this schema begins and ends with antithetical discursivities recommending 'educational' empowerment for women, especially through the education of 'rights'.[8] This is the understanding of patriarchy from which national and international women's non-governmental organizations (NGOs) and advocacy-based social movements are predominantly organized. The agenda of the 'development' agencies for women is concerned with the 'issues' rather than the social organization that gives rise to them. Thus, feminism is incorporated in patriarchal corporate agencies and managerial bureaucracies of the state, which create a class of women experts who hold power over other women. In their role as technical/administrative policy-makers or service providers they help build the ruling apparatuses that oppress the very women they want to 'empower'. In this way, even unintentionally, feminists can become ideologues for patriarchal capitalism's reproduction and for constructing an ideological feminism for its legitimation. Such a feminism is a competing ideology within patriarchal social relations and consciousness. Feminist political struggles are reduced to struggles between two sets of antithetical ideologies.

Ideology, feminist theory and women's standpoint

If liberal feminism with its emphasis on the socially and materially ungrounded primacy of consciousness is a subjectivist reductionism, its opposite, a dominantly structuralist viewpoint, is an objectivist materialism. It would be absurd to argue that any form of knowing is unconnected to either the knower's experiences and activities, her location and participation in society or her subjective apprehension of them. The idea of a humanly uncreated social or economic 'structure', a system with its own 'laws' which affect people foundationally, is patently fabulous, as is the notion of an absolute subjectivism which can create the world as it pleases. Experience, social location, relations and history serve as the standpoint of knowledge for a materialist understanding of the world. Thus, the ideology of an objectivist knowledge created from the 'outside' has to be counterposed by knowledge produced from the 'inside' by social insiders. This ushers in the question of the standpoint of knowledge being treated differently by different schools of feminist thought. Investigating the issue of 'standpoint' of knowledge prompts us to compare non-Marxist and Marxist-feminist approaches. Non-Marxist women's standpoint theorists emphasize the direct nature of knowledge which arises from women's experience, thus removing the role played by epistemological mediation. It assumes a single axis of standpoint produced by lived patriarchy as the overall social determinant. This location of the woman subject is claimed as the clearest vantage point for knowing social reality. The woman subject seen as situated at the greatest distance from the 'centre' of power thus becomes the ideal knower. This version of standpoint theory puts us in a quandary because it posits an unmediated existential experience as being both the problem to be understood as well as the endpoint for the search for truth. If we challenge this presupposition of an unmediated truth born of direct experience, then within this schema we are left with multiple and relative competing truths. Such an epistemological position cannot provide a solid ground for any project of social transformation. The different locations and relations of women across society with their different experiences do not add up to an overall character of social organization.

The feminist Marxist version of standpoint theory, however, can be the best epistemological choice because it takes into account not only direct, non-mediated experiences but also social relations and forms of mediation that enter into the process of knowledge production. Dorothy E. Smith's *A Feminist Sociology* (Smith 1987) provides us with this position. Using Marx's anti-ideological/materialist method of beginning our social inquiry from the everyday lives and experiences of women (people), Smith accords a crucial role to women's experiences in the creation of a transformative knowledge. But these experiences are not left as 'individual' but are socialized instead, thus integrating finite forms of social organization and relations with their diversities and contradictions as components of an individual's experience. Smith clarifies how specificity of women's experiences arises as she shows that they inhabit a social organization of which patriarchy is a vital organizing component. It is this complex and contradictory social organization which accounts for actual and ideological unevennesses and ruptures that women experience. Women's feeling of being at odds with what is around them comes from the social relations and ideas which are both implicated in and at odds with each other. This practical consciousness of contradiction between what women live and what they are told creates what Smith calls a 'fissure' integral to women's (people's) consciousness. This 'fissure' or 'the line of fault' (ibid.) is markedly evident among all social groups who are oppressed and marginalized, but in others as well. There is a daily experience of a double message between actual social relations, practical consciousness and ideology. The situation is further complicated by the fact that an 'outsider' of one group could be the 'insider' of others. The challenging question that arises in this context is what is ideological and what is actual in our lives? How can we grasp what conceals the ongoing organizational relations and ideas and instead presents us with a seamless account of our lives? These questions do not arise in liberal standpoint theory but are indispensable to a Marxist anti-ideological feminism because the actual and concrete social relations are considered in this approach both contradictory and convergent.

Generally speaking, women and patriarchy and social and biological reproduction entered relatively late into Marxist theorization. Early socialists/communists considered patriarchy lower on the scale of the revolutionary agenda. Thus self- and social emancipation are by default seen as masculine prerogatives and, therefore, more fundamental to the revolutionary project. Here certain versions of Marxism evince an ideological occlusiveness because an ideological perception of production has disconnected it from reproduction. The naturalization of this division has continued to hide constitutive relations between production and reproduction, of different kinds of labour as well as public and private spaces. Though practically experienced as integrated, their integrity remained theoretically invisible. The social forms of class and class struggle were consequently set apart and even at variance in forging a revolutionary project based on a dynamic constitutive conception of the social. To think non-ideologically would be to note the pre-existing sexual and social division of labour bequeathed by patriarchy to capitalism. Capitalism with its respatialization of women and reproduction to 'private' life, redefining labour as wage labour, became common sense, an internalization of ideology in daily life. Yet a reflexive and critical reading of Marx also provided the basis for focusing on patriarchy as a major social problematic. The self-reflexivity of his method and his search beyond bourgeois conceptual axioms offered the possibility of fresh epistemological critiques and analyses. Social analysis grounded in comprehensive notions such as the mode of production, social formation and their accompanying forms of consciousness all provided a historical materialist understanding. It was evident that patriarchy could not be understood on its own without being placed within the social formation as a whole, nor could social practices or ideas and norms be conceived without socio-sexual division of labour, enabling 'gender' with masculine and feminine imperatives. Feminist political economy disclosed how patriarchal sexual division of labour is indispensable in the realization of surplus value.

It is important to note that feminist political economy holds a tension in trying to reconcile the structural imperatives of political economy with the subjective and agentic dimensions of the concept of the 'woman' found in feminist theorization. It is this tension which was expressed by Heidi Hartmann in her formulation of the problem as an 'unhappy marriage' of feminism and Marxism (1981). As I have noted elsewhere: 'If we assess Marxist/socialist feminism in terms of agency or representation, we find little interest in either. We are clearly pitted in the midst of an unresolved relationship between two social projects premised on different grounds' (Bannerji 1995: 75). Until recently, Marxist-feminist uses of class analysis have been economistic, structure based, with an assumption of a male working class. But in their feminist incarnation, Marxist feminists have had to rely on women's experiences and responses, where their subjectivities and agencies provide the central theoretical focus. Much of the influence in the area of non-subjectivism and displacement and introjection of ideology into the social structures comes from the work of Louis Althusser.[9] The point is to go beyond the binary formulation of structure and subjectivity, which cannot be done 'through either a subsumption of feminism in Marxism or through arithmetic exercise which constructs a social whole by adding together qualitatively different epistemological stances' (Bannerji 1995: 79). To get over this binary formulation, we need to have a theory of consciousness in which experience is grounded in concrete forms of social being and knowing. Experience or the subjective moment arising in daily lives of people must be our point of entry, but not the endpoint. We must extend our understanding of an individual's experience, intention and location on to social and historical levels. Then it will become evident that the local and immediate experiences are specific forms of a general larger social organization and relations. It is by reading my experience in these historical, social terms that the standpoint of my knowledge would allow for deeper social understanding. The objective and subjective moments will come together through a progressive revelation of how the larger social organization and forms of consciousness contain and shape our lives. Our experiences in the local can become truly comprehensible within that framework. We would go beyond self-referentiality and connect with others in time and space.

It should be obvious how feminists and Marxists could both benefit enormously from using Marx's own version of critique of ideology, as it is possible to deploy categories such as 'woman' or 'class' in critical, expository or in ideological and occlusive ways. Eschewing ideology, we could step out of the various false perceptions of 'women' and socialize the 'woman question'. Marx's critique of ideology could offer the richest method for apprehending the social. We could see how the social, reduced to the market economy, disconnected the economic aspect of society from all others. Extrapolating ideas from their social contexts and content is the essence of ideology. Substituting a part of the social for the whole, or an ahistorical whole which denies specificity of the constitutive parts, are both ideological enterprises. Formulation of the social whole in terms of the base (the 'economic' infrastructure) and the superstructure (the sociocultural forms), or a 'corresponding' or 'reflective' relation between society and culture, all arise from such an epistemology. The hierarchic ranking of class and gender cannot capture the nature of social formation. The answer to this dualist problem does not lie in appending the 'woman question' to the 'class question'. An ideological view of society which breaks the social into fragments without constitutive relations, or homogenizes or essentializes social reality, makes both social analysis and revolutionary social transformation inconceivable. It is interesting to note how non-Marxist feminists and economistic Marxists both suffer from this dualist ideological approach.

The process of development of ideology lies in the division of mental and manual labour at its most developed. The thought products – the intellectual objects that mental labour produces – enter as 'things' into relations with each other. They achieve a status similar to commodities in their circulation. They also have their dead labour and living labour dimensions and create an ever-growing edifice of self-serving conceptual products. As such, it is no surprise, especially in their alienated and intellectual forms, that thoughts become reified realities. Keeping this in mind might lead us to use categories in an investigative manner, exploring the concrete nature of social formations.

This is of course a very difficult thing to do. As Marx puts it in the 'Afterword' to the second German edition of the first volume of *Capital*, the mode of presentation has the danger of obscuring the mode of production.[10] The category or concept 'capital' is thus in need of analysis so that its formational complexities correct the ideological vision of seeing capital as a 'thing' rather than a particular social relation and concomitant formation. The same can be said of 'commodity', 'money', 'wage-labour' and so on.[11] If concepts are not 'things' or ground-level realities, they are ways of talking about something. It is this 'something' that we need to address in discussing a raced, patriarchal class formation. Critique of ideology also needs ideas, but these ideas send us out of the category into a lived, socio-historical world. They must point outward rather than deeper into themselves – they are, after all, names burdened with the content of reality.

Notes

1 See throughout Gramsci (1971).

2 See Arthur's introduction to Marx and Engels (1970).

3 Marx and Engels write: 'The ideas of the ruling class are in every epoch the ruling ideas, i.e. the class which is the ruling *material* force of society, is at the same time its ruling *intellectual* force. The class which has the means of material production at its disposal, has control at the same time over the means of mental production, so that thereby, generally speaking, the ideas of those who lack the means of mental production are subject to it. The ruling ideas are nothing more than the ideal expression of the dominant material relationships, the dominant material

relationships grasped as ideas; hence of the relationships which make the one class the ruling one, therefore, the ideas of its dominance' (Marx and Engels 1970: 64, emphasis in original).

4 See Marx and Engels: 'Once the ruling ideas have been separated from the ruling individuals and, above all, from the relationships which result from a given stage of the mode of production, and in this way the conclusion has been reached that history is always under the sway of ideas, it is very easy to abstract from these various ideas '*the* idea,' the notion, etc. as the dominant force in history, and thus to understand all these separate ideas and concepts as 'forms of self-determination' on the part of *the* concept developing in history. It follows then, naturally, that all the relationships of men can be derived from the concept of man, man as conceived, the essence of man, *Man*' (Marx and Engels 1970: 66–7, emphases in original).

5 In this context, see Abigail Bakan (2008) for an interesting way of conceptualizing the social as a 'dialectical totality' relying on reconceptualizing 'the politics of difference', with the claim that major forms of difference are categorized 'by human suffering identified in [Marx's] work' (ibid.: 239). The main forms of human suffering are exploitation, alienation and oppression. 'Race', gender and class are seen as 'categories' of difference. However, it is important to note that from our point of view Bakan does not move the critique of ideology any farther than connecting the notion of difference with that of categories.

6 Marx says in the *Grundrisse*: 'The concrete is concrete because it is the concentration of many determinations, hence the unity of the diverse. It appears in the process of thinking, therefore, as a process of concentration, as a result, not as a point of departure, even though it is the point of departure in reality, and hence also the point of departure for observation (*Anschauung*) and conception' (1993: 101).

7 See Michèle Barrett (1988), for example. For Barrett, the interest is in ideology as content, a body of connected ideas, discourses and stereotypes. As summarized in a piece on the blog Survivingbaenglish, 'Barrett develops a detailed account of what she identified as the four key mechanisms by which textual representation reproduced ideology: stereotyping; compensation by the discourse of the supposed moral value of femininity; collusion i.e. manipulation of consent; and recuperation – the negation of challenges to the dominant gender ideology' (Survivingbaenglish 2014). While all these mechanisms are valuable points of inquiry for reproduction of patriarchy as ideological content, no use is made by Barrett of ideology's process of production, which Marx considers so important.

8 Catherine MacKinnon, who has read Marx and understood some aspects of materialist critique, provides us with the most interesting version of the liberal feminist account of difference between Marxism and feminism (MacKinnon 1982). An interesting but deeply dualistic reading of both Marxism and feminism, this essay illustrates both the useful and the misleading sides of liberal feminist thinking. 'As Marxist method is dialectical materialism, feminist method is consciousness raising ...' (ibid.: 543). It sees feminism as an essence of collective subjectivity of women, while Marxism 'refers to a reality outside thought which it considers to have been an objective – that is, truly non-socially perspectival – content' (ibid.: 543). It is this version of Marxism and feminism which I critique in this essay.

9 See Althusser (1971). On close examination Althusser's understanding of ideology and Marx's are not the

same. Whereas for Marx ideology is only one aspect of forms of consciousness, Althusser's concept of ideology occupies the entire mental space, thus making it impossible to develop a qualitatively different set of critiques and concepts that lead to socialist/communist revolution.

10 To put it in Marx's words: 'Of course the method of presentation must differ in form from that of inquiry. The latter has to appropriate the material in detail, to analyse its different forms of development, to trace out their inner connexion. Only after this work is done, can the actual movement be adequately described. If this is done successfully, if the life of the subject-matter is ideally reflected as in a mirror, then it may appear as if we had before us a mere a priori construction' (Marx 1971: 28; see also pp. 26–9).

11 To understand this process of reification of ideas and their circulation through mutual exchanges, it is useful to read Section 4, Chapter 1 of the first volume of *Capital*, 'The fetishism of commodities and the secret thereof'. In the production of ideology, as in the production of commodities, 'the social character of men's labour appears to them as an objective character stamped upon the product of that labour; because the relation of the producers to the sum total of their own labour is presented to them as a social labour, existing not between themselves but between the products of their labour' (Marx 1971: 77). This could be said of ideology as well, as there is an independent relationship conceived between the reified ideas.

References

Althusser, L. (1971) 'Ideology and ideological state apparatus (notes towards an investigation)', in *Lenin and Philosophy and Other Essays*, trans. B. Brewster, New York: Monthly Review Press, pp. 127–86.

Bakan, A. B. (2008) 'Marxism and antiracism: rethinking the politics of difference', *Rethinking Marxism*, 20(2): 238–56.

Bannerji, H. (1995) *Thinking Through: Essays on Feminism, Marxism and Anti-Racism*, Toronto: Women's Press.

— (2011) 'Building from Marx: reflections on "race," gender and class', in S. Carpenter and S. Mojab (eds), *Educating from Marx: Race, Gender and Learning*, New York: Palgrave Macmillan, pp. 41–60.

Barrett, M. (1988) 'Ideology and the cultural production of gender', in *Women's Oppression Today: The Marxist Feminist Encounter*, New York: Methuen, pp. 65–85.

Berger, J. (1972) *Ways of Seeing*, London: BBC.

Gramsci, A. (1971) *Selections from the Prison Notebooks*, ed. Q. Hoare and G. Smith, New York: International.

Hartmann, H. (1981) 'The unhappy marriage of Marxism and feminism: towards a more progressive union', in L. Sargent (ed.), *Women and Revolution*, Montreal: Black Rose, pp. 313–38.

MacKinnon, C. (1982) 'Feminism, Marxism, method, and the state: an agenda for theory', *Signs: Journal of Women in Culture and Society*, 7(3): 516–44.

Marx, K. (1971) *Capital*, vol. 1, Moscow: Progress.

— (1993) *Grundrisse*, Harmondsworth: Penguin.

Marx, K. and F. Engels (1970) *The German Ideology*, ed. C. J. Arthur, New York: International.

— (1976) 'Theses on Feuerbach', in K. Marx and F. Engels, *The German Ideology*, Moscow: Progress, pp. 615–17.

Smith, D. E. (1987) *The Everyday World as Problematic: A Feminist Sociology*, Toronto: University of Toronto Press.

— (1990) *Conceptual Practices of Power:*

A Feminist Sociology of Knowledge, Toronto: University of Toronto Press.

— (2005) *Institutional Ethnography: A Sociology for People*, New York: Rowman and Littlefield.

Survivingbaenglish (2014) 'Michele Barret [sic]: ideology and the cultural production of gender', Blog, survivingbaenglish.wordpress.com/michele-barret-ideology-and-the-cultural-production-of-gender/.

Williams, R. (1977) *Marxism and Literature*, Oxford: Oxford University Press.

8 | IMPERIALISM AND PRIMITIVE ACCUMULATION

Judith Whitehead

In the past fifteen years, Marxist and Marxist-feminist scholars have given increased attention to the process of primitive accumulation (De Angelis 2001; Perelman 2000; Harvey 2003, 2005; Hartsock 2006; Federici 2004, 2012; Glassman 2006; P. Patnaik 2005, 2008, 2012; U. Patnaik 2008). A number of scholars have recognized that neoliberalism, the dominant global economic and social policy of the past thirty years, has fuelled new rounds of privatization of common resources. This process is especially marked in peripheral and sub-imperial regions of the world economy, but it has reappeared to some extent in formerly core regions as well (Glassman 2006). In addition, core regions have experienced a widespread assault on the social wage, including a reduction and dismantling of pensions, benefits and unemployment insurance, day care provisioning, education and health systems, and so on (Harvey 2005). Both the privatization of common resources and the assault on the social wage have highlighted that dispossession is not simply a historical artefact of the transition from feudalism to capitalism. Rather, it recurs throughout the history of capitalism as a means of overcoming contradictions – for example, where capital faces a declining rate of profit, or where working-class and feminist organizations were historically strong enough to compel the state and capital to share some of the costs of social reproduction. Both conditions were notably present in Atlantic Fordism during the 1970s and 1980s: globalized neoliberal capitalism, with its assault on both the social wage and remaining global commons, is viewed by many analysts as a response to that crisis of profitability. David Harvey (2003), for example, views neoliberalism as representing the restoration of class power under conditions of an accumulation crisis.

This chapter will review the major contributions to the revived debates on dispossession and primitive accumulation. My review is a critical reflection on current literature with a particular goal in mind: to show how primitive accumulation is shaped by, and shapes, contemporary gender, race and class relations. To do so requires a rapprochement not only with contemporary Marxist and Marxist-feminist analyses of primitive accumulation, but also with contemporary literature on imperialism. This is because imperialism is the force that first created the racialized and ethnicized world division of labour through military/mercantile colonialism. It also continues to influence both patriarchy and class relations today.

My interest in primitive accumulation was stimulated by two research projects in India during the past decade. The first focused on the dispossession of mainly subsistence-oriented Adivasi (or aboriginal) populations from a major dam in western India (Whitehead 2010), and the second dealt with how processes of gentrification in Mumbai are displacing former textile workers and their families from their sites of informal habitation (Whitehead and More 2007; Whitehead 2014). Both involved the dispossession of groups of people in an important emerging economy. Both populations were marked by multiple forms of difference – including gender, 'tribal' and caste distinctions. Hence, analysing their dispossession required an intersectional understanding of gender, class and ethnicization/racialization.

Contemporary rethinking of dispossession

Most recent analytical work on dispossession and primitive accumulation challenges the orthodox historical stage-interpretation of Soviet Marxism that viewed primitive accumulation as a temporary phase enabling capitalism to emerge from the confines of feudal land tenures and subsistence provisioning. The orthodox interpretation held that all societies passed through four stages (primitive communism, feudalism, capitalism and socialism), with primitive accumulation being the historical springboard for the emergence of capitalism in general. Most contemporary writers, however, believe that primitive accumulation is a continuous feature of capitalism, and constitutes a logical rather than a historical precondition for capitalist relations to be reproduced (De Angelis 2001; Harvey 2003; Patnaik 2005). As De Angelis notes, Marx defined primitive accumulation as the process by which producers were separated from the means of production. This process created on the one side a class of people who had only their labour-power to sell, and on the other side a class who owned the means of production and could purchase labour-power through the wage contract. Once the separation of the majority from their means of subsistence was established, the compulsions of economic necessity drove the dispossessed to seek wage work. The 'classic' example Marx gave of this process was the enclosure of tenant farmers' land and the privatization of common land in England during the period 1500–1800. This process of commodification, enclosure and privatization involved widespread dispossession of rural producers. In addition, Marx referred to the Atlantic slave trade and the looting of gold and silver mines in the Americas as examples of primitive accumulation. He also mentioned the use of taxation policy and credit as levers of dispossession in colonies during the period 1700–1900, with colonial India being an important example. Marx's extension of the term to these essentially mercantile and military processes was perhaps due to the fact that both the Atlantic slave trade and the increased circulation of bullion and specie in Europe from colonies were major conduits for the accumulation of capital in England. Indeed, as Williams has documented, overseas mercantile profits from the slave, sugar and rum trades virtually financed England's Industrial Revolution, transforming Liverpool and Bristol into major world commercial ports (Williams 1945).

De Angelis argues that primitive accumulation and its associated 'extra-economic compulsion' is potentially present in all capital/labour relations and is structured by the degree and level of class conflict, the degree of technical intensification of production, and so forth (De Angelis 2001: 8). For him, class struggle determines whether primitive accumulation presents itself as either the foreground or the background of capitalist strategies in differing geographies and historical periods. This point has been elaborated by Brass in his analysis of the rise of 'unfree labour' in contemporary capitalist agriculture in India and Latin America (Brass 1999). In addition, De Angelis argues that primitive accumulation should be understood as a logical a priori for capitalism to occur, rather than a temporal phase that was overcome once 'the ordinary economic compulsions of market fetishism' held sway (De Angelis 2001: 10). Since capital itself represents a logical expansion of the contradictory commodity form, so too do 'accumulation' and 'expanded reproduction' represent a logical expansion of the original separation between the owners of capital and owners of labour-power (ibid.: 13).

Accumulation by dispossession

David Harvey provides perhaps the best-known revision of Marxist thinking on primitive accumulation. He introduces the concept of 'accumulation by dispossession' to fuse both the assault on social wage and the privatization of the commons into a single universe of dispossession discourse. Harvey argues that the process of the expropriation of means of production is not only the starting point but also accompanies the capitalist accumulation process through time. Although haphazard and contingent, contemporary forms of accumulation by dispossession are the most dominant feature of neoliberal globalization. They include the dispossession of peasant populations in Asia, Africa and Latin America, the privatization and commodification of land and water, bioprospecting, structured asset depreciations, the privatization of nationalized industries, credit and stock manipulations, Ponzi schemes, the depletion of the global environmental commons, the privatization of community culture, knowledge and resources through intellectual property laws, the privatization of public assets, the rolling back of regulatory frameworks, the re-emergence of unfree labour, and the erosion of pensions and the social wage. They also include the transformation of the socialist economies such as those of the former USSR and China in a capitalist direction. Basically, accumulation by dispossession entails a process whereby the sectors of the economy or the factors of production which thus far have not been in the fold of the capitalist logic of profit-making are subjected to it. This process entails dispossessing the previous owners of these means of production. In Harvey's reading, these diverse processes of dispossession represent attempts by contemporary capital to overcome an over-accumulation crisis, and all represent a transfer of resources, wealth and rights from the global working and middle classes to a narrow capitalist elite (Harvey 2005: 145–50).

Harvey's theory of over-accumulation identifies lack of opportunities for profitable investment as the fundamental problem for capital. Thus non-capitalist sectors or territories need be opened up not only for trade but also to permit capital to invest in profitable ventures using cheaper labour power, raw materials, low-cost land, and the like. Finance capital becomes the driving force in this process, to the extent that even large and monopoly industrial firms have become financialized (Harvey 2003; Patnaik 2005). In a reprise, but also in a revision of Luxemburg's thesis that capitalism needs an outside to manage its value realization problems, Harvey expands the outside of capitalism to include not only pre-capitalist regions, but also non-capitalist sectors or domains within capitalist economies. Here, we can see that Harvey's emphasis on non-capitalist sectors within capitalist relations offers an avenue for a new discussion of the role of housework and the gender division of labour in contemporary globalized capitalism, typically seen as an 'outside' inside the heart of advanced capitalism.

Hartsock attempts to further Harvey's analysis of accumulation by dispossession by centring the global process of accumulation on gender divisions. Her starting point is that 'global accumulation is a new moment of primitive accumulation, and primitive accumulation is significantly marked by gender' (2006: 180). Hartsock draws largely from the Marxist-feminist literature on export processing zones (EPZs) during the early phase of globalization, particularly that of Mies (1986) and Ong (1987). During this early phase, especially in South-East Asia and Mexico, young women made up the predominant workforce. Generalizing from such studies, Hartsock notes that: 'women have become "models" for the more generally feminized virtual workers demanded by flexible accumulation, such that primitive accumulation becomes simultaneously a moment of the feminization of the labour force' (2006: 179). She also draws on Mies' discussion of the 'othering' of women, nature and the colonies to argue that women's lives are in some ways outside capital and therefore constitute a continuing site of primitive accumulation. Echoing Luxemburg, Hartsock argues that capitalism requires interchange with non-capitalist sectors, and both women and colonies provide an ongoing externality that exchanges with capitalism and thus solves problems of over-accumulation and underconsumption. The spatial shift of labour-intensive work to former colonies and the use of women's low-paid labour in export production suggests that non-Western women are the optimal labour force for global restructuring because they are primarily defined as housewives, thereby cheapening their labour-power and decreasing the overall political militancy of the working class (ibid.; see also Mies 1986). For Hartsock, the global generalization of flexible labour-power is based on an increasing convergence between the sexual and international divisions of labour, with (women) producers being located in the global South and consumers in the global North.

Critiques of accumulation by dispossession

Previous critiques of the concept of accumulation by dispossession have turned on the broadness of its scope and the fact that aspects of it relate to qualitatively different social and class processes. Brenner, for example, argues that the concept has inflated itself out of existence. He notes that mergers and acquisitions actually belong to the centralization of capital, while withdrawals of social security and pensions are processes normally included within the expanded reproduction of capital: neither necessarily involves the subjection of non-capitalist sectors to the logic of accumulation (Brenner 2004: 10). Both McNally (2009) and Glassman (2006) have noted that the most salient feature of primitive accumulation highlighted by Marx – that is, that the separation of producers from their means of production constructs new types of class relations – does not characterize many aspects of accumulation by dispossession as elaborated by Harvey. Fine (2004) has noted that while Harvey believes accumulation by dispossession is fundamental to contemporary accumulation by providing 'spatial fixes' to problems of accumulation, he has confused cause with effect. The lack of dynamism in productive sectors is due to the predominance of finance capital, not vice versa, and many of the processes that Harvey clubs together under accumulation by dispossession are a consequence of this lack of dynamism.

Similar criticisms on the grounds of overgeneralization can also be made of Hartsock's (2006) analysis. First, it is unusual to see employment either in export or domestic industries by women analysed as a form of primitive accumulation. Rather, employment acquisition has usually been defined by Marxists as either the formal or real subsumption of labour to capital under conditions of expanded reproduction, with the distinction between formal and real subsumption depending on the technical composition of capital. In other words, the process of primitive accumulation is seen as logically if not temporally prior to the formal or real subsumption of labour. Secondly, literature on the gender division of labour in export industries during the past twenty years notes an increasing uptake of male workers, so that the gender division of labour is now nearly equal in most export-oriented manufacturing sectors, at least in Asia (Ghosh 2009). Thirdly, there is a metaphorical equation in Hartsock's analysis between colonies and post-colonies, with both being seen as 'in some ways outside capital', enabling Hartsock to invoke Luxemburg's argument on the reliance of capitalism on non-capitalist sectors. Yet most analysts would not place China, South Korea, Taiwan, Indonesia, Turkey or India as somehow 'outside' capitalism even during the colonial period. Indeed, many neo-Marxist analyses unpacked their unequal incorporation as colonies into a global division of labour under the aegis of imperialism (Bagchi 1982, 2007; Lenin 1999; Patnaik 1972, 1997, 2010). In addition, new world economic histories have placed Asian economies at the centre of developing mercantile capitalism during the immediate pre-colonial period (Arrighi 2009; Frank 1998; Bagchi 2007). Fourthly, since only a tiny proportion of women in Asia, Africa and Latin America are actually employed in export industries or free trade zones, the generalization of these workers to the entirety of women's experiences in emerging economies erases the diverse ways that gender relations have been impacted by different forms of primitive accumulation. Hartsock bases much of her analysis of women's work in the new international division of labour on Mies' classic work *Patriarchy and Accumulation on a World Scale* (1986). There, Mies too tended to essentialize women's work in emerging economies as being located primarily in world-market factories or export processing zones. However, in most emerging economies only a small minority of women have found work in such factories, and none of the women I worked with in India had done so. There are varied but differential impacts of dispossession by gender in core and non-core capitalist regions. In order to address these differences, and to provide a more grounded reading of diverse interweavings of contemporary primitive accumulation with gender and race, it is necessary to review contemporary literature on the role of imperialism in shaping primitive accumulation and the international division of labour. In bringing contemporary theories of imperialism into alignment with the concept of accumulation by dispossession, I hope to show how the diverse processes included in the concept of accumulation by dispossession occlude significant differences in the way that women and men from different geopolitical and class locations experience dispossession.

Accumulation by dispossession, primitive accumulation and imperialism

A cursory glance at aspects of accumulation by dispossession linked to crises of expanded reproduction – for example, decline of the social wage, privatization of state services, mergers and acquisitions,

Ponzi schemes – and those linked to primitive accumulation proper, such as privatization of land, water, community intellectual property, bioprospecting and land grabbing, shows that these two processes are spatially differentiated. While some forms of primitive accumulation proper have sporadically emerged in agricultural sectors of the capitalist core (Glassman 2006), the majority of cases of primitive accumulation, including non-economic coercion, are occurring in former colonized regions. Conversely, forms of accumulation by dispossession associated with the sphere of expanded reproduction – reductions in the social wage, Ponzi schemes, privatizations of state sectors of production – are more marked in the older, core capitalist regions. Indeed, it was the experiential difference of my own forms of AbD (accumulation by dispossession) – the reduction in my pension pot between 2008 and 2011 – and those experienced by the people I had previously done research on – that is, South Asian Adivasis dispossessed of their land and water rights by large infrastructure projects – which led me to first question the broadness of the accumulation by dispossession concept. I think it safe to say that the most coercive, jaw-dropping aspects of AbD, usually associated with primitive accumulation, including land grabs and the dispossession of land, water, forest and other resources, are occurring largely in the agricultural sectors of tropical and semi-tropical regions of the world and are often, but not exclusively, centred on those populations previously termed 'indigenous'. For example, the World Commission on Dams noted in 2002 that two-thirds of all people displaced by dams since 1970 have consisted of populations deemed 'indigenous' by the UN definition of the term. Contemporary land grabs, in which large areas of land are sold to private developers or state actors, have predominantly occurred in agrarian regions of Africa, Latin America and parts of South-East Asia. Indigenous populations of North America, still living in a colonial relationship with settler states, are also experiencing primitive accumulation in the contemporary period, as treaty rights are overridden by transnational trade agreements or as governments appropriate land for military or infrastructural development.

Hence, while the concept of accumulation by dispossession broadens our understanding of the multiple ways in which both wealth and capital are being concentrated in the contemporary period, there are significant conceptual, social and legal differences in the range of processes that are occurring. One of the most important is the systemic difference between those affected by accumulation by dispossession in expanded reproduction, on the one hand, and primitive accumulation through enclosure and privatization of land, water and resources, on the other hand. The ongoing spatial divisions between these two forms of accumulation by dispossession indicate that imperialism still remains a force in the contemporary world, since primitive accumulation involving separation of producers from the means of production has been more intense and continuous in formerly peripheral countries and also in emerging regions, such as India, China and Brazil. In addition, peripheral and emerging regions continue to experience demand compression and deflation, such that their agricultural commodities are released to world markets (and contemporary capital) at a price below their value (Patnaik 2010).

Harvey generally sees imperialism involving attempts at defusing tensions in accumulation through spatial fixes, with the Iraq war being an example. He sees imperialism as evolving through a territorial logic, while capitalism evolves through an economic logic. This separation made in Harvey's thinking between economic and territorial imperatives precludes an understanding of the role that finance capital plays in contemporary forms of imperialism, although it was at the centre of classical debates between Lenin, Hilferding and Luxemburg. Indeed, some contemporary writers question whether or not imperialism exists at all in the current period. For example, Hardt and Negri (2000) have posited an overarching, nebulous empire that has no geographical or class location. However, since many of my research subjects still used the word, without having a fully developed theory of it, I felt obliged to search further, as well as to understand why dispossession was harsher in some social and geopolitical locations than in others.

Prabhat Patnaik, a South Asian economist, argues that finance capital and financialization have become the predominant fractions of capital in the past thirty years, as well as the driving force of neoliberal globalization. As in previous periods, finance capital is closely connected to imperialism. However, imperialism has changed its form since Lenin's time. Rather than imperialism consisting of the merging of finance and industry, finance capital today is not only predominant, but it is largely delinked from the needs of productive capital. It is also more footloose – that is, not tied to any particular location, although New York and London remain primary centres of operation. Rather, it has evolved into a separate, transnational class fraction that includes financiers from emerging regions as well. Patnaik understands contemporary imperialism as consisting in policy controls over national governments to suit the specific interests of finance, over and above national development goals or the security and welfare of populations. In such a form, the overall controls of finance imperialism over national governments have increased since the early twentieth century: if finance lacks 'confidence' in a particular country, then that country will face a liquidity crisis, so that pleasing finance, no matter how oppressive it is, is a precondition for economic survival (Patnaik 2010).

Patnaik sees imperialism as taking new forms, but as ultimately rooted in the money relation, the monetary system and the unequal interdependence of central and peripheral regions of the world. Unequal interdependence was instituted during the colonial period, which marked a specific phase of imperialism in which extra-economic coercion was used to institute a global division of labour between primary agricultural producers and manufacturing centres. Colonized regions also contained the largest labour reserves, which also provided, and continue to provide, stability to the overall global system. In other words, capitalism has always been accompanied by imperialism, with colonialism being just one phase of it – a coercive phase that was required to institute the unequal interdependence that then reproduced itself automatically (Patnaik 1997). The demand depression of rural producers, starkly illustrated in increased famines after the British East India Company (a mercantile, joint-stock monopoly trading venture) conquered Bengal in 1757, has largely continued today (Bagchi 2007). The continuity in demand depression through ongoing bouts of primitive accumulation in India's and Africa's countryside is a remarkably stable feature of the world history of capitalism. It can be explained by the reproduction of the relations of unequal interdependence established during the rise of capitalism, which is perhaps why Marx included these phenomena in his initial discussion of primitive accumulation.

Patnaik argues that, today as well as in the past, rural producers in ex-colonial regions remain important to the overall global stability of finance capital (Patnaik 2014). Owing to the large overhang of financialization through securitization and derivatives, which can be seen as new and complex forms of the money relation, the entire structure is unbalanced and vulnerable to various shocks (Bryan and Rafferty 2006). Hence, the values of certain primary commodities, such as oil, and also those originating in tropical and semi-tropical land masses, have to remain stable if the derivative monetary values of finance capital are to be secured. Since the tropical and sub-tropical land mass is constant, the commodities produced have a fixed character. Rather than their price increasing, as one could expect from a theory of comparative advantage, their prices have been either not risen, or have declined in the past thirty years. Because the value of certain primary commodities has to remain stable for finance capital to be secure, there has been an ongoing impetus to squeeze the absorption of domestic producers. Indeed, Patnaik (1997) shows that the existence of a mass of unorganized workers at the periphery has enabled capitalism at the centre to enjoy relative wage and price stability until recently. Policies of income deflation in peripheral regions, including a withdrawal of support for petty commodity producers and the former small and middle peasants, have unleashed new rounds of primitive accumulation: multinational retail chains displace petty traders; agribusiness squeezes petty commodity producers so that they have to sell their land; land-grabbing finance displaces small farmers; and petty producers are trapped by rising input prices and declining output prices (Patnaik 2010). In some cases, such as parts of South Asia, indebtedness has led to the phenomena of 'farmer suicides', showing that primitive accumulation sometimes includes the dispossession of life itself (Leech 2012). Patnaik's analysis explains, among other phenomena, the growing schism in India between the urban middle classes, which have largely benefited from neoliberal globalization and constitute the poster children for India's recent GDP growth, and the continuing poverty of the unorganized sector, particularly but not exclusively located in rural areas.

Patnaik's emphasis on the role of transnational finance capital as the coordinator of contemporary imperialism also helps explain another distinctive feature of primitive accumulation in India and in other ex-colonial tropical regions. In Marx's England, primitive accumulation resulted either in full-scale proletarianization or the emigration of 'surplus populations' to lands that had been 'cleared' of indigenous inhabitants. However, the recent rounds of primitive accumulation in rural areas in India, Africa and Latin America have resulted in an incomplete process of proletarianization. This is because the level and extent of industrialization in peripheral regions, despite their export orientation, have not been sufficient to absorb all those 'released' from agriculture (Sanyal 2007; Chatterjee 2008; Smith 2011; Whitehead 2013). Pauperization has occurred, but not full proletarianization, which many writers see as a blocked transition with many and diverse policy implications (Sanyal 2007; Smith 2011). The semi-proletarianized will therefore be a long-term feature of capitalist transition in many ex-colonial countries; and the management of their expectations will constitute a core feature of the political resolution of these ongoing contradictions. These political resolutions can take the form either of welfarist measures targeting the semi-proletarianized, or of authoritarian political projects based on majoritarian ethnic exclusivity (see Bannerji 2011).

Imperialism and sub-imperialism

Another set of writers have sought to explain the continuing spatial divisions between accumulation by dispossession and primitive accumulation, along with the rise of the BRICs (Brazil, Russia, India, China), through a theory of sub-imperialism. Mayo and Yeros (2011: 4) argue that by ignoring centre–periphery contradictions in the overall accumulation process, Harvey has failed to analyse the economic tendencies resulting from the dominance of finance imperialism. They further point out that his theory lacks attention to the historical dimension of colonialism that produced global spatial inequalities in the past four centuries – that is, to the development of underdevelopment and the creation of a world division of labour in which formerly colonized regions supplied cheap raw materials to Europe and North America (Amin 1977).

Mayo and Yeros (2011) have termed the endpoint of primitive accumulation in Africa, much of Asia and Latin America as semi-proletarianization, while others have referred to it as pauperization, the creation of a relative surplus population, or even deproletarianization (Brass 1999; Mayo and Yeros 2011; Bannerji 2011; Smith 2011). Neoliberal scholars speak of the burgeoning 'informal sector' in Asia, Africa and Latin America. In India, an important example of sub-imperialism where the informal sector comprises the vast majority of those employed, the predominant form of production in rural areas in the past two decades has been marginal agriculture, combined with micro-scale home businesses as a means of survival. Indeed, Sanyal (2007) has argued that the process of semi-proletarianization in India today means that the trajectory of capitalism in peripheral and sub-imperial regions will be markedly different from that taken in Europe. Various authors have debated whether the new semi-proletarianized constitute a reserve army of labour or a relative surplus population. However, all agree that primitive accumulation without full proletarianization is occurring in many regions. One of its consequences has been large-scale rural–urban migration, creating, in the process, a 'planet of slums' in the cities of peripheral and semi-imperial regions (Davis 2006).

Mayo and Yeros (2011) argue that the major emerging countries, the BRICs, share certain features with the peripheral countries, but also constitute what they term sub-imperial states. Sub-imperialism is based not on a national class pact, which implies a positive and independent relationship between productivity and wage growth, but rather on export production involving the super-exploitation of labour-power through demand compression, as Patnaik has previously noted (Marini 1965). Sub-imperialism is also characterized by regional economic dominance combined with an overall alignment with finance imperialism. The demand constraints of wage suppression in sub-imperial countries entail that export industries are their primary engine of growth and that capital export (spatial fixes) will be an important feature of future development. While it is too early to judge whether sub-imperialism heralds a multipolar world that might challenge imperialism, a modest realignment of imperialism's hierarchies, or the emergence of new core regions of accumulation, the concept does explain the harsher trajectories that primitive accumulation takes in what used to be termed peripheral and semi-peripheral regions of the world (see Wallerstein 1974). Super-exploitation of labour and demand compression in both sub-imperial and peripheral regions are translated into daily experiences of extra-economic coercion in the implementation of privatization drives, enclosure of the commons, the commodification of water, biopiracy, the clearing and 'redevelopment' of slums, the capitalization of agriculture, the forcible acquisition of agricultural land for industry, and other neoliberal nostrums. Meanwhile, in those regions that remain in the periphery, such as central Africa, primitive accumulation in the form of land

and resource grabs has sometimes assumed genocidal proportions in which both metropolitan finance and sub-imperial capital have been driving forces (Mayo and Yeros 2011).

Both Patnaik (2005) and Mayo and Yeros (2011) see finance capital as the driving force behind the subordination of national governments to finance-friendly policies. Wage compression and demand depression in sub-imperial and peripheral regions help to explain the harshness of dispossession in those regions. The difference between Patnaik and Mayo and Yeros is that the latter differentiates between emerging and still-peripheral regions. Through both Patnaik's and Mayo and Yeros' understanding of the underlying causes of spatial differentiation of accumulation by dispossession and primitive accumulation, it is possible to develop a more nuanced analysis of the role of gender in primitive accumulation on a global scale that does not erase the specificities of imperialism (and sub-imperialism) and its twinned ideologies of racialization/ethnicization. Indeed, it might be useful to name the process 'differential primitive accumulation' in order to capture its racialized and gendered character: land grabs, land dispossession, and even ethnocide often fall most severely on already marginalized populations outside the imperial core, as Leech (2012) has noted, while the reduction of the social wage is most prominent in the older, capitalist countries.

Federici, gender and differentiated primitive accumulation

An important contribution to understanding gender and differentiated primitive accumulation has been made by Sylvia Federici (2012). She, along with Fortunati (1995) and Mies (1986), had earlier analysed the expropriation of women's sexual and reproductive powers for the accumulation of labour power that suited capital's valorization requirements in Europe (Federici 2004). Federici had previously also analysed the witch-hunt terror in the sixteenth and seventeenth centuries as a means for the state to control demographic rates and the reproduction of labour in the European transition to capitalism. This she viewed as a specifically gendered form of primitive accumulation. She, like Mariarosa Dalla Costa (2004) and Maria Mies, started from the 'wages for housework' debate in Europe, with its analysis of how unpaid domestic work subsidized overall costs of reproduction of labour and thus increased the rate of exploitation for capital. This debate drew on the classical formulation by Engels of the changing relationship between the domestic and public realms – that is, on the connections between relations of production and reproduction due to the emergence of private property and the state. As Engels noted, the reproduction of the workforce, including its subsistence, education and healthcare, has both a biological and a social aspect. The social aspect of reproduction includes a patriarchal division of labour in which women are primarily concentrated in unpaid domestic work, while men worked in the public realm in which the wage contract defined the socially productive character of their work. The patriarchal, direct control of women's bodies, choices and lives that produced unpaid domestic work was directly analysed by Mies and Dalla Costa as a specifically gendered instance of primitive accumulation (Mies 1986; Dalla Costa 2004).

Federici (2012) has extended her analysis of gendered primitive accumulation in Europe to the contemporary international division of labour, taking unpaid subsistence and reproductive work as her focus. However, this time she situates her analysis on the role of women's unpaid work in Africa, where she lived and worked for several years. By using the subject position of women's unpaid work in a peripheral region as an a priori subject position, Federici has implicitly aligned herself with feminist standpoint theory and critical feminist race theory, often referred to as intersectional thinking (Hooks 2012; Bannerji 1995; Khosla 2005; and relevant chapters in this volume). The intersectional perspective argues for feminist analyses which begin from the starting point of the lives of women, which are shaped in multiple ways by gender, race and class, in order to show how women's lives are differentially shaped by all three sets of relations (Davis 1983; Bannerji 1995). Incidentally, Federici's analysis, like those of Bannerji and Davis, does not succumb to the linguistic essentialism that has characterized much critical feminist race theory of a deconstructive trend: her analysis is materialist, focusing on the changing and varied relations between productive and reproductive work. An intersectional perspective can suture forms of differentiated dispossession with the alignments of race and patriarchy without reducing one to the other. As Marx noted, the concrete is concrete because it is the condensation of multiple relations, and it is this multiplicity which intersectional feminism seeks to unravel.

Federici's reflections on the relation between unpaid subsistence-oriented work – whether domestic work, subsistence-oriented agriculture or caring work outside the home – and the international division of labour enables her to draw a number of startling connections (and critiques) that have, as yet, not been widely discussed in feminist analyses. For example, she draws a direct temporal link between the wages for housework campaign, capital's inability to subsidize domestic work in core regions in the 1970s, and the neoliberal assault on the social wage of the late seventies and early eighties. Her analysis helps to explain how cultural patriarchal forms and norms have reappeared in many regions of the world. Her focus on unpaid work also allows her to draw links between the destruction of subsistence agriculture in peripheral regions and the suppression of non-commodified production through structural adjustment programmes, thus leading to migratory movements to the global North. She also analyses the role of global remittances for domestic economies which primitive accumulation and migratory labour have set in motion. While at first movements of international migration from Africa involved mainly male migrants, with rural women's work combining both subsistence production and reproduction, they later involved wide-scale female migration in the 1990s. She also draws links between structural adjustment programmes and the restructuring of the global circuits of reproduction in the form of female migrants who take up commodified domestic work or poorly paid service work in affluent regions and countries.

Federici analyses the multiple connections that tie primitive accumulation and gender in peripheral regions to the global division of labour. She notes the connection between extra-economic forms of coercion embedded in the destruction of subsistence agriculture, the massification of the international sex trade, and the increasing prevalence of war and genocide in Africa in the 1980s and 1990s as a scramble for resources and land followed the introduction of neoliberal policies. She analyses the prevalence of extra-economic coercion in structural adjustment and austerity programmes as a means for finance capital to pry open non-commodified sectors for global accumulation:

> Endless wars, massacres, entire populations in flight from their lands and turned into refugees, famines: these are not only the consequences of a dramatic impoverishment that intensifies

> ethnic, political and religious conflicts ... They are the necessary complements of the privatization of land relations and the attempt to create a world in which nothing escapes the logic of profit ... (Federici 2012: 77)

Fedirici draws numerous connections between neoliberalism, gender and global accumulation that have been often ignored in feminist literature, although these are often rather sketchily mapped. She notes how structural adjustment and austerity programmes have adversely affected both productive and reproductive work in Africa, creating large sections of the population divorced from the means of production without alternative wage work. In other words, they are becoming part of the semi-proletarian or relative surplus population as discussed by Mayo and Yeros (2011), Sanyal (2007), Patnaik (2005), and Smith (2011). The implication for gender relations is that unpaid domestic and subsistence labour necessary for mere survival becomes intensified. She criticizes the role of global feminist NGOs in disciplining and containing feminist demands in Africa for livelihood and reproductive rights by diverting these demands into 'income-generating projects' that rely heavily on women's unpaid work. She discusses a further expression of centre–periphery linkages in the rise of 'global adoption factories' in which women from sub-imperial and peripheral regions produce babies primarily for export to childless women in wealthy regions, a new twist on the primitive accumulation of women's bodies and reproductive capacities. In addition, she discusses the increasing appropriation of young women's bodies from peripheral and sub-imperial regions in the burgeoning international sex trade, often under conditions of near-slavery. She also discusses the role of women workers in poorly paid jobs in export processing zones, but does not see this as the singular or major impact of neoliberal globalization on gender relations.

In addition to the connections she draws between finance-led neoliberalism, primitive accumulation and gender, Federici offers criticisms of feminist movements of Europe and North America, which have not reckoned with the changes the restructuring of the world economy has produced in the material conditions of women. She argues that this is largely because they have often settled for a reformist position that criticizes gender discrimination, but leaves the hegemony of capitalist relations intact. In withdrawing from anti-capitalist struggles and critiques, she argues that feminism has often been reduced to a vehicle for the rationalization of the contemporary global order. She concludes that neoliberal policies have created a system of global apartheid, transforming peripheral and sub-imperial regions into immense pools of cheap labour. For Federici, these regions play the same role with respect to metropolitan economies as the 'homelands' played in relation to the white areas in South Africa. She argues that a new feminism must emerge that recognizes the role of primitive accumulation for contemporary capitalism and especially the immense role that unpaid productive and reproductive labour plays in buttressing high rates of profit for global monopoly capital: 'If the destruction of our means of subsistence is indispensable for the survival of capitalist relations, this must be our terrain of struggle' (Federici 2012: 137).

Federici's work opens up new spaces for analysis and activism, drawing some new connections between the differentiated forms of primitive accumulation, the evolving contradictions between centre, sub-imperial and peripheral regions, and the diverse impacts of primitive accumulation on the spheres of both production and reproduction. Although some of her insights remain sketchy, she does provide a map to situate future work showing how both productive and reproductive labour are being reshaped in the global economy, so as to dramatically cheapen its overall costs for capital.

Federici's concluding section proposes a reclamation of 'the commons' and a commoning of the material means of production and reproduction as a solution for contemporary ecological, economic and social crises that are expressed most dramatically through increased rounds of primitive accumulation. As a 'materialist-feminist', she lays great stress on the means of reproduction as the basis from which the process of social production emerges. Her examples of the maintenance, defence and/or reclamation of 'the commons' include tontines (credit associations) in Africa, urban farming in America and Europe, and the defence of subsistence farming against neoliberal planning by women in west and central Africa. Also included are communities of care to meet the needs of elderly people in the United States, the women's association of the Landless Workers' Movement (MST) in Brazil, which insisted on a communal compound for organizing domestic work, and landless women's associations in both Paraguay and Bangladesh that have expanded women's subsistence agricultural activities in those countries.

While such examples illustrate local forms of resistance against the deepening of primitive accumulation, they do not provide a systematic or general form of resistance to it. Most of Federici's examples are locally based and relate to a single movement. Acknowledging that 'commoning the world may be as difficult as passing through the eye of a needle' (ibid.: 144), Federici does not examine the role that wider social movements could play in decommodifying sectors of reproduction such as childcare and elder care, land use, agricultural production, water provisioning and housework. Indeed, one of the most successful movements against primitive accumulation, the Landless Workers' Movement in Brazil, achieved its successes through resistance to and later engagement with a developmentalist state. In another well-known case, the movement against resistance to water privatization in Cochabamba, Bolivia, success was achieved when the movement widened its base to include rural cocoa farmers. It then became a nationwide protest against neoliberal privatization and primitive accumulation. Since forms of primitive accumulation are diverse and geographically separate (a water privatization scheme here, gentrification elsewhere, a dam or a land grab in still yet other locations), purely local forms of resistance run the risk of becoming isolated, marginalized and easily repressed (Whitehead 2013). National and international umbrella coalitions that link up the various sites of primitive accumulation showing how they are all aspects of the same process sutured through the commonality of dispossession might help overcome spatial and temporal separations through a common understanding of the relation of primitive accumulation to accumulation in general.

Conclusions

Work that draws out the connections between the new economy of semi-proletarianized productive and reproductive labour, on the one hand, and the ongoing dependence of capital upon such unpaid work, on the other hand, is an important future task for Marxist-feminist scholarship and activism. A recent volume of *Feminist Economics* examining the gendered aspects of large-scale land acquisition (or land grabs) provides an important contribution that unpacks the relations between different aspects of dispossession and gender, class and radicalized vulnerabilities (Doss et al. 2014). Intersectional theory can provide the framework that sutures an array of relations of domination to the process of global accumulation that, in turn, influences contemporary trajectories of primitive accumulation. As Brenner and Holmstrom note in their analysis of the anti-globalization movement: 'The theoretical challenge is to connect the notion of "intersectionality" to a Marxist feminist framework; the strategic challenge is to actually implement a political discourse and organizing practice that is not only intersectional but also moves toward a critique of capitalism and the necessity of an alternative' (Brenner and Holmstrom 2013: 283). Contemporary Marxist-feminism must turn against all forms of discrimination along with a rejection of the world that finance capital has made. Theories of imperialism can precisely help Marxist feminists to 'connect the notion of intersectionality to a Marxist-feminist framework' (ibid.: 285). It is only by simultaneously confronting capitalism, imperialism and patriarchy that the twinned problems of essentialism and reformism that have plagued previous feminist movements and scholarship can be overcome.

References

Amin, S. (1977) *Imperialism and Unequal Development*, New York: Monthly Review Press.

Arrighi, G. (2009) *Adam Smith in Beijing: Lineages of the Twenty-first Century*, London: Verso.

Bagchi, A. (1982) *The Political Economy of Underdevelopment*, Cambridge: Cambridge University Press.

— (2007) *Perilous Passage: Mankind and the Global Ascendancy of Capital*, London: Rowman and Littlefield.

Bannerji, H. (1995) *Thinking Through: Feminism, Marxism, Anti-racism*, Toronto: Women's Press.

— (2011) *Demography and Democracy*, Toronto: Canadian Scholars' Press.

Brass, T. (1999) *Towards a Comparative Political Economy of Unfree Labour: Case Studies and Debates*, London: Frank Cass.

Brenner, J. and N. Holmstrom (2013) 'Socialist-feminist strategy today', *Socialist Register*, 49: 266–87.

Brenner, R. (2004) 'What is and what is not imperialism?', *Historical Materialism*, 14(4): 3–67.

Bryan, D. and M. Rafferty (2006) *Capitalism with Derivatives*, New York: Palgrave Macmillan.

Chatterjee, P. (2008) 'Democracy and economic transformation in India', *Economic and Political Weekly*, 19 April, pp. 53–60.

Dalla Costa, M. (2004) 'Capitalism and reproduction', *The Commoner*, 8, Autumn/Winter, www.thecommoner.org.

Davis, A. (1983) *Women, Race and Class*, Toronto: Random House.

Davis, M. (2006) *Planet of Slums*, London: Verso.

De Angelis, M. (2001) 'Marx and primitive accumulation: the continuous character of capital's "enclosures"', *The Commoner*, 2, September, www.thecommoner.org.

Doss, C., G. Summerfield and D. Tsikata (2014) 'Land, gender, and food security', *Feminist Economics*, 20(1): 1–23.

Emmanuel, A. (1972) *Unequal Exchange: A Study of the Imperialism of Trade*, New York: Monthly Review Press.

Engels, F. (2004) *The Origin of the Family, Private Property and the State*, Chippendale, Australia: Resistance Books.

Federici, S. (2004) *Caliban and the Witch: Women, the Body and Primitive Accumulation*, New York: Autonomedia.

— (2012) *Revolution at Point Zero: Housework, Reproduction and Feminist Struggle*, Oakland, CA: PM.

Fine, B. (2004) 'Debating the "New Imperialism"', *Historical Materialism*, 14(4): 241–78.

Fortunati, L. (1995) *Arcane of Reproduction: Housework, Labour, Prostitution, and Capital*, New York: Autonomedia.

Frank, A. G. (1998) *Reorient: Global Economy in an Asian Age*, Berkeley and Los Angeles: University of California Press.

Ghosh, J. (2009) 'Informalization and women's work force participation: an examination of recent trends in Asia', in S. Razavi (ed.), *The Gendered Impacts of Liberalization: Towards 'Embedded Liberalism'?*, New York: Routledge, pp. 163–90.

Glassman, J. (2006) 'Primitive accumulation, accumulation by dispossession, accumulation by "extra-economic" means', *Progress in Human Geography*, 30(5): 608–25.

Harding, S. (1991) *Whose Science? Whose Knowledge? Thinking from Women's Lives*, Ithaca, NY: Cornell University Press.

Hardt, M. and A. Negri (2000) *Empire*, Boston, MA: Harvard University Press.

Hartsock, N. (2006) 'Globalization and primitive accumulation: the contribution of David Harvey's dialectical Marxism', in N. Castree and D. Gregory (eds), *David Harvey: A Critical Reader*, Oxford: Blackwell, pp. 167–90.

Harvey, D. (2003) *The New Imperialism*, Oxford: Oxford University Press.

— (2005) *A Brief History of Neoliberalism*, Oxford: Oxford University Press.

Hooks, B. (2012) *Writing beyond Race*, New York: Routledge.

Khosla, P. (2005) 'Privatization, segregation, and dispossession in Western, urban space: an anti-racist, Marxist-feminist reading of David Harvey', MA thesis, submitted to the Faculty of Environmental Studies, York University.

Leech, G. (2012) *Capitalism: A Structural Genocide*, London: Zed Books.

Lenin, V. I. (1999) *Imperialism, the Highest Stage of Capitalism*, Sydney: Resistance Books.

Marini, R. M. (1965) 'Brazilian subimperialism', *Monthly Review*, 23(9): 14–24.

Marx, K. (1967) *Capital*, vol. I, New York: International Publishers.

Mayo, S. and P. Yeros (2011) 'Rethinking the theory of primitive accumulation: imperialism and the new scramble for land and natural resources', Paper presented to the 2nd 'International Initiative for Promoting Political Economy' conference, Istanbul, 20–22 May.

McNally, D. (2009) *Global Slump: The Economics and Politics of Crisis and Resistance*, London: Merlin.

Mies, M. (1986) *Patriarchy and Accumulation on a World Scale: Women in the International Division of Labour*, London: Zed Books.

Ong, A. (1987) *Spirits of Resistance and Capitalist Discipline: Factor Women in Malaysia*, Binghampton: State University of New York Press.

Patnaik, P. (1972) 'On the political economy of development', *Economic and Political Weekly*, February, pp. 197–212.

— (1976) 'Lenin and imperialism: an introduction', in P. Patnaik (ed.),

Lenin and Imperialism: An Appraisal of Theories and Contemporary Reality, London: Sangam.
— (1997) *Accumulation and Stability under Capitalism*, Oxford: Clarendon Press.
— (2005) 'The accumulation process in the period of globalization', www.networkideas.org/feathm/may2008/ft28_Globalization.htm.
— (2008) *The Value of Money*, New Delhi: Tulika.
— (2010) 'Notes on contemporary imperialism', mrzine.monthlyreview.org/2010/patnaik201210.html.
— (2012) 'For the value of money', Contribution to a panel discussion, 'Is imperialism a useful concept in the age of financial globalization', reprinted in *Monthly Review*, mrzine.monthlyreview.org/2012/patnaik281212.html.
— (2014) 'For the value of money', mrzine.monthlyreview.org/2012/patnaik281212.html.
Patnaik, U. (2008) *The Long Transition*, New Delhi: Tulika.
Perelman, M. (2000) *The Invention of Capitalism: Classical Political Economy and the Secret History of Primitive Accumulation*, Durham, NC: Duke University Press.
Rodney, W. (1972) *How Europe Underdeveloped Africa*, Washington, DC: Howard University Press.
Sanyal, K. (2007) *Rethinking Capitalist Development: Primitive Accumulation, Governmentality and Post-colonial Capitalism*, New York: Routledge.
Smith, G. (2011) 'Selective hegemony and beyond, populations with "no productive function": a framework for enquiry', *Identities*, 18(1): 2–38.
Wallerstein, I. (1974) *The Modern World System*, New York: Academic.
Whitehead, J. (2010) *Development and Dispossession in the Narmada Valley*, New Delhi: Pearson.
— (2013) 'Accumulation through growth and accumulation by dispossession', in M. Ekers, G. Hart, A. Loftus and S. Kipfer (eds), *Gramsci: Space, Nature and Politics*, London: Routledge, pp. 279–300.
— (2014) 'Flexible work, flexible housing: the transformation of Mumbai into a global city and the fate of its working class', in S. Kashmir and G. Carbonella (eds), *The New Anthropology of Labour*, Oxford: Berghahn, pp. 123–66.
Whitehead, J. and N. More (2007) 'Revanchism in Mumbai? Political economy of rent gaps and urban restructuring in a global city', *Economic and Political Weekly*, 42(25): 2428–34.
Williams, E. (1945) *Capitalism and Slavery*, Chapel Hill: University of North Carolina Press.

9 | INTERSECTIONALITY

Delia D. Aguilar

The place of intersectionality as a key concept or principle in feminist studies is well established at this particular moment. Originally employed to refer to the trilogy of gender, race and class conceived as systems and, later, as a multiplicity of identities, the term has become a catchword, the easy utterance of which tends to presume a commonly shared, agreed-upon understanding. But this is far from the case. Almost twenty-five years after intersectionality was first articulated by critical race scholar Kimberlé Crenshaw, discussions and debates devoted to its exploration continue unabated at conferences and in journals, both in the United States and in Europe.[1] Much academic energy continues to be expended in its revision, elaboration or questioning, at the same time that attempts to pin down its precise meaning have proved unsuccessful. Its status remains unclear. Is it a theory? A heuristic device? A methodology?

In spite of its lack of coherence and the disparate uses to which it has been put, however, intersectionality has a few relatively invariant features that signal complicity with the conservatism of the historical period. This will be the subject of this chapter. To this end, it will trace the roots and evolution of intersectionality as a conceptual tool. It makes the assumption that only by recognizing the changing socio-political environment accompanying its development – alterations in its meaning, constituent properties and purpose or application – can its mutation in the hands of academic practitioners make sense. A further assumption is that, given intersectionality's centrality in the field of women's studies, taking into account shifts in the political climate will also serve to highlight feminism's trajectory and delineate the deradicalization that contemporary feminism itself has undergone since its inception in the late 1960s. Put more sharply, the reformulations of intersectionality by feminists today merely reflect the corporatization of the academy and its increasing subservience to a neoliberal global regime.

The women's liberation movement and 'triple jeopardy'

Although Crenshaw is credited with the introduction of the term 'intersectionality' in 1989, its conceptual roots can be traced back to the 'triple jeopardy' slogan launched by Third World activists when the women's liberation movement reached its apex. Historians of the era describe this moment in US history as unparalleled in its exuberance and optimism, when no institution was sacrosanct, everything was subject to interrogation, and the overthrow or at least radical overhaul of the system seemed possible.[2] Schooled in the civil rights and anti-Vietnam war movements, women's liberation activists drew ideas as well as inspiration from the socialist politics of the New Left and from then burgeoning national liberation and independence struggles in the Third World.[3] Information about covert intervention and outright military suppression of these struggles by the United States was widely disseminated among movement people. In particular, what feminists learned about US policies regarding Vietnam and later the invasion of Cambodia in Asia, along with overt and covert interventions in Central and Latin America, forced a collective questioning of the humanity of capitalism as a social system. It was in the larger context of capitalism, therefore, that the newly awakened awareness and ensuing anger over women's subordination was situated, leading to a rethinking of quotidian gender relations in public and private spheres.

In the euphoria of the discovery in consciousness-raising sessions that dissatisfaction with their lives rested not in themselves but in gender inequality, white middle-class women projected their own experiences of female oppression as universal. This presumption was promptly met with resistance by women on the margins who detected its tacit racism. Third World women (a designation used by women of colour to indicate the existence of an internal colony), taking their cue from Vietnamese women freedom fighters, asserted that their experience of subordination did not come solely from gender but consisted, instead, of 'triple jeopardy'. This referred to three systems of oppression: sexism, racism and capitalism or imperialism. Among the groups taking this stance was the Black Women's Alliance in New York City which later united with Puerto Rican women to set up the Third World Women's Alliance (TWWA) in 1970, an organization that became a major player in 1970s activism. The Alliance presented their views in a newsletter entitled *Triple Jeopardy*. Subtitled 'racism, imperialism, sexism' (in that order), it displayed a fist and rifle inscribed on a Venus symbol at its masthead (Women of Color Resource Center 2013). The newsletter covered a wide range of issues including welfare, the US class structure, struggles of women in China, Guinea Bissau, Chile, and so on.

The jeopardy motif was simultaneously pursued by others seeking to develop the concept along Marxist lines. The first was Beal, who wrote a 1969 paper expounding on double jeopardy (Beal 1970). She begins by indicting 'the system of capitalism ... and its afterbirth, racism' for the destruction of 'the humanity of all people, and particularly the humanity of Black people' (ibid.: 340). She situates black women at the very bottom of the social relations of production. Yet the brutalization of black men, she observes, distorts their thinking to the extent that they imagine black women contributing to their emasculation. Applauding the ascent of men in the black power movement, she exhorts women's participation in the struggle together with the entire black community. This would not only redress women's 'double jeopardy' but also engender the black revolutionary struggle.

Following Beal's polemic, 'A Black feminist statement', written in 1977 by the Combahee River Collective (with Barbara Smith as main author), stands as a major document in women's liberation history (Combahee River Collective 1981), enjoying broad circulation and discussion in women-of-colour groups as well as leftist women's liberation circles. Like Beal's period piece, it revamped radical feminists' declaration of 'the personal is political' by pressing for the inclusion of race and class. It moved the jeopardy theme forward by depicting the 'multiple oppressions' suffered by black women as both 'simultaneous and interlocking'. Members of the Collective described themselves as socialists who viewed 'the destruction of the political-economic systems of capitalism and imperialism as well as patriarchy' as necessary for 'the liberation of all peoples' (ibid.: 213). The Collective broke ground in many significant ways. The first to enunciate identity politics, it legitimized lesbianism while rejecting white-lesbian separatism, and called itself feminist when the term was a pejorative label with 'bourgeois' connotations.

Capitalist triumphalism

If these forerunners of intersectionality bore the unambiguous imprint of the 1960s and 1970s, when Marxism enjoyed purchase among activists and academicians alike, it was the repudiation of Marxism which stamped those that were to follow not too long afterward. The collapse of social movements and the onset of neoconservatism with the Reagan/Bush administration in 1980 swept away the once prevailing belief that a meaningful exposition of gender, race and class demands an understanding of the system's operations. Economic restructuring that resulted in deindustrialization, the disintegration of cities, suppression of unions, and cutbacks in public spending dampened the optimism that had once ignited huge sectors of the population, especially the youth, optimism that had them take to the streets in legions to clamour for change. In 1989 the Soviet Union would collapse, causing many progressives to lose hope in an alternative, more humane social order.

These events were not without impact on feminism. This impact is tangible in King's essay on 'multiple jeopardy' (King 1988). Gone were any references to capitalism as a system to be dismantled; missing too is any allusion to the anti-imperialism that was ubiquitous during the anti-war movement of the 1970s. But the most glaring symptom of accommodation to an increasingly conservative *zeitgeist* was a conceptual one, and that was King's assertion that Marxism is no more than one of those 'monistic' liberation ideologies to be carefully avoided. Monism, her axe to grind, is the tendency to privilege one category of oppression over another; for feminists it is gender, for people of colour it is race, and for Marxists it is class, labour or the economy. This projection of Marxism as a simplistic theory that collapses everything into class or 'the economy' was soon to become a commonplace, an unquestioned premise in academic and popular discussions. Suddenly race, gender and class (now meaning status) emerged as co-equal in impact and significance, their levelling a sign of their conceptual potency. The thrust of King's argument – and its failings – forecast that of others to follow, the subject of a later section.

Refusing their subsumption under the generic label 'women', King, Beal, the Combahee Collective and other women of colour called attention to the narrowness, insularity and parochialism of white feminism by counterposing the very different circumstances governing their own lives. In her essay, King addresses the spurious 'race–sex' comparison resorted to by white women by emphasizing the substantive differences between racial and gender experiences of oppression. Such an analogy, she rightly claims, results in the disappearance of black women, the predicament that Crenshaw's 'intersectionality' metaphor is to likewise address. King proposes the notion of multiple jeopardy to replace Beal's 'double jeopardy', which she regards as simplistic and additive in that it suggests that racism + sexism = black women's experience. She charges that Beal ignores class ('double jeopardy' referencing only gender and race), a mistake King makes because she fails to understand that the relations of production in capitalism, the context of Beal's argument, are the very ground on which class is formed. (King has now substituted the Weberian sociological concept of stratification – that is, status, income, lifestyle, and so forth – for class or production relations.)

King asserts that it is the multiplicative effect of multiple oppressions which can adequately capture the interactions of three interdependent 'control systems' – racism, sexism and 'classism' – so that black women do not get caught in the tensions between nationalist, feminist and class liberation politics. King believes that, formulated as an interactive model, multiple jeopardy will allow the relative weight of gender, race or class to surface, depending on the context and issue under investigation. To illustrate its efficacy, she gives the example of the sexual exploitation of black women in the slave system, to wit: black slave women shared the hard labour and physical punishment endured by slave men but suffered rape in addition; their reproductive labour abetted the slave economy; and as sexual slaves of white men, their experience differed from that of white women. It is not clear how Beal or the Combahee River Collective could not have arrived at the exact same account. What is clear is that they might have been able to explain that different modes of production (in this case, the slave system) give rise to different social relations. They would have understood enough of the logic of profit-making to refrain from the statement: 'The legacy of … slavery under capitalism is the fact that employers, and not black women, still profit the most from black women's labor' (King 1988: 50). Or they could have grasped enough about ideological hegemony to comprehend why members of oppressed groups may desire 'a piece of the American Dream, not its destruction' (ibid.: 68).

Intersectionality as a juridical intervention

It should be acknowledged right off that when Crenshaw wrote her landmark 1989 article, she had very specific practical applications in mind. She did not consider intersectionality as she devised it to be a theory, much less a totalizing theory, or even a methodology, and certainly had no inkling of the controversies it would provoke or the voyage across disciplines and continents it was to make.[4] She stated as much at a 2009 conference held in Frankfurt to celebrate intersectionality's twenty years of existence and to continue the discussion attendant upon the approach since its arrival on the academic scene (Crenshaw 2011: 221–33). In her response to the proceedings, where she baulks at attempts to evaluate or measure the effectiveness of intersectionality in the abstract, she lays out her own personal predilection: she is not so much inclined to making theory as she is to engaging in practical application.

It might be salutary to elucidate the kernel of the project Crenshaw applied herself to. On examining cases filed by black women, she found that the courts had the same blind spot dealing with their 'compounded identities' as ordinary people do. In *De Graffenreid* vs. *General Motors*, the court in 1977 ruled against five black women who alleged that GM's seniority system perpetuated the effects of past discrimination against black women. It was found that all black women hired after 1970 had lost their jobs on account of lack of seniority, and that while GM had not hired black women before the Civil Rights Act of 1964, it had, in fact, hired white women before that year. The court's judgment was that GM's seniority system could not have perpetuated sex discrimination since GM did hire women (just not black women) during the period in which no black woman was hired. With the sex discrimination case dismissed, the court recommended that the women's case be consolidated with another alleging race discrimination, also against GM. When the women claimed that their case was not one of either sex or race but sex *and* race, the court responded that nothing in the law indicated the goal of creating a new classification of 'black women'.

If nothing else, this court's judgment decisively disposed of the 'woman as black' analogy previously seized upon by white women to make their case as an oppressed group. The single-axis categories of race or gender, as this court decision illustrates, can only function to erase black women out of existence: where race discrimination is under consideration, sex- and class-privileged black men sally forth; with gender discrimination, it is race- and class-privileged white women. (Observe that, in both cases, class privilege is a given.) It is this quandary which inspired Crenshaw to devise the metaphor of intersectionality, picturing a literal crossroads in which the damage inflicted on a black woman can only be judged as a consequence of either gender or racial discrimination, but not both.

Having thus pinpointed black women's dilemma as based on their compounded identities, which the junction metaphor is meant to illustrate, Crenshaw faults both the feminist movement and civil rights communities for accepting the prevailing paradigm that upholds privilege. She rues the remarginalization that occurs when suppression of privilege produces the image of black women as the emblem of intersectionality. Viewing her work as the product of a collaborative enterprise in critical race theory, she sketches a narrative of its origins that owes much to the formation of a critical mass of African-American feminist legal scholars which the civil rights movement made possible. She observes that critical race theorists brook no illusions about the law as a discourse of domination, but nevertheless see it as a site for contestation. This being the case, it is curious that those whose innovations built upon Crenshaw's seem oblivious of the legal and thus necessarily circumscribed parameters within which the concept was articulated, with some imagining a transformative potential far beyond its reach.

Lutz, Herrera Vivar and Supik observe how it was Crenshaw's intersectionality which captured the attention of scholars when several formulations designed for similar aims did not (Lutz et al. 2011a: 4). After all, Crenshaw's was a juridical intervention limited in its goal by its very nature. For example, she excludes class because class is not actionable – there is no redress for it within the court system or, for that matter, within capitalism. But perhaps this is precisely its appeal. It is more easily adapted and built upon than King's 'multiple jeopardies' or Hill Collins' 'interlocking systems of oppression', both of which speak distinctly of embeddedness in the African-American community and its marked stigmatization (Hill Collins 1991).[5]

Marxist-feminist critique

Davis declares that 'intersectionality offers a new *raison d'être* for doing feminist theory and analysis' (Davis 2008: 72). It might not be far fetched to interject that, given the challenge posed by women of colour and other women on the margins, feminism would have floundered without recourse to just such a conceptual tool. While the fear was that the deconstruction of 'women' might delegitimize the field, the outcome has been the opposite; intersectionality has been named as women's studies' most important theoretical contribution to other disciplines. As it turns out, African-American women have once again performed a role following closely on a historical pattern: abolition as impetus for women's suffrage and civil rights as spur for second-wave feminism.

There is no mistaking that those seeking to elaborate on Crenshaw are primarily academics whose interests lie in theory-making and scholarly research. In view of the prevailing political climate, it is not surprising that only a minority evince social justice concerns. Three pronounced features may be said to characterize writings on the subject. The first is that intersectionality scholars have been unable to move much beyond dissecting the intellectual puzzle that they interpret Crenshaw to have presented; that is, how to adequately conceptualize the manifold ways in which the categories of gender, race and class interact, with complexity and fluidity serving as criteria. The second is the vigorous push for the categories to be of equivalent importance. The third, but not least significant, is the avoidance of anything that might hint of Marxism. For the most part anti-Marxism is simply assumed.

Here, then, is a sampling of proposals on how best to advance the theorizing of intersectionality. Hancock vigorously opposes what she calls an 'Oppression Olympics'. From her point of view, one project is of necessity dominant as in the unitary approach, but when different oppressions are under consideration, these should all be equal (Hancock 2007). Yuval-Davis contends that intersectionality should include not simply society's marginalized sectors but all members, in which case it can, when fully developed, supplant social science stratification theory (Yuval-Davis 2011). She refers to gender, stage in the life cycle, ethnicity, class and so on as social divisions and insists on historicity and location in analysing such intersections. Unlike most, she gestures to the social and political developments that led to the decline of socialist thinking.

Reviewing approaches to intersectionality, McCall arrives at three broad classifications: intra-categorical, as in Crenshaw, where the focus is on the complexity within particular groups; anti-categorical, as in the post-structural rejection of identity as unity; and inter-categorical, which she favours. According to her, the latter is attentive to both inequalities within the categories and the larger structures (not specified) that generate these inequalities (McCall 2005). For her part, Walby (who worries about the fragmenting effects of postmodernism but refuses 'the totalizing framework of traditional Marxism' – Walby 1992: 33), along with Armstrong and Strid, summons critical realism and complexity theory to address several problems, among them: the balance between fluidity and stability; how to address class without leaving it out or giving it undue importance; and how to address oppression while making the powerful visible (Walby et al. 2012: 33). In the end, they dispose of 'mutual constitution' in favour of 'mutual shaping' because of its ability to show how social relations shape each other but do not become wholly changed in the interaction (ibid.). A rare contribution is one by Carastathis in which she asks whether representation, identity politics or difference should be the goal of transformative politics, and posits that feminist subjectivity can only arise from solidarity; that is, engagement in concrete political practice in 'oppositional politics … [to] actively transform structural relations of power' (Carastathis 2008: 29). The burden of these preoccupations is distilled in Lykke's proposal:

> we need to take seriously the metatheoretical potential of the concept of intersectionality to break up fixed theoretical frameworks, and in a positive rhizomatic sense to follow the non-hierarchical lines of light within, between and across different social categorizations and intersections as the concept asks us to do … (Lykke 2011: 212)

Conspicuously absent from these discussions is any reference to capitalism. The identities that intersect (and, on the macro level, the oppressive systems that interlock) are divested of their structuring material ground, resulting in a purely discursive analysis characteristic of postmodernism/post-structuralism. To paraphrase Meiksins Wood, the strategy here is to centre all arguments on the plurality of identities and social divisions, as if doing so denies the totalizing logic of capitalism (Meiksins Wood 1995: 246). The existence of a multiplicity of modes of domination and oppression, the litany of which can be lengthy, is incomprehensible when dissociated from capitalism as a system.

It is the capitalist mode of production and the social relations underlying it which provide the key to understanding why gender, race and other identity markers evolve into oppressions to begin with. It is in the context of capitalist social relations, where the capitalist must extract the surplus labour of those without property in the means of production, that these identity categories are activated as mechanisms to facilitate exploitation. The key issue pivots around the fraught concept of class. Meiksins Wood argues that class is 'not only a specific system of power relations but also the constitutive relation of a distinctive social process, the dynamic of accumulation and the self-expansion of capital' (ibid.: 246). From a Marxist perspective, class is not merely another form of inequality or the equivalent of stratification – the latter implying social integration, the former conflict or irresoluble antagonism – as postmodernists would have us believe. Worthy of note is that even with this culturalized notion of class, interest in it has waned in intersectionality studies, with the scope having narrowed to gender and race (Walby et al. 2012: 231).

It must be understood that the insistence on equivalence and the vehement objection to the primacy of class are the driving factors in intersectionality arguments based on postmodernism. Heavily influenced by Laclau and Mouffe and their advocacy of new social movements, these theorists postulate that difference or identity is not coherent or unified and has no particular connection to the mode of production as it does in Marx (Laclau and Mouffe 1985). Hall contrasts the postmodern to the Enlightenment subject in this manner: while the latter has a unified and stable identity, the postmodern subject 'is becoming fragmented … Identity becomes "a moveable feast": formed and transformed continuously in relation to the ways we are represented or addressed in the cultural systems which surround us' (Hall 1992: 275). The social, then, has no fixed or single determining point like production or the economy, no one major source of conflict and no historical agent of change like the working class.

Confronting such indeterminacy head-on, Meyerson refutes the economic reductionism charge levelled at Marxists (Meyerson 2011). He insists on the *explanatory* primacy of class analysis as the way to comprehend gender, race and class oppression. For him, not only is class the primary determinant, it is the only structural determinant. Driving this point home, he sets up an unmistakable distinction between the gender and racial division of labour on the one hand and, on the other, the ideologies of racism and sexism that justify the oppression of people of colour and women respectively. For how can one sensibly declare, for instance, that it is race which causes racism, or gender which causes sexism? To make the status of class as a structural determinant profoundly clear, Meiksins Woods asks pointedly: 'Is it possible to imagine class differences without exploitation and domination?' (Meiksins Wood 1995: 258). And Meyerson restores the concept of struggle to theory with this straightforward, unambiguous declaration: 'The primacy of class means that building a multiracial, multigendered international working-class organization ... should be the goal of any revolutionary movement: the primacy of class puts the fight against racism and sexism at the center. Oppression is multiple and intersecting but its causes are not' (Meyerson 2011: 2).

In an incisive Marxist critique of Hill Collins' 'interlocking oppressions' that readily applies to the body of intersectionality studies as a whole, Gimenez points out that the flattening of oppressions and their lack of anchor shed no light whatsoever on their possible causes or why they persist (Gimenez 2001). While Collins acknowledges that institutional bases of power need to be identified – a concern that current discourse-leaning theorists hardly even pay lip-service to any longer – she fails to do so. Instead, she proposes as an overarching *ideological* frame a 'matrix of domination', which, quoting bell hooks, refers to 'a belief in domination ... in notions of superior and inferior' (Hill Collins 1991: 226). Since no structure is named, Gimenez is led to conclude that the categories are regarded as invariant and taken for granted, leaving the relations of power unexplained. She similarly questions Collins' reliance on experience as the source of knowledge. Our social existence, Gimenez reasons, is shaped by the capitalist mode of production and the forces and relations producing it, knowledge of which individuals may not necessarily possess. What she is alluding to here is the Marxist concept of alienation in which individuals become self-alienated because they have no control over their own labour, and the products of their labour are alienated from them by the private ownership or control of the means of production. Alienated labour 'alienates man from his own body, external nature, his mental life ...' (Petrović 1983: 11). This is why Ebert, agreeing with Gimenez, believes that inquiry must proceed into the genealogy of power in the capitalist system rather than depend on experience, which can succeed in yielding nothing more than ethnographies of power as effects of the status quo (Ebert 2005: 40). De-alienation (and, by extension, the reliability of experience), in contrast, can only be reached both through the abolition of private property and a thoroughgoing reorganization of economic and social life so that the producers themselves become the self-managers.

In light of the foregoing critiques, we may pose the following questions: Why do proponents of intersectionality avoid macro-level perspectives and focus obsessively on micro-politics and heterogeneity? Why has exploitation been replaced by oppression in their lexicon? And what precipitated such a strong distaste for Marxism if, as Eagleton and others like him continue to believe, it remains 'the most searching, rigorous, comprehensive critique [of capitalism] … ever to be launched' (Eagleton 2011: 2)? What in the material conditions of capitalism have changed to lead to discursive inflections of intersectionality in which the system itself has been made to disappear and, by its disappearance, made eternal?

As mentioned previously, significant changes have, indeed, transpired in the capitalist economy now gone global. To more fully grasp the transition to cultural reductionism, let us turn to Eagleton's description of these changes:

> There was a shift from traditional industrial manufacture to a 'postindustrial' culture of consumerism, communications, information technology and the service industry. Small-scale, decentralized, versatile, non-hierarchical enterprises were the order of the day. Markets were deregulated, and the working-class movement subjected to savage legal and political assault. Traditional class allegiances were weakened, while local, gender and ethnic identities grew more insistent. (Ibid.: 3)

Eagleton notes that it is the new information technologies which made globalization possible, allowing for the outsourcing of manufacturing to cheap labour in the global South. Marshalling international financial institutions such as the International Monetary Fund and the World Bank with their structural adjustment programmes, US capitalism has been able to restructure the world economy for the benefit of the corporate class. This in turn has resulted in a maldeveloped, impoverished periphery, inducing massive migration to the metropolis. Within the United States, Eisenstein refers to this economic transformation as no less than 'a political and economic sea change' that drew unprecedented numbers of women into the labour force, with the majority in the low-wage service sector and a token minority in upper-level occupations (Eisenstein 2009). Such adjustments are to be comprehended as a response to a failing economy, a reaction to the bust of the post-Second World War boom.

Some of the manifest changes in globalization were initially hailed by cultural critics because they perceived in these an emancipatory potential, a 'de-centering' of the Western subject (Miyoshi 1993). The disintegration of Fordist production and its replacement by finance capital similarly indicated the disappearance of the working class, thus giving way to theories postulating the arrival of identity-affiliated cultural movements stemming from a variety of social antagonisms, no longer that of worker versus capital. Laclau and Mouffe discerned in these 'highly diverse struggles: urban, ecological, anti-authoritarian, anti-institutional, feminist, anti-racist, ethnic, regional or sexual minorities' a rupture from class war into a 'rapid diffusion of social conflictuality to more and more numerous relations which is characteristic today of advanced industrial societies' (Laclau and Mouffe 1985: 159). Class demarcation was thus erased by foregrounding all kinds of difference as equally salient. This is precisely the world view of current intersectionality studies.

As Marxists have pointed out, although capitalism has altered in form it has not changed in essence, nor has the working class altogether dissolved. It does not take scholarly investigation to know that consumer products flooding the US market come from sweatshop labour in China and so-called developing countries. Eagleton opines that what accounts for the acquiescence to the status quo (as mirrored in conceptualizations of intersectionality, for instance) is not the transformations capitalism has undergone but the hopelessness of intellectuals in the face of a vanished alternative.[6] This is a situation that is most unfortunate because, as any present-day progressive (Marxist or not) will have to concede, capitalism as a system has become ever more brutal, more predatory. In this arrangement, the victims are increasingly female, of colour and of the global South, the very subjects intersectionality claims investment in. Against this backdrop, the disconnect of intersectionality theory is stark and deeply shameful.

A felicitous example

All that said, one study departs from the rest, serving as an example of how – *contra* intersectionality theorists – difference and multiple identities can in fact be elucidated and made meaningful when securely anchored in class, gender and racial/national relations of power on the world stage. This is Anderson's study of migrant domestic workers, women of colour of different nationalities, in six European cities in the mid-1990s. Herself a member of a UK domestic workers' organization, Anderson examines the women's experiences as workers, their relationship with their female employers and with the state of which they are non-citizens, the nature of reproductive work and its connection to production in capitalism, the work of organizing, and so on (Anderson 2000).

Anderson's singular contribution (one made possible with a materialist approach) is her contention that paid domestic work, particularly when it includes care, involves not the sale of labour power but the sale of the self, of personhood.[7] Caught in the liminal space between the traditional and the modern, the private and the public, migrant domestic workers (regardless of their individual traits or characteristics) are personally dependent on their female employers, a condition reinforced by state laws. Here Anderson summons the history of slavery in the US South to emphasize its connection to the current practice of hiring domestic workers from the global South. In taking over the reproductive work traditionally assigned to the wife, it is obvious that domestic workers are enabling their employers to participate in lucrative work in the public sphere; mitigating tensions inherent in the household gender division of labour; and taking over the task of a diminishing welfare state. Less evident is that what they are reproducing, over and above everything else, is the social status of the woman who pays them. In Anderson's words, they are servicing lifestyles that are otherwise impossible to sustain, a situation in which racialization is an essential component of migrant domestic workers' imposed servitude.

With the above as her conceptual frame, Anderson is able to get into the narratives of the women in a way that makes their daily negotiation of the power relations in which they are embedded (class, racial/national) at once striking and poignant. While several studies have been conducted of female migrant workers, the vast majority have as their guideposts the culturalization prescribed by intersectionality theorists. In particular, these have steered far away from scrutiny of their actual work lives, fearing this would spotlight their 'victimization' and, instead, deliver them into the realm of an imagined existence in which they are projected as subjects purportedly with agency and choice. Here, for example, is an excerpt from a recent book on Filipina entertainers (read: prostitutes) in US military bases in South Korea:

> In their labor migration, Filipina entertainers come to explore their own sense of self as romantic, desirous, and sexual subjects through the language of romantic love … The realization of the self is accomplished in an emotional relationship unencumbered by rational calculations and material concerns … The passionate drive of love is … anti-structural, entailing a partial abandonment of normative values made particularly pertinent in a migration site. Love in this analysis is … an authentication of the autonomous self. (Cheng 2010: 135)

Conclusion

But there are signs of a break in the conservative tide. The economic meltdown of 2008, not to mention US imperialism's unending wars as well as protest movements in the United States (for example, Occupy) and elsewhere, send warning signals that things cannot proceed as they have. The calamity that corporate globalization has turned into, both in its merciless ravaging of the ecology and of people's lives, has sparked a renewed interest in Marxism. Marxist feminist interventions, though sparse, have never been absent; for example, Gimenez's retheorizing of what was seen as the 'unhappy marriage' of Marxism and feminism constitutes a much-needed attempt to resume aborted discussions about the relationship between capitalism and patriarchy, but on new terrain (Gimenez 2005). In an exemplary book detailing the ways in which global elites have successfully co-opted hegemonic feminism's fundamental principles, Eisenstein urges the termination of feminism's subservience as a 'capitalist handmaiden' (Eisenstein 2009: 199–229). She challenges feminists to learn how capitalism operates, insists on the recognition of the significance of class, and advocates for the return of socialism to the feminist agenda. Following the lead of activist women of the global South, she issues a call for a kind of feminism that, fully conscious of its location in the world capitalist system, cannot but take a position that is unswervingly anti-racist and anti-imperialist. This is a stand that could not be farther removed from that assumed by intersectionality scholars.

Notes

1 A conference to mark the twentieth anniversary of intersectionality was held at Goethe University in 2009, with Kimberlé Crenshaw in attendance along with 300 participants. Selected presentations were compiled in Lutz et al. (2011b).

2 Notable for its assemblage of documents from the women's liberation movement from the mid-1960s to 1977 and for its pointed introduction and headnotes is Baxandall and Gordon (2000). See also Evans (1979); Rosen (2006).

3 Martha Gimenez writes that second-wave feminists conducted a 'dialog ... not with the real Marx ... but with a "straw Marx"' (Gimenez 2005: 12). Judith Orr shares this sentiment (2010).

4 She followed this article with another centring on violence against women of colour (1991).

5 A collection of writings illustrating the gender, race and class theme is the anthology by Moraga and Anzaldua (1981). An excellent example of a qualitative study of gender and race as squarely situated in capitalism of the late 1970s can be found in Joseph and Lewis (1981).

6 Eagleton describes this as 'a creeping sense of political impotence' among former Marxists (Eagleton 2011: 6). Michael Lebowitz attributes this loss of hope to the deformities of then-existing socialism (Mingliang 2013).

7 Shortly after this book's publication, Arlie Hochschild coined the now universally accepted term 'global care chain' to describe this growing phenomenon: how migrant domestic workers entrust their children to parents or relatives back home while caring for the offspring of well-off families in the metropolis (Hochschild 2001). Reverting to the pre-feminist conception of housework/childcare as a 'labor of love', it wipes out the gains won by activists and scholars seeking valuation for reproductive work as in, for instance, the wages-for-housework campaign and the domestic labour debate. Such a turnaround from inconvenient truths – for who wants class conflict that is up close and personal? – must contain a lesson in unconscious racism somewhere.

References

Anderson, B. (2000) *Doing the Dirty Work: The Global Politics of Domestic Labour*, London: Zed Books.

Baxandall, R. and L. Gordon (eds) (2000) *Dear Sisters: Dispatches from the Women's Liberation Movement*, New York: Basic Books.

Beal, F. (1970) 'Double jeopardy: to be Black and female', in R. Morgan (ed.), *Sisterhood is Powerful*, New York: Vintage, pp. 340–53.

Carastathis, A. (2008) 'The invisibility of privilege: a critique of intersectional models of identity', *A Multidisciplinary Journal on the Normative Challenges of Public Policies and Social Practices*, 3(2): 23–38.

Cheng, S. (2010) *On the Move for Love*, Philadelphia: University of Pennsylvania Press.

Combahee River Collective (1981) 'A Black feminist statement', in C. Moraga and G. Anzaldua (eds), *This Bridge Called My Back*, Watertown, MA: Persephone, pp. 210–18.

Crenshaw, K. (1989) 'Demarginalizing the intersection of race and sex: a Black feminist critique of antidiscrimination doctrine, feminist theory and antiracist politics', *University of Chicago Legal Forum*, 139: 139–67.

— (1991) 'Mapping the margins: intersectionality, identity politics, and violence against women of color', *Stanford Law Review*, 43(6): 141–99.

— (2011) 'Postscript', in H. Lutz, M. T. Herrera Vivar and L. Supik (eds),

Framing Intersectionality: Debates on a Multi-faceted Concept in Gender Studies, Surrey: Ashgate, pp. 221–33.

Davis, K. (2008) 'Intersectionality as a buzzword: a sociology of science perspective on what makes a feminist theory successful', *Feminist Theory*, 9(1): 67–80.

Eagleton, T. (2011) *Why Marx was Right*, New Haven, CT: Yale University Press.

Ebert, T. (2005) 'Rematerializing feminism', *Science & Society*, 69(1): 33–55.

Eisenstein, H. (2009) *Feminism Seduced: How Global Elites Use Women's Labor and Ideas to Exploit the World*, Boulder, CO: Paradigm.

Evans, S. (1979) *Personal Politics: The Roots of Women's Liberation in the Civil Rights Movement and the New Left*, New York: Vintage.

Gimenez, M. (2001) 'Marxism and class, gender and race: rethinking the trilogy', *Race, Gender & Class*, 8(2): 23–33.

— (2005) 'Capitalism and the oppression of women: Marx revisited', *Science & Society*, 69(1): 11–32.

Hall, S. (1992) 'The question of cultural identity', in S. Hall, D. Held and T. McGrew (eds), *Modernity and Its Future*, Cambridge: Polity, pp. 273–325.

Hancock, A. (2007) 'When multiplication doesn't equal quick addition', *Perspectives on Politics*, 5(1): 63–79.

Hill Collins, P. (1991) *Black Feminist Thought: Knowledge, Consciousness, and the Politics of Empowerment*, New York: Routledge.

Hochschild, A. (2001) 'The nanny chain', *American Prospect*, 19 December, prospect.org/article/nanny-chain.

Joseph, G. and J. Lewis (1981) *Common Differences: Conflicts in Black and White Feminist Perspectives*, New York: Anchor.

King, D. (1988) 'Multiple jeopardy, multiple consciousness: the context of a Black feminist ideology', *Signs*, 14(1): 42–72.

Laclau, E. and C. Mouffe (1985) *Hegemony and Socialist Strategy: Towards a Radical Democratic Politics*, London: Verso.

Lutz, H., M. T. Herrera Vivar and L. Supik (2011a) 'Framing intersectionality: an introduction', in H. Lutz, M. T. Herrera Vivar and L. Supik (eds), *Framing Intersectionality: Debates on a Multi-faceted Concept in Gender Studies*, Surrey: Ashgate, pp. 1–22.

— (eds) (2011b) *Framing Intersectionality: Debates on a Multi-faceted Concept in Gender Studies*, Surrey: Ashgate.

Lykke, N. (2011) 'Intersectional analysis: black box or useful critical feminist thinking technology?', in H. Lutz, M. T. Herrera Vivar and L. Supik (eds), *Framing Intersectionality: Debates on a Multi-faceted Concept in Gender Studies*, Surrey: Ashgate, pp. 207–20.

McCall, L. (2005) 'The complexity of intersectionality', *Signs*, 3(3): 1771–800.

Meiksins Wood, E. (1995) *Democracy against Capitalism*, Cambridge: Cambridge University Press.

Meyerson, G. (2011) 'Rethinking Black Marxism: reflections on Cedric Robinson and others', *Cultural Logic*, 3(2), clogic.eserver.org/3-1&2/meyerson.html.

Mingliang, Z. (2013) 'The relevance of Marxism today: an interview with Michael A. Lebowitz', 29 April, mrzine.monthlyreview.org/2013/lebowitz210313.html.

Miyoshi, M. (1993) 'A borderless world? From colonialism to transnationalism and the decline of the nation-state', *Critical Inquiry*, 12(4): 726–51.

Moraga, C. and G. Anzaldua (eds) (1981) *This Bridge Called My Back*, Watertown, MA: Persephone.

Orr, J. (2010) 'Marxism and feminism

today', *International Socialism*, 27, 29 April, www.isj.org.uk/index.php4?id=656.

Petrović, G. (1983) 'Alienation', in T. Bottomore, L. Harris, V. G. Kiernan and R. Miliband (eds), *A Dictionary of Marxist Thought*, Cambridge, MA: Harvard University Press, pp. 9–15.

Rosen, R. (2006) *The World Split Open: How the Women's Movement Changed America*, New York: Penguin.

Walby, S. (1992) 'Post post-modernism? Theorizing social complexity', in M. Barrett and A. Phillips (eds), *Destabilizing Theory: Contemporary Feminist Debates*, Stanford, CA: Stanford University Press, pp. 31–52.

Walby, S., J. Armstrong and S. Strid (eds) (2012) 'Intersectionality: multiple inequalities in social theory', *Sociology*, 46(2): 224–39.

Women of Color Resource Center (2013) 'Triple jeopardy – Third World Women's Alliance', 29 April, www.flickr.com/photos/27628370@N08/sets/72157605547626040.

Yuval-Davis, N. (2011) 'Beyond the recognition and re-distribution dichotomy: intersectionality and stratification', in H. Lutz, M. T. Herrera Vivar and L. Supik (eds), *Framing Intersectionality: Debates on a Multi-faceted Concept in Gender Studies*, Surrey: Ashgate, pp. 155–69.

10 | LABOUR-POWER

Helen Colley

Introduction

This chapter discusses the keyword 'labour-power', considering both its role within the capitalist system and also the process of its production and reproduction. Labour-power is the term by which Marx referred to our creative, productive and reproductive capacities. The chapter begins with his understanding of labour-power as a uniquely human characteristic, distinguishing us from other species. It goes on to summarize Marx's understanding of labour-power under capitalism and how labour-power is exploited to fuel capitalism's creation of surplus value (profit). It next discusses how Marxist feminists have extended the notion of labour-power to include not only the mental and manual capacities by which Marx himself defined it, but emotional capacities too. The rest of the chapter considers issues related to the reproduction of labour-power by women. It looks at the historical emergence of capitalism from within feudalism, which required a massive expansion of labour-power, and the mass witch-hunts used for centuries to ensure this expansion by imposing state control over women's reproductive capacities. It then reviews debates between and within Marxism and feminism about the social reproduction of labour-power and the nature of women's oppression: is it an issue of class, gender or both? Inevitably, the chapter summarizes very briefly a range of lengthy and complex analyses, but it does so in the hope of prompting the reader to engage with the original works on which it draws.

Labour-power is what makes us human

In his *Economic and Philosophical Manuscripts of 1844*, Marx spells out his view of human nature, which he terms our 'species-being' (Marx 1959: 31). He argues that there is one fundamental and essential aspect of human nature that is transhistorical (that is to say, it does not change throughout the ages, whatever the mode of production or type of society we live in). While all other animals have the ability to labour in order to meet their immediate needs for survival – obtaining food and building nests, for example – humans are the only species who can do this consciously, purposively and freely. Our labour is not just instinctive, nor is it confined to meeting our basic survival needs. We have the capacity to labour also for spiritual, social, intellectual and aesthetic purposes, with a vision of the future and of *transforming* rather than just utilizing the world we find around us – and being transformed ourselves as we do so. It is this distinctive and inherently human capacity which Marx terms 'labour-power' and which inspires his unswerving belief in our potential to create a future society in which freedom, security and development of our abilities to the full could be guaranteed for all. He defines it thus in Chapter 6 of the first volume of *Capital*, on the buying and selling of labour-power: 'By labour-power or capacity for labour is to be understood the aggregate of those mental and physical capabilities existing in a human being, which he exercises whenever he produces a use-value of any description' (Marx 1999). We shall return to this definition in considering the ways in which feminists have extended Marx's thought. For now, though, we focus on the ways in which Marx understands that this transhistorical essence of human nature is also profoundly shaped by the specific historical and material conditions in which we live; that is to say, by the mode of production which dominates in any particular era of human society. The way in which this happens under capitalism is, of course, a profound and complex argument, expounded fully in *Capital*, but which can be studied more fully but accessibly in some of the works I also draw on here: Marx's pamphlets for working people (such as *Wages, Price and Profit* [1975]; *Wage-labor and Capital* [1902]), and in the work of Allman (1999, 2007, 2010), Harvey (2010) and Rikowski (2002). Here, we can only review briefly some of the key elements of this argument, before going on to explore how feminist thought has developed and debated Marx's concept of labour-power.

Marx's concept of labour-power under capitalism

In the 1844 manuscripts as well as in *Capital* and elsewhere, Marx sees labour-power as being the engine at the very heart of capitalism, 'fuel for its living fire' (Rikowski 2002). In this society, which is driven by the exchange of commodities for profit, labour-power itself is commodified:

> Labour-power is the ... very special commodity, the commodity that actually makes capitalism possible ... Between the fifteenth and eighteenth centuries, the land from which the peasant population secured their subsistence was increasingly privatised. These people came to the point of having only one commodity, which they could sell in order to purchase the necessities of life. That commodity was their labour-power, the commodity that serves the same purpose for the vast majority of human beings in the 21st century. (Allman 2007: 12)

As capitalism came to control all means of production, working people were left with no other means of subsistence than to sell their labour-power. They were 'free' of slavery and of feudal relations, but this 'freedom' was only that of being able to sell their creative, productive capacities in the labour market. When people's labour-power is sold for a wage and put to work in capitalist society, it transforms raw materials into other commodities in a twofold way: it invests them *both* with a use-value (or usefulness) *and* with an exchange-value (when sold in the market). The latter allows the capitalist owner of the commodity – and the commodified labour-power now congealed in it – to realize 'value'. This value is 'the substance of capital's social universe' (Rikowski 2002: 181), capitalism's very lifeblood. This understanding of the commodity under capitalism, which distinguishes it from the forms that commodities took in previous societies with different modes of production, is the 'germ-seed' of Marx's explanation of capitalism. But how do this transformation of commodities and the subsequent creation of value by labour-power function?

Typically, working people imagine that they sell their *labour* – the work that they do – to the employer; and that there is a direct relationship between the number of hours or days that they work, and the wage or salary they receive for it. This leads to notions such as 'a fair day's pay for a fair day's work', which assume that there is or can be some proportionate sharing between employer and employee of the proceeds from selling the commodities produced, after taking into account the employer's initial investment and production expenses. These assumptions of a direct and potentially fair and just exchange of labour for a wage are reinforced by the employment contract.

However, such ideas represent an *ideological* understanding of the employer–employee relationship – that is to say, one that obscures and distorts a deeper reality (Allman 1999). In fact, Marx explains, we need to think about the labour process very differently. First, we must understand that the capitalist is purchasing *labour-power* – our capacity to work productively – rather than labour itself. This means that the employer always has an interest in seeking to intensify productivity – that is, to make workers produce more within each hour of labour-time. Labour-power is separated from workers and becomes congealed in the commodity that they produce, but the capitalist now owns the latter. When this commodity is sold in the market, the capitalist reaps its entire exchange-value, which is more than the wage that is returned to the workforce. Only a proportion of the proceeds, therefore, is paid back to the employees who have created the commodity. This is not determined as a proportion of the market price of the product at all, but rather *in relation to the costs of ensuring that the labourers can socially reproduce themselves and continue to supply labour power* (sustain themselves physically and mentally, raise a family, and so on – costs which are relative to particular expectations about standards of living and which therefore vary around the world and in different historical periods).

If it is the overall time in which labour-power is expended on a commodity which generates its entire exchange-value, this produces a very different view of the relationship between labour-time and the wage received. The wage accounts only for the exchange-value realized during a proportion (often a small one) of working time. The rest of the day (or week, month, year), employees are working for free, and employers will enjoy all of the fruits of this portion of their labour-power to themselves. There is no possibility of a 'fairly' negotiated share for the worker here. The value realized from this unpaid proportion of the labour-power deployed is what Marx calls 'surplus-value', or profit. This is capitalism's *raison d'être*, and human labour-power is the only force that can create it. (Although new technology may also increase productivity, unlike human beings technology cannot reproduce itself relatively cheaply: the capital costs of developing, maintaining and replacing it mean that technology consumes surplus value rather than generating it. That is why there are limits to capitalism's ability to replace human beings by, for example, robotics in manufacturing.) Capitalism therefore constantly seeks to extort a greater amount of surplus value from labour-power, and it can do so in two ways: first, by extending the length of the working day; secondly, by increasing productivity – that is, the intensity with which labour-power is deployed.

This exploitation of labour-power has powerful negative effects on working people, since it estranges them from their own labour. Marx discusses in the 1844 manuscripts four different types of alienation this creates: alienation from the products of their labour; alienation from the labour process; alienation from themselves; and alienation from other workers. Alienation can therefore result in serious mental and physical health problems for many working people (Marx 1959). It also pervades lives beyond the workplace, creating broader social problems; as Rikowski (2002) argues, value is not only produced in the workplace, it has become our 'social universe' under capitalism. However, alienation can also act as a double-edged sword for capitalism, since within it lie immanent possibilities of workers developing a more critical consciousness of the labour process; exercising resistance to the incorporation of themselves into capital; and moving towards a more radical, transformative praxis (Allman 1999; Brook 2009a, 2009b).

Emotional labour: extending Marx's concept of labour-power

As we have seen above, Marx (1999) defined labour-power as the mental and physical capabilities humans have for producing use-values. But this definition overlooks the domain of the emotional, and from the 1970s throughout the second-wave women's movement, Marxist feminists contributed important extensions to the understanding of labour-power in this regard. Agnes Heller's *A Theory of Feelings* (1979) advanced an understanding that emotions are *neither* natural and innate, *nor* undifferentiated resources to which different genders or social classes have differential access and affordances. However universal, inevitable and irresistible emotions may appear to us, Heller argues that in fact quite different repertoires of feeling are available to different class fractions and genders. They are related to the mode of production in any given society, to multiple divisions of labour within it, and to different relationships to the means of production.

Building on these insights, Arlie Russell Hochschild (1983) offered a radical new extension of Marx's concept of labour-power by introducing the notion of 'emotional labour'. She argued that in caring and other human service occupations – education, healthcare, customer service, and so on – the management of one's own and others' feelings is not a private adjunct to work, nor a sub-category of caring. It is a key feature of the work process, a form of paid labour, and therefore emotional capacities are an aspect of labour-power. Emotional labour 'requires one to induce or suppress feeling in order to sustain the outward countenance that produces the proper state of mind in others' (ibid.: 7), so that the 'emotional style' of providing a service is central to the use-value of that service. But since this emotional capacity is bought in the labour market, and is therefore controlled and prescribed in its manner of deployment by employers, it can result in a particularly intense form of alienation from the self and from others. Some of the most intimate aspects of our humanity are commodified and exploited for profit (exchange-value) rather than for the mutual benefit of others (use-value). To give just a few examples, comforting and pleasure (sometimes even sexual attraction) are promised by airlines from their cabin crew (ibid.); love is often explicitly offered as part of the package for sale by childcare providers (Colley 2011a); and emotional as well as physical caring for patients is expected of female doctors and nurses (James 1989; Smith 1992, 2012). This could be seen as a particular form by which late capitalism seeks to intensify the exploitation of labour-power as it relies ever more heavily on the service sectors and the drive for consumerism. Not only must service be given, but it must also now be given 'with a smile' or with an exhortation to 'have a nice day'. It draws into the production of surplus value not only our heads and our hands, but our hearts as well.

Even where caring service work is undertaken in public rather than privately owned services, as with every aspect of our lives, these are suffused with capitalist social relations (Rikowski 2002) that are intensified as privatization is prepared for and driven through in the current economic climate. Although often conceived of as work 'for people', the commodification of human service work recasts it as a service 'to consumers' (Goffman 1969; Stacey 1984). The labour of practitioners within these services then becomes: 'subsumed within the social relations of capitalist production … their work has become more controlled, supervised or managed, and often deskilled or … de-intellectualised' (Allman 2010: 55). Given this permeation of our whole society by capitalist values, emotional labour can extend beyond paid work in public services to voluntary work. Youth mentoring projects, for example, such as Big Brothers Big Sisters in North

America, have involved millions of adult volunteers (around 80 per cent of whom are women) and often take the form of 'engagement mentoring' (Colley 2003a, 2003b). This approach is determined top-down by policy-makers and is tied to 'welfare-to-work' outcomes for disadvantaged youth as well as increasing the transferable skills of mentors. It therefore tends to prescribe very closely the ways in which mentors should relate to their mentees, so that the building of trusting, caring relationships between an adult and a young person is viewed as a vehicle for reforming the characters of both to produce an ideally 'employable' set of attitudes, values, behaviours and beliefs. Mentoring thus becomes a type of emotional labour in which the raw material to be worked on is the very personhood of those taking part: a deeply alienating process which can damage both parties (Colley 2011b).

It is vital to recognize, then, that alienation is not at all confined to the traditional realm of commodity production alone, but also extends to work that demands emotional labour, including the work of social reproduction. Although Marx often used industrial examples to illustrate the social relations of capitalism, he held a much more inclusive and fluid view of them both flowing out into and drawing in other spheres of social life. As Allman notes, discussing educational work, capitalism

> reaches out into every aspect of our social existence, sometimes impacting on and influencing these other dimensions of our lives. At other times, its effects work in the opposite direction. *It pulls or incorporates factors that seem to be external to the production process into its frame – encompassing them within the 'essence' of capitalism.* (Allman 2010: 63, emphasis added)

In the context of the unequal distribution of power and authority in capitalist patriarchal society, Hochschild (1983) argued that the alienation generated by emotional labour is experienced differentially according to gender and social class and increases as institutional mechanisms seek to intensify and regulate the management of feelings. It can be most easily recognized when the individual senses a clash between what they actually feel and what they know they 'ought' to feel. In these circumstances, if a worker continues to try to put her 'heart and soul' into the job, she risks stress and burnout. If she tries to protect herself by distancing her 'real' self from her work identity and trying to 'act the part', she risks detachment from her own emotions and low self-esteem for her insincerity. If she tries to separate her 'real' and 'work' selves without succumbing to self-blame, she risks cynicism and guilt.

Of course, male workers can also experience the demand for emotional labour. But Hochschild argued that patriarchal social relations within capitalism render women particularly vulnerable to its pressures. First, women have learned to exchange emotion as a resource or gift, because they often lack material resources. Secondly, women are expected to specialize in one aspect of a gendered division of labour: caring. Thirdly, the subordinate status of women as a gender renders individual women more vulnerable to the displacement of feelings by others. Finally, the power difference between men and women means that 'women's work' is more likely to be invisible. Not only does emotional labour go largely unrecognized, but its very quality depends on its invisibility, so that women who display too much evidence of its efforts and its costs are likely to be stereotyped as 'inadequate' or 'hysterical'.

Hochschild's thesis has been challenged by liberal and post-structural feminists (e.g. Bolton 2005; Price 2001) advancing depoliticized ideas of 'emotion management' or the concept of 'emotional intelligence' most famously promoted by Goleman (1996). Such critiques argue that the commodification of emotion in capitalist enterprises is overstated in the concept of emotional labour; or that the exploitation of feelings in the workplace can be explained in individualized moral and psychological terms; or that workers retain substantial agency, empowerment even, in choosing how to deploy their feelings at work. Nonetheless, these positions can be maintained only by ignoring capitalist social relations and the exploitative labour processes that Marx so thoroughly analysed in his work.

There is, however, another aspect of Hochschild's work that points to more fundamental controversies in Marxist-feminism. She argues that there is a key difference between 'emotional labour' and what she terms 'emotion work' – that is, the caring and nurture that women undertake within the home and family: 'emotional labor is sold for a wage and therefore has *exchange value* … the synonymous terms emotion work or emotion management [are used] to refer to these same acts done in a private context where they have use value …' (Hochschild 1983: 7, emphasis in original). The questionable assumption Hochschild makes here is that social relationships within the family, as well as the work entailed in them, somehow lie outside the realm of capitalist social relations. This raises issues about the work of social reproduction, especially unpaid work within the family, which have generated sharp debates within and between Marxism and feminism, to which we shall return in a later section of this chapter. Next, however, let us turn to the question of the reproduction of labour-power, how crucial a necessity this is for capitalism, and why this means patriarchy remains fundamental to it.

Ensuring the reproduction of labour-power: a condition for capitalism's emergence

Through the Industrial Revolution, which sealed the establishment of capitalism as the dominant mode of production, the family's role as a unit of production – both in agriculture and in the craft production of other commodities – was brought to an end. It became a privatized sphere devoted to the social reproduction of labour-power, relying on the unpaid labour of women. Because Marx's own work concentrates predominantly on the more public sphere of capitalism, that of industrial production and the generation of surplus value through the direct exploitation of labour-power in the employed workplace, mainstream Marxism has tended to work with a masculinist and unhelpful hierarchical distinction between 'productive' labour (which produces surplus value directly) and 'non-productive' labour (which does not), in which the notion of 'non-productive' has become ideologically entangled with capitalism's undervaluing of women's work (Mies 1998). This in turn has led to a focus on class oppression as the primary issue for struggle and a view of gender (as well as racism and other oppressions) at best as a secondary issue and at worst as a divisive distraction from the class struggle. It is impossible to discuss here the whole range of these debates, which are amply addressed in this book. But the reproduction of labour-power offers a crucial focus of analysis for understanding the relationship between capitalism and patriarchy and therefore between class and gender. This requires a historical materialist explanation of the emergence of capitalism, and in particular the process of primitive accumulation by which it could develop within and eventually overthrow the feudal mode of production.

While the primitive accumulation of capital was pursued brutally through the invasion and colonization of the Americas, Africa and Asia, central to this process in Europe were the torture and execution of hundreds of thousands of women charged with witchcraft and infanticide throughout several centuries in the Middle Ages (ibid.; Federici 2004). Despite the social and legal inequalities which women faced under feudalism, a wide layer of women had come to enjoy independence and status as craftspeople and traders as well as healers and midwives, the latter two enabling women to control their fertility and reproductive functions. But as the old feudal order began to collapse under the rise of capitalism in the fifteenth and sixteenth centuries, destitution drove many women into prostitution and vagabondage. The rationalization of agriculture dispossessed masses of people from what had been common land; war, disease and starvation took their toll on a declining population; but the dawn of capitalist production required a means to ensure that sufficient labourers could be available for waged labour. The emerging capitalist class needed a vast supply of labour-power to put to work on its accumulated capital in order to generate surplus value and further expand its rule. In this respect, the witch-hunts of the Middle Ages can be seen as 'one of the mechanisms to control and subordinate women, the peasant and artisan, women who in their economic and sexual independence constituted a threat for the emerging bourgeois order' (Mies 1998: 81). Accusations of witchcraft were associated closely with the practices of contraception and abortion, showing that 'witch-hunting in Europe was an attack on women's resistance to the spread of capitalist relations and the power that women had gained by virtue of their sexuality, their control over reproduction, and their ability to heal' (Federici 2004: 170).

It was vital for capitalism to ensure that women were subordinated to its need to expand and ensure a continually growing supply of labour-power – that special class of commodities which only women's bodies could reproduce. Patriarchal social relations within capitalism, then, are not simply some latent vestige of previous modes of production, but absolutely essential to the reproduction of the 'fuel for capitalism's living fire' (Rikowski 2002). As Federici argues: 'Witch hunting was … instrumental to the construction of *a new patriarchal order* where women's bodies, their labor, their sexual and reproductive powers were placed under the control of the state and transformed into economic resources' (Federici 2004: 170, emphasis added). The reproductive labour of women is discussed more fully in Michelle

Murphy's chapter in this book. Here, however, we can note that not only, as Murphy shows, does the capitalist state and its agencies intervene to curtail the reproductive capacities of women of colour both in its heartlands and in the neocolonial world, but also in the global North the struggle for women to access free contraception and abortion on demand if they so choose has never been definitively won, and has repeatedly been brought under attack – politically, legally and indeed with physical violence – by right-wing forces. The struggle, then, for women to control their bodies – free of any coercion either to reproduce or be prevented from doing so – is one that strikes at the patriarchal heart of capitalism. It is an issue in which class and gender, together with race, are thoroughly inseparable.

The social reproduction of labour-power: an issue of gender *and* class

The centrality of controlling women's sexuality and reproductive capacities in order to guarantee an adequate supply of labour-power demonstrates capitalism's 'abject dependence' (Fortunati 1995) on the social reproduction work of women in the home and family – a dependence which the capitalist system has to obfuscate as far as possible, because of its potentially explosive capacity to spark resistance and rebellion. However, this returns us to Hochschild's (1983) questionable distinction between 'emotional labour' exploited in the workplace and what she sees more benignly as 'emotion work' within personal relationships. Indeed, understanding women's work (mental, physical and emotional) to reproduce labour-power in the home and family and the ways in which this connects with the oppression and exploitation of women has been a major line of division within and between Marxism and feminism. As we have already noted, dominant masculinist interpretations of Marx have subordinated the struggle against women's oppression to a narrow view of the class struggle or resisted any movement for women's liberation as a distracting or even divisive obstacle to revolutionary change (Mies 1998; Arruzza 2013). From such perspectives, women's work in reproducing labour-power is 'non-productive' and creates only use-values rather than exchange-values or surplus value; it is not, therefore, central to the capitalist system or its rule.

A diametrically opposing line of argument came from the radical feminist strand of the second-wave women's movement. Their view was that patriarchy has for millennia been the prevalent form of society, whatever the economic mode of production. Gender, and not class, should therefore be the focus of struggle; and men, rather than the capitalist class, are seen as the main proponents of oppression and exploitation across all sections of society:

> Within the patriarchal system all women suffer oppression by all men, all men benefit from the subordination of women and all the other forms of exploitation, hierarchy and supremacy are only the extensions of male supremacy. Patriarchy, therefore, pre-dating capitalism, racism and colonialism represents women's principal, common enemy. (Arruzza 2013: 99)

Leading radical feminists such as Kate Millett (1970) and Shulamith Firestone (1970) emphasized biological differences between men and women as the source of women's oppression. Their separatist perspective called for a revolution against male domination, one that could separate sexuality from childbearing and -rearing, and challenge societal norms of heterosexuality and the nuclear family. Without this, they believed, none of the other injustices in society could be addressed. However, this focus on gender as the primary issue fails to address differences among women along lines of class and race. Nor can it account for the ways in which the capitalist mode of production mobilizes patriarchy in its quest for profit and the decisive role that the exploitation of labour-power plays in producing surplus value.

A very different perspective has been developed by Marxist feminists such as Mariarosa Dalla Costa and Selma James (1972) and Leopoldina Fortunati (1995), inspired (like Federici and Mies) by Italian autonomist Marxism. Although Marx himself had not analysed in depth how the reproduction of labour-power was related to the workings of capitalism, and in particular to the production of surplus value, such scholars argue that it is both possible and necessary to apply the dialectical historical materialist method he developed to this issue. Along with Federici (2004) and Mies (1998), they emphasize capitalism's absolute dependence on women's work in the family to socially reproduce labour-power. Mies puts this bluntly: 'Proletarianization of men is based on the housewifization of women' (Mies 1998: 110).

The essential nature of reproduction work is deeply obscured by being represented as 'non-work', as a 'natural' or 'personal' process –

socially as a matter simply of personal relationships and economically as a relation of individual consumption between the female homemaker and the male worker who typically brings in a wage from selling his labour-power. But although it *appears* as a dual exchange in which the woman exchanges reproduction work for a portion of the man's wage, according to this perspective the exchange can *actually* be seen as a three-sided one between women, capital and the male wage-earner who is only an intermediary. Through the vehicle of the male wage, capitalism transmits an 'indirect' wage to buy and exploit women's labour-power to reproduce existing and new labour-power for the labour market:

> [Capitalism] has been rendered so much more productive [than previous modes of production] not only by the extension of the working day to the humanly possible limits, but also through reproduction being posited as 'natural production,' which has enabled *two* workers to be exploited with *one* wage, and the entire cost of reproduction to be unloaded onto the labor force. (Fortunati 1995: 9, emphasis in original)

This illusion plays another role for capitalism in combating the alienation that people experience as they are dehumanized to nothing but their hired labour-power in the workplace. In recasting the social reproduction of labour-power in the family as loving care, as a private process which rehumanizes workers and reasserts their individual uniqueness and personhood (Marx 1959), capitalism also defuses the impetus to struggle against exploitation.

Whereas Fortunati (1995) has sketched emotion work in general terms, Marjorie DeVault (1991, 1999) has used Dorothy Smith's institutional ethnography (2005) to offer perhaps the closest 'excavation' of emotion work *as work* within the family. In her book *Feeding the Family: The Social Organization of Caring as Gendered Work* (1991), she showed the multitude of tasks (often so taken for granted that they were indiscernible by women themselves) through which wives and mothers not only ensured that their families were reproduced by providing edible meals, but also provided their partners and children with pleasure and feelings of being cared for as they were fed and coordinated opportunities in and around mealtimes for them to interact and relate to each other in positive ways that built the family as a cohesive social unit.

Much feminist scholarship has studied these activities only within the context of white, middle-class women in the standard North American family, or 'SNAF' (Smith 1993). But while drawing attention to gender oppression, such an exclusive focus ignores divisions of class and race, disability and sexuality, which DeVault was concerned to address through a more expansive view of emotion work: 'some family groups, compared to others, are asked to do more or different work, producing forms of social inequity rendered invisible by the most common ways of thinking about family life' (DeVault 1999: 56). She considers examples such as the advocacy that mothers have to mobilize skilfully to ensure that disabled children receive appropriate support in their schooling; the survival and identity work which creates particular emotional demands on mothers in racialized groups to support their children to cope with oppression; and the work of either 'passing' as a socially acceptable 'SNAF' or resisting that norm, a challenge that arises for gay and lesbian parents as well as for single mothers and blended families. In highlighting this broad range of issues necessitating emotion work, such scholarship has 'put on the public agenda a range of previously neglected activities and made a matter for debate the questions of how such work is to be done and how to support those doing it' (ibid.: 61).

Some of these analyses have been associated with the rise of a movement for 'wages for housework'. By making visible the work that women undertake in the home and family, by demystifying it and demonstrating its exploitative nature, and by calculating the costs which capitalism would have to bear if this work were done on a directly paid-for basis, this movement drew powerful attention to women's oppression as a central issue for the class struggle as a whole. Yet this perspective also has important flaws. In particular, it seems to accept a gendered division of labour in which the reproduction of labour-power remains women's work, and it fails to challenge women's confinement to its often mundane and isolating tasks. It poses the question of why women's work in rearing children and maintaining the home and family should need to be viewed as 'productive' rather than 'reproductive' work in order to validate its centrality to class struggle as well as to the struggle against gender oppression.

Kathi Weeks' book *The Problem with Work* (2011) responds to such critiques of 'wages for housework' by proposing an extension of the autonomist analysis through a challenge to the primacy of all forms of work in shaping our lives and identities. She argues that it is better to focus on broader power relations of employed and family work rather than on the exploitation of labour-power in paid work and on the division of labour of all types of work rather than on class (which she views as an outmoded issue of identity). From this perspective, the normative and moralistic work ethic of capitalism is perpetuated in the analyses hitherto offered by liberal feminism, 'classical' Marxism and Marxist-feminism: 'Feminists … should focus on the demands not simply or exclusively for more work and better work, *but also for less work*; we should focus not only on revaluing feminized forms of unwaged labor but also challenge the sanctification of such work that can accompany or be enabled by these efforts …' (ibid.: 13, emphasis added). This leads to a utopian anti-work or post-work vision for a society in which all people would have greater choice and freedom over their creative activities, and labour – whether in employment or in the home – would be a far less dominating and defining aspect of humanity. Two immediate political demands are associated with this vision: for a basic living income for all people to socially reproduce themselves, irrespective of their contribution to productive work, and for a reduction of the working week to thirty hours with no loss of pay, allowing those in work to have more time and energy to engage in other political and creative activities. Weeks suggests that fighting for these relatively modest reforms could inspire people to collective action and raise their consciousness about the need for social transformation. However, it is difficult to see how such tactics might form part of a more revolutionary strategy when Weeks' approach downplays an understanding of both the exploitation of labour-power and the work of producing and reproducing labour-power as fundamental to capitalist patriarchy and its incessant drive for profit. Although challenging masculinist readings of Marx, she seems to be throwing the Marxist-feminist baby out with the bathwater. If, as she suggests, the struggle should be to do only 'what we will', and to throw off any sense of moral obligation to work, one could ask how such an approach might really benefit women when they already have to do many forms of work that others do not wish to do. An alternative vision for revolutionary transformation is offered by Frigga Haug (2010), who argues that *all* people's time should be divided equally between four principal domains of activity: employed work; social reproduction work; personal self-development; and political activism.

In this way, not only can a more equitable distribution of reproductive labour be fought for, but women's need to organize themselves through political activism to engage in these struggles is highlighted.

Conclusion

Marx understood labour-power as the creative capacities, mental and manual, that make us distinctly human. Under capitalism, however, workers have no means of subsistence other than to sell their labour-power for a wage. The capitalist then extracts their living labour-power, congeals it into dead commodities, exchanges these for profit, and thus exploits labour-power to fuel surplus value for himself – a process that results in profound alienation for the worker. Marxist-feminist scholars have extended this notion of labour-power to include emotional as well as mental and manual capacities and have shown how the exploitation of labour-power has been intensified by increased demands for emotional labour in human service work. They have also demonstrated the crucial role of patriarchy in enabling nascent capitalism to subjugate women and their bodies to ensure that sufficient labour-power was available for industrial-scale production.

Further debates between Marxism and feminism have sought to analyse the status of the work that women do to reproduce labour-power in the home and family. Masculinist interpretations of Marx have viewed this as a secondary or even divisive issue in relation to the class struggle, while radical feminists have argued that gender is the primary question and that class divisions have always been secondary to the oppression of women by men. Marxist feminists refuse this 'class or gender' divide. Some see women's reproduction of labour-power not as unpaid, but as work that is indirectly paid for and exploited by capitalism through the medium of men's wages. Others, however, are concerned that this 'wages for housework' movement abandons women to the isolation and mundanity of much social reproduction work and argue therefore for a more equitable distribution of both employment and social reproduction in ways that allow all people to engage in self-development and political activism as well. Analysing both labour-power and its reproduction in a coherent way is a challenging task, but as we have seen from this brief review, these issues lie at the heart of understanding capitalist patriarchy and the class and gender oppression it spawns.

References

Allman, P. (1999) *Revolutionary Social Transformation: Democratic Hopes, Political Possibilities and Critical Education*, Westport, CT: Bergin & Garvey.

— (2007) *On Marx: An Introduction to the Revolutionary Intellect of Karl Marx*, Rotterdam: Sense.

— (2010) *Critical Education against Global Capitalism: Karl Marx and Revolutionary Critical Education*, 2nd edn, Rotterdam: Sense.

Arruzza, C. (2013) *Dangerous Liaisons: The Marriages and Divorces of Marxism and Feminism*, Pontypool: Merlin.

Bolton, S. C. (2005) *Emotion Management in the Workplace*, Basingstoke: Palgrave.

Brook, P. (2009a) 'The alienated heart: Hochschild's "emotional labour" thesis and the anticapitalist politics of alienation', *Capital and Class*, 98: 7–31.

— (2009b) 'In critical defence of "emotional labour": refuting Bolton's critique of Hochschild's concept', *Work, Employment and Society*, 23(3): 531–48.

Colley, H. (2003a) *Mentoring for Social Inclusion: A Critical Approach to Nurturing Mentor Relationships*, London: RoutledgeFalmer.

— (2003b) 'Engagement mentoring for "disaffected" youth: a new model of mentoring for social inclusion', *British Educational Research Journal*, 29(4): 505–26.

— (2011a) 'Learning to labour in the nursery', in P. Jones (ed.), *Marxism and Education: Renewing Dialogues*, vol. 3: *Pedagogy and Culture*, Basingstoke: Palgrave Macmillan.

— (2011b) 'Mentoring young people: a saintly vocation or an alienating praxis?', in S. Carpenter and S. Mojab (eds), *Educating from Marx: Race, Gender, and Learning*, Basingstoke: Palgrave Macmillan, pp. 87–112.

Dalla Costa, M. and S. James (1972) *The Power of Women and the Subversion of Community*, London: Wages for Housework, radicaljournal.com/books/maria_dalla_costa_power.

DeVault, M. L. (1991) *Feeding the Family: The Social Organization of Caring as Gendered Work*, Chicago, IL: University of Chicago Press.

— (1999) 'Comfort and struggle: emotion work in family life', *Annals of the American Academy for Political and Social Sciences*, 561: 52–63.

Federici, S. (2004) *Caliban and the Witch: Women, the Body and Primitive Accumulation*, Brooklyn, NY: Autonomedia.

Firestone, S. (1970) *The Dialectic of Sex: The Case for Feminist Revolution*, New York: William Morrow.

Fortunati, L. (1995) *The Arcane of Reproduction: Housework, Prostitution, Labor and Capital*, Brooklyn, NY: Autonomedia.

Goffman, E. (1969) *Asylums*, London: Penguin.

Goleman, D. (1996) *Emotional Intelligence: Why It Can Matter More than IQ*, London: Bloomsbury.

Harvey, D. (2010) *A Companion to Marx's Capital*, London: Verso.

Haug, F. (2010) 'A politics of working life', in T. Seddon, L. Henriksson and B. Niemeyer (eds), *Learning and Work and the Politics of Working Life*, London: Routledge, pp. 217–25.

Heller, A. (1979) *A Theory of Feelings*, Assen: Van Gorcum.

Hochschild, A. R. (1983) *The Managed Heart: Commercialization of Human Feeling*, Berkeley and Los Angeles: University of California Press.

James, N. (1989) 'Emotional labour, skills and work in the social relations of feeling', *Sociological Review*, 31(1): 15–42.

Marx, K. (1902) *Wage-labor and Capital*, New York: New York Labor News, https://archive.org/details/cu31924002370181.

— (1959) *Economic and Philosophical Manuscripts of 1844*, Moscow: Progress, www.marxists.org/archive/marx/works/download/pdf/Economic-Philosophic-Manuscripts-1844.pdf.

— (1975) *Wages, Price and Profit*, Peking: Foreign Languages Press, https://ia600304.us.archive.org/8/items/WagesPriceAndProfit/wpp.pdf

— (1999) *Capital*, www.marxists.org/archive/marx/works/1867-c1/ch06.htm.

Mies, M. (1998) *Patriarchy and Accumulation on a World Scale*, 2nd edn, London: Zed Books.

Millett, K. (1970) *Sexual Politics*, New York: Doubleday.

Price, H. (2001) 'Emotional labour in the classroom: a psychoanalytic perspective', *Journal of Social Work Practice*, 15(2): 161–80.

Rikowski, G. (2002) 'Fuel for the living fire: labour-power!', in A. C. Dinerstein and M. Neary (eds), *The Labour Debate: An Investigation into the Theory and Reality of Capitalist Work*, Burlington: Ashgate, pp. 179–202.

Smith, D. E. (1993) 'The Standard North American Family: SNAF as an ideological code', *Journal of Family Issues*, 14: 50–65.

— (2005) *Institutional Ethnography: A Sociology for People*. Lanham, MD: Altamira.

Smith, P. (1992) *The Emotional Labour of Nursing*, Basingstoke: Macmillan.

— (2012) *The Emotional Labour of Nursing Revisited: Can Nurses Still Care?*, Basingstoke: Palgrave Macmillan.

Stacey, M. (1984) 'The division of labour revisited', in P. Abrams, R. Deem, J. Finch and P. Rock (eds), *Development and Diversity: British Sociology, 1950–1960*, London: George Allen & Unwin, pp. 172–90.

Weeks, K. (2011) *The Problem with Work: Feminism, Marxism, Antiwork Politics, and Postwork Imaginaries*, Durham, NC: Duke University Press.

11 | NATION AND NATIONALISM

Amir Hassanpour

Marxism emphasizes the class nature of nations and nationalisms, anchoring them in the emergence of the bourgeoisie in the process of transition from feudalism to capitalism.[1] Gender is missing in this theoretical claim. Feminism highlights the gendered nature of nations, considering them as a form of patriarchal organization of society.[2] In this theorization, class is generally overlooked.

Marxism seeks the elimination of nations and nationalism in the process of socialist revolution leading to classless communist society. While feminism emphasizes the patriarchal nature of capitalism, the dismantling of patriarchy is usually not premised on the dismantling of the nation.

Marxist theorization

Marxism's interest in theorizing nation and nationalism is informed by its project of radically transforming the world and replacing class society, divided into numerous nations, with communism, conceived as a classless human society not fragmented by nationalism and national borders. Attachments to nation and ethnicity, as well as religion, tribe, territory, language and gender, are treated as predicaments of class society, which Marx called 'prehistory' (Marx 1970: 22). The consciousnesses, identities or particularities rooted in these cleavages are tied to class relations and serve the reproduction of these relations within the socio-economic formation to which they belong (e.g. feudalism, capitalism and socialism). Nations are a relic of the past, not the cornerstone of a new society.

It is not surprising, therefore, that Marxists detest nation(alism) ideologically and theoretically. Politically, however, nationalist movements are assessed according to three interrelated considerations: a) do they aim at the overthrow of pre-capitalist relations, feudalism, tribalism, slavery, etc.?; b) do they struggle against national oppression?; c) do they hinder or promote the proletariat's project of overthrowing capitalism? As early as 1948, Marx and Engels wrote in the Communist Manifesto:

> The communists are further reproached with desiring to abolish countries and nationality. The working men have no country. We cannot take from them what they have not got. Since the proletariat must first of all acquire political supremacy, must rise to be the leading class of the nation, must constitute itself the nation, it is so far, itself national, though not in the bourgeois sense of the word. (Marx and Engels 1976: 502–3)

Reading Marx undialectically, many commentators on Marxism do not make sense of why the proletariat should disown nation and, at the same time, constitute itself as nation. Commenting on the quotation, Lenin (1972: 166–7) noted that the phrase 'workers have no country' means that a) their economic position is not national but international, b) their class enemy and the conditions of their emancipation are international, and c) the international unity of the workers is more important than their national unity. Yet, the working class is formed and politically bound within the borders of the nation-state. Marx and Engels noted: 'Though not in substance, yet in form, the struggle of the proletariat with the bourgeoisie is at first a national struggle. The proletariat of each country must, of course, first of all settle matters with its own bourgeoisie' (Marx and Engels 1976: 495). Thus, the working class, divided by national borders, is under the direct economic, political and military rule of 'its own' bourgeoisie, and its struggle has to be directed first and foremost against its own class enemy. Thus, understood dialectically, the national and the international, like the bourgeoisie and the proletariat in which they are rooted, form a 'unity and struggle of opposites' – that is, they depend on and negate each other.

While the formation of nations takes different forms, Marxist theory anchors the advent of nations in the rise of capitalism. Nations emerged in the process of the disintegration of economically and politically fragmented feudal society and the concomitant formation of a single market, based on capitalist division of labour. This process involves the formation of a common territory (homeland; national market) in which both capital and labour can move freely. The capitalist market uproots the land-tied peasantry, transforms them into wage-earning labourers (the proletariat), and thereby mixes the population, a process that requires a national language, one that overcomes regional dialects and facilitates the forging of national ties, including a common, though still class-differentiated, cultural life. Before the First World War, when eastern European and Russian socialists, including Rosa Luxemburg, Karl Radek, Otto Bauer, V. I. Lenin and J. V. Stalin, were debating the national question, Stalin summed up the Marxist-Leninist position: '*A nation is a historically constituted, stable community of people, formed on the basis of a common language, territory, economic life, and psychological make-up manifested in a common culture*' (Stalin 1970: 68, emphasis in original). A people becomes a nation only if all the four characteristics are present.[3] Having a state is not a requirement of nationhood, although nationalists strive for statehood, and according to Lenin, 'the national state is *typical* and normal for the capitalist period'.[4]

Thus, the Marxist theory of nation is different from the traditional understanding, cherished in democratic theory, of 'ethnic' (cultural) and 'civic' (political) nations.[5] Although the literature on the topic considers language and culture as markers of ethnicity, they are, in Marxist theory, socio-historical phenomena rather than inherent or primordial features of nations. Marxist theory is also different from 'civic nation' theories, which equate the nation with political-juridical structures such as 'popular democracy' (or liberal or 'bourgeois democracy'), and in so doing conflate the nation with the state (for a critique of these theories, see, e.g., Yack 1999).

Capitalism and its nations develop unevenly, leaving the world divided into a hierarchy of small and big, developed and developing, colonizer and colonized, sovereign and dependent, or oppressor and oppressed nations. Under conditions of uneven development, there are more nations than states, most of which are multinational entities. The formation of nations and their states in the beginning of the capitalist era was progressive insofar as national statehood helped in the dismantling of feudalism. At the same time capitalism, especially in its later development, had to break down national borders, a situation that paves the road to socialism:

> Developing capitalism knows two historical tendencies in the national question. The first is the awakening of national life and national movements, the struggle against all national oppression, and the creation of national states. The second is the

> development and growing frequency of international intercourse in every form, the break-down of national barriers, the creation of the international unity of capital, of economic life in general, of politics, science, etc.
>
> Both tendencies are a universal law of capitalism. The former predominates in the beginning of its development, the later characterises a mature capitalism that is moving towards its transformation into socialist society. The Marxists' national programme takes both tendencies into account, and advocates, firstly, the equality of nations and languages and the impermissibility of all *privileges* in this respect (and also the right of nations to self-determination …); secondly, the principle of internationalism and uncompromising struggle against contamination of the proletariat with bourgeois nationalism, even of the most refined kind. (Lenin 1971a: 15, emphasis in original)

Marx, Engels and many of their followers assess nations, nationalisms and nationalist movements in terms of their contribution or opposition to revolution. Marxists see nation(alism) as a component of capitalism, both of which are, historically speaking, obsolete. According to Lenin, 'Bourgeois nationalism and proletarian internationalism – these are the two irreconcilably hostile slogans that correspond to the two great class camps throughout the capitalist world, and express the *two* policies (nay, the two world outlooks) in the national question' (ibid.: 14). At the same time, Marxists oppose national oppression not for moral reasons but because it inhibits the democratization of political life and holds back the struggle for socialism. According to Marx, 'any nation that oppresses another forges its own chains' (Marx 1971: 163). Lenin also emphasized: 'Whoever does not recognize and champion the equality of nations and languages, and does not fight against all national oppression or inequality, is not a Marxist; he is not even a democrat' (Lenin 1971a: 16). In defending the Bolshevik policy of supporting the right of oppressed nations to self-determination, Lenin elaborated:

> *Insofar* as the bourgeoisie of the oppressed nation fights the oppressor, we are always, in every case, and more strongly than anyone else, *in favour*, for we are the staunchest and the most consistent enemies of oppression. But insofar as the bourgeoisie of the oppressed nation stands for *its own* bourgeois nationalism, we stand against. We fight against the privileges and violence of

> the oppressor nation, and do not in any way condone strivings for privileges on the part of the oppressed nation. (Lenin 1971b: 55, emphasis in original)

National oppression is an obstacle to socialist revolution especially because it divides the working class according to national belongings and turns the class into the 'reserve army' of 'its own' bourgeoisie. While nationalists oppose national oppression, they benefit from it insofar as it facilitates class collaboration in the name of defending 'the fatherland', 'the nation' or 'national honour'. The alternative is internationalism:

> Marxism cannot be reconciled with nationalism, be it even of the 'most just,' 'purest,' most refined and civilised brand. In place of all forms of nationalism Marxism advances internationalism, the amalgamation of all nations in the higher unity, a unity that is growing before our eyes with every mile of railway line that is built, with every international trust, and every workers' association that is formed (an association that is international in its economic activities as well as in its ideas and aims). (Lenin 1971a: 22)

This claim about the conditions that favour internationalism has confused many critics of Marxism, who often quote Marx himself on the future of nations: 'National differences and antagonisms between peoples are daily more and more vanishing, owing to the development of the bourgeoisie, to freedom of commerce, to the world market, to uniformity in the mode of production and in the conditions of life corresponding thereto' (Marx and Engels 1976: 503). These developments in productive forces undermine national attachments, borders, territorial integrity and sovereignty. In fact, advances in 'the means of communication and transport' had allowed as early as the mid-nineteenth century, when Marx was penning *Grundrisse*, 'the annihilation of space by time' (Marx 1973: 524), so much so that the

> Constant revolutionising of production, uninterrupted disturbance of all social conditions, everlasting uncertainty and agitation distinguish the bourgeois epoch from all earlier ones. All fixed, fast-frozen relations, with their train of ancient and venerable prejudices and opinions, are swept away, all new-formed ones become antiquated before they can ossify. All that is solid melts into air, all that is holy is profaned ... The need of a constantly expanding market

> for its products chases the bourgeoisie over the entire surface of the globe. It must nestle everywhere, settle everywhere, establish connexions everywhere. (Marx and Engels 1976: 487)

However, capital's dynamic of 'expand or die' does not lead to the dismantling of the nation and the world order of nation-states. Political conditions – that is, the presence of the capitalist state and its nationalist politics as well as the prevalence of ideologies of nationalism, national chauvinism or fascism – will not allow the spontaneous or peaceful dissolution of nation-states. The superstructure guards the economic base, and in case the bourgeoisie feels threatened it will appeal to nation, nationalism, homeland, country, patriotism, fascism, xenophobia, racism, religious hatred, war and genocide in order to wreck any idea of coexistence, peace and internationalism. Marx's claim about the emergence of material conditions for the withering away of nations is borne out by, among other developments, the formation of the European Union, both its successes and failures. It is significant, also, that the EU emerged on the ruins of two Europe-based wars in which European imperialist powers devastated their continent and, together with other states, ruined much of the rest of the world. Another significant experience was the dissolution of the Second International of socialist parties after they all, with the exception of the Bolsheviks, joined the 'patriotic war' of their bourgeoisie in the course of the First World War. Hence, whether nationalist or internationalist politics prevails is not dictated by the economics of capitalism. It depends, rather, on the political and ideological outlook of communist parties; in other words, struggles in the superstructure, rather than the level of capitalist development, determine how the contradiction between the two politics and the two classes will be resolved.

Determined not to join 'their own' bourgeoisie in the First World War, the Bolsheviks turned the capitalist war into a revolution against capitalism, overthrew the Tsarist regime, and laid the foundations for socialism under conditions of famine, destruction and military intervention of imperialist powers. This was a revolution in the world's largest country, multinational Russia, which according to Lenin was 'a prison house of nations'. Freedom from this 'necessity' called for, consistent with Hegelian and Engelsian dialectics, its recognition and, according to Mao, its transformation, too (Mao Tse-Tung 2007b: 183). The Bolshevik party had the theoretical preparation to make what Engels called, in a different context, this difficult 'leap from the realm of necessity into the realm of freedom' (Engels 1976: 367). Before the revolution, Lenin had emphasized that it was '*impossible* to abolish national (or any other political) oppression under capitalism, since this requires the abolition of classes, i.e., the introduction of socialism', but socialism, itself a class society, only 'creates the *possibility* of abolishing national oppression ...' (Lenin 1971c: 116, emphasis in original). In other words, freedom from the nation was a question of transition not from capitalism to socialism but from the latter to communism. Many steps were taken to create the *possibility* of this transformation. One major issue of theory and practice was whether socialism could be built in one country or, as Marx had suggested, on the scale of developed capitalist countries of Europe. In the absence of successful socialist revolutions in Europe, the party, considering changes resulting from the transformation of capitalism into imperialism since the late nineteenth century, undertook the project of 'socialism in one country'. The world's only country with a non-ethnic and non-territorial name, the Union of Soviet Socialist Republics, was, however, divided into republics demarcated by and named after the major nationalities, nationalities such as Armenian, Georgian, Tajik and Turkmen, all of which had embarked on the road to national formation only a few decades before 1917. As part of the project of eliminating national oppression, in 1917 the party recognized the independence of Finland, and the constitution granted the nationalities' sovereign and equal status with the right to self-determination up to and including the right to secede. It was clear, in Lenin's theoretical work, that self-determination, like 'equal pay for equal work', is a 'bourgeois right' which reproduces the inequalities of capitalist relations. To give another example, in culture and arts, a policy of 'nationalist in form, socialist in content' was promoted. Although national antagonisms diminished, all these steps turned into sites of class struggle between communists and nationalists. Dialectically speaking, communists and nationalists or the proletariat and the bourgeoisie, far from being separated, exist in unity and struggle.

Not surprisingly, communists themselves advocated policies that were nationalistic and justified by 'necessities' such as the impositions of capitalist encirclement, the second imperialist war, or the Cold War. Nationalism was present in subtle ways when, for example, communist parties around the world were expected to support the 'headquarters of proletarian revolution', the USSR, even at the expense of forgoing revolution against their own bourgeoisie. Equally damaging was the appeal to nationalism during the Second World War and even the forcible transfer of some nationalities from the theatre of war in the west to central Asian republics. Less than a decade after the formation of a 'socialist camp' extending from China to Germany, Nikita Khrushchev, in a *coup d'état* in 1957, opened the way for capitalist relations, a situation which, within a few years, the Communist Party of China (CPC) identified as 'restoration of capitalism' leading to the transformation of the USSR into a 'social imperialist' country – that is, 'socialist in words, imperialist in action'. Summing up the experience of both the USSR and China, Mao noted that, in the process of class struggle under socialism, a 'new bourgeoisie' emerges inside the ruling communist party and its political and ideological line leads to a restoration of capitalism. This happened also in a *coup d'état* in China in 1976, which brought the 'capitalist roaders' to power and restored capitalism and its nationalism.

While in the theoretical-political positions summarized above there is no reference to the historical contradiction between the two genders, Marxism, as a general dialectical theory of society, allowed profound insights into the gender division of society. Marxists from August Bebel (*Woman and Socialism*, 1879) and Engels (*Origin of the Family, Private Property and the State*, 1884 [1985]) in the nineteenth century to leaders in the women's movement such as Clara Zetkin, Inissa Armand and Alexandra Kollontai in the early twentieth century created a body of theoretical and empirical knowledge on gender relations, which split feminist consciousness and practice into two class sites – liberal and socialist/communist. In connection with theories of nation(alism), liberal feminism aims at achieving equality within the framework of the capitalist nation and its political-juridical structure – that is, bourgeois democracy. By contrast, Marxism emphasizes that gender equality cannot be achieved under capitalism. This is the case because capitalism allows only for legal equality of women and men, which in the absence of social and economic equality inevitably reproduces the inequalities of the patriarchal regime. Marx argued, in dealing with equal rights of the workers, that because individual workers have different needs, equal right remains, even in socialism, 'a right of inequality, in its content, like every right' (Marx 1972: 16).

In contrast to liberal feminism's nation-centred political agenda, socialist women symbolically broke down the borders of the nation-state when in 1911 they launched 8 March as the International Working Women's Day. Two years after the October Revolution, Lenin highlighted, on 8 March 1920, unprecedented and swift progress towards legal equality in gender relations in the Soviet Union, warning that this was just one necessary but insufficient step towards real (extra-legal) equality. Even socialism, he emphasized, cannot uproot gender domination (Lenin 1982: 85). Instead of continuing the creation of conditions for the demise of nation and patriarchy, the Communist Party of the Soviet Union declared in the early 1930s, against the claims of Marxist-Leninist theory, that classes and patriarchal relations had disappeared.

Feminist theorization

Feminism, in the simple sense of consciousness and knowledge about gender relations and women's emancipation, was born together with nationalism and its first nation-states (e.g. the Netherlands, Britain, France and the United States) in the age of Enlightenment. The first generation of feminists found out that the bourgeois democratic state had no intention of treating men and women as equal members of the nation. Citizenship, the much-celebrated achievement of democratic revolutions, allowed full membership in the nation only to propertied or taxpaying men, and denied citizenship rights to women, male workers and religious, ethnic and racial minorities. Not only the male Robespierre, representative of the radical wing of the bourgeoisie, but also intellectual women realized that the revolutionaries' call for 'Liberty, Equality and Fraternity' was no more than a promise. It is remarkable that Olympe de Gouges (1748–93), a woman aristocrat, immediately rejected the French Revolution's hallmark, the 'Declaration of the Rights of Man and the [Male] Citizen', and issued, instead, the 'Declaration of the Rights of Woman and the Female Citizen'.

Feminists and women activists continued to struggle for raising the status of women by addressing their demands to the state and working within the framework of the nation. But the nation-state was reluctant to reform the hierarchical structure of nationhood. It took about a century of intellectual and political struggles of the suffragettes to impose on the state women's right to vote and to be elected. The gendered nature of the nation-state did not, however, visibly change as a result of reforms – even the most outstanding one, women's access to the main organ of democratic rule, the parliament. Opposed to the masculinist militarism and violence of the nation-state on the eve of the Second World War, Virginia Woolf (1882–1941) wrote about the antagonism between women and nation. A woman asks, she noted,

> 'What does "our country" mean to me, an outsider?' To decide this she will analyse the meaning of patriotism in her own case. She will inform herself of the position of her sex and her class in the past. She will inform herself of the amount of land, wealth and prosperity in the possession of her own sex and class in the present – how much of 'England' in fact belongs to her … 'Our country,' she will say, 'throughout the greater part of history has treated me as a slave; it has denied me education or any share of its possessions … in fact, as a woman, I have no country. As a woman I want no country. As a woman, my country is the whole world.' And if, when reason has its say, still some obstinate emotion remains, some love of England dropped into a child's ears by the cawing of rooks in an elm tree, by the splash of waves on a beach, or by English voices murmuring nursery rhymes, this drop of pure, if irrational, emotion she will make serve her to give to England first what she desires of peace and freedom for the whole world. (quoted in West 1997: xi)

De Gouges and Woolf were not alone in highlighting the conflict. Some six decades after Woolf, Kaplan, for instance, another feminist, noted that 'feminism and nationalism are almost always incompatible ideological positions within the European context'. As a result of this incongruity, western European feminism has been 'aligned with the parties of the Left' (Kaplan 1997: 3). In contrast to American 'liberal feminism' or the feminism of Western industrial nations outside Europe, western European feminism 'tends to be more radical and more marked by the language and ideas of Marxism, Leninism, communism, and socialism …' (ibid.: 22).

It would be appropriate, however, not to conflate the conflict between women and nation(alism) with that between feminism and nation(alism). Feminism is the conscious, theoretically and politically formulated component in women's struggle for emancipation; it consists of a diversity of positions ranging from liberal feminism's agenda for reforming gender relations within the framework of the nation-state to Marxist-feminism's platform for dismantling the patriarchal nation. Quite often feminist consciousness sets the agenda of women's movements. More recently, some feminists in the West have highlighted the conflict between women and nation in more theoretical ways than Gouges or Woolf. Yuval-Davis, for instance, identifies three modes of women's reproduction of nations – biological, cultural and symbolic. However, biological reproduction, in this study, is reduced to a question of reproductive rights – that is, the 'right of women to choose whether to have children, as well as how many to have and when ...' (1997: 22). Compared with the Marxist proposition of the dual nature of production,[6] this approach is much more limited in scope and significance. In fact, some feminists try to resolve the conflict by making nationalism more egalitarian through a reform of the regime of rights. West, for example, has devised a 'Theory of Feminist Nationalism', which consists of 'social movements simultaneously seeking rights for women and rights for nationalists within a variety of social, economic, and political contexts' (1997: xxx).

In non-Western contexts, too, feminists as well as nationalists aim at reconciling the conflict. Quite often both sides argue that women should not push for equality and gender justice as long as the whole nation is under colonial or external oppression (see, among a vast literature, Jayawardena 1986). This compromise is often rationalized by attributing its alternative – that is, no prioritization of nationalist demands over women's demands – to 'White', 'racist' or 'Western' feminisms (see, for instance, Yuval-Davis 1997: 117–18). While the existence of racism in Western feminisms is well established, the project of reconciling nationalism and feminism is universal, both Western and Eastern, and is a class position: the bourgeoisie's preference to keep in check all social, political and economic conflicts within the nation and ensure the loyalty of women to the nation-state. In this reconciliation, nationalism and its state have the upper hand.

In the absence of a compromise similar to that in national liberation movements, the social movements of the 1960s in the West, especially women's and feminist movements, were able to expand the regime of rights. By the end of the twentieth century in many Western states, a set of reforms had removed many obstacles to legal equality between the two genders. Women's and feminist movements envisage new rights all the time, and today the rights granted by the state are far more extensive than those contemplated by the early generations of feminists. In this sense, it is easy to demonstrate that constitutional and legal equality has been achieved in some nation-states, where, one may claim, liberal feminism has accomplished its mission. While the state can be pushed farther to grant other rights, Marxists argue that legal equality, far from eliminating extralegal equality, actually contributes to its reproduction. Although some strands in non-Marxist feminism, especially anarchist and radical, continue to be suspicious of the state, their alternatives to capitalism and nation(alism) distinguish them from Marxism. Marxist theory considers the state and its legal regime as one source for the reproduction of the contradiction between the genders. The regime of rights, a product of Enlightenment and bourgeois democratic revolutions of the late eighteenth century, was able to dismantle the feudal legal system by establishing capitalism's alternative, the juridico-political system of bourgeois democracy. Such a system is incapable, even in its most refined or radical form, of dismantling today's capitalism and its patriarchy (Lotta et al. 2009).

Marxist-feminist theorization: requirements and obstacles

We have seen in the last two decades important contributions, by both Marxist and non-Marxist feminists, to our understanding of gender relations during the rise of capitalism. For instance, Sylvia Federici's *Caliban and the Witch: Women, the Body and Primitive Accumulation* (2004) ties primitive accumulation to the expropriation of women's unpaid labour, including reproduction, rather than wage labour only. Leopoldina Fortunati's *The Arcane of Reproduction: Housework, Prostitution, Labor and Capital* (1995) argues that reproduction creates value and, as such, it should be treated as production. Mary Murray's *The Law of the Father: Patriarchy in the Transition from Feudalism to Capitalism* (1995) delves into relationships between patriarchy, property and kinship in the rise of the state in England during the transition period. However, these studies, inspired by Marxism, have no focus on the emergence of nations in the process of transition. By contrast, Dana Nelson's non-Marxist work *National Manhood: Capitalist Citizenship and the Imagined Fraternity of White Men* (1998) examines gender, nation and race and how 'white manhood' shaped the American nation from the Revolutionary War to the mid-nineteenth century.

These theoretically conscious empirical studies provide deep insight into interweaving social relations of capitalism, patriarchy and nationhood even though they do not aim specifically at developing

Marxist-feminist theorizations of nation. Such a goal requires theoretical work in its own right. But theory, far from being a simple summing up or generalization of empirical findings, is a site of political, philosophical and ideological struggles. Marxism as well as feminism is the outcome of such struggles on two fronts – externally against adversaries (patriarchal and capitalist outlooks) and internally among conflicting positions within its own territory. Marxism, for example, developed as a materialist outlook, in conflict with idealism, and at the same time in opposition to mechanical materialism. However, theoretical and even political positions, much like social classes, are not separated by mountains; Marxist dialectics was shaped more by the dialectics of Hegelian idealism than that of materialists, which was less advanced. In spite of or also because of this interpenetration of positions, Marxism has sought to distinguish itself as the world view of one class, the working class, rather than an eclecticism of the best.

Marxism and feminism were, from the beginning, separated as two conflicting class positions, although Marxist theorization of patriarchy became a component of feminist knowledge. It was clear, in early Marxism (e.g. in Engels), that gender was not a class formation, yet economistic Marxism, especially in the USSR from the late 1920s, reduced gender to class and gender oppression to class exploitation. By the early 1930s, the Communist Party was announcing that class struggle, women's oppression and national oppression in the USSR had come to an end. This claim moved the country and much of the international communist movement into a rightist or conformist direction with serious political consequences. While it is rather obvious in Marxist theory that gender is distinct from class and oppression and exploitation are different,[7] it is also known that projects to eliminate gender oppression or national oppression are political, and class politics at that.[8] Thus, one may claim that Lenin's idea that gender and national oppression would not be uprooted under socialism and Stalin's claim that by the early 1930s – barely the beginning of socialism – they had ended are two class positions, even though they emanate from the same party.

Given the seriousness of political struggles over gender relations, it is not difficult to explain the failures of 'marriage' projects between feminism and Marxism. Marxism was a serious challenge to liberal feminism at the end of the nineteenth and beginning of the twentieth centuries, and in the 1960s and 1970s reshaped feminist knowledge. Since the late twentieth century, however, while feminism is experiencing a 'knowledge explosion' (Kramarae and Spender 1992), Marxism has suffered setbacks, especially after the restoration of capitalism in China (1976) and earlier in the USSR (1957), the collapse of the Eastern Bloc (1989–92), the hegemony of neoliberalism, and growing conformism in the academy (see below). Marxism is experiencing, in the context of current economic crisis, a new phase of revival, though it cannot reclaim its twentieth-century status without extensive renovation in theory, especially in its approach to gender relations. It can incorporate the extensive knowledge created by feminisms much in the same way Marx and Engels embraced, enthusiastically and critically, advances in non-Marxist knowledge such as Darwin's theory of evolution and Henry Lewis Morgan's findings and insights on pre-class societies.

Marxism and feminism aim at changing reality (class society and patriarchy) and replacing it with alternative systems of social relations. This political goal distinguishes them from conformist theorizations such as post-structuralism, which rejects liberation or emancipation as 'grand narratives' and restricts human consciousness and action to 'here and now'. No doubt, while the conflict between Marxism and 'postality' cannot be reconciled, some feminist positions readily blend with post-structuralism.[9]

Feminism, in its post-structuralist versions, is constrained by a variety of epistemological positions. For instance, fear of essentialism robs post-structuralists of major building blocks of an adequate theory, including crucial concepts such as 'patriarchy' and 'woman' (see below), and restricts their participation in political struggles. The impact on activism is so debilitating that some anti-essentialists engage in theoretical tricks and, instead of admitting essences and rejecting essentialism, reject essence and make 'temporary and strategic' alliances with essentialism.[10] In order to make way for participation in resistance and solidarity politics, they take shelter in 'strategic essentialism', 'strategic universalism' (Burden 2012) and even 'strategic relativism' (Ryan 1995: 582).

Marxism posits the existence of essences, without which it would be difficult to distinguish between phenomena in society and nature. Essences are, however, historical and, like all phenomena, change. In dialectics, motion is absolute and rest is relative. Believing in essences does not make anyone essentialist unless essences are understood as unchanging or eternal. Marxist theorizations of 'nation', 'patriarchy' or any other social formation become even more complex and adequate insofar as they have to be understood through philosophical categories such as 'freedom and necessity', 'necessity and chance', 'essence and phenomenon', 'matter and consciousness', 'universal and particular', 'motion and rest', 'relative and absolute', 'possibility and actuality' and 'concrete and abstract'. When non-Marxists use these oppositions at all, they treat them as binary oppositions, dichotomies or dualisms. In Marxist dialectics, however, the two sides stand in relationships of 'unity and struggle' – that is, they depend on each other for their existence and under certain conditions may negate or transform into each other. From a Marxist perspective, for example, the diversity of 'nations' or 'patriarchies' is inevitable owing to their socio-historical nature, each formed or created under particular conditions; however, human thought, enabled by language, is capable of grasping universals in the midst of particulars. Every patriarchy is inevitably particular in the sense that it emerges in a distinct historical context owing to variations in consciousness, culture, geography, class system, socio-economic formations, language, religion, statehood, nationality, ethnicity, and so on. Obviously, human societies, some separated by physical divides such as oceans and continents, did not create gender relations according to any blueprint for a universal system. It is possible, however, to depict universality in the particularity of patriarchies. French, Cree, Spanish and Iranian patriarchies are different, but they can readily be seen as regimes of gender relations rather than, say, religion, class or kinship systems. Moreover, universals and particulars form a dialectical contradiction, and far from being inherent qualities or properties, they can be depicted as relations of mutual dependence and transformation into each other, and their status, as universal or particular, depends on the context: 'Because the range of things is vast and there is no limit to their development, what is universal in one context becomes particular in another. Conversely, what is particular in one context becomes universal in another' (Mao Tse-Tung 2007a: 85).

Thus, patriarchy (the regime of exercise of male power in hierarchically organized gender relations), while always particular, forms a universal in the context of class societies from the ancient to the modern period (it is found in all these societies), although it appears as a particular in the context of the longer span of history, from pre-class to the beginning of class formations.

Post-structuralism conflates dialectical contradictions with dualisms, and resolves them by discarding one side of the opposites, the universal, and, inadvertently though systematically, presenting the other side, the particular, as a universal. The following is an example of understanding essentialism and discarding the universal in favour of the particular:

> Despite patriarchy's heuristic value for theorizing hierarchical social structures, for feminists its usefulness is diminished by its essentialism, according to which male dominance of women is an inevitable response to natural differences. Such assumptions sustain ahistorical conceptions of 'woman' and 'man' as universal categories, ignoring racial, class, and other differences. Patriarchy's usefulness as a theoretical concept is contested around these issues. (Code 2000: 379)

Here a most important concept of feminist theory, 'patriarchy', is discarded because it is used essentialistically within discredited claims of 'natural differences'. In fact, Marxist and much non-Marxist social theory have rejected biological determinism. These reservations do not allow post-structuralist feminism to adequately theorize nation(alism), a task that calls into play a conceptual repertoire including 'liberation', 'independence', 'sovereignty', 'freedom', 'self-determination', 'imperialism' or 'internationalism', which are readily rejected as 'grand narratives' or 'essentialisms'.

In the context of globalization and ongoing technological revolution, non-Marxist literature entertains ideas of the erosion of borders and the withering away of the nation(-state), but theories of 'transnationalism', 'cosmopolitanism', 'post-nationalism' or 'feminist nationalism' fail to account for the way nations reproduce themselves by, among other measures, fortifying national borders even as they are eroding.

The conflict between Marxism and feminism over the question of nation(alism), briefly outlined in this chapter, points to the need for constructive interaction between these two major world views. While the material conditions for the withering away of nations have been present for a long time, nations continue to exercise sovereignty, in part through the exercise of patriarchal power, drawing hundreds of millions of women into the capitalist market and unleashing an ever-expanding 'war on women'. Resolving these contradictions is a major theoretical and political challenge of our time. Marxist theory advocates the withering away, through prolonged class struggle, of nations and all institutions and social relations of class society. Feminist theory's main preoccupation is elimination of gender hierarchy within the perimeters of the nation.

Notes

1 The focus of this chapter is on the theorization of nation(alism) in 'classical' Marxism, primarily the works of Marx, Engels and Lenin.

2 By 'feminism' I mean, except when prefixed by 'Marxist', its very diverse non-Marxist versions, some of which are identified here as 'liberal' and 'post-structuralist'.

3 Critics of this position fail to grasp the interrelationships between these four constituents of the nation dialectically, and reject it as the Stalin 'shopping list' (e.g. Yuval-Davis 1997: 19). The theoretical claims underlying the definition are: (a) nations are not eternal or primordial phenomena but, rather, have a beginning and an end; (b) they are products of capitalism ('common economic life'); (c) nations are not racial or tribal formations, but are made up of many ethnic or racial backgrounds; (d) nations are stable communities of people rather than 'casual and loosely connected conglomerations of groups' like pre-capitalist empires; (e) people living in a stable community without a common language cannot form a nation although different nations can have the same language, e.g. English in New Zealand, Australia and the United States; (f) a common language alone, e.g. English in England and the United States, does not lead to the formation of a nation (British or Spanish colonies separated from Britain and Spain in spite of community of language); (g) a common territory is necessary for 'lengthy and systematic' association, which depends on people living together generation after generation; (h) common territory and language do not by themselves create a nation; the casual union of principalities under a king did not create a nation; and (i) a common culture distinguishes nations that speak in the same language (Stalin 1970: 66–9).

4 Lenin noted that 'the tendency of every national movement is towards the formation of *national states*, under which these requirements of modern capitalism [i.e. connections between classes, the market and proprietors, and buyers and sellers] are best satisfied. The most profound economic factors drive towards this goal, and, therefore, for the whole of western Europe, nay, for the entire civilised world, the national state is *typical* and normal for the capitalist period' (1971b: 40–1, emphasis in original).

5 For a non-Marxist critique of the civic/ethnic dichotomy, see, e.g., among a vast literature, Spencer and Wollman (1998).

6 From early works such as *The German Ideology* (1846) to *Capital* (1867, vol. 1) to the latest ones including *The Origin of the Family, Private Property, and the State* (1884 [1985]), Marx and Engels thought of *production*, the most important distinguishing feature of our species, as consisting of two inseparable components: 'According to the materialist conception, the determining factor in history is, in the final instance, the production and reproduction of immediate life. This, again, is of a twofold character: on the one side, the production of the means of existence, of food, clothing

and shelter and the tools necessary for that production; on the other side, the production of human beings themselves, the propagation of the species' (Engels 1985: 71).

While this theoretical spark could lay the foundation of gendered theorization, Marx and Engels themselves did not pursue it further, and generations of later Marxists failed to grasp its significance and some opposed it (for a non-feminist survey of the struggle over this theoretical position in Marxist theory, see Guhr [1988]; see also Sayer [1987: 77–82]).

7 For a critique of economistic Marxism's conflation of class and gender, see Mojab (forthcoming).

8 Women are the source and engine in the struggle against patriarchal gender relations; however, in the rich history of this struggle, from the demand for enfranchisement to abortion rights, some women have supported the patriarchal regime; similarly, some workers, too, have opposed socialism. This is primarily the question of politics as a realm of consciousness and its autonomy from one's location in class, gender or nation.

9 For a critique of the conformism of contemporary feminist theories, see, among others, Ebert (1996) and Eisenstein (2009).

10 See, for instance, the dilemma of activists for indigenous rights: 'In the politics of indigenousness in international fora there are discourses and practices that strategically delimit the universe of meanings and that seek to define what are indigenous traditions, histories, collective memories, worldviews, present conditions, ways of life, and future aspirations. I argue that indigenous intellectuals and activists depict a strategically essentialized indigeneity to legitimize claims for social justice and rights; thus, this depiction should not be understood simply as an uncritical and retrograde essentialism. The (re)construction of peoplehood involves negotiating concepts used by nation states and, at the same time, a continuous conscious redrawing of cultural boundaries' (Escárcega 2010: 3).

References

Burden, B. (2012) 'Strategic universalism: dead concept walking on the subalternity of critique today', eipcp.net/transversal/0607/buden/en/.

Code, L. (2000) 'Patriarchy', in L. Code (ed.), *Encyclopedia of Feminist Theories*, London: Routledge, pp. 378–9.

Ebert, T. (1996) *Ludic Feminism and After: Postmodernism, Desire, and Labor in Late Capitalism*, Ann Arbor: University of Michigan Press.

— (2005) 'Rematerializing feminism', *Science and Society*, 61(1): 33–55.

Eisenstein, H. (2009) *Feminism Seduced: How Global Elites Use Women's Labour and Ideas to Exploit the World*, Boulder, CO: Paradigm.

Engels, F. (1976) *Anti-Düring (Herr Eugen Düring's Revolution in Science)*, Peking: Foreign Languages Press.

— (1985) *The Origin of the Family, Private Property and the State*, ed. E. Burke Leacock, New York: International.

Escárcega, S. (2010) 'Authenticating strategic essentialisms: the politics of indigenousness at the United Nations', *Cultural Dynamics*, 22(1): 3–28.

Federici, S. (2004) *Caliban and the Witch: Women, the Body and Primitive Accumulation*, Brooklyn, NY: Autonomedia.

Fortunati, L. (1995) *The Arcane of Reproduction: Housework, Prostitution, Labor and Capital*, Brooklyn, NY: Autonomedia.

Guhr, G. (1988) 'Production of life', in J. Herrmann and J. Kohn (eds), *Familie, Staat und Gesellschaftsforma-*

tion [Family, state and the formation of society], Berlin: Akademie-Verlag, pp. 51–61.

Jayawardena, K. (1986) *Feminism and Nationalism in the Third World*, London: Zed Books.

Kaplan, G. (1997) 'Feminism and nationalism: the European case', in L. West (ed.), *Feminist Nationalism*, New York: Routledge, pp. 3–40.

Kramarae, C. and D. Spender (1992) *The Knowledge Explosion: Generations of Feminist Scholarship*, New York: Teachers College Press.

Lenin, V. I. (1971a) 'Critical remarks on the national question', in V. I. Lenin, *Critical Remarks on the National Question [and] The Rights of Nations to Self-determination*, Moscow: Progress, pp. 7–38.

— (1971b) 'The right of nations to self-determination', in V. I. Lenin, *Critical Remarks on the National Question [and] The Rights of Nations to Self-determination*, Moscow: Progress, pp. 39–97.

— (1971c) 'The discussion of self-determination summed up', in V. I. Lenin, *Critical Remarks on the National Question [and] The Rights of Nations to Self-determination*, Moscow: Progress, pp. 112–50.

— (1972) 'Letter to Inessa Armand, November 20, 1916', in V. I. Lenin, *On Proletarian Internationalism*, Moscow: Progress, pp. 166–7.

— (1982) *On the Emancipation of Women*, Moscow: Progress.

Lotta, R., N. Duniya and K.J.A. (2009) 'Alain Badiou's "politics of emancipation": a communism locked within the confines of the bourgeois world', *Demarcations: A Journal of Communist Theory and Polemic*, 1, demarcations-journal.org/issue01/demarcations_badiou.html.

Mao Tse-Tung (2007a) 'On contradiction', in Slavoj Žižek (ed.), *On Practice and Contradiction*, London: Verso, pp. 67–102.

— (2007b) 'Talk on questions of philosophy', in Slavoj Žižek (ed.), *On Practice and Contradiction*, London: Verso, pp. 169–85.

Marx, K. (1970) *A Contribution to the Critique of Political Economy*, ed. M. Dobb, trans. S. W. Ryazanskaya, New York: International.

— (1971) 'Confidential communication', 28 March 1870, in K. Marx and F. Engels, *Ireland and the Irish Question*, Moscow: Progress, pp. 160–3.

— (1972) *Critique of the Gotha Programme*, Peking: Foreign Languages Press.

— (1973) *Grundrisse: Foundations of the Critique of Political Economy*, trans. M. Nicolaus, New York: Random House.

Marx, K. and F. Engels (1976) 'The Manifesto of the Communist Party', in *Collected Works*, vol. 6, New York: International, pp. 477–506.

Mojab, S. (forthcoming) 'Tavahom-e qanun va tasavor tabaq-e' [The illusion of law and the imagining of class].

Murray, M. (1995) *The Law of the Father: Patriarchy in the Transition from Feudalism to Capitalism*, London: Routledge.

Nelson, D. (1998) *National Manhood: Capitalist Citizenship and the Imagined Fraternity of White Men*, Durham, NC: Duke University Press.

Ryan, S. M. (1995) 'Errand into Africa: colonization and nation building in Sarah J. Hale's Liberia', *New England Quarterly: A Historical Review of New England Life and Letters*, 68(4): 558–83.

Sargent, L. (ed.) (1981) *The Unhappy Marriage of Marxism and Feminism: A Debate on Class and Patriarchy*, London: Pluto.

Sayer, D. (1987) *The Violence of Abstraction: The Analytical Foundations of*

Historical Materialism, London: Basil Blackwell.

Spencer, P. and H. Wollman (1998) 'Good and bad nationalisms: a critique of dualism', *Journal of Political Ideologies*, 3(3): 255–74.

Stalin, J. V. (1970) 'Marxism and the national question', in *Selections from V. I. Lenin and J. V. Stalin on National Colonial Question*, Calcutta: Calcutta Book House, pp. 65–107.

West, L. (1997) 'Introduction: Feminism constructs nationalism', in L. West, *Feminist Nationalism*, New York: Routledge, pp. xi–xxxvi.

Yack, B. (1999) 'The myth of the civic nation', in R. Beiner (ed.), *Theorizing Nationalism*, Albany: New York State University Press, pp. 103–18.

Yuval-Davis, N. (1997) *Gender and Nation*, London: Sage.

12 | PATRIARCHY/PATRIARCHIES

Kumkum Sangari

As a concept, patriarchy was characterized differently in and through women's movements in imperial and subordinate economies, and each definition encoded specific forms of resistance. Though its articulation with and imbrication in other structures, institutions and practices was always a pivotal issue, in British, western European and North American feminisms the concept hinged on the autonomy or relative autonomy of patriarchy, while the dependence of patriarchy/patriarchies on other forms and loci of systemic inequality preoccupied several currents in the women's movement in India. This chapter sketches these trajectories, traverses the disparate political locations of the term that have ranged, curiously, from renovation to relegation of Marxism, and argues for a fresh understanding of the regional, class, caste and colonial co-constitution of patriarchies, especially under the aegis of capitalism. It outlines the advantages of pluralizing the term and the corresponding alterations in patriarchy as an analytic abstraction. It suggests that the current crisis of social reproduction and the differential transnational dissolution, distribution and recomposition of patriarchal practices are best analysed through the concrete specificity of familial, state and market-led patriarchal regimes.

Looking back, the term patriarchy signals a number of breaks as well as a deep historicity construed as either a search for origins or as an explanation for continuity. Since the oppression of women was evidently not peculiar to capitalism yet evident within it, it was seen to have a separate history spanning distinct modes of production. And it was partly on the question of the absolute autonomy or relative autonomy of patriarchy that the term was tugged in different directions – used, reinflected or rejected in Euro-American feminisms. Some level or degree of autonomy was required from the term but also seemed to render it intractable or untenable. The double pressure to separate *and* relate it to a mode of production always returned to questions of imbrication. Is patriarchy connected, related, interdependent or embedded in other structures, institutions and practices – political, social, cultural, religious? Is it a parallel structure or does it depend on other forms of inequality? This latter emphasis in the women's movement in India, in which I have been shaped, carried the term beyond male domination into structural questions and resolutions.[1]

Autonomy: North American, British and western European currents

Patriarchy, literally the rule of the father, is commonly taken by feminists of different political persuasions to refer to oppression or domination of women by men (individually or collectively) through political, economic, social and discursive structures. The extension of the term can be traced to Engels. In his *The Origin of the Family, Private Property and the State*, a nascent political anthropology of origins, patriarchy is understood both as a break with the preceding 'mother right' (1981 [1884]: 73) of matrilineal and 'communistic households' (ibid.: 120) and as a prior social form that capitalism inherits and puts to work. Engels' thesis pointed to the mutual imbrication of production and species reproduction as well as changing forms of private property and marriage/the family. It has been challenged on the grounds of economism, historical specificity, reliance on a tendentious colonial anthropology, an inadequate understanding of the propertyless and of women who controlled means of production but were still oppressed (for instance, Karat 2005: 253–4), as well as reworked so that more relational concepts of production and social reproduction have emerged. Yet the universalization of a somewhat static idea of the domestic enslavement of women by men distilled from Engel's rhetoric became the underpinning of the concept of patriarchy.

The concept continued to elicit a search for historical origins. In the 1970s ethnographic accounts of primitive and tribal formations were framed as genesis stories and spliced with psychoanalysis. In the exegetical use of Freud, Gayle Rubin's 'The traffic in women' ([1975] 2011) and Juliet Mitchell's *Psychoanalysis and Feminism* (1975), psychoanalytic categories such as the unconscious double as an ahistorical and extra-economic theory of psychic origins and become an autonomous pathway to understanding the fashioning of sexual personalities, ideology and the subordination of women. Further, Rubin's method tacitly positions tribal groups as incompletely relegated pasts since there is little attention to what lies between industrialized societies and the pre-state or relatively sheltered tribal formations (Amazon valley, Trobriand islands, New Guinea) scrutinized by anthropologists (especially in Claude Lévi-Strauss's theory of the exchange of women between men), thus giving her essay an unfortunate quasi-evolutionary, colonial and Eurocentric cast.[2]

In the 1970s, discomfort with the concept was expressed by Marxist and other feminists, especially with the radical feminist interpretation of patriarchy as a political institution (for example, Kate Millett's *Sexual Politics* [1970], which also extended patriarchy from the rule of the father to the rule of men). For radical feminists, male power over women comprised a universal oppression and occurred primarily through biological sex and sexuality (as in Brownmiller's *Against Our Will* [1976]). Their thesis equated male domination with a transhistorical patriarchy, defined women as a class and men versus women as the primary social division, and was in turn vigorously critiqued for its biologism and skewed understanding of class.

The contentious splitting off of sexuality from class and of family from polity functioned as a theoretical and political separation that pushed patriarchy into a psycho-familial terrain, splittings off that intentionally separated feminist from socialist struggle. This was not confined to radical feminists. For instance, a 'neutral' anthropological terrain of 'gender systems' was inaugurated by Rubin as an alternative to patriarchy. She defines a sex/gender system as 'the set of arrangements by which a society transforms biological sexuality into products of human activity, and in which these transformed sexual needs are satisfied' (Rubin 2011: 589–93). She separates this domain of social life from the rest of 'material life' yet does not want to name it a 'mode of reproduction' or 'patriarchy' since these terms reductively bifurcate 'sexual' systems from 'economic' systems, whereas 'production' and 'reproduction' occur in both (ibid.: 664–74).[3] There is a curious double impulse here. On the one hand, Rubin wants to separate sex/gender system from mode of production and reject Marxist explanations of sex oppression as a reflex of economic forces – that is, she tacitly identifies the usage of the term patriarchy with economic determinism as well as separates the task of feminism from that of working-class movements.[4] On the other hand, she rejects the concept of patriarchy as indicating solely a distinct sexual system and wants, eventually, a 'political economy of sexual systems' since these are part of a 'total social system' and 'cannot, in the final analysis, be understood in isolation'. In effect, she proposes a return to and renovation of Engels' endeavour (ibid.: 775–80, 1022–6, 1048–52, 1057–8).[5] Yet, in her argument, there is an unresolved historical relation between the kinship system (the form that a sex/gender system takes), an archaic and stagnant pool of heteronormative obedience in tribal societies, and the family in developed societies, where kinship no longer has other organizing functions and is reduced to sex and gender.[6] On the one hand, kinship is the primary organizational and emblematic locus where 'conventions of sexuality are produced and maintained' and 'the economic oppression of women is derivative and secondary' (ibid.: 775–80). On the other hand, kinship is drastically truncated in Euro-America – an inordinately powerful remainder with *no* material base.

In the same decade, the term patriarchy acquired a political force because it was severally resignified in women's movements. Euro-American socialist and Marxist accounts pulled the term towards the sexual division of labour within class systems and, in a synthesis of Marxism and radical feminism, into a theory of *dual systems* in which capitalism and patriarchy were both interlocking and separate. The relation between patriarchy and the mode of production, and whether women's oppression was to be located in the base or the superstructure, was widely debated. Althusser's interpretation of Marx and Engels that posited a 'relative autonomy' of superstructures with 'determination in the last instance by the (economic) mode of production', which in turn is overdetermined by them (Althusser 1996: 87–128), facilitated definitions of the relative autonomy of patriarchy for some feminists. Others, especially Zillah Eistenstein, sought to establish a symbiotic if not dialectical relation between class and gender hierarchies in capitalist countries (see Eisenstein 1981: 339–62 and 1978). Christine Delphy theorized patriarchy as a virtually separate economic system concurrent with capitalism: it remained 'the system of subordination of women to men in contemporary industrial societies', but its economic base was 'the domestic mode of production' (Delphy 1988: 259–68; see also 1984). Subsequent analyses pointed to the gendering of the entire trajectory of capitalism from the formation of class societies (returning to and modifying Engels) and primitive accumulation (i.e. unwaged or indirectly waged work as the foundation of capitalism) to its unbroken reliance on (unwaged) social reproduction (Mies 1986;

Federici 2004).[7] Productive and reproductive household labour and subsistence production undergirded and enabled the accumulation of capital. Indeed, social reproduction was understood as crucial for the expanded reproduction of capital, and as social reproduction itself was redefined as social production – that is, unwaged value-producing labour[8] – it became evident that dual systems could be precarious even as an abstraction.

The term underwent contraction and elaboration. Barrett and McIntosh preferred the adjectival form to describe as patriarchal those social relations which combine 'a public dimension of power, exploitation or status with a dimension of personal servility' (Barrett and McIntosh 1985: 39). However, in *Theorizing Patriarchy*, Walby presented 'the concept and theory of patriarchy as essential to capture the depth, pervasiveness and interconnection of different aspects of women's subordination [that] can be developed to take account of different forms of gender inequality over time, class and ethnic groups' (Walby 1990: 3). The term was useful because it was structural and systemic, and she disaggregated six components (paid employment, household, state, male violence, culture and sexuality) as applicable to contemporary Britain and, more generally, Western societies.

The variety of historical forms that patriarchy has taken was frequently acknowledged and was the direct intention of materialist feminism, which sought to anchor itself in a renovated Marxism. Thus for McDonough and Harrison, patriarchal relations take their dominant form from dominant relations of production; for example, within the capitalist mode of production, patriarchy operates through class relations. The task of feminism was to establish the exact interrelation at specific moments of history between modes of production and structures of patriarchy. Their usage of the term also brought together relations of production with relations of human reproduction and control of labour, fertility and sexuality (McDonough and Harrison 1978).

As in dual systems theory, the problematic here was the transition to capitalism and the continuity of patriarchy – changes in the mode of production mutate the form of patriarchy but do not destroy it. Periodization was either introduced into the term (Eisenstein's 'capitalist patriarchy') or patriarchy itself became a pre-modern referent, while its modern form was named fraternity, a fraternity in which men become notional equals but retain the right to rule over their women (Pateman 1988).[9] In *Theorizing Patriarchy*, Walby's designation of private and public forms of patriarchy signified a transition from the pre-modern to the modern, and the shift to public forms refers primarily to the massive welfare state interventions (benefits, care provision) in Europe that decreased familial dependence for women. Substituting public and private patriarchy with public and private 'gender regimes', Walby's *Globalization and Inequalities* (2009) anchors the transition to the 'fully modern' on a combination of Weberian rationalization, defamilialized individuation, free wage labour, market rather than household production, and a public gender regime that can involve either state or market welfare (ibid.: 282, 261).[10] Neither version of transition can adequately interrogate the source and nature of accumulation that funds state welfare and the inherent unevenness of capitalism, or fully accommodate the history of its perpetual dependence on something 'outside of itself' (*pace* Rosa Luxemburg), its search, in order to stabilize itself, for an outlet in 'what remains still open of the non-capitalist environment' or unproletarianized sectors (Luxemburg 2003: 426). David Harvey has usefully posited a continuous relation between expanded reproduction and the often violent processes of accumulation by dispossession within this inside–outside dialectic, especially in the global South (2003: 141).

Patriarchy came to be seen as a theoretically inadequate term either because it was too abstract and static and lacked the internal dynamism of its partner, capitalism (see Gottfried 1998), or because it was interpreted solely as a familial and pyschosexual domain which now belonged to an outgrown European past. Thus for Slavoj Žižek, the demise of patriarchy is coterminous with the dissolution of a specific family form. Citing Marx and Engels from the first chapter of *The Communist Manifesto* – 'The bourgeoisie, wherever it has got the upper hand, has put an end to all feudal, *patriarchal*, idyllic relations' (emphasis added) – he sees the critique of patriarchal ideology and practice as misplaced because they are no longer hegemonic: patriarchy has been 'progressively swept away by market individualism of rights', and the 'family and parenthood itself are *de jure* reduced to a temporary and dissolvable contract between independent individuals' (Žižek 2011: 49–50).

As the category women came into question in anti-essentialist or anti-foundationalist feminisms, so did patriarchy since it also seemed to universalize and ontologize the category women (see Butler 1990).

Alternatively, patriarchy seemed too separate from other systems of oppression such as class and race. The relegation of the term on these grounds itself signalled a break within Euro-American feminisms, a break that replaced the concept of patriarchy with the concepts of gender, difference, intersectionality, gender systems or gender regimes. This break and these alternatives were implicated in a jettisoning of Marxism and its reduction of social inequality to a single category of class or capitalism, or crafted in specific opposition to its vaunted economic determinism, or intended to deprioritize class.

Ironically, the same double pressure to relate and separate persisted in the terms that replaced patriarchy. The meaning of the most widely used term, gender, rapidly moved beyond the social construction of difference and became instead a constitutive element of social relationships that included social institutions and organizations, the economy and polity, as well as a primary way of signifying relationships of power (Scott 1999: 42–5). Over time the analyticity of gender expanded further to take in intersectionality (of race and class),[11] relationality (of race and class), structure (as an organizing principle that determines allocations of resources and power, divisions of labour in the home and workplace) and practices of representation (see Glenn 1999). It seems, then, that the concepts of gender and intersectionality were pushing in the same direction and could be made to do much of the same work as the concept of patriarchy. I think, however, that gender works better as a verb that can signify a process: the production of differences that underwrite normativities, identities, representations and discourses, a variable and conflictual process that comes to be predicated on inequality because it is at work *within* a patriarchal system. Gender cannot, without becoming either overladen or diffuse, indicate the totality of a patriarchal system and its structural imbrications.

Scholars who have used other terms that replaced patriarchy have also found it difficult to shed the latter's referents or avoid the old and recurring question of imbrication. Intersectionality is tacitly committed to giving a separable social and discursive history, trajectory and ontological weight to gender, race, class and ethnicity, yet aspires to go beyond merely parallel or crisscrossing paths. Kimberlé Crenshaw perceives race and gender as different systems of oppression that intersect, modify each other, interlock or even converge. She describes intersectionality as a form in which 'systems of race, gender and class domination converge', and subdivides it into structural, political and representational intersectionality (Crenshaw 1991: 1245–6).[12] This impels intersectionality, like gender, to traverse much of the same ground as patriarchy. However, the singularity assigned to each system devalues or underestimates the connected processes (historical and contemporary) that shape and often co-constitute these same systemic inequalities.

Further, how and where would the undeniable multiplicity and simultaneity of oppressions be anchored? Walby's *Globalization and Inequalities* (2009) offers to pluralize the *base* – each social system has its own and all other extant social systems become its environment – as well as *expand* the base of gender regimes. In her discussion of Nira Yuval-Davis, Walby finds it problematic to connect each social inequality to a single and separate base:

> This approach segregates the bases of each of the categories: class is grounded in the economy; gender is a discourse about sexual and biological differences; ethnicity relates to discourses about exclusion and inclusion. The implication appears to be a relatively simple base–superstructure understanding of each set of social relations. (Ibid.: 62–3)

She also finds it segregationist and reductive to theorize gender as if it were entirely accounted for by the institution of the family. She describes instead regimes of inequality that may relate, intersect, interact, articulate or even 'coevolve' with each other in complex ways but which are conceptualized as separate systems that are not reducible to each other. Walby expands the base of gender regime and organizes R. W. Connell's gender structures, structures which were also inclusive but did *not* exist as either a systematic or a logical unity.[13] Her four-level model distinguishes between different forms and varieties of gender regime (domestic and public forms, with the latter subdivided into neoliberal and social democratic forms), while she finds gender relations in distinct forms in major institutional domains: the economic (subdivided into market and household, free wage labour and domestic labour), polities (including states, transnational bodies, organized religions), violence (gender-based, interpersonal, organized armies/militias), and civil society (including sexuality, knowledge institutions and contestatory social movements). She claims that a 'gender regime is constituted in all these [institutional] domains and is not reducible to just one base and at … all levels of abstraction: micro, meso and macro' (ibid.: 259). There are unresolved issues here since the ubiquity of gender, which has no single base, works chiefly to ensure that no domain can be privileged and that each domain contains multiple social relations: thus, analytic leverage can be gained only by establishing a sociological typology capable of infinite permutation while 'system' must be given the cohesive task of preventing a dispersal of gender relations. Yet Walby argues for a concept of system 'that does not insist that it necessarily saturates its territory, … [one that] allows for more than one set of social relations in the economy (and other domains) without insisting on a nested hierarchy in which all non-class relations were theoretically subordinated to class' (ibid.: 65–6). These mutually adaptive non-hierarchized systems, intended to discard both the base–superstructure and the Althusserian model, seem to depend on a version of relative autonomy and analytic separation for theorizing complex articulation. Can this model allow for the tensions or dialectical relation between different systemic structures of class, cross-class and non-class oppression?

The term heteropatriarchy renuanced male dominance to include the invisibilizing of lesbians and served briefly as a bridge between feminist and queer studies of sexuality. Later, in a post-feminist and/or post-Marxist inflection, the term was seen as passé because patriarchy had itself already been overcome in the 'West', sexual democracy and gender scrambling had successfully outmoded the sex/gender binary inherent in heteropatriarchy, and the category 'women' was no longer unifying. In the flipside of this locution – bureaucratic, conservative, racist or co-opted feminist – patriarchy deteriorated into alterity: it was no longer home grown, it functioned only in 'other' places (especially Islamic countries), and was carried into Euro-America by migrants. An alien life form nurtured elsewhere, it had to be eradicated among potential and actual migrants through lessons in sexual democracy.[14] Here patriarchy becomes synonymous with culture, or rather the term culture conflates 'civilizations', traditions, kinship, religions and patriarchies. Culture becomes the place of allegation, ascription and explanation and performs controlling functions. This reoriented culturalism (which has colonial antecedents and several disciplinary locations) hides its own political investments, works within the tradition/modernity framework, describes patriarchal violences as resting on tradition,[15] and produces what I term the blind traditional subject. The production of insulated 'traditions' from both settled populations and migrants strips their economic and political coordinates: the blind traditional subject (whether in honour killing or forced marriage) seems to require only cultural and religious anchorage or the sustenance of kinship.

The 'conflationary' perspective has at least two consequences. First, the kinship analytic reserved for 'others' (e.g. 'Islamic' countries, or northern India, where patriarchy is seen to be organized around patrilineage and patrivirilocality) can become stilted or tendentious since much that falls into the provenance of kinship and gender relations – rights of inheritance, ownership, transmission of property, degrees of mobility and autonomy, and choices regarding entry and exit into marriage – are also part of class processes. Secondly, the increasing drive for cultural alterity obscures the past and present albeit often contrary co-constitution of imperial and subordinate economies, nation spaces and patriarchies. This elision creates a default position that designates colonial and European patriarchal systems as pre-constituted, independent entities – despite the colonial aegis of capitalism – and the illusion that nation spaces can be 'culturally' insulated sites in a neoliberal era. In actuality, capitalism, class formation and with them patriarchies have worked across national boundaries for a long time.[16]

Co-constitution: a perspective from India

Historically, the difficulty of reading pre-capitalist patriarchies, processes of sedentarization and colonization from inside the frame of a singular pattern of transition to capitalism remains unless the spatial and temporal unevenness of capitalism compounded by that of colonization and neocolonialism is addressed. The implications of the absence of uniform transitions, the inherent logic of capital that expands through uneven differentiation of sectors, geographies and labour forces, the several 'economies' and 'cultures' created in the process of the dissolution or restructuring of pre-capitalist institutions, the ensuing histories of concurrence, disjuncture and systemic patterning of difference are well understood[17] but seldom elaborated in analyses of contemporary patriarchies.

Socialist and Marxist feminists in Europe and America were not unaware of the differences in non-capitalist or hitherto colonized regions but there were theoretical lapses, especially in the 1970s. First, the pertinence of historical and contemporary relationships between imperial and subordinate economies for understanding patriarchal structures was seldom scrutinized. Maria Mies made some provocative interventions in the 1980s by linking domestic work in the global North (characterized as a pre-capitalist mode of production) to subsistence farming in the global South as parallel resources or reserve armies for the primary accumulation of capital. Under the impetus of Wallerstein's world systems theory, she also linked housewifization in Europe to the process of colonization and expropriation of resources, suggesting an interpenetration of colonial practices, the gendering and racialization of divisions of labour, and labour markets. Though critiqued for simplifying the asymmetries within and between the global North and the global South, Mies' work drew attention to the connection of Third World subsistence and other unpaid labour with consumption and development in the First World and, along with others, foregrounded the contemporary international division of labour (Mies 1982, 1986; Mies et al. 1988; Pearson et al. 1981; Elson and Pearson 1997).[18]

Secondly, the theorization of capitalism was usually Eurocentric. It could not, for instance, be transposed to India, where capitalism had made, historically, a later entry; where it came in segmentary fashion and different modes of production coexisted for a long span of time; where historically the question of transition from a singular feudalism could not be posed; where labour regimes such as slavery and bonded labour persisted alongside wage labour; where caste was imbricated in class formation; where *several* residual, dominant and emerging family forms existed; and where pre-capitalist patriarchies had crystallized differently through the articulation of caste-based divisions of labour, regional economies and histories of state formation, tribal, matrilineal and patrilineal systems, multiple juridical or religio-legal systems, and varied customary laws, and as such no single origin could be proposed.

Thirdly, the recurring Euro-American emphasis on patriarchy as the binarizing rule of men or a theory of male domination rather than of structured dominance undermined the wider political potentials of the term and could not explain the unequal distribution of power among men, the crafting of class/caste divided masculinities, the consent or complicity of women or their conditional access to/agential exercise of patriarchal power. Women can be on both sides of the divisions between oppressed and oppressors, exploited and exploiters.

Conceptually, then, should we settle for a host of quasi-anthropological gender regimes, a singular patriarchy with variants, or multiple patriarchies? Is patriarchy an abstract unity with different modes of functioning, an abstract unity with concrete variants, or an abstract unity with multiple concrete and systemic modes? If the problematic is to see patriarchal systems in specific social formations and historical locations, their interlocks with different modes of production and the precise relation with class processes, then the category should be pluralized. Abstract unity would refer to core distributive structures that are never left behind but may not all exist simultaneously: sexual division of labour, regulation of sexuality and procreation, unequal access to social and economic resources, property and public space, and gendered violence and ideologies. Wherever a set of patriarchal arrangements cohere into a systemic repertoire one can speak of a patriarchy; this could encompass some variations and define the threshold at which the variations, reformulations or changes begin to cohere into another set of systemic arrangements. Pluralizing the term makes it a capacious, non-ethnocentric and non-Eurocentric concept that can indicate unities and differences – both ideological and systemic – in terms of class, caste, region and family forms within and across nation spaces. The term multiple patriarchies has the advantage of giving access to the historical specificity and colonial co-constitution of both non-European and European societies within the uneven disposition of capital.

Finally, instead of male domination, a psycho-familial ensemble, dual systems or the knee-jerk reaction against Marxist prioritization of class, it may be more productive to conceptualize a patriarchy not as an irreducibly *separate* system but as *co-constituted* at many levels with other systemic equalities within and across nation spaces. If co-constitution is understood as generating *different* forms (that instantiate class, caste, race and region divisions) as well as *new* entities, and the patriarchal systems so produced are seen as both discrete and articulated, then patriarchy as an abstraction must carry the presence, the force and the dynamic of both pluralization *and* articulation.

In Marxist theory, an analytic abstraction is a universal capable of apprehending particularity, heterogeneity, historical specificity and variable instantiation. Does the concept of a singular patriarchy have the same purchase on the dynamic *processes* prior to and within capitalism – historical interrelation, co-constitution, reciprocal determination or the instrumental mutuality of patriarchal systems (as in the production of interdependent distinctions between castes, between owners and slaves, or colonizers and colonized)? And can it distil the millennial yet irregular temporality in which patriarchies depend on distinct modes of production but may not operate at the same frequency, have the same tempo of change, or coincide with the precise duration of a single mode? Multiple patriarchies are to be grasped not as variants, subtypes or deviations from a *classic* form, but as a vast and variegated field of practices straddling different modes of production that are recognizable by the properties they have in common but not necessarily or fully comparable across time and space in every respect. The efficacy of an abstraction lies in its capacity to distil, explain and return to the concrete. Historically, Marxist abstractions were largely made from a European concrete. Now they must perforce extrapolate from a concrete world rather than Europe and its anthropological others, shed regional limitation, and answer to the wide resistances that challenge patriarchal systems. Unless processes of pluralization and articulation are implicit in patriarchy as an abstraction, it cannot stand in dialectical relation to the concrete – that is, in a mutually dependent and mutually transforming relation. Indeed, if a Marxist-feminist abstraction is to be dialectical, it must always be under revision since the properties of an abstraction can alter in correspondence with concrete changing structures and unresolved processes.

The simultaneous particularization, resignification and pluralization of the term patriarchy in the specificities of the women's movement in India as it struggled against the state, civil society, the economy, the construction of religious and caste antagonism and several colonial legacies may anchor these assertions. The founding moments of the second phase of the women's movement in India in the late 1970s centred on hierarchized violence: the rape of poor/low-caste women, custodial rape, dowry-related deaths and widow immolation. Family violence was not seen as a private affair: campaigns against domestic and sexual violence centred as much on women's rights as on the state's duties, and gendered violence was seen to be imbricated in caste and class inequalities as well as linked to economic and distribution issues – especially women's lack of economic independence, rights to residence, property and agricultural land, and unequal access to household and social resources. This initial identification of forms of patriarchal power 'outside' the family – power that was seen to be vested in the state and to inhere in class stratification, village elites and caste-based 'communities' – has continued to undergird most feminist analyses (for an early example, see PUDR 1984). If questions of labour and livelihood were conventionally embedded in political economy, feminist analyses and activism propelled what were usually seen as 'family' or 'social' issues – dowry, sex-selective abortion, birth control – in the same direction and showed how existing and emerging patriarchal arrangements were articulating with changes in the economy as a whole. Critiques of domestic violence such as dowry-burning expanded into gendered critiques of capitalism. In this sense, the women's movement enlarged the theoretical ambit of left-wing analyses.

The concept of patriarchy/patriarchies, which now cohabits with gender and intersectionality, has had a sustained life in the women's movement in India both because it emerged from the ground and because it was resignified, theoretically expanded and made more flexible through successive redefinitions. Those women on the organized and independent left who had also grappled with the question of the articulation of patriarchy and capitalism in the late 1970s and 1980s clung to the concept because patriarchy signified systemic oppression and not merely male domination; because it could indicate the structured control of reproduction, procreation and sexuality; and because a theoretical relocation of patriarchy into *both* base and superstructure allowed for a critique of divisions of labour and resources as well as all forms of ideological representation.

The old left-wing characterization of patriarchy as a feudal relic that would surely be surpassed was questioned by Marxist feminists beginning in the early 1980s on the ground that old practices were being recast and renovated.[19] This led to substantial redefinition of patriarchy both as a static and as a singular formation as well as of its relation to the caste order and class formation. In the ongoing resemanticization, patriarchy emerged as subject to constant reconstitution, and the term itself was pluralized. This redefinition first emerged from the empirical necessity of accounting for the regional, class, caste and tribal differences in patriarchal practices in India (for example, dowry had not yet overridden bride price in the 1980s) that did not have identical histories of emergence; the rapid and ceaseless reformulation of patriarchal practices from the colonial period; and the role of the state in historical and contemporary transitions – as well as from the recognition that patriarchies were intrinsic to the formation of, and changes within, caste and class.[20] The latter recognition sharpened into seeing patriarchies as squarely a *part* of (rather than as a supplement of) class formation, as governing access to productive and survival resources, and as determining divisions of domestic labour, conditions of wage work and entry into the labour market. As a result, class mobility could be seen as a point of maximization of patriarchal oppression and patriarchal arrangements seen as occurring at different points in the class/caste hierarchy rather than as effects of illiteracy, ignorance or poverty, while the visible slide of patriarchal practices and especially ideologies across castes, classes or religions introduced a new problematic of their proliferation and homogenization (Sangari 1993, 1995: 3289–90).

There were many arguments during and after the 1980s on how to simultaneously alter class and gender relations, on whether class struggle would enable a fight against those patriarchal ideologies that were carried within left political movements, whether rape was more than a class weapon, as well as about the precise understanding of the nature of the state, the transition to capitalism, and the forms of political mobilization that followed upon a class analysis. Another fraught question about and inside mass movements and political parties was the perception of women's issues as a 'divisive' question, one that could be skirted by forming separate women's cells or wings rather than confronted as being integral to a broad left analytic of structural change. However, even though this was seldom consciously or theoretically articulated, the notion of patriarchy as crucial to the understanding of social inequality along with the desire to transform all social institutions were the symbolic horizon of the women's movement in India and, in hindsight, made it much closer to those transformative aspirations and agencies that go under the name of Marxism.

Patriarchy thus reconfigured and pluralized could work as a secular and materialist theory to account for patriarchal structures, both within the same country and transnationally, and have an analytical edge for vexed questions of religious identity, caste hierarchies, regional differences and differential constructions of sexuality.[21] Multiple and overlapping patriarchies could stand as the concrete ground of feminism as an elective affinity, as the material history of the structuring of gender relations embedded in extant grids of inequality that positioned women, paradoxically, as caste- and class-divided but not as governed by separate patriarchies belonging to sealed Hindu, Muslim or Christian religious communities. Rather, the systemic operations of multiple overlapping patriarchies both aggregate and disaggregate women (according to situation, subject position, social location). An understanding of the continuous articulation or co-constitution of patriarchal regimes with caste and class processes could be counterposed to identitarian disaggregations of the category women which endorse or essentialize a primary identity, especially in a heteronormative context where women are already conscripted to reproduce social, caste and religious boundaries. Caste as the continuation of gross hierarchized injustice involves all women, and is not only about 'different' women facing 'different' kinds of oppression; that is, caste can be seized as a category which paradoxically dismantles the unified category 'women' as well as reconstitutes it, but now within patriarchal relations of structured inequality.

The term patriarchy rhetorically evokes 'women' as a category, but in fact patriarchy is not interchangeable with women, and nor is it an ontological category. Patriarchal systems are predicated on practices of oppression which wrap women *and* men, dominated and dominant, into their operations. They are structurally related to or depend on other axes of social division and other systems of inequality; neither self-sustaining nor epiphenomenal, they work along the grain of social divisions, use and reinforce existing divisions, and are a crucial part of the emergence of new social tensions. Patriarchies are relational, occupy different historical configurations, have been continuously reformulated in changing conjunctures (social, political, economic, transnational), and have also been altered by varied forms of resistance – that is, they are not reproduced mechanically. In sum, there is no historical essentialism available to women.

As I understand it, patriarchies are at once relatively autonomous and a satellite. They have till now accompanied most modes of production, and these modes of production in turn have depended on them to varying extents. They have gained a relative autonomy, in part, through sheer duration – that is, their persistence in successive modes of production in which earlier forms of material, ideological and institutional discrimination have been adapted, transmuted or recycled. And, in part, because they do not seem to synchronize fully with a mode of production – historically 'the relation between changing modes of production, patriarchal structures and class positions is both aligned and disjunct', and patriarchies 'appear to have no single one to one relation with a given mode of production but seem to change through overlap and reformulation' (Sangari and Vaid 1989: 5). They are satellites in the sense that the concrete form of any patriarchal system is imbricated in and depends on a mode of production and does not have a separate or separable existence.

Distributions: familial, state and market patriarchal regimes

Politically, the concept of patriarchies is an important oppositional concept because it foregrounds structural inequality; patriarchies have not disappeared and will not do so without resistance and struggle. Elaborated with historical precision and theoretical rigour, the concept of multiple patriarchies can provide a way of understanding abstract unities, historical specificities and practical differences in a way that valorizes neither similarity nor difference, but instead can see the latter in a dialectical fashion as discrete relations of overlap, interdependent difference and divergence. Pluralization deepens the historicity of the concept, but does it answer to the time–space compression of a neoliberal era? And what would now be the most salient lines of pluralization and articulation?

Multiple patriarchies can designate relatively autonomous or co-constituted regional entities shaped over long periods of time. The accelerated subsumption into a crisis-ridden yet deepening neoliberal capitalism has generated rapid overlaps and reshaping of patriarchal practices and ideologies across and within classes, regions and nations in the past three decades. Patriarchies seem too solid, bulky and durational an entity to grasp the speed and intensity of many mutually constitutive interactions. Perhaps multiple patriarchal regimes that retain a political force and emphasize their systemic location in base and superstructure, production and reproduction, labour and sexuality may serve as a more agile term that can mark or periodize the shifts within this phase of a neoliberal capitalism. Walby has defined a gender regime as analytically separate from other regimes of inequality (2009: 259). A patriarchal regime, however, by definition *depends on* and articulates with other forms of inequality, especially those anchored in social divisions of labour. An analytic based on concrete familial, community, state-led and market-led patriarchal regimes may prove useful in addressing the more patent and apprehended loosening of region-specific practices, the global circulation of images and ideologies in televisual and social media, the more vivid formation of transnational regimes of accumulation and dispossession in the global North and South, and finally the simultaneous dilution and sharpening of regional differences with transnational redistributions of manufacture, labour and services. Familial, state and market regimes are not identical everywhere but function as mechanisms of dissolution and recomposition, the affirmation and creation of homogeneous or heterogeneous patriarchal practices.

The changes in forms of production and labour organization accelerated by the post-Fordist disaggregation of production and outsourcing of services, the private sector intensification and adaptation of older gendered forms of labour (such as home-based production), and the export of domestic and reproductive labour by remittance economies[22] have all led to the emergence of new and often feminized proletariats composed of legal and illegal migrants who provide low-wage services in the informalized global economy. At the same time, labour migration has generated visible reaggregations of production and services inside host countries. This reaggregation and disaggregation of production, labour, peoples and families is accompanied by a recouping of familial, sexist and racist ideologies which circulate or recombine across national territories. The class relations of this new proletariat do not answer to the place of origin or the place of labour alone. These relations have to be read in terms of relations to domestic production as well as a gendered repositioning of labour and survival in the global economy, an economy in which many forms of women's labour are resituated as a flexible resource for transnational exploitation.

Contemporary capitalism can destabilize the family in the interests of market individuation and labour migration, but it can also perpetuate and reconfigure the link between the family/household and women's waged labour. Despite the greater market absorption of the work hitherto supervised in the household, the market has not released the vast majority of women from unpaid domestic and care work, which remains intractable or non-negotiable. Given the crisis and transformation in social reproduction accompanying increasing capitalist penetration, a contradiction is emerging between the global accumulation of capital and the provisioning of stable conditions for social reproduction (see Bakker and Gill 2003: 20, 27).[23]

As neoliberalism eviscerates social democratic projects, the shift within North American and European welfare states – which had decreased familial dependence partly in response to labour and feminist struggles – to workfare and austerity can revolve around either refamilialization or the transfer of some aspects of social reproduction to the market – that is, return some women to the home and unwaged work and prise others into the transnational migrant service and care labour market. In subordinate economies that never provided more than minimal welfare and in which the state is morphing into an agent of mandated deregulation, patriarchies are being repositioned and reformulated in complex and formative conjunctions of familial, state-induced and market-led patriarchal regimes. The labour of social reproduction – domestic, household, subsistence – has been picking up the slack of development and attempting to make up for the lack of social services, education, security, adequate wages and employment. It not only acts as a buffer when minimal state welfare recedes, but is part of the 'dependable' social relations in which the domestic and transnational market is and will continue to be embedded. Social reproductive labour in the South subsidizes consumption in the North.[24] And as social reproduction itself becomes a transnational field, one still in formation, several patriarchal regimes can collude or collide to form new constellations. The double positioning of nation-states in subordinate economies as points of entry for global capital and internal extraction requires both governed labour/services and individuated consumption. Thus as it supervises the transition to neoliberalism, the state too can batten on familial patriarchal regimes, regimes that produce governed labouring subjects, control access to  domestic resources, and assume unwaged social reproduction.

Since patriarchies articulate with other forms of inequality and the political economy as a whole, they have been and remain a part of the uneven geopolitical and economic relationships *between* regions. The co-constitution of patriarchies and wider ideological ensembles began with colonization and financing of the global North by the global South and now has new coordinates for consolidating transnational regimes. In the current regime of capital *some* developing countries are crucial to sustaining a regime of accumulation;[25] they provision Euro-American lifestyles at the cost of their own people and reserves (such as India or China), replicate extractive relations internally, cede economic territory (natural resources, markets, labour, environment), and become broker states that make nation spaces safe for transnational capital and corporate extraction. To what extent, then, should we continue to think of patriarchies as *entirely* specific to or cordoned by a region or nation? If patriarchies constitute the given and mutating social field which facilitates the functioning of neoliberal capitalism, can they be segregated from the globalized economy? Neoliberal capital exploits existing labour conditions and invents new ones and, as regulatory mechanisms, patriarchies are part and parcel of existing labour conditions and are reformulated in the creation of new regimes. As has been evident for a while, markets sectorally exploit gendered, ethnicized, racialized and caste-segregated labour.[26] Global labour market operations (home-based work, multinational factories, outsourcing of service or manufacture, export processing zones, special economic zones) draw on regions governed by familial protocols; indeed, these assume and shop for discriminatory patriarchal regimes as guarantors of cheap labour, and can deploy or produce vulnerabilities. The market is not, after all, an unambiguous anti-traditional force that loosens familial patriarchal practices – it can also sustain, alter or resuscitate them; it may dissolve familial patriarchal practices to an extent but maintain or reinstate caste, ethnic and racial hierarchies that in turn depend on gendered subordination.[27] The market and market-led states may not only have a stake in familial patriarchal regimes, but the market emancipation of some women may depend on the *continuation* of familial regimes elsewhere. Thus the question of location does not rest on an imperious world map of more and less patriarchal regions; rather, it is a material question of *differential and shifting patriarchal distributions*. Even as Euro-American labour markets benefit from familial patriarchal regimes in the global South, the same familial regimes are exhibited by Euro-American states as cultural stigmata to devalue migrant and *in situ* labour; to turn welfare mechanisms into patriarchal controls on migrants (either as routine, national security or neoliberal austerity measures); and to rationalize political and/or military intervention. These cultural stigmata can be instrumentalized as economic conditionalities (posed in the language of human rights) for 'disobedient' countries.

The two images compressed in the blind traditional subject – one who carries patriarchal practices in a suitcase to Europe or one who lives in his/her ancestral homeland mired in old habits – are both misleading. Not only are seemingly old patriarchal practices being produced and renovated on the fraught ground of resident/migrant interactions *inside* Euro-America, they are also being produced and renovated within subordinate economies through the generation of differential citizenships with graded entitlements and through the deepening of structural violence. The conditions for structural violence can be engendered transnationally even as its instantiation in acts of gendered violence may occur at home. As a terrain of global capital accumulation, familial, neoliberal state and market patriarchal regimes connect migrant with domiciled labour and are a crucial part of class and regional contradictions.

Given the sluggish persistence and the mercurial shifts in patriarchies, our critical apparatus must constantly be under revision if it hopes to characterize the complexity of the social field and demarcate incipient contradictions. The analytic advantage of the concept of multiple patriarchal regimes might lie in the ability to seize the complex and formative conjunctions as well as the shifts, overlaps and restructuring of family, state and (trans)national market to understand differential co-constitution across regions, classes and communities. As the material base of patriarchies is patchily eroded or recomposed by state or market interventions, there is a concurrent mobilization *and* immobilization of women's labour, a simultaneous move to defamilialize *and* refamilialize, and power/control shifts from familial to state regimes and back, as well as from familial to state and market regimes. The proximities, alignments, confluences, loops, tensions and disjunctions between familial, state and market patriarchal regimes may be the material terrain of Marxist-feminist critique – given its commitment to connect and analyse seemingly disparate social processes and structures of power – while the abrasions and emerging contradictions between these regimes may become sites of resistance.

Notes

1 The term also had significant trajectories in Arab and Chinese feminisms and in the Soviet Union, trajectories that I cannot discuss here on account of space limitations.

2 Rubin acknowledges that psychoanalysis and structural anthropology can be dangerous as they are 'sophisticated ideologies of sexism' (2011: 951–4), yet she finds the work of Freud and Lévi-Strauss useful because it 'enables us to isolate sex and gender from "mode of production" and to counter a certain tendency to explain sex oppression as a reflex of economic forces' (ibid.: 975–8).

3 Rubin does discuss Marxist applications of patriarchy to explain the oppression of women: women as a reserve

labour force for capitalism; women as conduits of capitalist consumerism; and the relationship between housework and the reproduction of labour which puts women squarely into the terrain of extraction of surplus value from labour by capital (2011: 602–5). Yet since capitalism is not the genesis of the oppression of women, which can be found in feudal Europe and non-capitalist tribal societies (ibid.: 630–5), she concludes that every society has a sex/gender system – 'a set of arrangements by which the biological raw material of human sex and procreation is shaped by human, social intervention and satisfied in a conventional manner' (ibid.: 658–61). She sees patriarchy as a term used to distinguish the forces maintaining sexism from other social forces such as capitalism (ibid.: 672–7). Further, Rubin sees patriarchy as a term that collapses the human necessity of organizing sexual worlds with the empirically oppressive ways in which it has been organized. Thus, the sex/gender system carried in kinship systems is preferable as a 'neutral' term that refers to the domain and, unlike patriarchy, indicates that oppression is not inevitable within it (ibid.: 678–83). At the same time, she calls for a political economy of sexual systems that can point to the limits of Lévi-Strauss's notion of the exchange of women (ibid.: 772–81) and calls for a study of each society to determine the exact mechanisms of its sexual systems.

4 Rubin wants to give full weight to sexuality and marriage so that the women's movement addresses 'a different source of human discontent' from the working-class movement (2011: 978–82).

5 Rubin also asks for a Marxian analysis of sex-gender systems along the lines of the evolution of money and commodities since the economics and politics of sex-gender systems are obscured by the concept of the exchange of women (2011: 991–6).

6 Rubin calls for a 'revolution in kinship' (2011: 938–42) because these organizations of exchange and sexuality belong to 'the dim human past' but 'still dominate our sexual lives'. However, they no longer have a 'functional load' since kinship has been 'systematically stripped of its functions – political, economic, educational, and organizational. It has been reduced to its barest bones – *sex and gender*' – and is part of 'the archaic relationships which deform [human sexual life]' (2011: 940–9).

7 Mackintosh, noting the continuous reconstitution of the sexual division of labour, argued that since women's subordination is independent of capitalism and a product of capitalism, the intersection of the two needs to be examined (1981: 3–17).

8 See, for instance, Fortunati (1995). Mitchell, Marston and Katz argue against separating the work of production and social reproduction since substantive distinctions between them are blurred. They define domestic labour as part of the process of social reproduction, integral to the overall process of production and accumulation, and thus thin the distinction between base and superstructure (Mitchell et al. 2004).

9 Earlier, Rubin had delimited patriarchy as referring only to the rule of the patriarch/father and not to men as a collective adult body, and as such a specific and restricted form of male dominance (2011: 680–7).

10 Walby concedes that gender regimes can also be shaped by their intersection with regimes of inequality in other countries but this is defined merely as a matter of international and regional 'influences' that include 'emergent global institutions, global hegemons, networks, and waves' (2009: 264).

11 Drucilla Cornell notes that gender was used to illuminate the construction of differences but soon became a social identity for all women, and could function as the ultimate ground of feminist analysis and critique. This deployment was called into question by women of colour. Kimberlé Williams Crenshaw introduced the idea of intersectionality to demonstrate how race, class and gender are all part of how black women lived their blackness and their womanhood, and how they are discriminated against through the intersection of these three forms of oppression. As a theoretical as well as a philosophical matter, intersectionality demanded that feminists expand the very analyticity of gender; it could no longer be used to name a social identity. It ceased being *sui generis* a category of analysis; it had to be seen as intersecting with other categories of analysis (Cornell 2004).

12 Interestingly, in 'The Combahee River Collective statement' (Combahee River Collective 1977), black feminists had argued much earlier that it was 'difficult to separate race from class and sex oppression because in our lives they are most often experienced simultaneously' and set out to produce an 'integrated analysis' of racial, sexual, heterosexual and class oppression.

13 Connell, moving away from monolithic male domination, tied gender structures to the beliefs, customs, ideologies, laws, institutions and social practices of domestic and waged labour, power and cathexis that structure women and men's participation in civil society, the economy and the state (Connell 1987). In *Gender* (2003), Connell's notion of the gender order of a society comprises production relations, power, emotional relations, especially sexuality, and symbolic relations.

14 On the involvement of some feminists in an anti-immigrant consensus in the European Union, see Fekete (2006: 1–22). On sexual democracy 'tests' for potential immigrants, and the creation of homophobic 'others', see Fassin (2010: 507–29).

15 See, for instance, the statement of the UN General Assembly in 2000 cited in Coomaraswamy (2004: 33).

16 On the mediation and repurposing of familial patriarchies by British colonization in India in a complex field of institutional and class/caste interaction or collaboration, the selective preservation and reform of patriarchies that locked into the creation and reproduction of classes, class boundaries and labour pools, the new entities produced at sites of interaction in the colony that returned in different registers to remake gender formation and ideologies in the metropolis, see Sangari (1999: xxxii–xxxiv, xlii–xlviii, 184–7, 300–7). On reciprocal currents between European witch-hunts and the racist charges of devil-worshipping in the Americas to break local resistance and to justify colonization and the slave trade, see Federici (2004: 198–200, 233). On motherhood and domesticity as an imperial construct in the United Kingdom and the United States, see Burton (1994) and Kaplan (1998). On the formation of European sexuality in colonial sites, see Stoler (1997) and Levine (2000). On how 'old' values are reinvented and invoked by Chinese working-class patriarchy and how these are connected to and negotiate racial and class inequalities in the contemporary United States, see Shi (2009: 31–60).

17 See, for instance, Luxemburg (2003: 368–418); Bloch (1994: 90–1); Bagchi (1991); Sangari (1999: xxvi–xxviii).

18 On the links between enslaved workers and waged workers in colonial England, see Federici (2004: 104). For a recent examination of the dialectical shaping of semi-proletarian households

by the contradictory processes of proletarianization and housewifization (as a functional requirement of capitalism) and the mechanisms through which capitalists extracted surpluses from and externalized the costs to these semi-proletarian households from the sixteenth century in the world system, see Dunaway (2012).

19 This characterization was the broad position taken by parliamentary left parties, a position expressed in speeches, pamphlets and articles. Subsequently, the All India Democratic Women's Association (AIDWA), the women's wing of the Communist Party of India (Marxist) (CPI(M)), made nuanced and structural definitions of patriarchy that acknowledged the 'new life' of seemingly old practices such as dowry and casteism (see Karat 2005: 253–4).

20 These themes, along with a pluralization of the term, first appeared in Sangari and Vaid (1989: 1–26). The concept of multiple and overlapping patriarchies was later sporadically amplified as a historically specific as well as contemporary analytic in Sangari (1995, 1999, 2007: 40–2, 57–60, 62).

21 On the historical emergence and contemporary contours of systemic caste-distinct patriarchal practices, see Ambedkar (1989); Chakravarti (1993, 2003); Anandhi et al. (2002); Rege (2006: 1–7). For a discussion of multiple patriarchies in relation to caste and religious differences as well as overlaps in the customary domain, see Sangari (1995, 1999: 231–47, 276–8). There are ideological similarities among texts from different religions, or different texts can be used to support similar customary practices. The shared patriarchal, proprietorial and class codes, the small variation in core arrangements – dowry, chastity, seclusion, domestic roles and obedience – disclosed that major correlates of a patriarchal system were region, class and urbanization rather than religions, and that there was no such thing as a singular Muslim, Hindu or Christian patriarchy in India.

22 Sassen notes that large-scale migration to cities and other countries is a consequence of foreign investment in export production because it displaces subsistence farmers in many parts of the world (1998: 41). Federici also notes that the migration from South to North follows the transfer of capital caused by payment of foreign debt, and she directly links the dismantling of state welfare in Europe with the employment of migrants in domestic work and global care (2012: 70, 73, 87).

23 Federici attributes the crisis in social reproduction in Africa, Asia and Latin America to globalization of the world economy (structural adjustment, trade liberalization, attack on material conditions of social reproduction and subsistence agriculture) and sees the new international division of labour as built on this crisis, a crisis which harnesses the labour of women for reproduction of a metropolitan workforce and builds new divisions among women (2012: 66, 86, 70).

24 On the vested interest multinational firms have in preserving or encouraging the new development of indigenous social structures that play a vital role in social reproduction in order to maximize their profits, see MacCormack (2000: 45–6). According to Rai, the domestic sector is as large in the South as in the North but the input from state benefits in the South is less and overall wages are lower. This in turn subsidizes consumption in the North which benefits both men and women in the North at the expense of social reproductive labour in the South (2013: 28–81).

25 I owe this insight to C. P. Chandrasekhar. On the precursive transfers of surplus from the colonies to Britain and

the present situation, see Patnaik (2006, 2012: 1–12).

26 Labour market segregation and the exploitation of existing patriarchal practices are well known. For instance, on the reliance of multinational sneaker companies on women's marriage strategies in Korea, see Enloe (2004: 57–68). On ethnicized production networks in the United States, see Applebaum (1999: 297–316); Ong (2008: 104).

27 Lourdes Beneria also notes that the market can accelerate the diffusion of both 'liberating' and 'sexist' practices. It can break up patriarchal traditions or have negative consequences for those who suffer from discrimination and market exploitation as well as create new constraints and exacerbate patriarchal practices, as in Russia after 1989 (Beneria 1999: 73–4).

References

Althusser, L. (1996) 'Contradiction and overdetermination', in *For Marx*, trans. B. Brewster, London: Verso.

Ambedkar, B. R. (1989) *Writings and Speeches*, ed. V. Moon, Bombay: Government of Maharashtra Education Department.

Anandhi, S., S. Jeyaranjan and R. Krishnan (2002) 'Work, caste and competing masculinities: notes from a Tamil village', *Economic and Political Weekly*, 37(43): 4397–406.

Applebaum, R. P. (1999) 'Multiculturalism and flexibility: some new directions in global capitalism', in A. F. Gordon and C. Newfield (eds), *Mapping Multiculturalism*, Minneapolis: University of Minnesota Press, pp. 297–316.

Bagchi, A. K. (1991) 'From a fractured compromise to a democratic consensus', *Economic and Political Weekly*, 26(11/12): 611–28.

Bakker, I. and S. Gill (2003) 'Ontology, method and hypothesis', in I. Bakker and S. Gill (eds), *Power, Production and Social Reproduction: Human In/Security in the Global Political Economy*, New York: Palgrave Macmillan, pp. 17–41.

Barrett, M. and M. McIntosh (1985) 'Ethnocentrism and socialist-feminist theory', *Feminist Review*, 20: 23–47.

Beneria, L. (1999) 'Globalization, gender and the Davos man', *Feminist Economics*, 5(3): 61–83.

Bloch, E. (1994) *Heritage of Our Times*, Oxford: Polity.

Brownmiller, S. (1976) *Against Our Will: Men, Women and Rape*, Harmondsworth: Penguin.

Burton, A. (1994) *Burdens of History: British Feminists, Indian Women and Imperial Culture, 1865–1915*, Chapel Hill: University of North Carolina Press.

Butler, J. (1990) *Gender Trouble*, New York: Routledge.

Chakravarti, U. (1993) 'Conceptualising Brahminical patriarchy in early India: gender, caste, class and state', *Economic and Political Weekly*, 28(14): 579–85.

— (2003) *Gendering Caste: Through a Feminist Lens*, Kolkata: Stree.

Combahee River Collective (1977) 'The Combahee River Collective statement', www21.adrive.com/file-manager/downloadfile/194738 94-Combahee1979/pdf.

Connell, R. W. (1987) *Gender and Power*, Stanford, CA: Stanford University Press.

— (2003) *Gender*, Cambridge: Polity.

Coomaraswamy, R. (2004) 'Identity within: cultural relativism, minority rights', in A. Hussain (ed.), *Race: Identity, Caste and Conflict in the South Asian Context*, Colombo: ICES.

Cornell, D. (2004) 'From America: gender in America', in R. Ben-Slama et al. (eds), *Keywords: Gender*, New York: Other Press, pp. 33–54.

Crenshaw, K. W. (1991) 'Mapping the margins: intersectionality, identity politics and violence against women of colour', *Stanford Law Review*, 43: 1241–99.

Delphy, C. (1984) *Close to Home: A Materialist Analysis of Women's Oppression*, trans. D. Leonard, Amherst: University of Massachusetts Press.

— (1988) 'Patriarchy, domestic mode of production, gender and class', in C. Nelson and L. Grossberg (eds), *Marxism and the Interpretation of Culture*, Urbana: University of Illinois Press, pp. 259–68.

Dunaway, W. A. (2012) 'The semiproletarian household over the *longue durée* of the modern world-system', in R. E. Lee (ed.), *The Longue Durée and World-Systems Analysis*, Fernand Braudel Center Studies in Historical Social Science, Albany: State University of New York Press, pp. 97–136.

Eisenstein, Z. (1978) *Capitalist Patriarchy and the Case for Socialist Feminism*, New York: Monthly Review Press.

— (1981) 'Reform and/or revolution: towards a unified women's movement', in L. Sargent (ed.), *Women and Revolution: A Discussion of the Unhappy Marriage of Marxism and Feminism*, Boston, MA: Southend, pp. 339–62.

Elson, D. and R. Pearson (1997) 'The subordination of women and the internationalization of factory production', in N. Visvanathan et al. (eds), *The Women, Gender and Development Reader*, London: Zed Books, pp. 191–202.

Engels, F. (1981 [1884]) *The Origin of the Family, Private Property and the State*, Delhi: People's Publishing.

Enloe, C. (2004) *The Curious Feminist*, Berkeley and Los Angeles: University of California Press.

Fassin, É. (2010) 'National identities and transnational intimacies: sexual democracy and the politics of immigration in EU', *Public Culture*, 22(3): 507–29.

Federici, S. (2004) *Caliban and the Witch: Women, the Body and Primitive Accumulation*, Brooklyn, NY: Autonomedia.

— (2012) *Revolution at Point Zero: Housework, Reproduction and Feminist Struggle*, Oakland, CA: PM.

Fekete, L. (2006) 'Enlightened fundamentalism? Immigration, feminism and the right', *Race and Class*, 48(2): 507–29.

Fortunati, L. (1995) *The Arcane of Reproduction: Housework, Prostitution, Labor and Capital*, trans. H. Creek, Brooklyn, NY: Autonomedia.

Glenn, E. N. (1999) 'The social construction and institutionalization of gender and race: an integrative framework', in M. Max-Ferree, J. Lorbder and B. Hess (eds), *Revisioning Gender*, Delhi: Sage, pp. 70–96.

Gottfried, H. (1998) 'Beyond patriarchy? Theorizing gender and class', *Sociology*, 32(3): 451–68.

Harvey, D. (2003) *The New Imperialism*, Oxford: Oxford University Press.

Kaplan, A. (1998) 'Manifest domesticity', *American Literature*, 70(3): 501–606.

Karat, B. (2005) *Survival and Emancipation: Notes from Indian Women's Struggles*, Delhi: Three Essays Collective.

Levine, P. (2000) 'Orientalist sociology and the creation of colonial sexualities', *Feminist Review*, 65(1): 5–21.

Luxemburg, R. (2003) *The Accumulation of Capital*, trans. A. Schwarzchild, London: Routledge.

MacCormack, C. (2000) 'Land, labour and gender', in A. Lugo and B. Maurer (eds), *Gender Matters: Rereading Michelle Z. Rosaldo*, Ann Arbor: University of Michigan Press, pp. 37–53.

Mackintosh, M. (1981) 'Gender and economics: the sexual division of labour and the subordination of women', in K. Young, C. Wolkowitz and R. McCullagh (eds), *Of Marriage and the Market: Women's Subordination Internationally and Its Lessons*, London: Routledge, pp. 1–15.

McDonough, R. and R. Harrison (1978) 'Patriarchy and relations of production', in A. Kuhn and A. M. Volpe (eds), *Feminism and Materialism: Women and Modes of Production*, London: Routledge, pp. 42–67.

Mies, M. (1982) *The Lacemakers of Narsapur: Indian Housewives Produce for the World Market*, London: Zed Books.

— (1986) *Patriarchy and Accumulation on a World Scale: Women in the International Division of Labour*, London: Zed Books.

Mies, M., V. Bernholdt-Thomsen and C. von Werlhof (eds) (1988) *Women: The Last Colony*, London: Zed Books.

Millett, K. (1970) *Sexual Politics*, New York: Doubleday.

Mitchell, J. (1975) *Psychoanalysis and Feminism: Freud, Reich, Laing and Women*, New York: Vintage.

Mitchell, K., S. E. Marston and C. Katz (2004) 'Life's work: an introduction, review and critique', in *Life's Work: Geographies of Social Reproduction*, Oxford: Blackwell, pp. 1–26.

Ong, A. (2008) *Neoliberalism as Exception: Mutations in Citizenship and Sovereignty*, Durham, NC: Duke University Press.

Pateman, C. (1988) *The Sexual Contract*, Stanford, CA: Stanford University Press.

Patnaik, U. (2006) 'The free lunch: transfers from the tropical colonies and their role in capital formation in Britain during the Industrial Revolution', in K. S. Jomo (ed.), *The Long Twentieth Century: Globalization under Hegemony: The Changing World Economy*, Delhi: Oxford University Press, pp. 30–70.

— (2012) 'Capitalism and the production of poverty', *Social Scientist*, 40(1/2): 3–20.

Pearson, R., A. Whitehead and K. Young. (1981) 'Introduction: The continuing subordination of women in the development process', in K. Young, C. Wolkowitz and R. MacCullagh (eds), *Of Marriage and the Market: Women's Subordination Internationally and Its Lessons*, London: Routledge, pp. ix–xix.

PUDR (People's Union for Democratic Rights) (1984) 'Inside the family', Delhi: People's Union for Democratic Rights, March.

Rai, S. M. (2013) 'Gender and (international) political economy', in G. Waylen, K. Celis and L. Weldon (eds), *The Oxford Handbook of Gender and Politics*, Oxford: Oxford University Press, pp. 263–88.

Rege, S. (2006) *Writing Caste, Writing Gender: Narrating Dalit Women's Testimonies*, Delhi: Zubaan.

Rubin, G. (2011) 'The traffic in women: notes on the "political economy" of sex', in G. Rubin (ed.), *Deviations: A Gayle Rubin Reader*, Durham, NC: Duke University Press, pp. 33–65.

Sangari, K. (1993) 'The "amenities of domestic life": questions on labour', *Social Scientist*, September–November, pp. 244–6.

— (1995) 'Politics of diversity: religious communities and multiple patriarchies', *Economic and Political Weekly*, 30(51/52): 3381–9.

— (1999) *Politics of the Possible: Essays on Gender, History, Narratives, Colonial English*, Delhi: Tulika.

— (2007) 'Shaping pressures and symbolic horizons: the women's movement in India', in N. de Mel and S. Thiruchandran (eds), *At the Cutting Edge: Essays in Honour of Kumari Jayawardena*, Delhi: Women Unlimited, pp. 36–67.

Sangari, K. and S. Vaid (1989) 'Introduction', in K. Sangari and S. Vaid (eds), *Recasting Women: Essays in Colonial History*, Delhi: Kali for Women, pp. 1–26.

Sassen, S. (1998) *Globalization and Its Discontents: Essays on the New Mobility of People and Money*, New York: New Press.

Scott, J. W. (1999) *Gender and the Politics of History*, New York: Columbia University Press.

Shi, Y. (2009) 'The formation of a Chinese immigrant working-class patriarchy: reinventing gendered expectations within the structural confines of U.S. society', *Meridians*, 9(1): 31–60.

Stoler, A. N. (1997) 'Making empire respectable: the politics of race and sexual morality in 20th-century colonial cultures', in A. McClintock, A. Mufti and E. Shohat (eds), *Dangerous Liaisons: Gender, Nations and Postcolonial Perspectives*, Minneapolis: University of Minnesota Press, pp. 344–73.

Walby, S. (1990) *Theorizing Patriarchy*, Oxford: Blackwell.

— (2009) *Globalization and Inequalities: Complexities and Contested Modernities*, London: Sage.

Žižek, S. (2011) *Living in the End Times*, London: Verso.

13 | REPRODUCTION

Michelle Murphy

How might we build new forms of life out of the old? This simple yet pressing question animates this revision of the keyword 'reproduction'. According to the *Oxford English Dictionary*, in its most general sense reproduction means 'the action or process of forming, creating, or bringing into existence again'. Pointing to the possibility of re-creation, the history of the term has been tossed between the worlds of manufacture and life. Since the 1970s, reproduction has been a crucial keyword for Marxist-feminist theorizations of family forms, care labour, heterosexual divisions of labour, domestic work, unpaid work and even patriarchy. In this vein of theorization, reproduction is typically conflated with childbirth and childcare, thereby concentrating the theorization of reproduction on the ways sexed embodied difference has been mobilized in the history of capitalism to create new divisions and stratifications of labour through patriarchy. In contrast, this chapter asks: Why do we think we know what reproduction is? What does reproduction encompass? How does it stretch beyond bodies or heterosexuality? Reproduction needs to be retheorized, yet again, to account for the ways living-being is remade in contemporary capitalist formations.

The interconnected terms production (the act of creation) and reproduction (the act of creating again) both acquired new meanings during the rise of industrial capitalism in eighteenth-century Europe.[1] Production first became a term in economics through the works of François Quesnay and Adam Smith, who used it to describe the achievements of new arrangements of labour, raw materials and machines in emergent industrialism.[2] At the same historical juncture, European scholars of natural history and comparative anatomy began to use the term reproduction to name the ways life, especially species-life, regenerated itself. In particular, reproduction began to name the conservation of form within a species across generations.[3] Significantly, reproduction came to describe the capacity of all living things to regenerate themselves out of their own animacy, without human labour. It was a process of generating more, which historian Martina Schluender has characterized through the equation '1+1=3': life's capacity to create the 'more' of plants and animals that could multiply ownership, provide the raw materials to be transformed through industry, or sold as commodities for profit (Schluender 2010).

As an identification of a process of life itself, separable from human manufacture but also providing the raw materials for all economic activity, the concept of reproduction reflected a larger history of delimiting realms as inside and outside of economics within liberal capitalism. For example, at the very same time that a new legal regime defined the rights of man in terms of property and ownership of one's labour in eighteenth-century Europe, designations of sexed and raced living-being carved out domains where women and children could be ruled under distinctive patriarchal family law, while racialized persons and their children could be enslaved as a living property owned by others. Simultaneous with the refinement of chattel slavery as a capitalist system that commodified humans via race, with the elaboration of colonialisms validated through designations of raced and primitive life, and with the invention of new patriarchies within family forms, the concept of reproduction indicated life's own capacity to generate surplus, a natural process external to and prior to economic activity, but which could nonetheless be subsumed into capitalism as its raw materials.[4]

Within the evolutionary epistemologies of the nineteenth century, 'reproduction' took on new significance for capitalism. It still referred to a process of living-being, but now encompassed extensive spans of time resulting in evolutionary changes that did not simply maintain species-kind, but also produced the difference that natural selection destroyed or multiplied. Reproduction, thus, did not merely remake life as more of the same; it generated constellations of variation, more or less adapted, more or less primitive, and more or less valuable. Reproduction became a living difference engine. As a living source of variation, evolution was thus imputed as the well from which capitalism's divisions of labour by sex and race could draw (McClintock 1995). It naturally sliced life into differences that justified accumulation through patriarchal colonialisms, enslavements and apartheids. By the end of the nineteenth century, however, evolutionary forces were imagined as open to rational human direction, giving rise to an explosion of eugenic projects around that world that actively sought to rationalize race through reproduction for the sake of improved and purified forms of life, resulting in the horrors of genocide, concentration camps and mass sterilization.[5] In other words, the conceptual distinction of production-as-economic and reproduction-as-living was a forceful ruse that facilitated the demarcation of racial, sexual and colonial difference as 'natural', legitimizing acts of violence and oppression.

Writing in the nineteenth century in the belly of an empire, Marx retheorized reproduction at the crossroads of economics and living-being. In *Capital*, reproduction named the ploughing back of some of the products of accumulation into maintaining the means and forces of production. Without reproduction, capitalist society could not maintain itself over time. It happened in the business of a factory, where worn machines were replaced, and also in the life of workers, who must spend wages in order to pay for their own subsistence and maintain their life. Labourers must reproduce themselves from day to day, and thus must work in order to live. Thus, reproduction, for Marx, was also the name for the process by which human life and its labour power were regenerated, both in terms of eating and the daily sustaining of an individual body, and in terms of aggregate life, the life of workers across generations. Succinctly put, 'If production be capitalistic in form, so too will be reproduction' (Marx 1977: 711). The term reproduction, when used by Marx, was integral to political-economic processes (rather than separate from economics) and further extended to the maintenance of the social relations that capitalism required. As a system of relations that assembled together machines, bodies and nature, capitalism was continuously remaking those relations through 'a process of reproduction, [that] produces not only commodities, not only surplus-value, but it also produces and reproduces the capitalist relation itself; on the one hand the capitalist, on the other the wage-labourer' (ibid.: 724). Marx notes, but does not elaborate, that the activities of women and children in contributing to the subsistence of the family are a form of 'supplementary labour' that produces the 'labour power' of the worker for capitalism (ibid.: 517–18). In Marx, then, reproduction was explicitly retheorized as existing within capitalist relations. Nonetheless, his work largely saw the generative, embodied capacities of animals, plants and living-being as part of the external natural world that capitalism subsumed as its raw materials through human interaction; but this was not explicitly theorized as part of reproduction itself.

Over the course of the twentieth century, capitalism developed and multiplied into something quite different from the British industrial form under which Marx theorized reproduction. By the mid-twentieth century, the epistemic figure of the 'macroeconomy' – the model of the total economy within the container of the nation-state – was invented by economists like John Maynard Keynes. In turn, state institutions began to gather quantitative data about the macroeconomy with new measures like gross national product (GNP) (Murphy 2013a; Bergeron 2004; Mitchell 2005; Waring 1999). By the second half of the twentieth century, the primary tasks of the nation-state became the care of 'the economy' and the increase of GDP. With decolonization, the globe was covered with an uneven patchwork of nation-states, each tending its own macroeconomy with a GDP to feed. Through the globalization of the epistemic figure of 'the economy', states were charged in a new way with creating, manipulating and governing the milieu in which capitalism could most effectively thrive (even if in practice this control over a national economy was illusory and instead at the mercy of transnational circuits of value extraction and capital accumulation). This shift to the fetish of the macroeconomy in the history of capitalism manifested itself in the rise of economic development as a new transnational formation, one that tied nationalism and neocolonialism to projects (such as structural adjustment) of rearranging life and land. So too was the fetish of the macroeconomy accompanied by the rise of neoliberal governmentalities that sought to rearrange the nation-state so as to maximize capitalist activity in order to foster, stimulate and free 'the economy'. This process of economization called for the massive rearrangement of life and governance in the name of amplifying the productive forces of capitalism.

Though a tyrannical global metric, GDP counted only some activities and forms of life as productive, thereby drawing into new legibility zones of undervalued life that could be politicized. In relation to labour, GDP measures only *waged* labour, and thus the labour of caring for children or labour put towards subsistence were hegemonically designated as forms of non-productive work. More broadly, both mid-twentieth-century liberal economic logics and much Marxist theory relied on this division between paid 'productive' work (which counted as contributing towards the economy) and unpaid 'unproductive' work, such as domestic and subsistence work often done by women, which was not counted as properly economic. It was in this historic moment of economization that Marxist feminists of the 1970s retheorized the 'relations of reproduction' as a sexual division of labour, relations that capitalism both relied on and undervalued. Mariarosa Dalla Costa and Selma James (1975), Selma James (1980), Maria Mies (1998), Claudia von Werlhof (2007), Leopoldina Fortunati (1989) and Sylvia Federici (2012), among others, argued that decolonization needed to simultaneously address colonialism's racism and capitalism's sexual division of labour, in which women lived in poverty doing the unwaged work of sustaining human life by caring for children, feeding families, and practising subsistence agriculture. Capitalism, they argued, not only devalued this labour, but relied on it as the free work that reproduces the labour force. Women were both a reserve army of labour that capitalism could call upon or dump as need be, and a source of free labour that made labourers. Capitalism relied on women's embodiment itself, their breasts, wombs and feelings, their fleshy vitality, to create future workers. Marxist feminist Selma James coined the term 'unwaged work' to describe the devaluation of reproductive labour (James 1980); thus, feminists organized campaigns, such as Wages for Housework or the Global Strike of Women, which attempted to revalue reproductive work and rearrange the values of the nation-state that counted killing over caring (Trotz 2007). As an epistemological effect of this political work, Marxist feminists helped to carve out 'reproduction' as a politicized domain. Reproductive labour, which under capitalism happened in the shadow space of economy, needed to be brought to light.

The emergence of Marxist-feminism in the 1970s and its theorizing of the 'relations of reproduction' comes out of this long history of considering reproduction as distinct from, or in the shadow of, capitalism. In this work, reproduction exists in a domain not fully subsumed by capitalism, not yet fully brought into commodification, and therefore it is a domain with the potential to generate other ways of living: caring versus killing. Yet this important era of Marxist-feminist theory has fundamental problems. First, it has tended to enshrine heterosexuality as natural, rather than as an effect of relations of power. Secondly, and relatedly, it posits the domain of 'nature' as external to and prior to the economic and the social, rather than considering designations of 'nature' as profoundly political. This tendency comes to the fore in ecofeminist versions of Marxist-feminisms that hold that Nature and Woman are similarly exploited under capitalism (Mies and Shiva 1993). Thirdly, Marxist-feminist arguments about reproductive labour have tended to conflate reproduction with childbirth, child rearing and labour within the family, thereby narrowing the ambit of the relations of reproduction. Fourthly, these arguments have failed to challenge the division of labour that condemns women to undertake mundane and devalued labour within family forms.[6] Fifthly, this work has tended to cherish labour as the singularly crucial category by which to theorize difference and value, as well as to organize and imagine activism and resistance. In doing so, it has been faithful to traditional Marxian analytics born of nineteenth-century Europe. Yet, in the twenty-first century, what are the sites and practices through which to theorize reproduction in an elaborated capitalism of the contemporary? What is reproduction now, how does it come to matter? Is it desirable, or even possible, to hold reproduction as a life process external to, ignored or undervalued by capitalism either conceptually or materially? How might we elaborate on Marx's expansive sense of reproduction, in which capitalist worlds are 'in the constant flux of its incessant renewal, every social process of production is at the same time a process of reproduction' (Marx 1977: 711)?

Remaking reproduction

Why do we think we know what reproduction is? If commodities and capital appear as a fetish that the critical analyst, aided by subjugated knowledges and critical theories, reveals as a congealment of obscured relations, so too might we see reproduction in its hegemonic form (as merely embodied, as primarily about childbirth) as also a fetish produced in an assemblage of social, economic, technoscientific, subjectivating and political relations. How have the powerful categories of Woman, Man, Child, Species, Organism, Individual, Sex, Race and even Life been variously materialized as necessary for understanding animacy and violence in capitalism's relations of reproduction? The Marxist-feminist tradition forged in the 1970s operates through a legacy of units of analysis little changed since the nineteenth century. Reproduction, as a keyword, demands to be unwound from premises of individually embodied childbirth, Darwinian versions of race and sex, or industrial accounts of labour value.

This is not to say that childbirth, women and labour are no longer salient categories; rather, they are just limited points of entry for the task of bringing a feminist critique of capitalism to bear on the twenty-first century. In fact, at the very moment that Marxist feminists crafted an analysis of how capitalism operated through undervalued, yet necessary, reproductive labour, the status of 'reproduction' in the form of 'population' was undergoing profound rearrangement as a domain of intensive intervention crucial to national economies, while technoscience was disaggregating reproduction into generative forms of biotechnology.

For example, the 1970s saw the global distribution of cheap contraceptives in the name of managing future population for the sake of national (and global) macroeconomies. Population control, in its many liberal, authoritarian and neocolonial guises, was overwhelmingly a project to increase the national metric of GDP per capita. The globalized project of preventing poor and raced future life was geared towards the goal of increasing future economic prosperity, made manifest in the task of improving GDP. American economists even calculated that an averted birth in the decolonized 'Third World' was worth more to GDP than a life lived (Enke and Zind 1969). An enormous global investment – by the United States, recently decolonized countries and East Asian nation-states such as Japan and China – sought to pre-emptively avert living-being, thereby turning reproduction into a domain of intensive capitalist investment, generating new forms of governmentality and enrolling political ideologies from communism to feminism in the process.[7] In so doing, new ways of explicitly calculating living surplus as unwanted excess life were accompanied by soon-to-be-hegemonic governmentalities of development, population control, family planning and public health. Such governmentalities sought both to reduce the birth of future life for the sake of macroeconomic futures and at the same time to 'develop' and manage poor people as aggregate populations of disposable life still available for subsumption into capitalism as labourers.[8] Reproduction, as a process of living-being in time, became an explicit, highly charged concern of governmentality in which economy, and hence the expansion of capitalism, was at stake. Through governmentalities such as population control, capitalism would come to actively shape its own conditions, its own milieu.

In this way, and many others, reproduction in the late twentieth century was far from an undervalued and ignored domain. It was intensely activated and exploited, subsumed and resubsumed by forms of capital. The very status of reproduction as a life process thereby shifted. Life was not held as prior to or outside of capitalism – life was instead a form of capital. Thus, we can historicize 'life' as a non-innocent domain first articulated by the sciences of the eighteenth century at the dawn of European industrial capitalism and racial systems of colonialism and slavery. By the end of the nineteenth century, reproduction was understood as a process capable of rationalization, one that generated new value for capitalism by virtue of creating difference and surplus. And by the late twentieth century reproduction was a process open to social engineering at macro and micro registers and was generative of new biotechnologies and forms of life that served as commodities and even forms of capital. Life was not just a living raw material, or a source of labour power in workers. Through technoscience, life's capacities for animation, generation, recombination and rearrangement directly created value. For example, the twentieth-century life sciences disassembled reproduction into rearrangeable micro-logical and molecular units of amino acids, proteins and cells; altered and isolated genes, viruses, bacteria and enzymes became commodifiable biotechnologies that could move between species and rearrange the very fabric of life – or even generate new forms of life. Moreover, the animate qualities of life, its capacities to exude chemicals, create more of itself and recombine, became ways of producing commodifiable substances of life itself. This generative capacity, moreover, was brought into technicity as a new kind of biocapital (Waldby and Cooper 2008; Helmreich 2008; Rajan 2006; Franklin 2007). Micro-logical forms of life were like machines that could create drugs, new organisms or other chemicals. Oocytes, tissue cultures and algae were heralded as non-human sources of biovalue that created new products for capitalism. In contemporary technoscience, reproduction expands beyond sex to include cloning, lateral gene transfer, polymerase chain reaction, forms of symbiosis, and even kinds of digestion. The reproduction of life has become a source of novelty, invention, animation, connectivity, responsiveness and difference that could be harnessed through technoscience. Reproduction became queered, existing beyond norms of heterosexuality. Reproduction multiplied the actors and sites involved in bringing life into existence. Even human childbirth became assisted, such that the absence of assisted childbirth became ethically charged as a kind of structural violence. For example, high rates of maternal and infant mortality have become entirely avoidable with biomedical infrastructures, and hence the continuing existence of such high rates is the ethically charged geopolitical effect of neglecting, destroying, or not building such infrastructures.

In addition to turning the micro-logical features of life into commodities and biocapital, reproduction has crucially also been financialized. The generative capacities of life as embodied particularly in female bodies became a domain for explicit speculation. For example, at the turn of the twenty-first century, 'The Girl', typically poor and brown, has become highly prized as a form of human capital that provides high rates of return on investment (Murphy 2013b) because such investment intervenes in a particular moment of female development and alters probabilities of reproduction. From Nike's Girl Effect campaign to Plan's Because I am a Girl project to Hillary Clinton's call for investing in girls as a way to combat terrorism, in the contemporary era 'The Girl' has become abstracted as a site of investment that offers the purportedly highest rates of return in the 'developing' world. Her rates of return are so high because investing in her life chances has implications for reducing her future fertility and raising her future wages, thereby providing a double benefit to GDP. In twenty-first-century development projects, logics of human capital have largely replaced population control and family planning as the means to alter the economy by virtue of altering sex and gender. In this formulation, embodied attributes ranging from learning and obedience to health become individualized forms of capital that states invest in for the sake of good rates of return. In the process, forms of life that do not offer promising rates of return, such as poor brown boys, have become a form of uninvestable surplus life, open to violence instead of salvation.

While any revitalized theorization of the relations of reproduction needs to take into account economization and financialization, there are aspects to capitalism's violence that are externalized from its own logics. Thus, in addition to the ways life is explicitly turned into forms of value for capital, the conditions of life are also being transformed by industrial chemicals, radiation and climate change. Landlessness, displacement, flooding and drought, deforestation and the aftermath of war on ecologies and infrastructure all profoundly alter the conditions for sustaining life in time. The terraforming consequences of capitalist activities are hegemonically rendered in economic logics as 'externalities' that companies and perpetrators are not responsible for. In other words, they are 'free' forms of violence that companies or states are allowed to distribute without accountability, such that human and non-human life are burdened with the material, often intergenerational, costs. With climate change, moreover, the externalization of the violent effects of capitalist activity has altered life on a planetary scale. Geologists now call our era the Anthropocene, an era beginning in the Industrial Revolution in which the entire planet has been altered by human activities. In other words, there is no life, no nature, not already altered by capitalism at the molecular level. Thus any retheorization of the relations of reproduction needs to be accountable to struggles to preserve the conditions of life, such as indigenous fights against extraction, subsistence land claims and critiques of environmental racism.

Thus, from the economization of life as manifest in population control, to the engineering of the generative capacities of life in technoscience, to the financialization of life in human capital, to the destruction of ecologies needed to sustain life, over the course of the twentieth century the conjugations between life and capital have been multiplied and expanded. By the 1970s, for feminisms too, the imperative to politicize the practices and conditions of 'seizing the means of reproduction' became urgent, giving rise to transnational feminist health movements that sought to develop technologies, protocols and laws by which women would be individually charged with the right and responsibility to shape reproduction within their own bodies (Dreifus 1977). For some feminists, this project took the form of feminist health clinics, NGOs and human rights protections directed at women's reproductive health, while still other feminists have embraced the logic of human capital to celebrate girls as investments, thereby positioning feminism as an expression of the purportedly liberating effects of capitalist logics. Yet other feminists began to theorize a more extensive ontology for reproduction that exceeded the individual body, heterosexuality and other normative categories of human life.

Two important feminist interventions that rearticulated the very premise of reproductive politics were the 1989 Comilla Declaration, written in Bangladesh, and the Reproductive Justice concept developed by activist US feminists of colour. The Comilla Declaration resulted from a conference co-organized by the transnational feminist organization Feminist International Network of Resistance to Reproductive and Genetic Engineering (FINRRAGE) and the Bangladesh organization Unnayan Bikalper Nitinirdharoni Gobeshona (UBINIG), led by Farida Akhter. The declaration theorized a version of reproductive politics that went beyond the important denunciation of the imperialist and nationalist violence of population control. It did so by tying together the rearrangement of sexed living-being in population control with the rearrangement of non-human life in the green revolution as well as the commodification of seed and organisms in agricultural biotechnology (FINRRAGE-UBINIG International Conference 1991). For Farida Akhter, human and non-human reproduction were not separable. The capacity to become and maintain life in time is not confined to childbirth, but extends to the means of sustaining and maintaining life through eating, agriculture and ecological relations to plant and animal life (Akhter 2007). Thus the relations of reproduction extend to the ways seeds, for example, have become fully subsumed as commodities in industrial capitalism. Relations of debt through loans for commodified seed amplify life's precariousness for people who grow food and make ecologies vulnerable to biodiversity loss. As such, the Comilla Declaration addressed reproductive politics in terms of 'engineering and industrialization of the life processes' (Akther 1989: 45) more broadly, and called for a reappropriation of the relations of reproduction from capitalism (Akhter 1992; FINRRAGE-UBING International Conference 1991).

Put another way, the declaration drew together the ways property relations, via technoscience, extended to the molecular registers of life in seeds and the ways economization extended to the macro-logical registers of life in economy and population. For Akhter, the division between political struggles around human reproduction and struggles around agriculture, plants and subsistence was an artefact of late twentieth-century global capitalism. Instead of seeing human and ecological reproduction as distinct, Akhter argues that the capacity to maintain life entangles humans with the plants, animals, land and water that make possible collective existence in time (Akhter 2007). Thus, resisting the subsumption of seed into capitalist relations is reframed as integral to a more extensive sense of reproductive politics, one that reaches beyond the questions of childbirth, beyond individual rights, and beyond the human. For the Comilla Declaration, liberal feminists' emphasis on birth control, choice and individualized reproductive rights was inadequate for a struggle against the expansive reach of relations of reproductions.

The concept of 'reproductive justice', also fashioned in the late 1980s, likewise insisted on overflowing the body, childbirth and choice as the containers of reproductive politics. As theorized by Asian Communities for Reproductive Justice (ACRJ) and the Sister Song Collective in the United States, the concept builds on legacies of work by anti-racist feminists for radically expanding the reach of reproductive politics to 'issues such as sex trafficking, youth empowerment, family unification, educational justice, unsafe working conditions, domestic violence, discrimination of queer and transgendered communities, immigrant rights, environmental justice, and globalization' (Sister Song Women of Color Reproductive Health Collective 2007). Reproductive justice sought to address 'reproductive oppression', theorized as a crossroads where capacities to maintain life, family and community were embroiled with racialized economic inequality, immigration law, pollution and climate change, such that reproductive justice addressed community politics rather than women in particular. Thus, reproductive politics was a struggle around the conditions that allowed life, and thereby enrolled everyone – and not just women.

The concept of reproductive justice, moreover, elaborates on the critique of the focus on childbirth, abortion and contraception by some feminists in the West, particularly white liberal feminisms. Feminists such as Angela Davis (1983), Dorothy Roberts (1997) and Andrea Smith (2005) insisted on highlighting the ways reproductive politics were contiguous with the violent effects of capitalism, colonialism and racism as expressed through incarceration and criminalization, structural poverty, war and genocide, or histories of slavery and segregation. Reproductive politics could not be separated from the conditions that make life vulnerable or destroy life. Thus, this vein of work insists that the often racialized structural distributions of violence, vulnerability and death are not separable from the politics of sustaining life. In other words, the relations of reproduction include distributions of destructive forces as much as forces that selectively promote or rearrange life.

What these two interventions into the reach of reproductive politics demonstrate is how the relations of reproduction might be retheorized for the twenty-first century as a diverse and distributed process, stretching beyond embodied senses of human reproduction or reproductive labour, and including both destructive as well as generative forces. In this spirit, the anthropologist Shellee Colen's influential notion of 'stratified reproduction' demonstrates how 'kinship' is hierarchically rearranged and made geopolitically mobile by structures of race, sex and class in transnational political economies of circulating labour (Colen 1995). At a conceptual register, anthropologist Marilyn Strathern has developed a notion of 'dispersed kinship' in order to ask complex questions about the shifting range of 'procreators' who take part in, 'assist' and hence are in 'relation to' reproductive acts as mediated by technoscience, property forms and knowledge production (Strathern 1992). Feminist technoscience studies scholar Donna Haraway offers the concept of 'mess mates' as part of a project to unwind the Western-bounded human by attending to the ways humans are always something more by virtue of being knotted to the non-human others through which living is possible (Haraway 2008). For Haraway, to be one is always to become with many.

Such feminist reformulations have reconfigured what counts as reproduction in our current conjuncture of global capitalism and terraforming. The politics of living-being has been reframed as a profoundly distributed phenomenon, while contemporary capitalism comes in a cornucopia of forms. Hence the relations of reproduction need to also be seen as messy multiple and extensive processes that manifest in and connect bodies and labour, but are not reducible to bodies or labour. The relations of reproduction can be critically reimagined as already making up a complex non-innocent matrix of life and death entanglements to which many are accountable. If reproduction is a distributed process of living-being already transformed by racism, birth control, heteronormativities, biomedicine, biotechnology, infrastructures, patriarchies, legacies of slavery, pollution, housing, economic development, militarization, financialization, criminalization, nation-states, climate change, queer politics, industrialized agriculture, labour relations, and so on, what is a feminist ontological politics of reproduction that can critically show how life is constituted through these material relations in ways that encompass but also exceed sexed and raced bodies as such? How to stretch attention to the historically and spatially extensive matrices of technoscience and political economy that do not just converge on but are themselves the process(es) of reproduction?

Distributed reproduction

It is in this spirit that reproduction is retheorized as a constellation of geopolitically extensive 'relations of reproduction' that unevenly disperse and rearrange life in a world riven by capital flows, racialized geographies, sexualities, wars, imperialisms and nation-states. Such a retheorization participates in provoking a feminist politics that does not concentrate on the body as its scale (with liberal rights and biomedical access as solutions) and expands beyond the traditional Marxist-feminist focus on revaluing reproductive labour. How might a reformulated sense of distributed reproduction offer connections and solidarity across geopolitics? How might it bind disparately situated communities in the project of sustaining life in time? Theorizing reproduction as a matrix of multiple and extensive relations of reproduction, we might ask how relations of reproduction are subsumed by but not reducible to relations of production.

In other words, as for Marxist feminists of the 1970s, today the politicization of the relations of reproduction is crucial to the critique of capitalism and the project of imagining and struggling for other worlds. At the same time, a circumscribed conception of reproduction is a historical artefact conceived within capitalist and nineteenth-century logics. Any theorization of the relations of reproduction, as much as it may offer a critical diagnostic of capitalism, is also a historical symptom. It is with this awareness that the concept of relations of reproduction needs to be retheorized in the following ways:

- as a multiplicity of formations that are spatially and temporally extensive in historically specific ways. As such, relations of reproduction, in the plural, are characterized by colliding worlds, in which life can be simultaneously fostered and abandoned, reassembled and destroyed by virtue of inhabiting multiple and contradictory relations of reproduction;
- as generating uneven distributions of precariousness, violence, infrastructure, wealth, death and life chances. Relations of reproduction shape the conditions whereby lives become and are destroyed. In other words, reproduction does not create a safe haven of caring, but is instead a set of relations that can sustain, transform and extinguish life;
- as generating value for capital both through fostering new life forms

in technoscience (such as biotechnology or industrial agriculture) and through destructions of life (such as through practices of economization that avert, abandon or destroy some forms of life in order to enhance the prosperity of future other life);

- as stretching beyond bodies and childbirth to include infrastructures (of healthcare or water), non-human life and ecologies. In this way, a theorization of distributed relations of reproduction sees life as always and only existing in connection with the non-human others that make existence possible;
- as recognizing the contradictory possibilities of living-being's generative properties. Living-being's capacities to generate difference and more of itself are already subsumed by capitalism, yet this capacity for difference and excess can also be seen as animating new possibilities for creating other worlds, for finding elsewheres within here;
- as subsuming feminisms as inside historically specific relations of reproduction, particularly in practices of development that have often advocated for targeting sex, girls, reproductive health and gender as more ethicized ways of connecting life, states and economy. Feminisms are non-innocently entangled in relations of reproduction; and
- as including questions of labour, but not confined to them, such that relations of reproduction include the world-rearranging processes of economization, financialization, slavery, colonialism and dispossession, as well as practices of subsistence, of coexisting with humans and non-humans, of flourishing together in sustainable conditions, of reconciliation and of pleasure and desire.

In these ways and more, a recharged theorization of the relations of reproduction might have a better chance of grappling with the urgent material conjunctures of the contemporary. A re-energized Marxist-feminism might still hold reproduction as a crucial political concept because it pivots around life – the struggle to exist again but differently, a struggle for the material and conceptual relations of life that expansively draws in the entire planet but also reaches down into the smallest substrates of existence. This retheorization involves letting go of the fantasy that women, sex and reproduction might provide special escapes from capitalism. Instead, the relations of reproduction are better theorized as already subsumed by capitalism and as thereby provoking the political task of looking towards ways of 'becoming with many' that can proliferate possibilities towards other forms of life.

Notes

1 For a useful genealogy of reproduction in the eighteenth century, see Jordanova (1995).

2 Early use of production as a term describing the creation of products from raw materials through manufacture dates to several foundational texts that inaugurated the European discipline of economics, or what was then called 'political economy', in the eighteenth century. In English, the OED dates one of the earliest uses of 'production' to Adam Smith's 1784 edition of *An Inquiry into the Nature and Causes of the Wealth of Nations*. In French, François Quesnay's *Tableu Économique* of 1758, which began the physiocratic tradition of political economy, was another influential early use.

3 The earliest use of the term reproduction to describe generation in life was by the French comparative anatomist Buffon in his history of animals (1749: 18). On the history of the shift from generation to reproduction, see Roger (1997: 116–31).

4 On the elaboration of race and sex within slavery and colonialism as capitalist systems, see Baucom (2005) and McClintock (1995).

5 Exemplary works on these topics include Briggs (1998); Mbembe (2003); Smith (2005): Stern (2005); Stoler (2003).

6 On this point, see Haug (2010).

7 On governmentality, see Foucault (1991); Scott (1995); Murphy (2012).

8 For exemplary analyses of the gendered and raced creation of subsumable and disposable labour, see Wright (2006) and Tadiar (2012).

References

Akhter, F. (1989) 'On the question of the reproductive right: a personal reflection', in *Proceedings of the FINRRAGE-UBINIG International Conference, 1989*, Dhaka: UBINIG, pp. 45–9.

— (1992) *Depopulating Bangladesh: Essays on the Politics of Fertility*, Dhaka: Narigrantha Prabartana.

— (2007) *Seeds of Movements: On Women's Issues in Bangladesh*, Dhaka: Narigrantha Prabartana.

Asian Communities for Reproductive Justice (2005) 'A new vision for advancing our movement for reproductive health, reproductive rights, and reproductive justice', Oakland, CA: Asian Communites for Reproductive Justice.

Baucom, I. (2005) *Specters of the Atlantic: Finance Capital, Slavery, and the Philosophy of History*, Durham, NC: Duke University Press.

Bergeron, S. (2004) *Fragments of Development: Nation, Gender, and the Space of Modernity*, Ann Arbor: University of Michigan Press.

Briggs, L. (1998) *Reproducing Empire: Race, Sex, Science, and U.S. Imperialism in Puerto Rico*, Berkeley and Los Angeles: University of California Press.

Buffon, G. L. L. (1749) *Histoire générale des animaux* [History of animals], Paris: Imprimerie Royale.

Colen, S. (1995) 'Like a mother to them: stratified reproduction and West Indian childcare workers and employers in New York', in F. Ginsburg and R. Rapp (eds), *Conceiving the New World Order: The Global Politics of Reproduction*, Berkeley and Los

Angeles: University of California Press.
Dalla Costa, M. and S. James (1975) *The Power of Women and the Subversion of the Community*, Bristol: Falling Wall.
Davis, A. Y. (1983) *Women, Race and Class*, New York: Vintage.
Dreifus, C. (1977) 'Introduction', in C. Dreifus (ed.), *Seizing Our Bodies*, New York: Vintage, pp. xvii–xxxi.
Enke, S. and G. R. Zind (1969) 'Effect of fewer births on average income', *Journal of Biosocial Science*, 1(1): 41–55.
Federici, S. (1973) *Wages against Housework*, Bristol: Falling Wall.
— (2012) *Revolution at Point Zero: Housework, Reproduction, and Feminist Struggle*, Oakland, CA: PM.
FINRRAGE-UBINIG International Conference (1991) 'Declaration of Comilla', *Journal of Issues in Reproductive and Genetic Engineering*, 4(1): 73–4.
Fortunati, L. (1989) *Arcane of Reproduction: Housework, Prostitution, Labor and Capital*, Brooklyn, NY: Autonomedia.
Foucault, M. (1991) 'Governmentality', in G. Burchell, C. Gordon and P. Miller (eds), *The Foucault Effect: Studies in Governmentality*, Chicago, IL: University of Chicago Press, pp. 87–104.
Franklin, S. (2007) *Dolly Mixtures: The Remaking of Genealogy*, Durham, NC: Duke University Press.
Haraway, D. J. (2008) *When Species Meet*, Minneapolis: University of Minnesota Press.
Haug, F. (2010) 'A politics of working life', in T. Seddon, L. Henriksoon and B. Niemeyer (eds), *Learning and Work and the Politics of Working Life*, London: Routledge, pp. 217–25.
Helmreich, S. (2008) 'Species of biocapital', *Science as Culture*, 17(4): 463–78.
James, S. (1980) *Sex, Race and Class*, Bristol: Falling Wall.
Jordanova, L. (1995) 'Interrogating the concept of reproduction in the eighteenth century', in F. Ginsburg and R. Rapp (eds), *Conceiving the New World Order: The Global Politics of Reproduction*, Berkeley and Los Angeles: University of California Press, pp. 369–86.
Marx, K. (1977) *Capital: A Critique of Political Economy*, vol. 1, New York: Vintage.
Mbembe, A. (2003) 'Necropolitics', *Public Culture*, 15(1): 11–40.
McClintock, A. (1995) *Imperial Leather: Race, Gender, and Sexuality in the Colonial Contest*, New York: Routledge.
Mies, M. (1998) *Patriarchy and Accumulation on a World Scale: Women in the International Division of Labour*, New York: Palgrave Macmillan.
Mies, M. and V. Shiva (1993) *Ecofeminism*, Halifax: Fernwood.
Mitchell, T. (2005) 'The work of economics: how a discipline makes its world', *European Journal of Sociology*, 47(2): 297–320.
Murphy, M. (2012) *Seizing the Means of Reproduction: Entanglements of Feminism, Health, and Technoscience*, Durham, NC: Duke University Press.
— (2013a) 'Economization of life: calculative infrastructures of population and economy', in R. Peg (ed.), *Relational Ecologies: Subjectivity, Sex, Nature and Architecture*, London: Routledge, pp. 225–54.
— (2013b) 'The Girl: mergers of feminism and finance in neoliberal times', *Scholar and Feminist Online*, 11(3).
Rajan, K. S. (2006) *Biocapital: The Constitution of Postgenomic Life*, Durham, NC: Duke University Press.
Roberts, D. (1997) *Killing the Black Body*, New York: Pantheon.
Roger, J. (1997) *Buffon: A Life in Natural History*, Ithaca, NY: Cornell University Press.
Schluender, M. (2010) '1+1=3: genealogies

of reproductive medicine in the German speaking countries, 1900–1990', Workshop paper, Economies of Reproduction Workshop, Berlin, 7 May.

Scott, D. (1995) 'Colonial governmentality', *Social Text*, 43: 191–220.

Sister Song Women of Color Reproductive Health Collective (2007) *Reproductive Justice Briefing Book*, Atlanta, GA: Sister Song.

Smith, A. (2005) *Conquest: Sexual Violence and American Indian Genocide*, Cambridge: South End.

Stern, A. M. (2005) *Eugenic Nation: Faults and Frontiers of Better Breeding in America*, Berkeley and Los Angeles: University of California Press.

Stoler, A. L. (2003) *Carnal Knowledge and Imperial Power: Race and the Intimate in Colonial Rule*, Berkeley and Los Angeles: University of California Press.

Strathern, M. (1992) *After Nature: English Kinship in the Late Twentieth Century*, Cambridge: Cambridge University Press.

Tadiar, N. (2012) 'Life times in fate playing', *South Atlantic Quarterly*, 11(4): 783–802.

Trotz, A. (2007) 'Red thread: the politics of hope in Guyana', *Race & Class*, 49(2): 71–9.

Von Werlhof, C. (2007) 'No critique of capitalism without a critique of patriarchy! Why the left is no alternative', *Capitalism, Nature, Socialism*, 18(1): 13–27.

Waldby, C. and M. Cooper (2008) 'The biopolitics of reproduction: post-Fordist biotechnology and women's clinical labour', *Australian Feminist Studies*, 23(55): 57–73.

Waring, M. (1999) *Counting for Nothing: What Men Value and What Women are Worth*, 2nd edn, Toronto: University of Toronto Press.

Wright, M. (2006) *Disposable Women and Other Myths of Global Capitalism*, New York: Routledge.

14 | REVOLUTION

Maryam Jazayeri

Let me begin by a straightforward observation and, based on this observation, a proposal for a clear political position and solution. Humanity is grappling with inequality, poverty, political oppression, wars and occupation, global conditions created by the capitalist system. This condition must not continue; it must end. So we must think *how* to reverse the course of this situation and *what* social force can usher in a new chapter in a human history that has a radically different social organization, thus emancipating humanity from the carnage of capitalism. This I call revolution.

After the 'Arab Spring' and the anti-austerity movements in Europe, the word 'revolution' became popular. From a concept that has been vilified, especially over the last three decades, it has become a highly respected one among diverse sections of the public. While this return on to the political scene of the concept of 'revolution' as aspiration is refreshing, its content and meaning remain dangerously vague. Most conceive of revolution in a way that in actuality leads away from it. The popular and distorted understanding of revolution is either 'going from worse to bad' or else some kind of manoeuvring within the structure of power, and in either case the social relations of capitalism, including patriarchy, remain fundamentally unfettered. Therefore, the challenge is to bring a clear and sharp theorization to the concept of revolution.

Revolution is not a moral objective, and its content in each epoch is not decided arbitrarily. As Marx argued, socialist revolution is *necessary* and *possible* because of the inner contradictions of capitalism. Revolution is a complex class struggle, with many contradictory elements simultaneously in unity and struggle with each other. In this chapter, I argue that revolution in the era of capitalism can only be a total one, one that dismantles the capitalist state, in particular, its institutions of organized violence and political repression – such as its armed forces, its police and its prisons, as well as its bureaucracies and administrative power. The private appropriation of social production must also be abolished with this total revolution. Revolution has to be led by the social forces that have the deepest interest in abolishing class distinctions, the production relations which produce those class distinctions, the social relations corresponding to those production relations, and the culture which works as the scaffolding and façade of this whole exploitative and oppressive social system. This can only be accomplished through a theory, practice and consciousness which are revolutionary.

I write as a revolutionary communist from the Middle East with a rich experience in the women's movement of Iran. The present theocratic state in Iran came into power in February 1979 and marked its rule by imposing the veil on women. Women rebelled and organized a mass protest on 8 March 1979. The slogan 'We didn't make revolution to go backwards' summed up their protest. We know today that the rise of theocracy in Iran had worldwide reverberations, and it still continues to shape and influence the ideological landscape, especially in terms of women's oppression. My sharper understanding of the concept of 'revolution' is very much influenced by this history. I will focus on the works of Marxist feminists such as Silvia Federici and Maria Mies for a more in-depth theoretical engagement with the subject of revolutionary transformation of society and the role of the women's movement in this process. Therefore, this chapter is not a review of the vast literature on women in social movements, a literature that is extensively covered in influential works by authors such as Ahmed (1982), Davies (1983), Rowbotham (1972, 1992), Sanghatana (1989) and Mary Ann Tétreault (1994). To make my argument clear, I lay out some of my thoughts on the interrelations between patriarchy and capitalism as well as the relationship between women's liberation and the emancipation of humanity.

Some philosophical considerations[1]

Marxist-feminist scholars have long sought to bring together Marxism and feminism as two poles of a conception that would have the ability to go beyond a gender-*particular* view of society. Through this process, they have made valuable contributions to the understanding of patriarchy in the (re)production of class society as a whole. However, I argue that they have not been successful in overcoming the problematic represented by hyphenation in the term Marxist-feminism.

Even though the merging of Marxism and feminism has been intended to overcome the 'particularism' of gender, most of the time it has turned into 'class reductionism' – the opposite pole of gender 'particularism', by which I mean the reducing of complex social relations having many interacting parts solely to one of the parts and then claiming it as the basis of all other social relations. This is a linear, mechanical view of a complex social reality. My argument is that capitalism indeed weaves together each and every oppressive power relation and mode of exploitation into one *universal* system.

I explain this dynamic – that is, the relationship between particular and universal – in philosophical terms. Patriarchy did not emerge with capitalism, it is descended from pre-capitalist social relations, but capitalism has integrated patriarchy in its dynamics. Therefore, while women's oppression, expressed in patriarchal relations, has a character distinct from class relations of exploitation, it has intense interactions with class relations in capitalism. To put it differently, women's oppression under patriarchal rule and exploitative class relations under capitalism are not phenomena external to each other; they are interrelated but separate, and their separateness is relative and not absolute. The patriarchal and class oppressions and exploitations are integrated in the overall body of capitalism and, while they are discernible as separate, they are intrinsically connected. The properties of each depend on their organic life within this whole and their inner connections with each other in the framework of the totality of social relations of capitalism. In understanding the contradictions and inner relations of different forms of oppression and exploitation in this dialectical way, it becomes clear that individuating but relating particular forms of oppression and exploitation, such as class, national identity/race, gender and their related social movements will not create the universal theorization and a social movement that can lead to the undoing of capitalism, patriarchy and all other forms of oppression.

Patriarchy is not reducible to class exploitation and oppression, nor should we adhere to an instrumentalizing of class analysis in explicating patriarchal relations. Patriarchy has its own particularity, all the while being part and parcel of the inner dynamics of class society. It is important to note that there is a contradiction between class oppression and women's oppression. By contradiction, I mean that they are not the same social relations within class societies. They each possess a distinct characteristic and rely on their particular features to constitute a universally oppressive system. In this dialectical articulation, 'universal' does not snuff out the 'particular'; in fact, the universal resides in each particular, and at certain junctures of the spiral process of this dialectic, one of the particulars can become a sharper expression of the universal than other particulars. For example, we can see that the oppression of women today has become a glaring concentration and embodiment of the workings of capitalism to such a degree that one is tempted to rephrase Marx on the proletariat and say that women's oppression represents whatever is done wrong to the whole of humanity and to nature. As such, the revolutionary subject of patriarchy is women as compared to the revolutionary subject of capitalism, which is the working class. But neither the working class nor women are ready-made revolutionary subjects. They have to be forged into such subjects, both theoretically and practically, through a revolutionary movement.

Patriarchy is the oldest relation of private appropriation of women's life activity. Under capitalism, social connections are established through the comprehensive and mutual dependence of people who are total strangers to each other. This social link is mediated by exchange value. Within capitalist relations, everyone carries their social power as well as their links to society in their pockets (Marx 1973: 157). Thus, social relations specific to capitalist relations are called value relations. Patriarchal relations are not capitalist value relations, but they serve the realization and reproduction of value relations. On the one hand, capitalism, in its relentless expansion of value relations into every corner of human existence, has the tendency to eliminate the man–woman divide, pulling women's life activity into the maelstrom of value relations; but on the other hand, capitalism chains women to patriarchal relations. This tension can never be mitigated or resolved under capitalism as long as the fundamental contradiction of capitalism is not resolved: the contradiction between social production and its private appropriation and control.

Without the abolition of patriarchy, there is no abolition of capitalist private appropriation. These combined world-historic relations of social production create different kinds of proletariat – the social force that has the deepest interests in uprooting private ownership of the means of production and, finally, all varieties of commodity relations and bourgeois rights. Under capitalism, women's oppression is not a transitional feature. It is everlasting. This makes women a subject of communist revolution – a subject to *become* – just like the working class, which has to become the subject of revolution. But becoming the subject of revolution is a conscious process on the part of the oppressed.

On commons: communism within capitalism?

Reading Silvia Federici's *Caliban and the Witch* (2004) made me enthusiastic for more learning and understanding. The book provides deep insights into how capitalist relations, as they developed and consolidated the rule of the bourgeoisie, systematized and raised to new heights violence against women – for the purpose of controlling her reproductive activity as well as restraining her revolutionary potential. I followed the historical trajectory of relations between the capitalist state and women through Federici's historical explorations and through other valuable works by other feminist scholars, in particular Selma James (2012), Michèle Barrett (1988) and the early work of Zillah R. Eisenstein (1979), which provoked in me deeper questions around the issue of how the bourgeoisie consolidated its power. The capitalist state even calibrated labour wages based on the 'household' – not to allocate a wage for the housework done, but to take advantage of women's familial affections in order to cheapen the labour costs for capitalist enterprises as well as to create an institution for ensuring the uninterrupted reproduction of labour power. Federici's explorations and observations about the history of capitalism and of resistance to it, and her sharp eye for detecting the great potential that exists for radically different social relations – including communist production relations – are thought provoking and inspiring.

But Federici's concept of commons, which is proposed as a political project or means for realizing that potential, sourly dwarfs the goal. She misses two key elements in the workings of capitalism – namely, the state structure and the inner dynamics of capitalist production, both of which incessantly penetrate into and commodify even the most rigid and resistant forms of production relations. This base/superstructural context makes it impossible for communist social production relations to take root under capitalism. In fact, one of Federici's logical but incorrect conclusions is that such production relations can take root just as bourgeois relations took root within feudalism (Caffentzis and Federici 2013). This analogy with feudal society, in the belly of which capitalist relations and the bourgeois class developed, is a mechanical comparison. A replication of this – with communist relations taking shape in the womb of capitalism – will not occur for the basic reason that bourgeois relations within the framework of class society are not radically different from feudal relations. But communist relations can come about only as a result of two radical ruptures signalled by Marx: first, a radical rupture from old property relations, and secondly, a radical rupture from old ideas arising from those relations. These ruptures are possible, according to Marx and Engels, only with the communist revolution, which allows

> separate individuals [to] be liberated from the various national and local barriers, be brought into practical connections with the material and intellectual production of the whole world and be put in a position to acquire the capacity to enjoy this all-sided production of the whole world (the creations of man). All-round dependence, this natural form of the world-historical co-operation of individuals, will be transformed by the communist revolution into the control and conscious mastery of these powers, which, born of the action of men on one another, have till now overawed and governed men as powers completely alien to them. (Marx and Engels 1970: 55)

Federici presents the commons as a substitution for such a revolution. She considers the idea of commons 'a logical and historical alternative to both the state and private property, the state and the market' (Federici 2012: 138–9). In capitalism, however, private property and the market cannot exist without the state. The capitalist state is an inseparable extension of capitalist production relations. It is the common executive body of the capitalist class. This reality dictates that, to realize the potential existing for a communist society, the state machinery of the capitalist class has to be destroyed. How does this reality figure in the commons strategy? It does not. The proponents of the idea of commons as an anti-capitalist political project praise the Zapatistas for not attempting to overthrow the state machinery. For example, Negri and Hardt declare in their *Multitude* that the goal of the Zapatistas 'has never been to defeat the state and claim sovereign authority but rather to change the world without taking power' (Hardt and Negri 2004: 85).

Even though there are slight differences between the anti-capitalist forces that have adopted this political project, what all of them share is the idea of changing the world without overthrowing the capitalist state. Therefore, they see no need for a radically different kind of state and no need to pose questions such as how it should be organized as the executive body of the oppressed and exploited people, how it will impose on the defeated bourgeoisie new non-exploitative relations of production; indeed, how it should organize and carry forth the world historic process of, to paraphrase Marx, the 'Four Alls': abolition of all class distinctions; abolition of all production relations which produce these class distinctions; abolition of all social distinctions which arise on this basis; and abolition of all ideas which sanction this context and help to reproduce it (Marx 1960: 117).[2]

Federici dismisses this total revolution on the grounds that it would be statist and believes (or speculates) that the commons strategy could be a way to evade this necessity. She – like Kropotkin[3] earlier in the twentieth century – is against the revolutionary strategy that Marx arrived at by applying historical materialism to the study of human society: that the passage from capitalism to communism makes it necessary to smash the old state and to build a radically different kind of state in order to carry forward this world historic passage – and eventually to abolish the state itself.[4] Marx clearly criticized two tendencies: those of the utopian socialists who believed that within the context of capitalist society it was possible to build communistic production relations, and those of the social democrats who thought they could compete with the bourgeoisie for control of the bourgeois state. Opposing social democrats, Marx argued that a revolution against capitalist society needs to smash the bourgeois state machinery rather than take it over (Marx and Engels 1973).

Now, the smashing of the state does not imply that this process is seamless and non-contradictory. Actually, the society which will emerge after the overthrowing of private property and its state is very problematic, as the twentieth-century socialist revolutions in Russia and China have demonstrated. The problem is how to ensure that such a state does not turn into a bourgeois state. Therefore, such a proletarian state consciously works towards the 'withering away' of the state itself. The restoration of capitalism in these two former socialist countries resulted in the launching by left intellectuals of a torrent of denials of basic facts of class struggle, denials that were conceptualized by, among others, postmodern philosophers and thinkers. At the heart of this postmodern conceptualization lies a denial of the fact that in order to destroy old property relations the state safeguarding it must also be destroyed.

What is really behind the co-optation of the commons?

Federici gives an account of how capitalism can adopt the 'discourse' of the commons. As such, she warns against 'crafting the discourse on the commons' in such a way that it would present the capitalist class with such an opportunity (Federici 2012: 141). But until capitalism is ended, any spontaneous and creative efforts of the people to carry out the production of knowledge and material necessities will generally be brought into capitalist circuits, if not snuffed out of existence. It is impossible to bring together 'many proliferating commons ... to form a cohesive whole providing a foundation for a new mode of production'[5] for the simple reason that capitalism dominates the world and owns the means of production. It has the necessary means to build roads, factories and schools and to finance innovations – and most of all to mobilize and control labour power. Its power over the means of production enables it to control the life activities of humanity as a whole, and especially of the working people. To lay 'the foundations for a new mode of production', it must first be forcefully dispossessed.

Until the time when this has happened, every time the people bond together to found any form of cooperative, sooner or later they will become capitalists themselves or be put out of business by the 'invisible hand' of the market. No matter how large and expansive and cohesive such commons are made, they will not be able to escape from the social reality of the rule of private ownership and appropriation. No matter how far they seem to be from the market, they will still ultimately be directed by the capitalist system – by its production relations as well as its political power.

Therefore, I argue that the concept of commons itself flings open the doors for the capitalist class to not only adopt the 'discourse of the commons', but also to penetrate and commodify any collective production of the commons. In fact, this is what capitalism is: private appropriation of socialized production. The problem is not that we are not collectively producing our lives; we can see how we produce our lives collectively just by reading the labels on the goods that we consume daily. The basic and fundamental relation between billions of people around the world is the exchange of labour power. This is the fundamental contradiction of capitalism and its ever more socialized production on a world scale, with private appropriation of the product by the few, an appropriation which gives rise to movements among people to break free from the clutches of 'private appropriation' – movements such as the 'commons' that Federici and other scholars have documented and analysed (e.g. Federici 2012: 132–43; Caffentzis and Federici 2013).

In countries as diverse as Iran and the United States, we have seen how during natural disasters these kinds of communistic cooperative undertakings spring up among the people and how the state machinery jumps in order to suppress them and take control of the collective endeavours of people. These movements are gravitational pulls towards a potential as well as necessary alternative world and social system which we have come to call communism.

I agree with Federici that these movements show that the conditions – both materially as well as in terms of the longings, aspirations and resistance of millions around the world – create the possibility for the surpassing of the organization of society on the basis of exploitation and oppression. But there is a huge obstacle to materializing this potential: the capitalist political power or state which guarantees that those at the top of human society will continue their carnage and will do whatever is necessary to keep this status quo – as we have seen in their colonial and imperialist wars, the securitization of societies, in the assassinations, imprisonment and legal executions of anti-capitalist activists, and so on. Federici fails to take account of the most glaring obstacle in the way of achieving the kind of social relations that she is advocating: the brutal power of that minority – the capitalist imperialist class; and she fails to pose the issue of the revolutionary overcoming of this obstacle. While she is very much worried by the creeping power of this system in co-opting the commons, in fact, what makes a movement or resistance relatively immune to being easily co-opted by the system is placing at centre stage of every movement the goal of the revolutionary overthrow of the system – even if this is not on its immediate agenda. It is wrong to consider or formulate communism as something achievable within the limits of the capitalist system and in symbiotic relationship with its state power – or worse, as something that humanity can spontaneously slip into without requiring the conscious revolutionary act of destroying the old and conscious efforts of human beings to build the new society.

For more than four decades, some post-structuralist or post-modernist intellectuals have criticized and vilified revolution as a 'grand narrative' and, denying the possibility of revolution, declared the possibility of revolution 'dead'. For instance, Negri and Hardt, who almost praise US imperialism for being a power moving the world towards the transcending of capitalism and the withering away of the state. They go so far as to attribute the imperialist expansions of the United States to its 'democratic expansive tendency implicit in the notion of network power [which] must be distinguished from other, purely expansionist and imperialist forms of expansion' (Hardt and Negri 2000: 166).

As capitalism develops, it becomes an increasingly larger barrier to the liberation of humanity from commodity relations, and the larger it becomes, so too does the necessity of focusing on bringing down the political power of capitalism and its social system. Until this barrier ceases to exist, no matter how much resistance, large or small, is mounted, if it is not directed and led with the goal of bringing this barrier down, humanity will be consumed and absorbed by capitalism. As Marx and Engels showed, it is the private ownership of the means of production and the ever-expanding capitalist commodity production which turn all relations into commodity relations, make everything into a commodity to be bought and sold – and at the heart of these relations lies the transformation of the ability of human beings to produce and reproduce into commodities. And this is the incessant law governing our societies, backed by the power of capitalist states and their international governing institutions. Within this framework, there is no chance to develop a radically different social system – not even in an embryonic state. However, there is the possibility of overthrowing the rule of capital in different parts of the world and of starting to build new societies – and expanding this revolutionary process in leaps and bounds.

As Engels put it, the state will wither away when the conditions of its requirement – that is, the class and socially stratified society – cease to exist. The interrelation between class society, state and patriarchy was brilliantly synthesized by Engels in the title of his seminal work *The Origin of the Family, Private Property and the State* (1985). These are part and parcel of a package. But it seems that the ideologues and militants of the commons believe that a truly alternative world to capitalism can come into existence within the framework of capitalism, and therefore there is no need or basis for a revolution.

Autarky or revolution?

An impressive body of work has been produced by feminist scholars since the 1960s on patriarchy and its relationship to the class system generally and with the capitalist class system in particular. This is a tremendous resource for communists to learn from and for conceptualizing women's oppression more correctly and for comprehensively enriching communist theories in this regard. Over the whole period of more than 160-odd years since the time communism was first formulated by Marx and Engels – and thus a revolution took place in the human understanding of society and its ailments – this science[6] has been developing, like all other sciences which probe into different spheres of the material reality surrounding us and in which there have been real advances due in large part to learning from the accumulation of knowledge achieved in different spheres of human effort. But the communist movement since its inception has for the most part ignored or dismissed the tremendous amount of feminist research into, hypothesizing and exploration of, and grappling with the nature of women's oppression throughout history in general and within the world dominated by the capitalist imperialist system – a sign that even communists are under the influence of the whole superstructure of patriarchy, which is deeply ingrained in the ideological superstructure of current societies.

When I read Maria Mies' book *Patriarchy and Accumulation on a World Scale* (1998) for the first time, I was pleased to have discovered another feminist writing on the extremely important and decisive role that patriarchy has played in how the imperialist capitalist system works. This book has a number of insights into the fact that the man–woman divide is one of the essential features of present-day capitalism, one that is at least as important as other production relations of domination – or imperialist production relations between a few metropolitan capitalist countries (Mies calls them 'overdeveloped' capitalist countries) and other countries of Asia, Africa and Latin America, whose economies have been subsumed and integrated from a subservient position into the international network of capitalist accumulation. These two exploitative production relations provide qualitative elements in the dynamism and super-profitable capitalist accumulation worldwide, and these make up a very crucial part of the structure of the worldwide capitalist system. Maria Mies clearly establishes these inseparable synergic relations and moves away from a Eurocentric view of capitalism.

Maria Mies says that 'feminists can no longer have the illusion that women's liberation will be possible within the context of this social paradigm [i.e. capitalism]' (ibid.: 208). But surprisingly, her proposals fall short of this call and remain within the framework of the capitalist system. She does not bring this call to its logical conclusion – that is, to build the new, one should destroy the old. I posit that this is due to the fact that she leaves out of the equation the question of the state and ignores the problem that bourgeois society is an integral whole with an economic base and political superstructure – at the heart of which lies the capitalist state.

I have studied criticisms laid on Marx and Engels by scholars such as Mies and Federici and other feminists whom I have mentioned. I do not have space here to deal with them appropriately. But one thing is clear: Marx and Engels, through their dialectical materialist study of human society, discovered and posited not only the simultaneous emergence of the class- and gender-based stratification of society, but also the inseparable link between the relations of production and the state. This ever-present reality is overlooked in the works of the Marxist feminists who strive to go beyond the explanation of women's oppression and who strive to propose radical changes in the way human society is today organized, based on exploitation and oppression. This reality – the reality of the state as part of the dominant social relations – must be recognized in order to fully embrace the revolutionary solution to humanity's miserable social conditions. Otherwise, any strategy or project for radically changing the world will come back in a full circle to the fold of the system we are trying to change and instead will serve its continuation.

I argued this in the case of the commons as put forward by Federici, and I argue that the same holds true in the case of autarky (self-sufficiency) (ibid.: 219) and the argument that subsistence is the alternative as proposed by Maria Mies (ibid.: xviii) as well as other feminist scholars of the Bielefeld School, such as Claudia von Werlhof and Veronika Bennholdt-Thomsen. Maria Mies' intervention (Mies 2014) in debates around the commons (joined by Caffentzis and Federici [2013], among others) is a continuation of her 'subsistence is the alternative' argument. While welcoming the debate on the commons, she comments that what is being put forward as the 'new commons' is not the commons at all: 'What can we learn from the old commons? What has to be changed today? Is there a realistic perspective for new commons?' (Mies 2014: 106). Mies' main observation is that: 'no commons can exist without a community. The old commons were maintained by a clearly defined community where people had to do communal work in order to sustain themselves. This work was neither forced upon people nor was it a nice pastime or a luxury. It was necessary for people's survival or subsistence …' (ibid.: 106–7). She gives the example of the 'free work' of the village community in her small village in the Rhineland in West Germany in the aftermath of the Second World War. From her depiction, one would think that post-war West Germany was a socialist country within which different communities began building locally without being pushed and pulled by the market forces of capitalism. But the reality is that after the Second World War the defeated capitalist-imperialist Germany was being rebuilt as West Germany with the help of the victorious Western capitalist-imperialist powers as a fortress against the growing socialist countries and the spectre of more socialist revolutions in Europe and rest of the world. And 'the people', through hard work and austerity, had to chip in and tighten their belts in order to subsidize this imperialist project. But this was not all. Vast numbers of peasants from Kurdish and non-Kurdish parts of Turkey were brought in to rebuild West Germany and work in its factories while the semi-feudal economy back in Turkey took care of their families and the raising of future generations of this cheap labour. So 'the happy little German village' should not be seen in isolation from this army of cheap labour! The reconstruction of West Germany was related to separating villages in Turkey from their subsistence activities and, more generally, to the push of capitalist socialized production on a world scale.

Mies proposes an 'alternative framework for an economy not based on the exploitation of nature, women and colonies', and states: 'The first basic requirement of an alternative economy is a change over, both in the overdeveloped and in the underdeveloped societies, from dependency for their basic subsistence needs – food, clothing, shelter – from economies *outside* their national boundaries towards greater *autarky*' (Mies 1998: 219, emphasis in original). But the world is not divided in this way. Capitalism has woven together even the remotest areas of the world into one world process of capitalist accumulation. Exchange of labour between people of the world is the foundation on which this system works. This socialized production is not the problem. In fact, it is the material basis of a world revolution and the building of a communist world; the problem is when this worldwide social cooperation is realized not directly but through the medium of capitalist relations, which is to say the law of value. The capitalist class takes over and controls our socialized production and exchange worldwide and uses it for its own profitable accumulation of capital. What enables the capitalist class to take control of our life activity worldwide (including women's labour) is private ownership and control of the means of production. Here classes are involved. Under the capitalist mode of production, the capitalist class and the proletariat are two antagonistic poles that directly face off against each other. But capitalism sucks life from people in different forms – through colonialism, imperialism and patriarchy.

Mies correctly underlines the important place that colonial and imperialist oppression and exploitation occupy in the workings of the world capitalist system. In fact, controlling colonies and neo- or semi-colonies is part of controlling the means of production. For example, through monopolizing the oil under the land in the Middle East, the famous 'Seven Sisters' petroleum companies of the Western imperialist powers (see Sampson 1976) captured hundreds of millions of people in this region within the enslaving international division of labour. The problem is that Mies treats the dominated countries as though they are homogeneous and monolithic. These countries too are divided into classes and are run on a class basis. The ruling classes in these countries are part and parcel of the combined capitalist class in the world and, regardless of their subservient status relative to those sitting at the summit of the capitalist system, they run these countries on behalf of the world capitalist imperialist system. The inequality in the world order is rooted *inside* these countries, and it is not just a matter of their *external* 'dependency'. Therefore, a revolution has to change the social relations within different countries as well as between them and the world imperialist capitalist system.

I agree with Mies that there has to be 'independence' in the sphere of subsistence in order to resist 'political blackmail and hunger' (Mies

1998: 219). But this independence can be achieved only on the basis of a total revolution and is one of the formidable tasks of any revolution. Socialist China (1949–76) was able to resist imperialist pressure and materially support the well-being of its people as well as support other revolutions. Even this kind of genuine and true independence will only be relative as long as revolution has not made inroads into most of the world.

A different kind of labour

Maria Mies also calls for 'a different kind of labour'. But this emancipatory goal cannot be achieved through the 'subsistence' strategy. It can be achieved only when the labour on a societal scale is directly social and not mediated by commodity exchange, the law of value. Mies uses a very important passage from Marx and interprets it to say that, according to Marx, the 'realm of freedom' comes when human beings are not governed by the necessity of labour. Agreeing with Schmidt, she quotes him: 'The problem of human freedom is reduced by Marx to the problem of *free time*' (Schmidt, cited in ibid.: 213, emphasis in original). On the contrary, Marx clearly states in the same passage that human beings must 'wrestle with nature' in order to maintain and reproduce life and must do so under 'all possible modes of production'. He emphasized that 'Freedom in this field can only consist in socialized man [sic]. But it nonetheless still remains a realm of necessity' (quoted in ibid.: 213).

Marx clearly demonstrated the dialectical relationship between the productive forces of human beings and their relations of production – the relations through which they organize their productive forces. And ownership of the means of production is at the heart of these production relations. Not a few Marxists have distorted Marx on this subject. They have reversed the relationship between productive forces and relations of production, positing that in order to do away with exploitative production relations and the ensuing social and class distinctions, the productive forces must develop. This is nothing but pseudo-Marxism. Marx has explained that the productive forces in their development at one point come into conflict with their 'outer shell', which is production relations. People become aware of this situation, start conceptualizing the problem, and seek a solution to it. Class struggle arises between the class which potentially has the ability to break out of this suffocating 'shell' and the class which wants to keep it in place. This is the material basis which gives rise to revolution, which demands it, and which makes it potentially possible.

During the 1980s, the feminists of the Bielefeld School put out a daring and thought-provoking challenge to mainstream notions within the left on how capitalism works. In her 'No critique of capitalism without a critique of patriarchy! Why the left is no alternative to capitalism', Claudia von Werlhof provided a clear explanation of what they think the 'problem' is and therefore what 'the solution' should be (Von Werlhof 2007).[7] The Bielefeld group, through their explorations into how capitalism functions, has made important observations. For example, they have discussed how different forms of slavery, unpaid labour, forced labour and serfdom, and so on, are used in the process of capitalist accumulation. This is a correct observation, and, in fact, capitalism has never relied solely on waged labour for the purpose of accumulation. Today, at the height of capitalism, almost all technological gadgets that we use on a daily basis contain some sort of slave labour congealed within them. Von Werlhof makes the point that 'None of these relations of production are to be misunderstood as pre-capitalist – they are all inherently capitalist' (ibid.: 8). I agree with this statement if it means that these different modes of exploitation, while having 'descended' from a different parental mode, have been transformed and subsumed by capitalism in its workings, and if it is understood to mean that they have become inseparable parts of the capitalist accumulation process. Capitalism is a different mode of production to slavery and feudalism; it is an extended commodity production at the heart of which lies the transformation of labour power itself into a commodity in order to accumulate private profit. Privately organized labour processes are linked together and forged into a social division of labour through exchange; these labour processes are bought and sold at prices that ultimately are decided by the socially necessary labour time to produce the labourers: 'This is the law of value, and social labour time is the regulator of prices and profits. The *quest for profit* dominates privately organized labor processes. Profit determines what gets produced – and how' (Lotta 2013).

This is the engine which drives capitalism, and it is on this basis that it transforms and sucks into its circuits labour that is unpaid, enslaved, forced, and so on. That is how capitalism turns all social wealth (no matter how and under what conditions that it is produced) into capital. I think it is well put by Von Werlhof herself that: 'The objective of capitalism is not the transformation of all labour into wage labour but the transformation of all labour, all life, and of the planet itself into capital – in other words, as Marx observed, into money, commodity, machinery, and the "command over labour"' (Von Werlhof 2007: 4). How to conceptualize the relation between a single world process of capitalist accumulation and the pre-capitalist modes of production existing in the continents of Asia, Africa and Latin America has been part of the debate within the communist movement as well as among left and feminist scholars from the 1960s on.[8]

The Bielefeld School's political economy delves into very important components of the capitalist mode of production, but fails to synthesize the latter's overarching organizing principle. The question remains: What are the collective principles of organization, or the universal laws of capitalism? Claudia von Werlhof claims that, contrary to the political economy of many on the left, theirs is not reductionist and that

> notions that long served as guidelines for a better future lose their meaning: the proletariat, the unions, left politics, technological progress, the 'development' of industrialized nations, the leading role of the North, the superiority of men over women. If we were to follow these notions, nothing would await us but a dead-end road. (Ibid.: 8)

I have noticed that Maria Mies as well as other scholars of the Bielefeld School integrate the 'left' into the power structure and/or blend the trade unionist left with revolutionary communists. However, the whole history of the left since Marx is marked by the struggle of revolutionary communists against 'revisionism'.[9] Therefore, for any serious challenge to Marxism it is appropriate to point to a definite body of theories put forward by a specific left. For example, Marx and Engels spent much of their time fighting against non-communist trends within the left. The *Communist Manifesto* carries a sharp critique of utopian socialists, and *A Critique of the Gotha Programme* is a critique of the draft programme of the United Workers' Party of Germany; Lenin fought against the alliance of the German Social Democratic Party with German imperialism during the First World War. And Mao, who recognized and exposed the restoration of capitalism in the USSR, analysed how socialism can be turned back on to the capitalist road, and he opposed the 'theory of productive forces' which made technical advance of the productive forces the criterion of 'socialism' rather than the ongoing revolutionizing of production/social relations and ideas and making these the criteria of 'progress' (Lotta 1978: 287). The list of these 'internal' struggles is long and is a reflection of the fact that the road to revolutionizing the world has been complicated and tortuous.

All that said, I turn to the final aspect of my critique of the Bielefeld School – that is, their alternative to this horrendous world of capitalism. From their analysis of what the 'problem' is, they derive their 'solution'. There is coherence between the two. Claudia von Werlhof claims that the 'solution' drawn from their analysis of capitalism is 'uncompromising' and should involve 'leaving commodity production behind and reviving a subsistence economy that has long been oppressed and largely destroyed' (Von Werlhof 2007: 9). The problem posed to humanity by capitalism can be solved only through a political revolution that defeats and overthrows the bourgeois state and its all-exploiting classes, a revolution that establishes a new revolutionary state, the mission of which is to build a new socialist economy – one that has radically different dynamics and principles to those of capitalism. Theoretical struggle to once again establish this truth is today of great importance for the future of humanity. To paraphrase Marx, the destruction of the present system in practice is not possible without first bringing it down in theory – in the consciousness of people.

The old and new commons are both old

The old and new commons are *both* old because they are enclaves – they are efforts within the framework of the old capitalist property relations which still dominate our societies throughout the world. The quest for 'space' under capitalism – be it in the form of 'commons' (old and new), 'autarky', Alain Badiou's 'points of autonomy' or Naomi Klein's 'worker cooperatives', even with genuine revolutionary intentions – is illusory at best, because these projects 'would not be able to free themselves from the surrounding commodity relations: at the level of input and exchange requirements, competitive pressures, and ideological influences (the narrowing perspective of "my/our" production unit, and so on)' (Lotta et al. 2009).

All of these theorizations fail to demonstrate that the capitalist *system* is comprised of an economic base and a political superstructure – the political rule of the capitalist class, their state as well as their ideological machine. Actually Maria Mies knows this, as she recounts how the 'old commons' were destroyed owing not to the self-interest, greed and competitiveness of individuals, but because of something which the 'capitalist landlords and industrialization *forced* upon villages and towns [in order] to appropriate and privatize common land, forests and brooks' (Mies 2014: 108, emphasis added). Any movement which is serious about changing the world for real needs to recognize that there is a class dictatorship which guards and imposes capitalist production and social relations, and that its pervasive ideological machinery works to bring people under the wings of the bourgeoisie. The state is part of the very fabric of bourgeois society.

To establish an alternative mode of production, 'a new kind of labour' (as Maria Mies calls for) in order to put an end to class exploitation, to patriarchy and to the shocking divide between the so-called 'South' and 'North', to end the dangerous destruction of the environment resulting from the destructive forces of capitalism and ugly imperialist and proxy wars, we need to make revolution and build socialist societies as the alternative to capitalism. Only after the dismantling of the capitalist state can a new state begin to socialize the ownership of the means of production. The socialist state is 'new' because it is guided by this goal and has the mission of eliminating the '4 Alls' that Marx identified in his *Class Struggles in France, 1848–1850* (1960: 117).

Why the revolutionary feminists retreated

All this said, I should argue that the moving away on the part of the feminists of the 1960s and 1970s from revolutionary universalism was not due to the insufficiency of Marxist-feminist concepts. In fact, the main trend of thought which has been influential has been relativism doled out by postmodernist theorizing. Many revolutionary feminists of the 1960s and 1970s have given up on revolution and have become content with taking 'small' steps. In the last four decades, the dominant intellectual and academic atmosphere has been a literary censorship and outright distortion of the real record of communist history and of the socialist revolutions of the twentieth century. Anti-communism is prized as 'objectivity'. This has robbed students of an understanding of what socialism and communism actually are, and instead has forced on them distortions and lies about that historical experience of socialism. Just take a look at how a most important revolutionary experience – the Cultural Revolution of China, its purposes and achievements as well as its real and not imaginary shortcomings – is depicted in bestsellers on China. 'Set the Record Straight', one of the rare internet sites committed to combating this scandalous fraud, puts it this way:

> From a thousand different directions, we are bombarded with the message that communism was a 'nightmare' and 'failure.' Go into a bookstore and look at the current titles on Mao, the Cultural Revolution, or socialism in the Soviet Union. Take a listen when commentators on TV and radio say something about communism. Leaf through a standard textbook on political theory or modern history. There's a highly distorted narrative of socialism in the 20th century, and it goes largely unanswered. (Set the Record Straight 2014)[10]

This intellectual landscape needs to change – and change urgently – because we are living through one of the harshest periods of capitalism, a period marked by imperial wars, tribal wars, heightened violence against women who are degraded by the rise of religious patriarchy and abhorrent pornography, massive hunger on a global scale, a planetary environmental emergency, and so on. People are resisting this horror, but they are being pulled by the strong and organized reactionary forces of all types, all around the world – as well as by the phony horizon of 'more democracy' administered by the imperialist capitalist system or the lure of religious fundamentalism.

Conclusion

Instead of despair and defeatism in the face of defeat and capitalist restorations in former socialist countries, there is a need for a serious grappling with revolutionary paradigms and for recasting them in order to achieve the conditions to pass the critical point of no return this time around. A new state power is profoundly necessary, but upon its formation it will immediately face the necessity of organizing society on a basis radically different to capitalism; at the same time, society carries with it the burden of the vestiges of old property relations and old ideas and is still surrounded by a world dominated by imperialist capitalism (Avakian 2006). Undoubtedly, most problematic of all is the fact that the new society would be obliged by the constraints of history to utilize state power – which historically is nothing but an outgrowth of the development of classes and class-based society, and is a specialized organ dedicated to preserving the political rule of a certain class over other classes. Marx called this new state power a 'dictatorship of the proletariat' which, according to him and Engels, will exist out of necessity in the whole worldwide 'transition period' from socialism to communism, when the state will 'wither away' along with all vestiges of class society. I am aware of the fact that Marx's phrase 'dictatorship of the proletariat' is very much despised by many feminists, scholars and left activists and is used by the bourgeoisie to depict Marx as being brutal. But this impression is far from being an objective and honest assessment of the revolutionary theory of Marx. The historical truth discovered and conceptualized by Marx and Engels is that the state in all forms is nothing but the dictatorship of one class over other classes. However problematic a new state power may be, it is a requirement, because the process of breaking with the old property relations and old ideas as well as of planting the new and guarding the burgeoning of new social relations necessarily involves replacing the rule of the exploiting classes with the rule of classes and other social forces that have the deepest interests in doing away with class society.

In the case of the new political rule which should rise on the ruins of the capitalist state, dictatorship can only mean that a new social organization based on the abolition of exploitation and oppression must be instituted, and it can only mean a new kind of political rule which aims at the abolition of state or class dictatorship for ever. I believe Marx is still correct on what the problems facing humanity are, and what the solutions to these are. He laid down clearly the framework of what the problems are with the capitalist organization of society. He explained its driving forces as well as its structures. However, like any other human endeavour, this 'science of revolution' also has to be summed up, developed and further synthesized.

Now, this scientific outlook was applied in the communist revolutions of the twentieth century, first in Russia (1917) and then in China (1949). The subsequent defeats of these revolutions and the restoration of capitalism within both proved that this process is much more complex than envisioned by Marx and Engels. Mao, who led the epical socialist construction in China through many tribulations after the 1949 revolution, was able to recognize and conceptualize this complexity. Against mechanical materialists and simplistic views of the state, he emphasized the fact that, throughout the long transition from socialism to communism, class struggle will continue until the time when all vestiges of old society and the state itself are abolished. In this long struggle, there will always be a danger of the restoration of capitalism.

The socialist revolutions in Russia and China, despite their defeats, for the first time in history launched humanity on the path of achieving a classless and non-stratified social organization. Their victories and defeats have shaped the left intellectual terrain and its divergent views, which can be grouped into three major categories: 1) these revolutions were horrendous; forget about them and just 'reform' the system; 2) they were flawless; just 'repeat' them; and 3) they were the first genuine steps in a long march towards a communist world, and their flaws were the flaws of any new endeavour and came from many sources – from the complexity of the road, historical limitations, backward ideas, missteps, and so on. I am a partisan of this latter dialectical materialist summation. An honest and objective search for truth about these revolutions will show that those societies, which each lasted for only a few decades and despite all their flaws, were incomparable to the capitalist nightmare that we are living through. But that said, they cannot and must not be repeated. Defeat of those revolutions brought to an end one stage in the long march for communism. A second stage should begin. This cannot take place without a dialectical materialist summation of both the positives and the negatives of those world-historic events.[11]

There is an urgent need, in academia and other intellectual institutions, for revolutionary courage and honesty in exploring the truth about the socialist revolutions of the twentieth century. This will clearly involve fighting back against the slanders which the ideological centres of the capitalist order have relentlessly spread about them – and in their efforts they have had the helping hand of relativistic postmodern epistemology. To quote Brian Lloyd: 'The primary task of any retrograde ideology is to represent appearance as reality. The surest sign that this work is proceeding smoothly is an outbreak of agnosticism regarding the possibility of distinguishing the two' (Lloyd 1997: 2). Socialist revolution with the aim of reaching communism will be a world-historic social upheaval – it will be a crossing of the Rubicon for human society. No wonder it is so viciously contested by the capitalist order and so passionately defended by a minority that has set its sights on a possible – even if seemingly far-off – future. The second stage of the communist revolution will come about only with a sharper understanding of what the problem is and what kind of revolution is the solution.

Notes

1 To develop these philosophical points, I have relied on the works of Ardea Skybreak and Bob Avakian. See, among others, Avakian (2009, 1999); Skybread (2006, 1984).

2 Federici emphasizes two outstanding reasons which, according to her, have made this concept – that of changing the world without taking power – popular internationally among the radical left. One is the 'demise of [the] statist model of revolution that for decades has sapped the efforts of radical movements to build an alternative to capitalism', and the other is the 'neoliberal attempt to subordinate every form of life and knowledge to the logic of the market'. She believes that, given enough clarification, the principle of the commons can be translated into a 'coherent political project'. She also remarks that the rise of Zapatistas in Mexico – beginning on 31 December 1993, to safeguard the dissolution of their communal lands – gave a new life to the concept of the 'commons' (Federici 2012: 138–9).

3 P. A. Kropotkin (1842–1921) was a Russian geographer and prominent theoretician of anarchism. He joined Bakunin's anarchist group in 1872, was jailed in 1874, escaped into exile two years later, and returned to Russia in 1917. He opposed Marxist ideas of class struggle, the dictatorship of the proletariat, and all forms of state rule. Although vehemently critical of the Bolsheviks, he called on the European workers in 1920 to oppose the military aggression of capitalist states against the Soviet Union.

4 Concerning 'withering away' and 'smashing' theories of the state: in the works of Marx and Engels, the approach of the proletariat to the question of state is treated clearly, especially in the trilogy *Class Conflicts in France*, *The Eighteenth Brumaire of Louis Bonaparte* and *The Civil War in France*. Later, Lenin elaborated on their work in his *The State and Revolution* (1981). Marx and Engels used the term 'smashing' to define the policy and approach of the revolutionary class regarding the old bourgeois state. Marx wrote to Kugelmann: 'If you look up the last chapter of my *Eighteenth Brumaire*, you will find that I declare that the next attempt of the French Revolution will be no longer, as before, to transfer the bureaucratic-military machine from one hand to another, but to *smash* it, and this is the precondition for every real people's revolution on the Continent. And this is what our heroic Party comrades in Paris are attempting' (Marx in Marx and Engels 1975: 247, emphasis in original).

However, they – specifically Engels – used the term 'withering away' to define the required but declining existence of proletarian state power during the long process of passage from socialism to communism in which a revolutionary state is required to safeguard the achievements of socialist revolution; but it has to vanish along with all vestiges of class society worldwide. Marx considered the state of the 'dictatorship of proletariat' as 'the necessary transition to the *abolition of all classes* and to a *classless society*' (Marx to J. Weydemeyer in ibid.: 64, emphasis in original).

5 In discussing the commons,

Federici sees the possibility of giving birth to an alternative production relation right in the womb of capitalism. For example, while discussing the case of 'urban gardens' in the United States which produce for neighbourhood consumption rather than for commercial purposes (Federici 2012: 142), she proposes that the left has to propose 'how the many proliferating commons, being defended, developed, fought for, can be brought together to form a cohesive whole providing a foundation for a new mode of production ...' She emphasizes that Hardt and Negri have raised this issue in *Empire* (2000) and *Multitude* (2004) as well as in their most recent publication, *Commonwealth* (2009).

6 By 'science', I do not mean a facilitator of technology, but a means of understanding the inner workings and dynamics of an object of study through vigorous objectivity based on observation.

7 See also Mies (1984); Von Werlhof et al. (1988); Von Werlhof (1978, 1985); and her *Wenn die Bauern wiederkommen: Frauen, Arbeit und Agrobusiness in Venezuela* (1985); and Salleh (1997).

8 One important work in this field is *America in Decline* by Raymond Lotta and Frank Shanon (1984). The book takes into account a wide array of debates that began in the 1960s, beginning with Marx and Lenin's political economy as the starting point, but synthesizes the latter's arguments and brings the functioning of capitalism – or rather imperialist capitalism – up to date in terms of the time of publication.

9 Since the time of Marx and Engels, a trend towards reformism, pragmatism and basically forgoing of the goal of revolution appeared within the Marxist movement. According to Lenin, revisionism is: 'To determine its conduct from case to case, to adapt itself to the events of the day and to the chopping and changing of petty politics, to forget the primary interests of the proletariat and the basic features of the whole capitalist system, of all capitalist evolution, to sacrifice these primary interests for the real or assumed advantages of the moment – such is the policy of revisionism' (Lenin 1977: 30).

10 The mission of 'Set the Record Straight' is to factually refute the lies spread in the media, mass-market books and mainstream scholarship about the Soviet and Chinese revolutions and to bring to light the overwhelming achievements of these revolutions as well as their real problems and shortcomings. Our mission is to reveal the actual history and experience of these revolutions, to open up a two-sided debate about socialism and communism, and to promote a conversation about why a radically different and liberating world is possible.

11 For more on this point, see Avakian (2006) and Lloyd (1997).

References

Ahmed, L. (1982) 'Feminism and feminist movements in the Middle East: a preliminary exploration: Turkey, Egypt, Algeria, People's Democratic Republic of Yemen', *Women's Studies International Forum*, 5(2): 153–68.

Avakian, B. (1979) *Mao Tsetung's Immortal Contributions*, Chicago, IL: RCP.

— (1999) *Marxism 'Embraces but Does Not Replace' in Observations on Art and Culture, Science and Philosophy*, Chicago, IL: Insight Press.

— (2006) 'Views on socialism and communism: a radically new kind of state, a radically different and far greater vision of freedom', www.revcom.us/bob_avakian/views/.

— (2009) 'Crises in physics, crises in philosophy and politics', *Revolution* (weekly journal of the Revolutionary Communist Party, USA), 161, 12 April.

Barrett, M. (1988) *Women's Oppression Today: The Marxist/Feminist Encounter*, revised edn, London: Verso.
Bennholdt-Thomsen, V. (1982) 'Subsistence production and extended reproduction: a contribution to the discussion about modes of production', *Journal of Peasant Studies*, 9(4): 241–52.
Caffentzis, G. and F. Federici (2013) 'Commons against and beyond capitalism', *Community Development Journal*, 49(1): 92–105.
Davies, M. (ed.) (1983) *Third World Second Sex: Women's Struggles and National Liberation*, London: Zed Books.
Eisenstein, Z. R. (1979) *Capitalist Patriarchy and the Case for Socialist Feminism*, New York: Monthly Review Press.
Engels, F. (1969) *Anti-Dühring*, Moscow: Progress.
— (1985) *The Origin of the Family, Private Property and the State*, Harmondsworth: Penguin.
Federici, S. (2004) *Caliban and the Witch: Women, the Body and Primitive Accumulation*, Brooklyn, NY: Autonomedia.
— (2012) *Revolution at Point Zero: Housework, Reproduction, and Feminist Struggle*, Oakland, CA: PM.
Hardt, M. and A. Negri (2000) *Empire*, Cambridge, MA: Harvard University Press.
— (2004) *Multitude*, New York: Penguin.
— (2009) *Commonwealth*, Cambridge, MA: Harvard University Press.
James, S. (2012) *Sex, Race and Class: The Perspective of Winning: A Selection of Writings 1952–2011*, Oakland, CA: PM.
Lenin, V. I. (1970) 'Imperialism, the highest stage of capitalism', in Lenin, *Selected Works in Three Volumes*, vol. 1, Moscow: Progress, pp. 667–768.
— (1977) 'Marxism and revisionism', in Lenin, *Selected Works in One Volume*, Moscow: Progress.
— (1981) *The State and Revolution: The Marxist Theory of the State and the Tasks of the Proletariat in the Revolution*, Moscow: Progress.
Lloyd, B. (1997) *Left Out: Pragmatism, Exceptionalism, and the Poverty of American Marxism, 1890–1922*, Baltimore, MD: Johns Hopkins University Press.
Lotta, R. (ed.) (1978) *And Mao Makes 5: Mao Tsetung's Last Great Battle*, Chicago, IL: Banner.
— (2013) '"Driving force of anarchy" and the dynamics of change', *Revolution Newspaper*, 4 November, revcom.us/a/322/on-the-driving-force-of-anarchy-and-the-dynamics-of-change-en.htm.
Lotta, R. and F. Shanon (1984) *America in Decline*, Chicago, IL: Banner.
Lotta, R., N. Duniya and K.J.A. (2009) 'Alain Badiou's politics of emancipation', *Journal of Demarcation*, 1, Summer/Fall, demarcations-journal.org/issue01/demarcations_badiou.pdf.
Marx, K. (1960) *Class Struggles in France, 1848 to 1850*, Moscow: Progress.
— (1973) *Grundrisse*, trans. M. Nicolaus, Harmondsworth: Penguin.
— (1981) *Capital*, vol. 3, trans. D. Fernbach, Harmondsworth: Penguin.
Marx, K. and F. Engels (1969) 'An address of the Central Committee to the Communist League', in *Selected Works*, vol. 1, Moscow: Progress, pp. 175–85.
— (1970) *The German Ideology*, London: Lawrence and Wishart.
— (1973) *Manifesto of the Communist Party*, 2nd edn, Peking: Foreign Languages Press.
— (1975) *Selected Correspondence*, Moscow: Progress.
Mies, M. (1984) 'Methodische Postulate

zur Frauenforschung – dargestellt am Beispiel der Gewalt gegen Frauen', *Beiträge zur feministischen Theorie und Praxis*, 1: 41–63.

— (1998) *Patriarchy and Accumulation on a World Scale: Women in the International Division of Labour*, New York: Zed Books.

— (2014) 'No commons without a community', *Community Development Journal*, 49(5): 106–17.

Rowbotham, S. (1972) *Women, Resistance and Revolution: A History of Women and Revolution in the Modern World*, New York: Vintage.

— (1992) *Women in Movement: Feminism and Social Action*, New York and London: Routledge.

Salleh, A. (1997) *Ecofeminism as Politics: Nature, Marx and the Postmodern*, London: Zed Books.

Sampson, A. (1976) *The Seven Sisters: The Great Oil Companies and the World They Made*, London: Coronet.

Sanghatana, S. S. (1989) *'We Were Making History': Women and the Telangana Uprising*, London: Zed Books.

Set the Record Straight (2014) 'Set the Record Straight', Home page, www.thisiscommunism.org.

Skybread, A. (1984) *Of Primeval Steps and Future Leaps: An Essay on the Emergence of Human Beings, the Source of Women's Oppression, and the Road to Emancipation*, Chicago, IL: Banner Press.

— (2006) *The Science of Evolution and the Myth of Creationism: Knowing What's Real and Why It Matters*, Chicago, IL: Insight.

Tétreault, M. A. (1994) *Women and Revolution in Africa, Asia, and the New World*, Columbia: University of South Carolina Press.

Von Werlhof, C. (1978) 'Frauenarbeit: der blinde Fleck in der Kritik der Politischen Ökonomie', *Beiträge zur feministischen Theorie und Praxis*, 1: 18–32.

— (1985) *Wenn die Bauern wiederkommen: Frauen, Arbeit und Agrobusiness in Venezuela*, Bremen: Periferia.

— (2007) 'No critique of capitalism without a critique of patriarchy! Why the left is no alternative to capitalism', *Capitalism – Nature – Socialism*, 18(1): 13–27.

Von Werlhof, C., V. Bennholdt-Thomsen and M. Mies (1988) *Women: The Last Colony*, London: Zed Books.

15 | STANDPOINT THEORY

Cynthia Cockburn

Standpoint theory is an epistemology, an account of the evolution of knowledge and strategies of action by particular collectivities in specific social relations in given periods. As a concept, standpoint derives from Karl Marx's exegesis of class relations in capitalism. The historical development of capitalism as a mode of production involved the disintegration of feudal hierarchies and their gradual replacement by a new class system. In the last few pages of volume three of *Capital*, Marx writes:

> We have seen that the continual tendency and law of development of the capitalist mode of production is more and more to divorce the means of production from labour, and more and more to concentrate the scattered means of production into large groups, thereby transforming labour into wage-labour and the means of production into capital. (Marx 1959: 885)[1]

Thus, though landowners remained in existence in the new era as a third class, it was the proletariat and the bourgeoisie – dynamic, mutually dependent, locked in antagonism – which were definitive of capitalism.

In his historical materialist analysis of capitalism, Marx stressed that the realities of life in the new mode of production shaped the consciousness of the individuals experiencing it. In *The German Ideology* he and Engels wrote: 'Life is not determined by consciousness, but consciousness by life' (Marx and Engels 1970: 47). Their distinctive understanding was that 'definite individuals who are productively active in a definite way enter into … definite social and political relations' (ibid.: 46). They continue in this vein,

> The social structure and the State are continually evolving out of the life-process of definite individuals, but of individuals, not as they may appear in their own or other people's imagination, but as

> they really are; i.e. as they operate, produce materially, and hence as they work under definite material limits, presuppositions and conditions independent of their will. (Ibid.: 46)

So too do awareness, understanding and theory evolve. Individuals 'developing their material production and their material intercourse, alter, along with this their real existence, their thinking and the products of their thinking' (ibid.: 46).[2]

This theme in Marx's work was later developed by Georg Lukács. In *History and Class Consciousness*, Lukács addresses Marx's account of, as he puts it, 'the special position of the proletariat in society and in history, and the standpoint from which it can function as the identical subject-object of the social and historical process of evolution' (Lukács 1968: 149).[3] He continues with a quotation from Marx and Engels' *The Holy Family*,[4] in which they represent the class relation as follows.

> The property-owning class and the class of the proletariat represent the same human self-alienation. But the former feels at home in this self-alienation and feels itself confirmed by it; it recognises alienation as its own instrument and in it possesses the semblance of a human existence. The latter feels itself destroyed by this alienation and sees in it its own impotence and the reality of an inhuman existence. (Cited in ibid.: 149)

As a consequence, Lukács himself continues, while class interests 'keep the bourgeoisie imprisoned within this immediacy', they force the proletariat to go beyond it, to become 'conscious of the social character of Labour'. It is 'only in the proletariat that the process by which a man's achievement is split off from his total personality and becomes a commodity leads to a revolutionary consciousness'. For the working class, therefore, recognizing the dialectical nature of its existence is, Lukács says, 'a matter of life and death' (ibid.: 164, 171). It necessarily pitches the class into struggle with its rulers. In this, the Marxian understanding of class standpoint can be heard to echo Hegel's account of the development of self-consciousness in which he employs the allegory of the 'master' and the 'servant', necessarily precipitated into existential conflict in which the stake is annihilation of self or other (Hegel 1977).[5]

One effect of class domination, therefore, is the emergence of a distinctive proletarian 'standpoint', or, as we might say today, a proletarian 'take' on life. What is more, because the view from below is capable of revealing 'the immanent contradictions' in the capitalist mode of production, the practical class consciousness of the proletariat has the revolutionary potential to disrupt the given structure, the unique 'ability to transform things' (Lukács 1968: 197, 205). Antonio Gramsci, also writing in the early twentieth-century tradition of 'Western Marxism', shared this understanding of class consciousness. Observing the capability of western European capitalist classes to sustain their rule over a potentially insurgent working class by hegemony – that is to say by culturally generated consent rather than coercion – he saw the potential for proletarian revolutionary thought to grow, find adherents among other elements in civil society, and eventually achieve counter-hegemonic capability, challenging the sway of ruling-class ideology (Gramsci 1971).[6]

The gendering of standpoint theory

Women do not feature in Marx's account of the creation of surplus value, the heart of his economic theory. Lukács and Gramsci for their part also seem to have conceived of the proletariat as male. They use masculine nouns and pronouns in referring to it, and rarely allude to female workers or female family members of male workers. In fact, the unthinking assertion of masculinity is sometimes so emphatic as to be laughable. Thus Lukács celebrating the proletarian achievement: 'From this standpoint alone does history really become a history of mankind. For it contains nothing that does not lead back ultimately to men and to the relations between men' (Lukács 1968: 186). Nonetheless, in the 1970s some feminist socialist thinkers began to see the usefulness of Marxist standpoint theory for understanding forms of thought emerging from women's exploitation and oppression in a patriarchal sex-gender order.

Dorothy Smith and Nancy Hartsock both began work on this theme in the 1970s, and published more substantial analyses in the following decade. In her major work *The Everyday World as Problematic: A Feminist Sociology*, Smith reprised the theme of earlier essays (Smith 1974, 1981), describing the 'brutal history of women's silencing' by authoritative male discourse. This marginalization of women's experience and thought she represented as part of 'the relations of ruling', a concept that, as she defined it, 'grasps power, organization, direction, and regulation as more pervasively structured than can be expressed in traditional concepts provided by the discourses of power'. It reflects, she says, 'the dynamic advance of the distinctive forms of organizing and ruling contemporary capitalist society, and the patriarchal forms of our contemporary experience' (Smith 1987: 3). Where was the sociology in which women would 'talk back' to power from the perspective of their everyday experience? Smith set out to make good the lack by creating 'a way of seeing, from where we actually live, into the powers, processes, and relations that organize and determine the everyday context of that seeing' (ibid.: 9). Referring explicitly to Marx's use of Hegel's parable of master and servant, Smith saw parallels between 'the claims Marx makes for a knowledge based in the class whose labour produces the conditions of existence, indeed the very existence, of a ruling class, and the claims that can be made for a knowledge of society from the standpoint of women' (ibid.: 79).

Similarly Nancy Hartsock, in an article on which she began work in 1978, brought a historical materialist approach to the understanding of 'the phallocratic institutions and ideology that constitute the capitalist form of patriarchy' (Hartsock 1985: 231).[7] She spelled out significant differences between men's and women's life activity. Where men have the singular role of producing goods, women as a sex produce both goods and human beings. Unlike those of men, women's lives are institutionally defined by the production of use-values in the home. She observed, therefore, that 'if life itself consists of sensuous activity, the vantage point available to women on the basis of their contribution to subsistence represents an intensification and deepening of the materialist world view available to the producers of commodities in capitalism, an intensification of class consciousness' (ibid.: 235).

Women's life activity, then, might be considered the source of a specific feminist standpoint. In proposing this, Hartsock spelled out some of the essential features of a 'standpoint' in Marxist theory. Material life, whether experienced by a given class or a given sex, both structures and sets limits on the understanding of social relations. In systems characterized by the domination by one group of another, the vision of each will be an inversion of that of the other. The view from above is likely to be both partial and perverse. Later, Hartsock would explain, 'By perverse I meant specifically both strange and harmful.'[8] On this reading, she concluded that women's lives surely 'make available a particular and privileged vantage point on male supremacy, a vantage point that can ground a powerful critique of the phallocratic institutions and ideology that constitute the capitalist form of patriarchy' (ibid.: 231). Most importantly, in Marxist theory, as Hartsock stresses, the standpoint of the oppressed group is an engaged vision, an achievement. It becomes available only through struggle. Finally, women's resistance to patriarchy, exposing the inhumanity of human relations, 'embodies a distress that requires a solution ... a social synthesis that does not depend on any of the forms taken by abstract masculinity' (ibid.: 246). Like the proletarian standpoint, it 'points beyond the present, and carries a historically liberatory role' (ibid.: 232).

Situated and plural knowledge

Recognizing 'standpoint' is to acknowledge that a plausible account of the world can be given from more than one positionality. In this spirit, a number of feminist theorists in the 1980s questioned the basis of knowledge claims (Rose 1983; Jaggar 1983; Harding 1986). Donna Haraway, addressing the multiplicity and diversity of feminist subjects and life experiences, developed the plural concept of 'situated knowledges' (Haraway 1988). She insisted on the embodied nature of all trustworthy seeing and knowing, dismissing 'unlocatable' knowledge claims as irresponsible. In particular, she stressed, one cannot expect to generate an understanding useful to subjugated groups from the universalizing standpoint of the master, 'the Man, the One God, whose Eye produces, appropriates, and orders all difference' (ibid.: 193). Diverse views from below, clearly rooted in life experiences, were a better bet for more reliable accounts of the world. 'The subjugated have a decent chance to be on to the god-trick and all its dazzling – and, therefore, blinding – illuminations. "Subjugated" standpoints are preferred because they seem to promise more adequate, sustained, objective, transforming accounts of the world' (ibid.: 191). 'Reliable', however, seemed to claim 'objectivity'. On what basis could partial and competing knowledges be considered objective? Haraway, and a little later Sandra Harding, reclaimed objectivity for situated knowledges. Harding had already contributed, in 1986, a major addition to feminist standpoint theory in her *The Science Question in Feminism*, in which she had savaged the androcentrism of the sciences and called for a feminist 'successor science' project (Harding 1986). Now she argued in defence of 'situated knowledges' that giving up 'the goal of telling one true story about reality' need not mean that 'one must also give up trying to tell less false stories' (Harding 1991: 187). Science had never been value-free, as scientists liked to claim. A stronger version of objectivity could be achieved by combining the standpoint from below with enquiry that was reflexive, by actors who named and clearly situated themselves, coming clean about power, interests and values, as informative about the subject and source of knowledge as about the objects of which they spoke.

Labour as Marxist-feminist problematic

Even within its own frame of reference, Marxist thought had clearly overlooked an important phenomenon. A distinctive feature of the division of labour is the sexual division of labour. This had been precisely Hartsock's project – to render an 'account of the sexual division of labour and its consequences for epistemology' (Hartsock 1985: 232). Capitalists reckon on, and profit from, both women's gendered disadvantage in the workplace and their unpaid labour in the home. This oversight has often enough been pointed out by women active in labour movements. It is possible, however, to represent the oversight as a shortcoming of socialist analysis, without positing a system of male supremacy in which men as men also benefit from women's labour. Lindsey German, for instance, dismissive of feminism as 'a limited political programme' (German 2007: 166), offers a thorough description of the position of women in capitalist labour relations while firmly rejecting the analysis of those feminist writers – she cites Heidi Hartmann (1981) in particular – who frame women's labour processes within patriarchal as well as capitalist relations. This, she writes, is 'an extremely partial reading' of women's history and a retreat from class analysis (German 2007: 154).

Other feminists challenging the gender blindness of Marxist thought have often tended, like Hartsock, to restrict their corrective analysis to labour processes and relations. Thus Heidi Hartmann, who, as Lindsey German noted, makes a cogent case for understanding patriarchy as a system of power relations distinct from, though deeply implicated in, the capitalist system of class relations, memorably defined patriarchy as 'a set of social relations which has a material base and in which there are hierarchical relations between men and solidarity among them which enable them in turn to dominate women'. Yet she continued immediately, 'The material base of patriarchy is men's control over *women's labour power*' (Hartmann 1981: 18, emphasis added). Elaborating on a point she had made two years earlier, that 'job segregation by sex is *the primary mechanism* in capitalist societies that maintains the superiority of men over women' (Hartmann 1979: 208, emphasis added), she writes:

> Job segregation by sex, by ensuring that women have the lower paid jobs, both assures women's economic dependence on men and reinforces notions of appropriate spheres for women and men. For most men, then, the development of family wages secured the material base of male domination in two ways. First, men have the better jobs in the labour market and earn higher wages than women ... Secondly ... women do housework, childcare, and perform other services at home which benefit men directly. Women's home responsibilities in turn reinforce their inferior labour market position. (Hartmann 1981: 22)

That many versions of feminist standpoint limit themselves to issues surrounding women's labour is in some sense a natural response to the fact that Marxist standpoint theory sees proletarian consciousness as resulting uniquely from the worker's experience of being forced to sell his labour power – something 'inseparable from his physical existence', as Lukács puts it – as a mere commodity (Lukács 1968: 166). Kathi Weeks' substantial recovery of feminist standpoint theory two decades after its founding moment is another case in which the analysis dwells on 'women's labouring practices' (Weeks 1998: 15). However, interestingly, she explicitly states that she does not propose 'labour as the fundamental source of women's oppression and the only site of feminist agitation'. Rather, the framing of this and earlier work (Weeks 1996) suggests a tactical choice, in the conflictual 1990s, to ground her argument in labour as a device for transcending the antagonism between modernism and postmodernism. Thus she writes:

> [I]f we take labouring practices, rather than signifying practices, as our point of entry into these configurations of gendered subjectivity, we can better account for the coercion under which gender is embodied; few would mistake labour for a practice that can be freely taken up or easily refused. Thus by privileging labour we are better able to keep sight of the constitutive links between systematic socioeconomic relations on the one hand and collective modes of practice and forms of subjectivity on the other. (Ibid.: 96)

Standpoint derived from other phases of life activity

Interestingly, Nancy Hartsock, at the start of the essay analysed above, seems to acknowledge a limitation implicit in her choice of focus. She writes: 'I argue that on the basis of ... the sexual division of labour, one could begin, though not complete, the construction of a feminist standpoint ...' (Hartsock 1985: 231). And indeed, some feminist thinkers did subsequently depart from the trope of 'work', the reiteration of the feminist standpoint's grounding in the exploitation of women's labour power and the struggle that evokes. They turned to other phases of women's lived experience to look for the emergence of feminist consciousness.

A highly innovative account came from Mary O'Brien, who, after many years as a practising midwife, turned academic and levelled her gaze on women's experience of conception, pregnancy and birthing. In *The Politics of Reproduction*, published in 1981, she suggested that an important impulse in patriarchy is control of offspring. Men's seed is alienated from them in copulation and conception. Women know their child as part of their own body, but if the man is to be sure of paternity, if he is to 'know' and appropriate the child, he must control the woman. In societal terms this requires cooperation between men. The biological process of reproduction, O'Brien argues, is a 'material substructure of history' necessarily giving rise to distinct forms of consciousness in men and women and accounting for systemic male supremacy as a historical phenomenon. Starting from this insight, she suggests, 'feminism must develop theory, method and strategy, and we must pursue this development from a fresh perspective, namely "the standpoint of women," women working from within women's reality' (O'Brien 1981: 188).

O'Brien is not the only feminist thinker to have noted that, while the subjection of the worker to the capitalist may hinge on labour and the working day, the subjection of women to men involves their whole being – physical, sexual, emotional, reproductive, aesthetic, relational – day and night. Others have looked to different aspects of oppression as potential sources of oppositional consciousness, feminist standpoints and movements. Towards the end of *The Science Question in Feminism*, published in 1986, Sandra Harding had already begun to question the singularity of 'the' feminist standpoint. It was the beginning of a period of postmodernist and post-structuralist emphasis on 'difference', on 'fractured identities' and 'hyphenized feminisms'.

Socialist-feminism, radical-feminism, lesbian-feminism, black-Marxist-feminism, black-lesbian-socialist-feminism, radical-women-of-colour – these hyphenizations, Harding couldn't help feeling, bespoke 'an exhilaration felt in the differences in women's perceptions of who we are and of the appropriate politics for navigating through our daily social relations'. Standpoint epistemology, she feared, if it stressed a singular feminist standpoint, might be taken to devalue that exhilaration (Harding 1986: 163).

Two decades later she would edit a reader that responded to this doubt, drawing together multiple accounts of feminist standpoints (Harding 2004b). The volume reproduced an important essay by Patricia Hill Collins which argued that the thinking of black feminists, the 'outsiders within' US society, must be seen as constituting a special standpoint on self, family and society (Collins 1986).[9] And Maria Mies and Vandana Shiva contributed a chapter arguing that women of different racial, ethnic, cultural and class backgrounds, notably in the 'global South', have evolved a distinctive shared analysis in confronting the threat posed by capitalist exploitation to the natural environment and ultimately to human and other life on earth. They represented this consciousness in terms of a rejection both of the Enlightenment notion that Man's freedom and happiness depends on 'his' eventual emancipation from Nature by the forces of reason and rationality, and of the Marxist concept of humankind's historic march from the 'realm of necessity' (i.e. the realm of nature) to the 'realm of freedom'. The feminist standpoint here takes the form of what the authors call the 'subsistence perspective' (Mies and Shiva 2004).[10]

Besides, by now it was no longer only diverse positionalities, in recognition of intersectionality, which were being proposed as sources of standpoints – it was also different phases of women's life activity. Another chapter in Harding's collection showed Sara Ruddick, for instance, arguing for maternal thinking, featuring 'preservative love', as generative of a feminist standpoint (Ruddick 1989).[11] In this vein, convinced by many years of empirical research in organizations of the women's peace movement, I entered this debate, proposing that the profoundly gendered phenomena of violence and war are significant features of women's 'life activity' and that resistance to them tends to generate a distinctive analysis. The social shaping of masculinity in patriarchy towards a readiness to prevail by use of force results in a marked predominance of men in violent criminality and in the ranks and commanding structures of armed forces. Women are a significant proportion of the victims of war and also experience gendered effects of militarization in everyday life in peacetime societies. I termed their critical analyses and mobilizations against violence and war a feminist anti-militarist standpoint (Cockburn 2007, 2010).

A further and somewhat startling Marxist-feminist innovation was that of Anna Jónasdóttir, who, in 1994, observed that we had been in error in so often reducing the 'material' in women's life experience to the economic. 'Work', she said, 'neither is nor ever can be life's only and total "prime want"' (Jónasdóttir 1994: 97). We were forgetting emotion. Empathy, attachment. In short, love. The activities around which the sexual struggle revolves, she maintained, are neither work nor the products of work, 'but human love – caring, ecstasy' (ibid.: 24). In making this case, Jónasdóttir represented herself as rendering reality 'from a standpoint best described as a certain kind of radical feminist stance' (ibid.: 17).

Women and men, Jónasdóttir believes, needing, seeking and practising love, 'enter into specific productive relations with each other in which they "quite literally produce new human beings."' Up to this point she was going no further than the 'conception and birthing' insight of Mary O'Brien, mentioned above. She went on to add, however, that women and men 'also produce (and reproduce) themselves and each other as active, emotional, and reasoning people' (ibid.: 63). It was in this process, she believed, that men became empowered. Adapting the Marxist theory of alienated labour, she suggested that:

> men can continually appropriate significantly more of women's life force and capacity than they give back to women. Men can build themselves up as powerful social beings and continue to dominate women through their constant accumulation of the existential forces taken and received from women. If capital is accumulated alienated labour, male authority is accumulated alienated love. (Ibid.: 26)

Truth or power?

An informative exchange of ideas on standpoint took place in the feminist journal *Signs* in 1997. In an article entitled 'Truth and method: feminist standpoint theory revisited', Susan Hekman tackled several problems for standpoint theory raised by postmodernism. She remarked that 'among younger feminist theorists, feminist standpoint theory is frequently regarded as a quaint relic of feminism's less sophisticated past'. Its inspiration, Marxism, had been discredited in both theory and practice. Standpoint theory seemed to 'be at odds with the issue that has dominated feminist debate in the past decade: difference' (Hekman 2004: 225).[12]

Hekman's aim, however, was not to dismiss but to reinstate feminist standpoint theory, by stressing a plurality of standpoints. She proposed Thomas Kuhn's 'paradigm shift' as a conceptual device capable of giving feminist standpoint postmodernist credibility. The new rejection of the possibility of absolute truth, the substitution of a notion of multiple and relative truths, should be read as a paradigm shift in the sense Kuhn intended. For Hekman, the theory as proposed by Hartsock and Harding stalled on an illogicality she found troubling in Marxist thought more generally: social constructionist and absolutist conceptions of truth are in contradiction. She argued that the lifeworld, like every other human activity, is discursively constituted. A 'standpoint', therefore, cannot claim to express the 'truth' about 'reality' – it must be understood as one representation among others, political and value-laden, 'a place from which feminists can articulate a counterhegemonic discourse and argue for a less repressive society' (ibid.: 239).

Hartsock, Collins, Harding and Smith fiercely countered Hekman's 'Truth and method' article, arguing in the same issue of *Signs*[13] that she was mistaken in prioritizing the matter of 'truth': what is at stake in 'standpoint' is not truth but power. It is specifically about challenging, from the position of the marginal, silenced and subjected, the conceptual practices of power, the 'view from above'. Furthermore, the subjects posited by standpoint theory are not a ragbag collection of individuals. Rather, they are groups sharing an experience of subjection to and by power – capitalist power, patriarchal power, white power. Trodden down, and looking upwards to the systemic level, they find themselves an oppositional consciousness[14] that enables them to become a resistant, challenging collective subject (Hartsock 2004; Collins 2004; Harding 2004a; Smith 2004).

Hekman's article was symptomatic of a body of feminist work on standpoint that was to follow in the first decade of the new millennium, much of it detached from its roots in Marxist thought. Indeed, already in 2005, Michael Ryan's entry on 'Standpoint theory' in *An*

Encyclopedia of Social Theory formulates it in its entirety as a product of feminist and 'multicultural' thought, without any reference to Marx or Marxism (Ryan 2005: 789). Prioritizing the issue of truth claims, many of these later authors found their primary inspiration less in Hartsock and Smith than in Donna Haraway's 'situated knowledges' mentioned above (Haraway 1988). Marcel Stoetzler and Nira Yuval-Davis, for example, proposed a strengthening of standpoint theory by the introduction of a concept of the 'situated imagination', in parallel with that of situated knowledge, arguing that it is only through a process of imagining that 'the transitions from positionings to practices, practices to standpoints, knowledge, meaning, values and goals, actually take place' (Stoetzler and Yuval-Davis 2002: 320).

A 2009 issue of *Hypatia* devoted to standpoint theory contained several articles in which the perspective of the social scientist, together with his or her problem in deciding how to evaluate competing truth claims, was largely substituted for the perspective of the feminist subject and her struggle to survive and thrive in capitalist patriarchy. Thus Janet Kourany tests standpoint theory against alternative methodological approaches in feminist studies, cautiously endorsing it as a usable academic resource despite the many questions she believes it leaves unresolved (Kourany 2009). Kristina Rolin problematizes the notion that the perspective of the disadvantaged is liable to be less partial and distorted than that of the powerful (the concept of 'epistemic advantage'). She proposes a lesser claim: standpoint theory may be understood as a resource for feminist epistemology and philosophy of science on the more modest ground that it simply 'urges feminist scholars to pay attention to relations of power as a distinctive kind of obstacle to the production of scientific knowledge' (Rolin 2009: 222). Joseph Rouse, in the same volume of *Hypatia*, traces the history of feminist standpoint theorization with the aim of moving 'beyond the constitutive tropes of standpoint theory' (Rouse 2009: 207). In doing so, he represents standpoints as competing knowledge claims generated by people 'as part of practical and perceptual interaction with one another in shared surroundings', without reference to power relations, subjugation or struggle. In historicizing standpoint theory, he notes that it dates back to the work of Smith, Hartsock and Collins, adding '*arguably … even to Marx and Hegel*' (ibid.: 202, emphasis added). By the end of the first decade of the twenty-first century, it seems, Marx had become, to the generation of social scientists educated in 1990s postmodernism, an obscure figure, no longer one but two centuries back in time.

The flaccidity of these recent accounts signals an amnesia, a forgetting that a standpoint is, in Kathi Weeks' words, 'a project, not an inheritance'. It is 'an ongoing achievement rather than a spontaneous attribute or consciousness …' It is 'both a product and an instrument of feminist struggle' (Weeks 1998: 8). In other words, it is in, and of, movements of resistance and revolution. And in the meantime new political insurgencies have been occurring in the second decade of the twenty-first century, sparked by life experiences very different from those of the industrial working class as known to Lukács in the early twentieth century, and of the women of second-wave feminism, among whom Dorothy Smith and Nancy Hartsock lived and worked half a century later. The World Social Forum events have mobilized activists from a wide range of global movements. Billion Women Rise has precipitated women into street protests against male violence from New Delhi to Kinshasa and London. Occupy has brought young people of many countries into city encampments and has squatted outside banks to protest against financial crime and austerity policies. They call themselves the 'ninety-nine percent'. We have to probe deeper into the collective subjectivities emerging. Who are they? Who are we? We need to pay careful attention to the specificity of the power relations against which we are rising in rebellion, as one conjuncture gives way to the next. How do these systems intersect with and amplify each other? It is not in the analyses of academics, but in the voices, leaflets, placards and tweets of new historic subjects, sparked to consciousness by new scandals of subjugation and exploitation, that contemporary standpoints are being expressed. And it is in these movements that a deeper understanding of the value of standpoint theory for future transformative change is likely to be forged.

Notes

1 First prepared for publication by Frederick Engels in 1894 after Marx's death. As is well known, Chapter 50, entitled 'Classes', is a fragment, no more than a couple of pages in length, and was destined to remain unfinished.

2 Written in 1845/46, the full work remained unpublished during the lifetimes of its authors.

3 *History and Class Consciousness* was originally published in 1923. In this passage, Lukács is referring to Marx's *Critique of Hegel's Philosophy of Right*, published in 1843.

4 A critique of the Young Hegelians, first published in 1845.

5 Hegel's book was originally published in 1807.

6 *The Prison Notebooks*, written by Antonio Gramsci in prison in Italy between 1929 and 1935, were first published in the late 1940s.

7 Nancy C. M. Hartsock's article 'The feminist standpoint: developing the ground for a specifically feminist historical materialism' was first published in 1983, in Hintikka and Harding (eds), *Discovering Reality: Feminist Perspectives on Epistemology, Methodology, Metaphysics and Philosophy of Science*. It was reprinted as Chapter 10 in her *Money, Sex and Power: Towards a Feminist Historical Materialism* in 1985.

8 Hartsock in an interview with Thonette Myking (see Myking 2007).

9 Originally published as an article of the same title in *Social Problems* (1986), Collins' argument was spelled out at greater length in Collins (1991).

10 An excerpt from the introduction to their book *Ecofeminism* published in 1993.

11 This chapter was an excerpt from her book *Maternal Thinking*, published in 1989.

12 Hekman's article, which originally appeared in *Signs* in 1997, was later republished, along with those of its discussants, in a collection edited by Sandra Harding (2004b).

13 The references given here are to their articles as republished in a volume edited by Harding (2004b).

14 The phrase 'oppositional consciousness' was coined by Chela Sandoval, who, in a seminal article in the Harding (2004b) collection, elaborated 'a topography of consciousness that identifies nothing more and nothing less than the modes the subordinated of the United States (of any gender, race, or class) claim as politicized and oppositional stances in resistance to domination' (Sandoval 2004: 200). Her stress on subjection, power and the multiplicity of resistant standpoints was an important contribution to transcending the antagonisms into which postmodernism had cast standpoint theory.

References

Cockburn, C. (2007) *From Where We Stand: War, Women's Activism and Feminist Analysis*, London: Zed Books.

— (2010) 'Gender relations as causal in militarization and war: a feminist standpoint', *International Feminist Journal of Politics*, 12(2): 139–57.

Collins, P. H. (1986) 'Learning from the outsider within: the sociological significance of black feminist thought', *Social Problems*, 33(6): S14–32.

— (1991) *Black Feminist Thought: Knowledge, Consciousness and the Politics of Empowerment*, New York: Routledge.

— (2004) 'Comment on Hekman's "Truth and method: feminist standpoint theory revisited." Where's the power?', in S. Harding (ed.), *The Feminist Standpoint Theory Reader: Intellectual and Political Controversies*, London: Routledge, pp. 247–54.

German, L. (2007) *Material Girls: Women, Men and Work*, London: Bookmarks.

Gramsci, A. (1971) *Selections from the Prison Notebooks*, London: Lawrence and Wishart.

Haraway, D. (1988) 'Situated knowledge: the science question in feminism and the privilege of partial perspective', *Feminist Studies*, 14(3): 575–99.

Harding, S. (1986) *The Science Question in Feminism*, Milton Keynes: Open University Press.

— (1991) *Whose Science? Whose Knowledge?*, Milton Keynes: Open University Press.

— (2004a) 'Comment on Hekman's "Truth and method: feminist standpoint theory revisited." Whose standpoint needs the regimes of truth and reality?', in S. Harding (ed.), *The Feminist Standpoint Theory Reader: Intellectual and Politi-*

cal Controversies, London: Routledge, pp. 382–91.
— (ed.) (2004b) *The Feminist Standpoint Theory Reader: Intellectual and Political Controversies*, London: Routledge.
Hartmann, H. (1979) 'Capitalism, patriarchy and job segregation by sex', in Z. Eisenstein (ed.), *Capitalist Patriarchy and the Case for Socialist Feminism*, London: Monthly Review Press, pp. 206–47.
— (1981) 'The unhappy marriage of Marxism and feminism: towards a more progressive union', in L. Sargent (ed.), *Women and Revolution: A Discussion of the Unhappy Marriage of Marxism and Feminism*, London: Pluto, pp. 1–41.
Hartsock, N. C. M. (1985) *Money, Sex and Power: Towards a Feminist Historical Materialism*, Boston, MA: Northeastern University Press, pp. 231–51.
— (1998) *The Feminist Standpoint Revisited and Other Essays*, Boulder, CO: Westview.
— (2004) 'Comment on Hekman's "Truth and method: feminist standpoint theory revisited." Truth or justice?', in S. Harding (ed.), *The Feminist Standpoint Theory Reader: Intellectual and Political Controversies*, London: Routledge, pp. 243–6.
Hegel, G. W. F. (1977) *Phenomenology of Spirit*, Oxford: Clarendon.
Hekman, S. (1997) 'Truth and method: feminist standpoint theory revisited', *Signs*, 22(21): 341–65.
— (2004) 'Truth and method: feminist standpoint theory revisited', in S. Harding (ed.), *The Feminist Standpoint Theory Reader: Intellectual and Political Controversies*, London: Routledge, pp. 225–42.
Jaggar, A. (1983) *Feminist Politics and Human Nature*, Totowa, NJ: Rowman and Allenheld.
Jónasdóttir, A. G. (1994) *Why Women are Oppressed*, Philadelphia, PA: Temple University Press.
Kourany, J. A. (2009) 'The place of standpoint theory in feminist science studies', *Hypatia*, 24(4): 209–18.
Lukács, G. (1968) *History and Class Consciousness: Studies in Marxist Dialectics*, trans. R. Livingstone, Cambridge, MA: MIT Press.
Marx, K. (1959) *Capital: A Critique of Political Economy*, vol. 3, London: Lawrence and Wishart.
Marx, K. and F. Engels (1970) *The German Ideology. Part 1*, ed. C. J. Arthur, London: Lawrence and Wishart.
Mies, M. and V. Shiva (1993) *Ecofeminism*, London: Zed Books.
— (2004) 'The subsistence perspective', in S. Harding (ed.), *The Feminist Standpoint Theory Reader: Intellectual and Political Controversies*, London: Routledge, pp. 333–8.
Myking, T. (2007) 'As we reoccupy Marxism as Feminism(s)', *Norsk filosofisk tidsskrift*, 42(4): 259–73.
O'Brien, M. (1981) *The Politics of Reproduction*, London: Routledge and Kegan Paul.
Rolin, K. (2009) 'Standpoint theory as a methodology for the study of power relations', *Hypatia*, 24(4): 218–26.
Rose, H. (1983) 'Hand, brain and heart: towards a feminist epistemology for the natural sciences', *Signs*, 9(1): 73–96.
Rouse, J. (2009) 'Standpoint theories reconsidered', *Hypatia*, 24(4): 200–9.
Ruddick, S. (1989) *Maternal Thinking*, Boston, MA: Beacon.
— (2004) 'Maternal thinking as a feminist standpoint', in S. Harding (ed.), *The Feminist Standpoint Theory Reader: Intellectual and Political Controversies*, London: Routledge, pp. 161–8.
Ryan, M. (2005) 'Standpoint theory', in G. Ritzer (ed.), *Encyclopedia of Social Theory*, vol. 2, London: Sage Publications.
Sandoval, C. (2004) 'U.S. Third World

feminism: the theory and method of differential oppositional consciousness', in S. Harding (ed.), *The Feminist Standpoint Theory Reader: Intellectual and Political Controversies*, London: Routledge, pp. 195–209.

Smith, D. E. (1974) 'The ideological practice of sociology', *Catalyst*, 8: 39–54.

— (1981) 'On sociological description: a method from Marx', *Human Studies*, 4: 313–37.

— (1987) *The Everyday World as Problematic: A Feminist Sociology*, Milton Keynes: Open University Press.

— (2004) 'Comment on Hekman's "Truth and method: feminist standpoint theory revisited"', in S. Harding (ed.), *The Feminist Standpoint Theory Reader: Intellectual and Political Controversies*, London: Routledge, pp. 263–9.

Stoetzler, M. and N. Yuval-Davis (2002) 'Standpoint theory, situated knowledge and the situated imagination', *Feminist Theory*, 3(3): 315–33.

Weeks, K. (1996) 'Subject for a feminist standpoint', in S. Maksisi, C. Casarino and E. K. Rebecca (eds), *Marxism beyond Marxism*, London: Routledge, pp. 89–118.

— (1998) *Constituting Feminist Subjects*, Ithaca, NY: Cornell University Press.

16 | EPILOGUE: GENDER AFTER CLASS

Teresa L. Ebert

Contemporary feminism is a ludic feminism (Ebert 1996). It is largely indifferent to material practices under capitalism such as labour, which shapes the social structures of daily life. In theory and practice, feminism has fetishized difference and erased the question of exploitation, diffusing knowledge of the root conditions of women's realities in particularities of oppressions. It has embraced the cultural turn – the reification of culture as an autonomous zone of signifying practices – and put aside a transformative politics, so much so that it is little more than a painfully parodic linguistic game.

A new (red) feminism is needed now: a feminism that clears out the undergrowth of bourgeois ideology which, by troping the concepts of class, history, theory and labour, has limited the terms through which feminism understands the condition of women. Red feminism is concerned not only with the 'woman question', but even more about the 'other' questions that construct the 'woman question' – the issues of class and labour.

For all the family quarrels in ludic feminism, as institutionalized by post-theories (e.g. Benhabib et al. 1995; Butler et al. 2000), its ways of understanding gender and sexuality are strategies for bypassing questions of labour and capital – the social relations grounded in turning the labour power of the other into profit. Feminism now dwells, instead, on matters of cultural difference. In reclaiming a materialist knowledge, red feminism contests the cultural theory grounding ludic feminism. Specifically, it argues that language – discourse in its social circulations – is 'practical consciousness' (as Marx and Engels write in *The German Ideology* [1976: 44]) and that culture, far from being autonomous, is always and ultimately a social articulation of the material relations of production. Ludic feminism localizes gender and sexuality in the name of honouring their differences and the specificities of their oppression. In doing so, it isolates them from history and reduces them to 'events' in performativities, thus cleansing them of labour. For red feminism, the local, the specific and the singular, namely the concrete, is always an 'imagined concrete' and the result of 'many determinations' and relations that 'all form the members of a totality, distinctions within a unity. Production (labour relations) predominates not only over itself … but over the other moments as well' (Marx 1973: 99–101).

Ludic feminism is gradually disappearing into the irrelevance of high-bourgeois caprice and humour interlaced with a defensive populism. It is turning into a Bakhtinian carnival in which playfulness, puns and corporeal analogies are substituted for transformative arguments (Probyn 2005), and the resignification of the world has taken the place of critique-al analysis for changing it (Gallop 2002).

Globalization, to take one specific issue that has had a serious impact on the lives of women and their families around the world but especially in the global South, is understood in ludic theory as 'a discourse, as the language of domination, a tightly scripted narrative of differential power' (Gibson-Graham 2006a: 120). The class contradictions of globalization are mystified in a 'politics that offers a compressed temporality – traversing the distance from "nowhere" to "now here"' (Gibson-Graham 2006b: xxi).

The consequences of reading globalization figurally have been disastrous for feminism. J. K. Gibson-Graham, for example, deploy Sharon Marcus' metaphors (1992) to compare globalization to rape (Gibson-Graham 2006a: 120–47). 'There are', Gibson-Graham write, 'many obvious points of connection between the language of rape and the language of capitalist globalization', and they list by way of example such words as 'penetration', 'invasion' and 'virgin territory' (ibid.: 124). Globalization, in their tropes, has the brutal force of the violence of rape and has become a discourse of power and oppression. Rape is understood not as domination but as a narrative (mis)representation of victimization and sexualization that can be resisted through resignification. Change, for them, is therefore changing representations – rewriting the script of rape/globalization. Thus, resistance to capitalism involves reinscribing the 'body of capitalism'. Elaborating on Elizabeth Grosz's troping of the male body (1994), they believe the power dynamics of globalization can be transformed by 'differently conceiv[ing] of the body of capitalism, viewing it as open, as penetrable, as weeping or draining away instead of as hard and contained, penetrating and inevitably overpowering' (ibid.: 135).

They thus rewrite 'finance capital (or money)' as 'the seminal fluid of capitalism' and as 'a spectacle of bodily excess, a wet dream', representing it as 'unleashing uncontrollable gushes of capital that flow every which way, including self-destruction' (ibid.: 135).

These analogies, however, cannot explain material exploitation, which is the root cause of globalization. Furthermore, this double move – treating rape as a matter of power relations and then turning power relations into linguistic associations – isolates rape from the social relations of production, making it into a local gender question that is, for them, simply a matter of the performativity of language (ibid.: 123). Playing with these supplementary tropes, their analysis drifts farther and farther away from globalization as an objective reality of contemporary labour relations. It becomes not only a frivolous troping of globalization, but also a trivialization of the fate of women and their sexuality under capitalism. The fight against globalization – the plundering of the labour of the other – turns into the question of 'how might we get globalization to lose its erection?' (ibid.: 126–7). This turns out to be not that difficult because, in the interpretation of Lisa Disch, who admires their arguments, their views of globalization amount to saying that 'what we know as globalization is less a rape … than … mutual masturbation' (Disch 1999).

Gibson-Graham's general argument uses feminism as a pluralizing strategy to claim that capitalism is not the sole source of exploitation in the global world. Therefore, 'the script of globalization', they write, 'need not draw solely upon an image of the body of capitalism as hard, thrusting and powerful' (Gibson-Graham 2006a: 138). Consequently the representation of the intervention of multinational corporations (MNCs) in the economy of the host country does not have to be read in terms of the standard script. They then ask the question which implies its own answer: 'Could we not see MNC activity in Third World situations in a slightly different light, as perhaps sometimes unwittingly generative rather than merely destructive?' (ibid.: 130). In other words, their ludic feminism ends up as an apologist for multinational corporations and leads to the climax 'that the economic "rape" wrought by globalization in the Third World is a script with many different outcomes. In this case we might read the rape event as inducing a pregnancy' (ibid.: 131). The grand finale of their discursive analysis of globalization as rape is that exploitation is good for women: 'For some women involvement in capitalist exploitation has freed them from aspects of the exploitation associated with their household class positions and has given them a position from which to struggle with and redefine traditional gender roles' (ibid.: 132).

This is too painful to call comical. The conclusion of their cutting-edge feminist 'analysis' is identical to the liberal banalities that are written day in and day out in the pages of such house organs of global capitalism as the *New York Times* (the main site for the dissemination of Thomas Friedman's views on globalization). In his 'In praise of the maligned sweatshop', Nicholas D. Kristof writes that the sweatshops in Africa set up by capitalists from the North are, in fact, 'opportunities', and he advises that 'anyone who cares about fighting poverty should campaign in favor of sweatshops' (Kristof 2006: A21). His argument is summed up by two sentences printed in bold font and foregrounded in his essay: 'What's worse than being exploited? Not being exploited' (ibid.: A21).

Globalization, for both the liberal writer and the ludic feminist, is the same: Gibson-Graham see it 'as liberating' a plurality of economic practices (Gibson-Graham 2006a: 139). Heterogeneity is what matters most. This view is indistinguishable – except in its corporeal metaphors – from the standard (very standard) neoliberal economic theory and its history in the North (Harvey 2005). Ludic feminists, along with neoliberals, declare that the 'revolutionary task of replacing capitalism' is now 'outmoded', and the only way to change it is by theorizing capitalism 'as fragmented' and not as a totality that enjoys unity and singularity (Gibson-Graham 2006a: 263). Feminist politics is, for them, essentially a 'language politics' (Gibson-Graham 2006b: 54–9). Ludic feminism is an ally of the old idealism grounded in the fantasies of a 'triumph over materialism' (Gilder 1989: 371–83) and the new pop-management theories that derive from it (Peters 1992). All their arguments are anchored in the rejection of totality in favour of a dispersed disorganization related by a network of metaphors (Gilder 1989: 370–81) aimed at a new spiritualism in which capitalism itself is not a decided reality but a nomadic 'fluid' (Gibson-Graham 2006b: 135).

Red feminism is, among other things, an argument that capitalism does not need the oppression of women, homophobia or racism in order to survive. It needs labour – cheap labour. Thus, for feminism to be a serious force in the struggle against global capitalism, it needs to be grounded in the labour theory of value, in class as the global relations of property, rather than in the 'local', the community (ibid.: 79–99). Gibson-Graham, of course, are not alone in being more interested in waging 'war on totality' and 'activat[ing] the differences' than in struggling against exploitation and for socialism (Lyotard 1984: 84).

Socialism presents a quandary for ludic feminists. They find they can neither reject nor accept it. In response to an interviewer who says he no longer knows 'what it means ... to say he ... is a socialist', but that he 'wouldn't take any pleasure in saying that [he is] not a socialist' either, Gayatri Chakravorty Spivak says she is not so much for socialism as she is not against it: 'Like you,' she says, 'I would not like to call myself an antisocialist' (Spivak and Plotke 1994: 18). Yet both agree that socialism, in some of its most fundamental aspects, is 'unacceptable' – because of what they and neoliberals regard to be its 'statist orientation' and 'narrowly economic focus', among other reasons. Their criticism is largely a defence of ludic individualism (ibid.: 17).

Gibson-Graham, Spivak and many other ludic feminists have moved a long way from the struggle to end capitalism. In fact, contemporary feminism has reached an impasse in which, as Gibson-Graham's *A Postcapitalist Politics* (2006b) clearly indicates, it cannot think of the future of humanity outside of capitalism. The freedom of women is now considered possible only by embracing capitalism – by accepting and working within the system rather than transforming it. This is one of the more telling aspects of Gayatri Spivak's interview on transnational resistance. Not only does she seem to readily accept 'capitalism with a small "d" development' (Spivak and Plotke 1994: 5) – that is, indigenous, low-growth capitalism in the Southern theatre, a version of the 'subsistence perspective' (Mies and Shiva 1993; Bennholdt-Thomsen and Mies 2000) – but she repeatedly suggests a form of 'enlightened benevolent' giving on the part of capitalist countries of the North. In other words, the post-socialist feminist's argument finally collapses into the clichés of bourgeois ethics: the 'unfinishable tug-of-war' between 'taking and giving', which 'relates to the ethical' (Spivak and Plotke 1994: 14). Global philanthropy, represented as ethics, becomes the social policy of transnational feminism not only for Spivak, but also for many non-governmental organizations (NGOs).

Even more common is the reification of the market economy in which consumption becomes the main arena of change. There is something of a North–South divide, however, around the 'politics of consumption'. Consumption is used in contemporary feminism and the left more generally as a means for displacing production and class. However, class conditions determine consumption. This is quite clear in the different ways consumption is understood in the North and the South. In the North, where liberty not poverty is the primary question, consumption is related to desire, while in the South, liberation from consumption and a voluntary simplicity are represented as the urgent response to poverty. The call for freedom from consumption, which is little more than an ahistorical and moralistic slogan, is at the heart of Mies and Shiva's micro-politics. As Mies argues, 'the only alternative' to the 'unending growth and profit' of the 'world market system' is 'a deliberate and drastic change of lifestyle, a reduction of consumption and a radical change in the North's consumer patterns' (Mies and Shiva 1993: 62). The authors, however, are silent on class and production. What they say is, in the end, not very different from 'Just say No'. It does little, if anything, to radically intervene in the capitalist structures of exploitation. Only in the most trivial sense does social change take place through consumption. Fundamental social transformation is always a change in production and its class relations.

Contemporary capitalism increasingly tries to secure its fundamental relations of profit by setting up a global civil society that is mapped out in terms of NGOs. These are used in many ways to secure the interests of global capitalism by displacing class and marginalizing production practices through entrepreneurship and the free market. It may be necessary to make a distinction here between transnational globalization and internationalism (Ebert 2009). By emphasizing transnational globalization, ludic feminism legitimizes a transnational order based on culture, at the centre of which is consumption. This is globalization in which transnationality is marked by observing that, for example, a clerk in Hong Kong listens to the same music and enjoys the same jeans and 'Gap clothes' as a teacher in Romania or a teenager in London. This new civil society is based on consumption, and the connections that it makes are connections among objects of desire. It is a civil society of commodification. In opposition to this, internationalism is based on a world-historical solidarity beyond the boundaries of nationality and consumption and founded upon class and production for freedom from necessity and the end to exploitation.

Red feminism argues against the view of globalization as a market order and a regime of consumption and for internationalism: the solidarity of all workers of the world beyond national boundaries.

Ludic feminism 'wages war' not so much against the exploitation of people by capitalism, but against repressing difference. In doing so, it is quite willing, as Spivak indicates, to form alliances with 'capitalism with a small "d" development' (Spivak and Plotke 1994: 5).

What is needed is not a new 'global-girdling' consumptionist feminism, but a red feminism. Instead of alliances based on ethics, which is a reification of individualism and individual desire(ing), a materialist international collectivity committed to emancipating women and all oppressed people from need and the exploitation of their labour needs to be constructed.

Red feminism

The cultural turn and its linguistic tendencies in feminism have isolated issues of gender and sexuality from their material conditions. Red feminism is an argument that gender and sexuality cannot be fully understood outside class relations. However, ludic feminism has obscured class and its relation to gender and sexuality by treating 'history', 'agency', 'modernity', 'postmodernity', 'essentialism', 'theory', 'labour' and the 'concrete' as cultural effects and as (semi-) autonomous sites of resistance as part of its claim to being a transformative practice. Culture, however, is never independent of the social relations of production, and cultural resistance, in and of itself, is not capable of transforming these relations. The most effective way to undertake such a transformation is by class struggle, which brings about 'root' changes through reorganizing the relations of labour and capital and which puts an end to social class. All social differences, such as gender, are effects of class – the inequality of labour. Red feminism is bringing class back to feminism. However, to do this requires rematerializing what ludic feminism has culturalized. We begin with theory.

Theory It has become a ritual for ludic feminism to dissociate itself from 'theory', which it regards as an abstract concern with little relevance to the actualities of gender and sexuality. Theory, in ludic discourses, is elitist (masculinist) and utopian. More specifically, theory is seen as an act of 'totalizing', which is synonymous in ludic circles with 'totalitarianism'.

Judith Butler distances herself from theory by assuming the familiar pose of 'ignorance'. 'Not knowing' has become the mark of genuine 'knowing' in ludic feminism, following Lacan, Žižek and others. Butler states that 'I do not understand the notion of "theory," and am hardly interested in being cast as its defender …' (Butler 1991: 14). Jane Gallop goes farther and devotes an entire book to refashioning theory into anecdote and turning concepts (the abstract) into tropes (the concrete) (Gallop 2002).

These ludic acts of distancing from theory are not only theoretical, but are also effects of a theory of theory. They put in question the idea of theory as an explanatory critique of social totality and instead privilege theory as play and as playful readings of the play of differences in sexuality, gender and texts of culture. Theory-as-play shifts the focus of analysis away from the material social relations of production to cultural representations. In a complex move, it quietly affirms the existing social relations of production through subtle and highly nuanced transgressive readings that put cultural norms in question. Material relations remain intact while cultural representations are textualized and their founding truth is shown to be a language effect and not objective reality (which, in the process of reading, is declared an objectivity effect).

Theory-as-play focuses not on gender relations as material social relations but on a critique of their representations. It shows how, for example, what are seen as natural gender and sexuality are performativities in/of language, and marks the incoherence of their seeming coherence by teasing out the working of tropes in these representations (Butler 2000, 2004).

Red feminism approaches theory as an explanatory critique. It is fundamentally different from theory-as-play in that theory-as-play is almost exclusively a critique of representation and, therefore, understands change as changing representations through, for example, resignification (as in Butler), remetaphorization (as in Cornell) and redescription (as in Rorty). In opposition to theory-as-play, theory-as-explanation argues that representation is always and ultimately determined by the relations of labour and capital. Social change that can transform gender relations is a matter of changing the relations of gender to class relations. For theory-as-play, culture is a linguistic chain – a staging of conflicting significations. Red feminism, in contrast, regards culture as always articulated by the social relations of production. Thus, culture is where people become aware of their objective class interests and fight it out. Culture, as E. P. Thompson puts it, is a 'way of *struggle*' not a chain of signification (1961: 33). Meaning, which is the focus of ludic feminism, is not the trajectory of nomadic signs but a social relation.

Why theory matters

Capitalist cultural politics produces a 'spontaneous' daily consciousness that perceives the social world as an assemblage of fragmented, (semi-)autonomous practices, each with its own unique and different 'cultural logic'. This is the view privileged in ludic theory in the name of honouring 'difference'. Red feminism demonstrates that the fragmentation of the social is an effect of the alienation of labour (Marx 1975). Its normalization in ludic theory (as, for example, the 'body without organs') is a response to capital's need to block any understanding of social totality that brings to the surface the fundamental contradictions of the capitalist regime – namely, the representation of the unequal exchange of wages for labour power as equal. This exchange – which is the ground of all capitalist institutions, from love to education, healthcare, imperialism and power – is mystified through cultural difference, which is valorized in ludic feminism.

Red theory is necessary for transforming gender relations. It provides a knowledge of social totality by which gender is grasped as class and feminism itself is rearticulated as a materialist theory: 'Without revolutionary theory, there can be no revolutionary movement. This idea cannot be insisted upon too strongly at a time when the fashionable preaching of opportunism goes hand in hand with an infatuation for the narrowest forms of practical activity' (Lenin 1961: 369). Ludic eclecticism – for example, in Rita Felski's *Literature after Feminism* (2003) – is a popular form of this practical opportunism now.

Agency Any mobilization of counter-hegemonic agency requires that one first theorize 'agency' itself. There is a tendency in ludic feminism to theorize agency in a pragmatic and local frame that is located in the specificity of situational actions. In other words, ludic feminism argues that all effective actions have a strong local dimension – at times it even claims that this locality is a form of materiality. However, while localizing the subject, it theorizes the subject in an unhistorical and idealist fashion. It somehow assumes that the subject, by the sheer power of its spontaneous experience, can undertake transformative action. In fact, the basis of ludic feminism's coalition politics is this idealist, but localized, subject: a subject that can enter into negotiation with other subjects and in a collaborationist mode bring about change. Change here is always a code word for opportunistic reform. This notion of agency – local, pragmatic, reformist and coalitionist – predominates in left ludic feminism.

To say it a different way: ludic feminism avoids the question of class, which is the only site of historical agency. It does so by first representing class as a dated view and then proposing, as an updated position, the subject of coalition located in identity politics. It multiplies the subject and regards this to be an emancipatory act: a feminist subject, an African-American, a Latino, and a queer subject, and so on. These isolated subjects are all masquerading as subjects of agency. Red feminism argues that a productive notion of agency has to be highly critique-al of such theories of agency which, in the final analysis, substitute lifestyle practices for class and then recognize this class-as-lifestyle as the main axis of human praxis.

This does not mean that sexuality, gender or race are not sites of struggle, but rather they are not autonomous spaces. Sexuality becomes a marker of social differences only in a class society. Race is the historical site of racism under capitalism wherein the cheap labour of the slave, the colonized and the racially different immigrant is the source of profit. In other words, although race, gender and sexuality are indeed spaces of historical agency and sites of social struggle – *they become so because of the divisions of labour and property relations (class)*. Therefore, in a world conquered by capital the *only* historical agent is the *other of capital*: the wage labourer. Any counter-hegemonic agency or human praxis that does not centre itself in this contradiction and this class antagonism will produce agency that might make the ludic writer feel empowered and enabled, but will leave the existing social practices intact. To be very clear, the route to social transformation does not pass through coalition – it is firmly centred in revolution.

Identity politics Identity politics puts forth an identity without class – one shaped by nomadic meanings of desire and experience. It is a subjectivity that does not put pressure on or threaten the existing social relations of labour. Even when the question of labour cannot be avoided – for example, in discussions of feminism and anti-racist struggles – labour becomes mostly a question of jobs and employment, that is to say, of income (e.g. 'equal pay'). But income, in and of itself, does not determine the relation of the subject of labour to the conflictual structures of labour. Income, to be more precise, can be from profit or from wages.

When the question of labour has been dealt with in ludic feminism or anti-racism, it has, for the most part, been reduced to how to increase the income of the subject – even the issue of domestic labour has been largely understood in terms of 'unpaid labour' and income for housework. Income is a matter of consumption; class is a question of production. Rarely has feminism or anti-racism struggled against the existing labour relations based on the hegemony of capital. The few exceptions have been those historical materialist feminists and anti-racists who have engaged the class constructions of gender, race and sexuality. But this work, especially in feminism in the 1970s and 1980s, has been largely cut off by the rise of ludic feminism and left identity politics.

Ludic theory grants autonomy or at least semi-autonomy to race, gender and sexuality and regards each in terms of its own assumed immanent logic, which is untranslatable into any other logic. The question therefore becomes *how* gender works, *how* race works, *how*, in effect, the cultural logic operates. The material logic of these relations – the question *why* gender works the way it does – is made marginal.

There is no immanent logic of race, gender and sexuality. There is only the single, inclusive logic of production that structures all. Most feminists, anti-racists and queer theorists have been quick to dismiss such a materialist theory by saying that the logic of labour cannot explain desire in sexuality, oppression in racism, and inequality in gender relations. However, gender, sexuality and race become social differences only when they become part of the social division of labour.

Racism, contrary to Foucauldian theory, is not simply a matter of asymmetrical power relations, nor is gender, nor is sexuality. Homophobia is not simply oppression – the exercise of power by heterosexuals over homosexuals. Gay-bashing is the articulation of violence, that is to say, the effect of power, but power cannot be understood in its own terms without inquiring into its genealogy in relation to property. Contrary to ludic theory, power is not the effect of discourse, nor is it simply the immanent condition of all relations. Power is the social and political manifestation of the ownership of the means of production. In other words, power is always generated at the point of production, and its effects should also be examined in connection to the relations of production. Racism is not simply oppression (the exercise of power by whites over blacks); sexism is not simply oppression (the exercise of power mostly by men over women). It is true that racism, sexism and homophobia are *experienced* by the subject (e.g. African-American, woman, lesbian) as effects of oppression and power. If we limit our inquiry to this experiential level, we will end up simply with ethnographies of power, which would be of very limited use. If, however, we move beyond regarding racism, sexism and homophobia as simply effects of power to understand why power is derived from ownership of the means of production, then we will be able to theorize relations of class, gender, race and sexuality in a more historical and transformative way.

Modernism/postmodernism Concepts of modernism/postmodernism and modernity/postmodernity are above all spaces of contradiction: they are concepts that have been used to come to terms with the history and shifts in cultures of capitalism. Modernity is the ensemble of all the conceptual strategies – from science to painting to music to sociology to psychoanalysis – used by the modernist subject to locate itself in the contradictions between wage-labour and capital. There are no ('modernist') styles in isolation from the historical unfolding of wage-labour and capital, from laissez-faire capitalism to monopoly capitalism.

To separate modernism from postmodernism or, for that matter, modernity from postmodernity may give the illusion of conceptual clarification and historical location, but it is eventually a species of what Marx and Engels in *The German Ideology* described as 'combating solely the phrases of this world' – that is, a politics of phrases (Marx and Engels 1976: 30). Postmodernity's various forms – in Jameson (1991), in Lyotard (1984), in Butler et al. (2000) – are all continuations of the attempt to understand capitalism without class. All of them are based, as we have already suggested, on the assumption that capitalism has changed – that there has been a fundamental structural change, a 'break' in capitalism demanding a new set of conceptual categories to understand the impact of capitalism on culture and society. The question of (post)modernity, however, is neither one of style nor of culture, because both style and culture are eventually the outcome of the primary contradictions of capitalism. Red feminism supersedes the well-worn categories of modernity/postmodernity, modernism/postmodernism, and their rehearsal in Habermas, Eagleton, Jameson and Butler, by returning to the main question. And the main question is mode of production. In place of positing that capitalism has changed, it is necessary to return to the basic issue: in what way has capitalism changed? Has the capitalism of modernity really been transformed into another capitalism (that of postmodernity) – what Jameson, borrowing Ernest Mandel's phrase, calls 'late capitalism'? Or does capitalism remain the same regime of exploitation – in which capitalists extract surplus labour from wage-earners. What has changed, as we have already argued, is not the fundamental factor of property relations, but the way that exploitation is articulated. Capitalist ontology remains the same; only its phenomenology has been modified. It is not exploitation which has been transformed – and this is the *only* index of the structure of change – but rather the *form* of exploitation has changed. If this simple 'fact' is recognized, then the whole debate about modernity/postmodernity, modernism/postmodernism turns out to be simply a politics of phrases.

In dealing with the question of history and the place of humans in history, the determining factor should not be modernity/postmodernity, but rather what cuts through the modern and the postmodern and places humans in their densely layered and complex history. *The relations of humans and history are the relations of labour.*

Referentiality Ludic theory, as we have argued, does not break free from the referent; rather it substitutes new modes and forms of reference and referentiality for those notions of the referent that have lost their historical usefulness for capitalism. To be more clear, traditional theories of the relation between language and reality (which have been the core of common notions of the referent and referentiality) were based on what might be called a 'Fordist' relation of correspondence between signifier and signified. This form of referentiality was more suitable for early industrial capitalism, the main features of which were Taylorism in management and the assembly line in production. However, with the emergence of cybertechonologies – which have brought with them new management techniques, such as plural organization and team management; substituted the post-Taylorist flexible workplace for the old Taylorist management, and opened up the labour force to women, African-Americans, Latinos and other marginalized groups – the mode of representation based on the adequation of signifier to signified has become historically irrelevant. One of the features of the new cybertechnologies is hypertextuality and pluralization of the sign. The sign – which in Fordist industrialism worked to a very large extent on mostly a single level – has become subject to various forms of doubling and self-referentiality, the effect of which is what Baudrillard calls 'simulation' and 'simulacra' (1994).

The fact that signs have become plural and the relations between signifier and signified have become relations of relays within relays does not mean the referent is lost. The referent, in response to social relations, has become plural. A new red theory of reference is needed. In reobtaining a more socially effective referent for language, we think the referent can be retheorized through *Capital*, specifically Chapter 10 in the first volume, in which Marx explicates labour in the working day. In brief, the discussion of the working day provides a very effective frame for establishing a theory of reference in which language is once again put in a relation of materiality to history in the form of labour. The new theory of reference should thus be based on a labour theory of language, which shows how meaning is a social relation.

'End of ideology' In left ludic theory, especially in the work of Ernesto Laclau and Chantal Mouffe, ideology is seen as undergoing a 'break'. In their writings, Laclau and Mouffe, through a heavy reliance on Lacan and Althusser, have erased the materialist theory of ideology articulated in Marx and Engels' *The German Ideology* and more emphatically reiterated in Marx's *Capital*. In order to dramatize the break, they have reduced the classical Marxist theory of ideology to a simple 'false consciousness' and have represented Althusserian and post-Althusserian views as groundbreaking conceptual feats. Ideology after this 'break' has become a generalized representation from which no one can escape and in which everyone is condemned to live their (social) life. One of the consequences of such a notion of ideology, of course, has been its erasure of the rigid clarity of class antagonisms.

Ideology has a very specific and materialist meaning in red feminism. In various chapters of the first volume of *Capital*, Marx explains the process by which the worker exchanges his or her labour-power for wages. In Chapter 10, he explains the precise mechanism of the working day during which the worker produces the equivalent of his wages and also surplus labour. In Chapter 6, he theorizes the difference between labour and labour-power and concludes that labour-power is that particular 'commodity whose use-value possesses the peculiar property of being a source of value, whose actual consumption is therefore itself an objectification of labour, hence a creation of value' (Marx 1976: 270). The exchange, he concludes, between the capitalist and the worker, is an exchange of labour-power for wages. This exchange is represented in bourgeois theory as a free, unfettered and equal exchange. In fact, at the end of Chapter 6, Marx makes a point of dwelling on this 'free-trader *vulgaris*' view of the exchange of wages for labour-power and concludes that it is anything but an equal exchange: it leaves the worker, Marx notes, 'like someone who has brought his own hide to market and now has nothing else to expect but – a tanning' (ibid.: 280).

The red feminist concept of ideology seeks to account for the representations of this exchange as an equal and fair exchange. This is the core of the red theory of ideology: how the relation between wage-labour and capital is represented as free and equal when it is anything but (it is 'a tanning'). False consciousness is a concept by which a materialist understanding marks the consciousness that regards this exchange to be an exchange among equals conducted in freedom. It is a false consciousness because it explains the material by the cultural (e.g. legal discourse). It thus sees the exchange as unfettered and non-coerced when, in fact, as Marx himself argues, this exchange takes place under 'the silent compulsion of economic relations' – a compulsion that 'sets the seal on the domination of the capitalist over the worker' (ibid.: 899). False consciousness is the consciousness that accepts the exchange of wages for labour-power as equal.

Essentialism Ludic feminism puts essentialism and anti-essentialism at the centre of contemporary gender theory. This move translates social struggle and its materialist understanding into epistemology. To translate social struggle – which is always over surplus labour – into epistemology is to reiterate a Hegelian move, at the core of which is the explanation of history by ideas rather than by labour. Therefore, any materialist theory that insists on the primacy of labour over ideas, the primacy of materiality over spectrality, is bound to be seen by ludic theory as essentialist. All cultural theory accounts for the way practices are mediated through innumerable cultural series. Yet any theory that understands practices and their cultural series as ultimately rooted in human labour is cast as 'essentialist'. On the other hand, to insist that such an accounting should always already be anti-essentialist – that is, to always only deal with specific situationalist practices – is to reify micro-politics and to cut off the relation between micro-politics and its underlying global logic of production. To put it another way, the ludic feminist debate on essentialism/anti-essentialism is a debate that eventually aims at severing the relation between the local and the global by positing the global as an essentialist, totalizing abstraction. Doing so blurs class lines and puts in place of class itself a series of fragmented, seemingly autonomous identities (race, gender, sexuality) – it marginalizes human solidarity, which is based on collective labour practices.

The intellectual The genealogy of the new intellectual begins with Foucault's statement in his interview 'Truth and power' in which he contests the notion of the universal intellectual with the idea of the specific intellectual. The specific intellectual, in contrast with the universal intellectual, is one who always works on the micro level and produces specific knowledges. She does not suffer from the illusion of any grand narratives, such as of human emancipation. For Foucault, it is unethical to make such grand gestures when one can engage specific issues in specific contexts. In his conversation with Gilles Deleuze, Foucault elaborates on his idea of the intellectual and intellectual practice by stating that the function of such an intellectual is essentially to enable the oppressed to find their voices and to be able to speak for themselves (Foucault 1977b: 205–17).

The notion of the specific intellectual has undergone a number of redescriptions in contemporary theory, and one of its more widely recognized forms is the idea of the new 'public intellectual'. A public intellectual is a person who is able to bridge the gap between academic disciplinary knowledge and larger public concerns. Both Foucault and contemporary theorists, who in response to him have focused on the public intellectual, are of course influenced by Gramsci and his notion of the role of the intellectual. The question of what constitutes an intellectual is not simply a matter of fixing an identity or prescribing a set of tasks (as Foucault and contemporary theorists all do). The role of the intellectual is most clearly marked by the Marxist tradition in which the intellectual is the person whose work is aimed at producing a theoretical consciousness. Theoretical consciousness in red feminism draws on Lenin's argument and its restatement by Lukács. Lenin regards this function – the production of a theoretical consciousness – to be so important that he writes: 'without revolutionary theory there can be no revolutionary movement. This idea cannot be insisted upon too strongly at a time when the fashionable preaching of opportunism goes hand in hand with an infatuation for the narrowest forms of practical activity' (Lenin 1961: 369). Lenin eliminates the artificial difference between the worker and the theorist. He argues that the worker is a theorist. Gramsci, of course, echoes Lenin when he talks about the role of common sense and philosophers. It is useful to quote at some length from Lenin's statement in *What is to be Done?*, because it clarifies the relation of the theorist and society, and the intellectual and the proletariat; it also sheds further light on the question of theory itself. Lenin writes:

> This does not mean, of course, that the workers have no part in creating a [socialist] ideology. They take part, however, not as workers but as socialist theoreticians, as Proudhons and Weitlings; in other words, they take part only when they are able, and to the extent that they are able, more or less, to acquire the knowledge of their age and develop that knowledge. But in order that working men [and women] may succeed in this more often, every effort must be made to raise the level of the consciousness of the workers in general; it is necessary that the workers do not confine themselves to the artificially restricted limits of 'literature for workers' but that they learn to an increasing degree to master general literature [i.e. theory]. It would be even truer to say 'are not confined,' instead of 'do not confine themselves,' because the workers themselves wish to read and do read all that is written for the intelligentsia, and only a few (bad) intellectuals believe that it is enough 'for workers' to be told a few things about factory conditions and to have repeated to them over and over again what has long been known. (Ibid.: 384)

Invoking Lenin's concept of the theorist-intellectual here may seem quite counterproductive given the extreme antagonism of ludic feminism to Lenin. It is thus necessary to address the relation of feminists, sexual theorists and Lenin. For bourgeois feminists, Lenin is the symbol of patriarchal oppression. This common antagonistic disdain for Lenin comes both from the widespread demonization of Lenin in bourgeois ideology and from a very basic and widely circulated misreading of Lenin by feminists – most notably of two of his letters to Inessa Armand (Lenin 1974). These letters are commonly taken as proof of Lenin's oppressive patriarchal and puritanical indifference to women's concerns and sexuality: specifically the issue of 'freedom of love' and his critique of feminist intellectual work – Armand's proposed pamphlet for proletarian women on love, marriage and the family. But such a reading of Lenin is quite ahistorical – it ignores the actual historical situation of Armand's work and Lenin's writing – and is blind to the fundamental erasure of class and bourgeois bias in feminism itself. Lenin is raising here the very basic question of class that feminists and sexual theorists, in nearly all their forms, have largely suppressed – what Lenin calls the 'objective logic of class relations in affairs of love' (ibid.: 39) as opposed to 'subjectively' understanding 'love' and sexuality as Armand and most feminists propose. Lenin critiques the notion of 'freedom of love' by enumerating a series of materialist understandings of the concept against the prevalent bourgeois notions dominant in the 'top-prominent classes' (ibid.: 38–9). He then argues that it will be the dominant bourgeois ideology which will prevail, resulting in misinterpretations of Armand's argument. In short, he is not suppressing Armand's project but critique-ally supporting it and, through a patient pedagogy, attempting to help Armand protect her project from the reality of bourgeois distortions that will 'tear out of it phrases … [to] misinterpret you' – that is, misinterpret the class distinctions and objective class realities of the conditions of sexuality as well as misinterpret the material needs of proletariat women *for sexuality free from material constraints*, as opposed to bourgeois demands for the *exercise of desire free from moral constraints*. This is a distinction that continues to be lost on feminist and sexual theorists today, and the continued antagonism towards Lenin's patient, but critique-al, pedagogy says considerably more about feminist intellectuals' own inability to engage critique and the class limits of their own understanding than it does about Lenin.

Totality In ludic theory, totality is either rejected in the name of pragmatism (which is sometimes called 'practice') or equated with totalization. Pragmatism's operational definition of truth – 'the true is the name of whatever proves itself to be good in the way of belief, and good, too, for definite, assignable reasons' – makes it difficult to argue for a post-capitalist society that would be inclusive in its economic access and its political and cultural freedoms. In other words, a pragmatist approach to truth will return us to a misrecognition of the relation of labour and capital (James 1974: 59). A pragmatist approach would have to say that such a relation is acceptable and truthful because, on the practical level, it works. It seems to us that any theorization of totality has to be very critique-al of such pragmatism and its various versions in ludic theory. The version of pragmatism that we just paraphrased is one developed most notably by Richard Rorty (1989). But Lyotard also puts forth a version of pragmatist social theory in his *Just Gaming* and *The Differend*. Lyotard's social theory takes as its point of departure his closing statement in *The Postmodern Condition*: 'Let us wage a war on totality; let us be witnesses to the unpresentable' (Lyotard 1984: 82). Lyotardian anti-totality social theory eventually leads to a notion of indeterminate judgement – that is to say, a judgement that is not based on any foundation of truth. This Lyotardian theory becomes the paradigm of ludic jurisprudence in which justice is separated from truth because truth is by definition a totalization, and justice has to attend to the 'differend', the 'unpresentable' and the untranslatable.

In contrast to a Rortyian anti-totality pragmatism and the Lyotardian 'differend' (judgement without truth), a more productive way to deal with totality is found in Lukács' writings. (One needs to be very careful, however, about Lukács' Hegelian idealism.) Lukács argues, in *History and Class Consciousness*, that bourgeois thought is by its very constitution detotalized and deotalizing: it is a fragmentary mode of knowing. This fragmentary consciousness he calls 'false consciousness'. Our point here is not to critique the way Lukács theorizes false consciousness, but rather to focus on what he proposes as the *other* of bourgeois thought: 'the relation to society as a whole' (Lukács 1983: 51). Totality is far from being an abstraction that forgets about specific differences – it is a concrete recognition of the diverse relations that produce the social. However, as Lukács insists and, of course, as Marx himself has indicated in his 'Introduction' to *Grundrisse*, the concrete of the totality is not identical with the empirical and the individual; the concrete 'is a concentration of many determinations, hence a unity of the diverse' (Marx 1973: 101). For Lukács, it is only by arriving at knowledge of society as a whole that it 'becomes possible to infer the thoughts and feelings which men would have in a particular situation if they were able to assess both it and the interests arising from it in their impact on immediate action and on the whole structure of society' (Lukács 1983: 51).

In theorizing social totality, red feminism shows how the particularities of gender and sexuality are specificities of class relations – as are the differences in feminism. The binary of ludic and red feminism is the rearticulation of the class binary, which is itself the outcome of the social relations of production.

References

Baudrillard, J. (1994) *Simulacra and Simulation*, Ann Arbor: University of Michigan Press.

Benhabib, S., J. Butler, D. Cornell and N. Fraser (1995) *Feminist Contentions: A Philosophical Exchange*, New York: Routledge.

Bennholdt-Thomsen, V. and M. Mies (2000) *The Subsistence Perspective: Beyond the Globalized Economy*, London: Zed Books.

Butler, J. (1991) 'Imitation and gender insubordination', in D. Fuss (ed.), *Inside/Out: Lesbian Theories, Gay Theories*, New York: Routledge, pp. 13–31.

— (2000) *Antigone's Claim: Kinship between Life and Death*, New York: Columbia University Press.

— (2004) *Undoing Gender*, New York: Routledge.

Butler, J., E. Laclau and S. Žižek (2000) *Contingency, Hegemony, Universality*, London: Verso.

Disch, L. (1999) 'Deconstructing "capitalism"', *Theory and Event*, 3(1).

Ebert, T. L. (1996) *Ludic Feminism and After: Postmodernism, Desire and Labor in Late Capitalism*, Ann Arbor: University of Michigan Press.

— (2009) *The Task of Cultural Critique*, Urbana: University of Illinois Press.

Felski, R. (2003) *Literature after Feminism*, Chicago, IL: University of Chicago Press.

Foucault, M. (1977a) *Language, Counter Memory, Practice*, ed. D. E. Bouchard, Ithaca, NY: Cornell University Press.

— (1977b) 'Truth and power', in C. Gordon (ed.), *Power/Knowledge: Selected Interviews and Other Writings 1972–1977*, New York: Pantheon, pp. 109–33.

Gallop, J. (2002) *Anecdotal Theory*, Durham, NC: Duke University Press.

Gibson-Graham, J. K. (2006a) *The End of Capitalism (As We Knew It): A Feminist Critique of Political Economy*, Minneapolis: University of Minnesota Press.

— (2006b) *A Postcapitalist Politics*, Minneapolis: University of Minnesota Press.

Gilder, G. (1989) *Microcosm: The Quantum Revolution in Economics and Technology*, New York: Simon and Schuster.

Gramsci, A. (1985) *Selections from Cultural Writings*, ed. D. F. Forgacs and G. Nowell-Smith, Cambridge, MA: Harvard University Press.

Grosz, E. (1994) *Volatile Bodies: Toward a Corporeal Feminism*, Bloomington: Indiana University Press.

Harvey, D. (2005) *A Brief History of Neoliberalism*, Oxford: Oxford University Press.
James, W. (1974) 'What pragmatism means', in *Pragmatism and Four Essays from the Meaning of Truth*, New York: New American Library.
Jameson, F. (1991) *Postmodernism or, The Cultural Logic of Late Capitalism*, Durham, NC: Duke University Press.
Kristof, N. D. (2006) 'In praise of the maligned sweatshop', *New York Times*, 6 June, p. A21.
Laclau, E. and C. Mouffe (1985) *Hegemony and Socialist Strategy*, London: Verso.
Lenin, V. I. (1961) *What is to be Done?*, in *V. I. Lenin Collected Works*, vol. 5, Moscow: Foreign Languages Publishing House, pp. 347–529.
— (1974) *On the Emancipation of Women*, 4th revised edn, Moscow: Progress.
Lukács, G. (1983) *History and Class Consciousness*, Cambridge, MA: MIT Press.
Lyotard, J.-F. (1984) *The Postmodern Condition*, Minneapolis: University of Minnesota Press.
— (1988a) *The Differend*, Minneapolis: University of Minnesota Press.
— (1988b) *Just Gaming*, Minneapolis: University of Minnesota Press.
Marcus, S. (1992) 'Fighting bodies, fighting words: a theory and politics of rape prevention', in J. Butler and J. Scott (eds), *Feminists Theorize the Political*, New York: Routledge, pp. 385–403.
Marx, K. (1973) *Grundrisse*, London: Penguin.
— (1975) *Economic and Philosophic Manuscripts of 1844*, in *Karl Marx Frederick Engels: Collected Works*, vol. 3, New York: International, pp. 229–443.
— (1976) *Capital*, vol. 1, trans. B. Fowkes, New York: Penguin.
Marx, K. and F. Engels (1976) *The German Ideology*, in *Karl Marx Frederick Engels: Collected Works*, vol. 5, New York: International, pp. 19–539.
Mies, M. and V. Shiva (1993) *Ecofeminism*, London: Zed Books.
Peters, T. (1992) *Liberation Management*, New York: Fawcett Columbine.
Probyn, E. (2005) *Blush: Faces of Shame*, Minneapolis: University of Minnesota Press.
Rorty, R. (1989) *Contingency, Irony, and Solidarity*, Cambridge: Cambridge University Press.
Spivak, G. C. and D. Plotke (1994) 'A dialogue on democracy', *Socialist Review*, 94: 1–22.
Thompson, E. P. (1961) 'The long revolution', *New Left Review*, 1: 24–39.

RECOMMENDED READING

Adlam, D. (1978) 'The case against capitalist patriarchy', *m/f*, 1(3): 83–102.

Adler, G., P. Hudis and A. Laschitza (eds) (2011) *The Letters of Rosa Luxemburg*, trans. G. Shriver, London: Verso.

Ahmed, L. (1982) 'Feminism and feminist movements in the Middle East: a preliminary exploration: Turkey, Egypt, Algeria, People's Democratic Republic of Yemen', *Women's Studies International Forum*, 5(2): 153–68.

Allman, P. (2007) *On Marx: An Introduction to the Revolutionary Intellect of Karl Marx*, Rotterdam: Sense.

Andermahr, S., T. Lovell and C. Wolkowitz (2000) *A Glossary of Feminist Theory*, New York: Oxford University Press.

Andreev, I. L. (1985) *Engels' 'The Origin of the Family, Private Property and the State'*, Moscow: Progress.

Andrijasevic, R., C. Hamilton and C. Hemmings (eds) (2014) *Feminist Review: Revolutions*, Hampshire: Palgrave Macmillan.

Bakan, A. and S. Smith (2013) 'Marxism, feminism and the fight for liberation', SocialistWorker.org, 10 July, socialistworker.org/2013/07/10/marxism-feminism-and-womens-liberation.

Bamforth, N. and D. A. J. Richards (2008) *Patriarchal Religion, Sexuality, and Gender: A Critique of New Natural Law*, Cambridge: Cambridge University Press.

Bannerji, H. (1995) *Thinking Through: Essays on Feminism, Marxism and Anti-Racism*, Toronto: Women's Press.

— (1995) 'But who speaks for us? Experience and agency in conventional feminist paradigms', in *Thinking Through: Essays on Feminism, Marxism and Anti-Racism*, Toronto: Women's Press, pp. 55–95.

— (2001) *Inventing Subjects: Studies in Hegemony, Patriarchy, and Colonialism*, New Delhi: Tulika.

— (2011) *Demography and Democracy: Essays on Nationalism, Gender and Ideology*, Toronto: Canadian Scholars' Press.

Barrett, M. (1980) *Women's Oppression Today: Problems in Marxist Feminist Analysis*, London: Verso.

— (1988) *Women's Oppression Today: The Marxist/Feminist Encounter*, Revised edn, London: Verso.

Beneria, L. (1989) 'Capitalism and socialism: some feminist questions', in S. Kruks, R. Rapp and M. B. Young (eds), *Promissory Notes: Women in the Transition to Socialism*, New York: Monthly Review Press, pp. 325–32.

Benhabib, S., J. Butler, D. Cornell and N. Fraser (eds) (1995) *Feminist Contentions: A Philosophical Exchange*, London: Routledge.

Biewener, C. (1999) 'A postmodern encounter: poststructuralist feminism and the decentering of Marxism', *Socialist Review*, 27(1/2): 71–96.

Brown, H. A. (2012) *Marx on Gender and the Family: A Critical Study*, Historical Materialism Series, vol. 39, Leiden: Brill.

Brown, N. (2008) 'Marxism and disability', *Mediations*, 23(2): 186–93.

Bruegel, I. (1978) 'Bourgeois economics and women's oppression', *m/f* 1(1): 104–11.

Burstyn, V. and D. E. Smith (1985) *Women, Class, Family and the State*, Toronto: Garamond.

Chattopadhyay, P. (2001) 'Marx on women's question', *Economic and Political Weekly*, 36(26): 2455–7.

Cotter, J. (2003) 'The class regimen of contemporary feminism', *The Red Critique*, www.redcritique.org/Spring2003/theclassregimenofcontemporaryfeminism.htm.

Coward, R. (1983) *Patriarchal Precedents: Sexuality and Social Relations*, London: Routledge and Kegan Paul.

Davies, A. (1983) *Women, Race and Class*, New York: Vintage.

Davies, C. B. (2007) *Left of Karl Marx: The Political Life of Black Communist Claudia Jones*, Durham, NC: Duke University Press.

Davies, M. (ed.) (1983) *Third World Second Sex: Women's Struggles and National Liberation*, London: Zed Books.

De Angelis, M. (2001) 'Marx and primitive accumulation: the continuous character of capital's enclosures', *The Commoner*, 2(1), www.commoner.org.uk/02deangelis.pdf.

De Beauvoir, S. (1957) *The Long March: An Account of Modern China*, trans. A. Wainhouse, London: Phoenix.

Draper, H. (2011) *Women and Class: Towards a Socialist Feminism*, ed. E. Haberkern, Alameda, CA: Center for Socialist History.

Draper, H. and A. G. Lipow (1976) 'Marxist women *versus* bourgois feminism', *Socialist Register 1976*, London: Merlin, pp. 179–226.

Duran, L. A., N. D. Payne and A. Russo (eds) (2007) *Building Feminist Movements and Organizations: Global Perspectives*, London: Zed Books.

Ebert, T. L. (1996) *Ludic Feminism and After: Postmodernism, Desire, and Labor in Late Capitalism*, Ann Arbor: University of Michigan Press.

— (2005) 'Rematerializing feminism', *Science & Society*, 69(1): 33–55.

Ebert, T. L. and M. Zavarzadeh (2008) *Class in Culture*, London: Paradigm.

Ehrenreich, B. (2005) 'What is socialist feminism?', *Monthly Review*, 57(3): 70–7.

Eisenstein, H. (2009) *Feminism Seduced: How Global Elites Use Women's Labor and Ideas to Exploit the World*, London: Paradigm.

Eisenstein, Z. R. (1979) *Capitalist Patriarchy and the Case for Socialist Feminism*, London: Monthly Review Press.

— (1981) *The Radical Future of Liberal Feminism*, New York: Longman.

Ennew, J. (1978) 'The patriarchal puzzle', *m/f*, 1(2): 71–84.

Epstein, B. (2001) 'What happened to the women's movement?', *Monthly Review*, 53(1): 1–13.

Evans, J., J. Hills, K. Hunt, E. Meehan, T. ten Tusscher, U. Vogel and G. Waylen (eds) (1986) *Feminism and Political Theory*, London: Sage.

Federici, S. (2000) 'War, globalization, and reproduction', *Peace & Change*, 25(2): 153–65.

— (2004) 'The great Caliban: the struggle against the rebel body', *Capitalism Nature Socialism*, 15(2): 7–16.

— (2004) *Caliban and the Witch*, Brooklyn, NY: Autonomedia.

— (2004) 'Women, land-struggles and globalization: an international perspective', *Journal of Asian and African Studies*, 39(1/2): 47–62.

— (2012) *Revolution at Point Zero: Housework, Reproduction, and Feminist Struggle*, Oakland, CA: PM.

Federici, S. and G. Caffentzis (2014) 'Commons against and beyond capitalism', *Community Development Journal*, 49(1): 92–105.

Feldman, S., C. Geisler and G. A. Menon (eds) (2011) *Accumulating Insecurity: Violence and Dispossession in the Making of Everyday Life*, London: University of Georgia Press.

Ferguson, A. (2004) 'Feminist perspectives on class and work', in *Stanford*

Encyclopedia of Philosophy, Stanford, CA: Stanford University Press, plato.stanford.edu/entries/feminism-class/.

Firestone, S. (1971) *The Dialectic of Sex: The Case for Feminist Revolution*, New York: Bantam.

Foord, J. and N. Gregson (1986) 'Patriarchy: towards a reconceptualization', *Antipode*, 18(2): 186–211.

Fortunati, L. (1995) *The Arcane of Reproduction: Housework, Prostitution, Labor and Capital*, Brooklyn, NY: Autonomedia.

Fraser, N. (2003) 'From discipline to flexibilization? Rereading Foucault in the shadow of globalization', *Constellations*, 10(2): 160–71.

— (2009) 'Feminism, capitalism and the cunning of history', *New Left Review*, 56(2): 97–117.

— (2013) *Fortunes of Feminism: From State-managed Capitalism to Neoliberal Crisis*, New York: Verso.

German, L. (1981) 'Theories of patriarchy', *International Socialism*, 2(12), www.isj.org.uk/?id=240.

— (1989) *Sex, Class and Socialism*, London: Bookmarks.

— (2007) *Material Girls: Women, Men and Work*, London: Bookmarks.

— (2012) *A People's History of London*, London: Verso.

— (2013) *How a Century of War Changed the Lives of Women*, London: Pluto.

Gimenez, M. E. (1998) 'Marxist/materialist feminism', *Feminist Theory*, www.cddc.vt.edu/feminism/mar.html.

— (2005) 'Capitalism and the oppression of women: Marx revisited', *Science & Society*, 69(1): 11–32.

Gimenez, M. and L. Vogel (2005) 'Marxist-feminist thought today', *Science & Society*, 69(1): 5–10.

Gingrich, A. (2003) 'Feminist social theory', leroy.cc.uregina.ca/gingrich/319m1703.htm.

Guettel, C. (1974) *Marxism and Feminism*, Toronto: Canadian Women's Educational Press.

Hanson, K. V. and I. J. Philipson (eds) (1990) *Women, Class, and the Feminist Imagination: A Socialist-feminist Reader*, Philadelphia, PA: Temple University Press.

Haraway, D. J. (1991) '"Gender" for a Marxist dictionary: the sexual politics of a word', in D. J. Haraway (ed.), *Simians, Cyborgs, and Women: The Reinvention of Women*, London: Free Association Books, pp. 127–48.

Hartsock, N. C. M. (1998) *The Feminist Standpoint Revisited and Other Essays*, Feminist Theory and Politics Series, Boulder, CO: Westview.

— (2004) 'Women and/as commodities: a brief meditation', *Canadian Woman Studies*, 23(3/4): 14–17.

Heitlinger, A. (1979) *Women and State Socialism: Sex Inequality in the Soviet Union and Czechoslovakia*, London: Macmillan.

— (1980) 'Marxism, feminism, and sex equality', in T. Yedlin (ed.), *Women in Eastern Europe and the Soviet Union*, New York: Praeger, pp. 9–20.

Hennessy, R. (2001) 'The challenge: from anti-capitalism to class consciousness', *Socialist Review*, 28(3/4): 81–92.

Holmstrom, N. (2003) 'The socialist feminist project', *Monthly Review*, 54(10), monthlyreview.org/2003/03/01/the-socialist-feminist-project/.

Hudis, P. (2010) 'Accumulation, imperialism, and pre-capitalist formations: Luxemburg and Marx on the non-western world', *Socialist Studies/Études Socialistes*, 6(2): 75–91.

Hunt, K. (1986) 'Crossing the river of fire: the socialist construction of women's politicization', in J. Evans et al. (eds), *Feminism and Political Theory*, London: Sage, pp. 47–65.

Incite! Women of Color against Violence (ed.) (2007) *The Revolution Will Not be Funded: Beyond the Non-profit*

Industrial Complex, Cambridge, MA: South End.

Jackson, S. (2001) 'Why a materialist feminism is (still) possible – and necessary', *Women's International Forum*, 24(3/4): 283–93.

James, S. (2012) *Sex, Race and Class: The Perspective of Winning: A Selection of Writings 1952–2011*, Oakland, CA: PM.

Jayawardena, K. and M. de Alwis (eds) (1996) *Embodied Violence: Communalizing Women's Sexuality in South Asia*, London: Zed Books.

Kabeer, N. (1994) *Reversed Realities: Gender Hierarchies in Development Thought*, London: Verso.

Kelly, G. (1992) *Revolutionary Feminism: The Mind and Career of Mary Wollstonecraft*, London: Macmillan.

Keohane, O. N., M. Z. Rosaldo and B. C. Gelpi (1982) *Feminist Theory: A Critique of Ideology*, Chicago, IL: University of Chicago Press.

Klotz, M. (2006) 'Alienation, labor, and sexuality in Marx's 1844 manuscripts', *Rethinking Marxism*, 18(3): 405–13.

Kuhn, A. and A. Wolpe (1978) *Feminism and Materialism: Women and Modes of Production*, London: Routledge and Kegan Paul.

Landes, J. B. (1989) 'Marxism and the "woman question"', in S. Kruks, R. Rapp and M. B. Young (eds), *Promissory Notes: Women in the Transition to Socialism*, New York: Monthly Review Press, pp. 15–28.

Lee, E. (1996) 'Marxism and feminist theory', in S. Wolton (ed.), *Marxism, Mysticism, and Modern Theory*, Oxford: Palgrave Macmillan.

Lerner, G. (1993) *The Creation of Feminist Consciousness: From the Middle Ages to Eighteen-seventy*, Oxford: Oxford University Press.

Luxton, M. (1985) *Feminist Marxism or Marxist Feminism: A Debate*, Toronto: Garamond.

Macdonald, L. (1997) *Feminism and Socialism: Putting the Pieces Together*, 2nd edn, New South Wales: Resistance Books.

MacKinnon, C. A. (1989) *Toward a Feminist Theory of the State*, Cambridge, MA: Harvard University Press.

Martin, G. (1986) *Socialist Feminism: The First Decade 1966–76*, Intro. K. Brodine, Seattle, WA: Freedom Socialist Publications.

Massel, G. J. (1974) *The Surrogate Proletariat: Moslem Women and Revolutionary Strategies in Soviet Central Asia, 1919–1929*, Princeton, NJ: Princeton University Press.

McNally, D. (1998) 'Gender, race, class and socialism: an interview with Himani Bannerji', *New Socialist*, 3(1): 12–14.

Melamed, J. (2011) *Represent and Destroy: Rationalizing Violence in the New Racial Capitalism*, Minneapolis: University of Minnesota Press.

Midgley, C. (ed.) (1998) *Gender and Imperialism: Studies in Imperialism*, Manchester: Manchester University Press.

Mies, M. (1986) *Patriarchy and Accumulation on a World Scale: Women in the International Division of Labour*, London: Zed Books.

— (2014) 'No commons without a community', *Community Development Journal*, 49(1): 106–17.

Mies, M., V. Bennholdt-Thomsen and C. von Werlhof (eds) (1988) *Women: The Last Colony*, London: Zed Books.

Miliband, R. and J. Saville (eds) (1983) *Socialist Register 1983: A Survey of Movements and Ideas*, London: Merlin.

Mitchell, J. and A. Oakley (eds) (1975) *The Rights and Wrongs of Women*, Harmondsworth: Penguin.

— (eds) (1986) *What is Feminism?*, New York: Pantheon.

Mohanty, C. T., R. L. Riley and M. Bruce Pratt (eds) (2008) *Feminism and War:*

Confronting US Imperialism, London: Zed Books.

Mojab, S. (1997) 'Crossing the boundaries of nationalism: the struggle for a Kurdish women's studies', *Canadian Woman Studies*, 17(2): 68–72.

— (2001) 'New resources for revolutionary critical education', *Convergence*, 34(1): 118–25.

Molyneux, M. and D. L. Steinberg (1995) 'Mies and Shiva's "ecofeminism": a new testament?', *Feminist Review*, (49): 86–107.

Nicholson, L. J. (1986) *Gender and History: The Limits of Social Theory and the Age of the Family*, New York: Columbia University Press.

Orr, J. (2010) 'Marxism and feminism today', *International Socialism*, 127, www.isj.org.uk/?id=656.

Page, M. (1978) 'Socialist feminism – a political alternative?', *m/f* 1(2): 32–42.

Phillips, A. (ed.) (1987) *Feminism and Equality*, New York: New York University Press.

— (2013) *Our Bodies, Whose Property?*, Princeton, NJ: Princeton University Press.

Ramazanoglu, C. (1989) *Feminism and the Contradictions of Oppression*, New York: Routledge.

Roberts, J. (2010) 'The state, empire and imperialism', *Current Sociology*, 58(6): 833–58.

Roman, L. G. (1993) 'Double exposure: the politics of feminist materialist ethnography', *Educational Theory*, 43(3): 279–308.

Rowbotham, S. (1974) *Women, Resistance and Revolution: A History of Women and Revolution in the Modern World*, New York: Vintage.

— (1992) *Women in Movement: Feminism and Social Action*, London: Routledge.

Rowbotham, S., L. Segal and H. Wainwright (2013) *Beyond the Fragments: Feminism and the Making of Socialism*, London: Merlin.

Sanghatana, S. S. (1989) *'We were Making History': Women and the Telangana Uprising*, London: Zed Books.

Schmidt, I. (2010) 'Rosa Luxemburg's "accumulation of capital": new perspectives on capitalist development and American hegemony', *Socialist Studies/Études Socialistes*, 6(2): 92–117.

Scott, H. C. (2010) 'Rosa Luxemburg's "reform or revolution" in the twenty-first century', *Socialist Studies/Études Socialistes*, 6(2): 118–40.

Slaughter, J. M. (1979) 'Feminism and socialism: theoretical debates in historical perspective', *Marxist Perspectives*, 2: 32–49.

Smith, A. (2005) *Conquest: Sexual Violence and American Indian Genocide*, Cambridge, MA: South End.

Smith, D. E. (1974) 'Theorizing as ideology', in R. Turner (ed.), *Ethnomethodology: Selected Readings*, Harmondsworth: Penguin, pp. 41–4.

— (1977) *Feminism and Marxism: A Place to Begin, a Way to Go*, Vancouver: New Star.

— (1983) 'Women, class and family', *Socialist Register 1983*, London: Merlin, pp. 1–44.

— (1990) 'The ideological practice of sociology', in *The Conceptual Practices of Power: A Feminist Sociology of Knowledge*, Northeastern Series in Feminist Theory, Boston, MA: Northeastern University Press, pp. 31–60.

— (ed.) (1990) *The Conceptual Practices of Power: A Feminist Sociology of Knowledge*, Northeastern Series in Feminist Theory, Boston, MA: Northeastern University Press.

— (2004) 'Ideology, science and social relations: a reinterpretation of Marx's epistemology', *European Journal of Social Theory*, 7(4): 445–62.

Smith, S. (2014) 'Women's liberation: the Marxist tradition', *International Socialist Review*, 93: 19–40.

— (2014) *Women and Socialism: Essays*

on Women's Liberation, Revised edn, Chicago, IL: Haymarket.

Sneed, M. (2010) 'Review of Roland Boer and Jorunn Økland, eds, *Marxist Feminist Criticism of the Bible*', *The Bible and Critical Theory*, 6(2): 1–3, novaojs.newcastle.edu.au/ojsbct/index.php/bct/article/view/320/303.

Stacey, J. (1983) *Patriarchy and Socialist Revolution in China*, Berkeley and Los Angeles: University of California Press.

Stites, R. (1978) *The Women's Liberation Movement in Russia: Feminism, Nihilism and Bolshevism 1860–1930*, Princeton, NJ: Princeton University Press.

Sutherland, K. (2005) 'Marx and MacKinnon: the promise and perils of Marxism for feminist legal theory', *Science & Society*, 69(1): 113–32.

Tétreault, M. A. (1994) *Women and Revolution in Africa, Asia, and the New World*, Columbia: University of South Carolina Press.

Thom, D. (2000) 'Marxism', in L. Code (ed.), *Encyclopedia of Feminist Theories*, London: Routledge, pp. 450–3.

Trincado, E. (2010) 'The current relevance of Rosa Luxemburg's thought', *Socialist Studies/Études Socialistes*, 6(2): 141–59.

Uppal, J. (2005) 'Teach feminist: pedagogy, politics, and process in women's studies', *Cultural Studies/Critical Methodologies*, 5(1): 30–44.

Van der Veen, M. (2001) 'Rethinking commodification and prostitution: an effort at peacemaking in the battles over prostitution', *Rethinking Marxism*, 13(2): 30–51.

Vogel, L. (2013) *Marxism and the Oppression of Women: Toward a Unitary Theory*, ed. S. Ferguson and D. McNally, Chicago, IL: Haymarket.

Von Werlhof, C. (2007) 'No critique of capitalism without a critique of patriarchy! Why the left is no alternative', *Capitalism Nature Socialism*, 18(1): 13–27.

Walby, S. (2011) *The Future of Feminism*, Malden, MA: Polity.

Weeks, J. (2011) 'Un-/re-productive maternal labor: Marxist feminism and Chapter Fifteen of Marx's Capital', *Rethinking Marxism*, 23(1): 31–40.

Weeks, K. (2011) *The Problem with Work: Feminism, Marxism, Antiwork Politics, and Postwork Imaginaries*, London: Duke University Press.

Weigand, K. (2001) *Red Feminism: American Communism and the Making of Women's Liberation*, Baltimore, MD: Johns Hopkins University Press.

Yelvington, K. A. (2010) 'The making of a Marxist-feminist-Latin Americanist anthropologist: an interview with Helen I. Safa', *Caribbean Studies*, 38(2): 3–32.

ABOUT THE AUTHORS

Delia D. Aguilar, now retired and an adjunct faculty member at the University of Connecticut, held tenured appointments in the women's and ethnic studies departments of Bowling Green State University and Washington State University. She was Irwin Chair of Women's Studies at Hamilton College (2008–09) and held a fellowship at the Bunting Institute of Radcliffe College (1992). She has also taught at the University of the Philippines and St. Scholastica's College in Manila. She has a history of engagement in encounters involving the women's movements in the Philippines and the United States, an engagement that continues to inform her work and thinking.

Himani Bannerji is a professor in the Department of Sociology at York University, Toronto. Her research and writing life extends between Canada and India. Her interests encompass anti-racist feminism, Marxism, critical cultural theories, and historical sociology. Publications include *Demography and Democracy: Essays on Nationalism, Gender and Ideology* (2011), *Of Property and Propriety: The Role of Gender and Class in Imperialism and Nationalism* (edited and co-authored with S. Mojab and J. Whitehead, 2001), *Inventing Subjects: Studies in Hegemony, Patriarchy and Colonialism* (2001), and *The Dark Side of the Nation: Essays on Multiculturalism, Nationalism and Racism* (2000).

Sara Carpenter teaches in the Women and Gender Studies Institute, the Equity Studies programme at New College, and Adult Education and Community Development programme, the University of Toronto. Her research focuses on the political economy of community development, ideologies of citizenship and democracy, and the extension of feminist-materialist analysis in community service provision. Currently, she is working with an international research collaboration exploring the impact of securitization policies on the material and social conditions of marginalized youth. She is co-editor with S. Mojab of *Educating from Marx: Race, Gender and Learning* (2012).

Cynthia Cockburn is a feminist researcher and writer living in London, where she is active in Women in Black against War and the Women's International League for Peace and Freedom. She is a visiting professor in the Department of Sociology, City University London, and honorary professor in the Centre for the Study of Women and Gender, University of Warwick. Her most recent books, products of action-research on gender in processes of war and peace, are *From Where We Stand: War, Women's Activism and Feminist Analysis* (2007) and *Antimilitarism: Political and Gender Dynamics of Peace Movements* (2012).

Helen Colley is a professor of Lifelong Learning at the University of Huddersfield, UK, and visiting professor of Adult Education at the University of Toronto. Her main research interests are the classed and gendered aspects of workplace learning. She is author of *Mentoring for Social Inclusion* (2003), an award-winning Marxist-feminist critique of youth mentoring. She has also published many articles and chapters on the super-exploitation of women through emotional labour. Her most recent research links this to the ethical pressures bearing down on human service workers – mainly women – as economic 'austerity' policies withdraw funding from this work.

Teresa L. Ebert is the author of the *Task of Cultural Critique* (2009) and *Ludic Feminism and After* (1996) as well as co-author of *Class in Culture* (2008) and the forthcoming *Marxism and the Work of (Post)Humanities* (2015). Her essays have appeared in such journals as *Rethinking Marxism*, *Cultural Critique*, *Textual Practice*, *Women's Review of Books*, and *College English*. She is a professor of Cultural Theory at the University at Albany, State University of New York.

Amir Hassanpour, a leading Marxist scholar of Kurdish Studies, has taught at Canadian universities, including the Department of Near and Middle Eastern Civilizations, University of Toronto (1999–2009). His research and teaching interests include communication and media studies, sociolinguistics, and Middle Eastern and Kurdish politics and history. He is the author of *Nationalism and Language in Kurdistan, 1918–1985* (1992), has published numerous articles in Kurdish and Persian, and has contributed to reference works such as the *Encyclopedia of Television* (1997, 2005), *Encyclopaedia Iranica* (1988–89, 1995–97), *Encyclopedia of Modern Asia* (2002), *The New Grove Dictionary of Music and Musicians*

(2001), *Encyclopedia of Modern Middle East* (2004), *Encyclopedia of Women and Islamic Cultures* (2005), *Encyclopedia of Diasporas* (2004), and *Encyclopedia of Genocide and Crimes Against Humanity* (2005). Professor Hassanpour has taught courses on Middle Eastern nationalisms and social movements and theory and methodology in Middle Eastern studies. In his research, he deals with a wide range of topics including genocide, peasant revolts, social class, and oral traditions.

Frigga Haug studied sociology and psychology in Berlin and started her political engagement in the German peace and student movement before she became an important figure in the German feminist movement. Based on her activism and her experience as an adult educator, she developed the feminist learning and research method of collective memory work. Haug became co-editor and co-publisher of the journal *Das Argument* and the *Historical Critical Dictionary of Marxism*, as well as co-editor of the journal *Forum Kritische Psychologie*. She co-founded the People's University Berlin and holds the positions of managing director of the Argument-Verlag and president of the Institute of Critical Theory Berlin. Haug was professor at Hamburg University of Economy and Politics, has taught at the Free University Berlin, and has been a visiting scholar in Kopenhagen, Innsbruck, Klagenfurt, Sydney, Toronto, and Durham. As a Marxist-feminist scholar, she is internationally renowned for her scholarship and interventions in the field of women's studies and feminist politics, work studies, women's socialization, and feminist methods and learning. In 2013 she was awarded the Clara Zetkin Women's Award by the German party Die Linke.

Maryam Jazayeri is a researcher and activist in the communist movement of Iran since the late 1970s. She contributes regularly to theoretical debates on women's movements and the renewal of communism.

Jamie Magnusson is an associate professor of Adult Education and Community Development at the Ontario Institute for Studies in Education, University of Toronto. Her activism and scholarship on precarity and dispossession examine militarized financialization in terms of urban development and social justice themes, with particular attention to women, youth, and LGBTQ communities. Recent journal publications include 'Precarious Learning and Labour in Financialized Times', 'Biosurveillance as a Terrain of Innovation in an Era of Monopoly Finance Capital', and, co-authored with Elisabeth Abergel, 'The Art of (Bio)Surveillance: Bioart and the Financialization of Living Systems'.

Michelle Murphy is a feminist technoscience studies scholar and professor of History and Women and Gender Studies at the University of Toronto. She is the author of *Seizing the Means of Reproduction: Entanglements of Feminism, Health, and Technoscience* (2012) and *Sick Building Syndrome and the Politics of Uncertainty: Environmental Politics, Technoscience, and Women Workers* (2006). Her work focuses on the entanglements of race and sex in technoscience, capitalism, and environmental politics. She is currently writing a book entitled *The Economization of Life* that traces an important twentieth-century history of the technoscientific practices by which sex, race, and economics were governed through the aggregate phenomena of 'population' and 'economy'. It traces a transformation from early twentieth-century eugenic projects that sought to govern evolutionary racial futures, to postcolonial technoscientific projects of the 1970s and 1980s that sought to govern fertility rates for the sake of national macro-economies, and on to contemporary projects to adjust racialized and sexed embodied futures of girls through investment into human capital.

Kumkum Sangari worked as a UGC professorial fellow at the Centre for Contemporary Studies, Nehru Memorial Museum and Library, and is the William F. Vilas Research Professor of English and the Humanities at the University of Wisconsin-Milwaukee. She has published extensively on British, American, and Indian literature, critical theory, religious conversion, medieval oral devotional traditions, nationalist figures such as Gandhi and Annie Besant, Bombay cinema and partition, televisual memory, and contemporary feminist art practice as well as contemporary gender issues such as personal law, domestic labour, the beauty industry, sex selection, dowry, domestic violence, widow immolation, and communal violence. She is the author of *Politics of the Possible: Essays on Gender, History, Narratives, Colonial English* (1999); the editor of *Trace Retrace: Paintings, Nilima Sheikh* (2013). She is co-editor with S. Vaid of both *Women and Culture* (1985) and *Recasting Women: Essays in Colonial History* (1990), and co-editor with U. Chakravarti of *From Myths to Markets: Essays on Gender* (1999).

Judith Whitehead is professor, Department of Anthropology, University of Lethbridge, and University Scholar 2011–13. She is currently working on issues of primitive accumulation relating to South Asia. Her publications include two books, *Development and Dispossession in the Narmada Valley* (2010) and *Property and Propriety: Gender and Class in Imperialism and Nationalism* (2001) (co-edited with H. Bannerji and S. Mojab), as well as thirty-five refereed articles. She won a prize for best article of 2012 in the *Journal of Contemporary Asia* for 'John Locke, Accumulation by Dispossession and the Governance of Colonial India'.

INDEX